HISPANICS IN THE UNITED STATES

An Agenda for the Twenty-First Century

HISPANICS IN THE UNITED STATES

Pastora San Juan Cafferty
David W. Engstrom
EDITORS

with a new preface and introduction by the editors

Transaction Publishers
New Brunswick (U.S.A.) and London (U.K.)

Library of Congress Catalog Number: 2001043733
ISBN: 0-7658-0905-2
Printed in the United States of America

Library of Congress Cataloging-in-Publication Data

Hispanics in the United States : an agenda for the twenty-first century /
  Pastora San Juan Cafferty and David W. Engstrom, editors ; with a new
  preface & introduction by the editors.
      p. cm.
   Includes bibliographical references and index.
   ISBN 0-7658-0905-2 (paper : alk. paper)
      1. Hispanic Americans—Social conditions   2. Hispanic Americans—Government policy. 3. Hispanic Americans—Social
   conditions—Forecasting. I. Cafferty, Pastora San Juan. II.
   Engstrom, David Wells, 1958-

E184.S75 H623   2001
305.8'68073—dc21   2001043733

For our parents:

Esther Lee Engstrom
George A. Engstrom
Hortensia Hourruitiner San Juan
Jose Antonio San Juan

who first taught us about the diversity that is American society.

Contents

List of Tables

Preface

When we decided to edit a collection of writings on Hispanics at the end of the twentieth century, to define an agenda of issues that must be addressed in this twenty-first century, we were aware that the then-unfinished United States Census of 2000 would certainly provide a much more accurate picture of the growing numbers of Hispanics in the United States. A year after the publication of *Hispanics in the United States*, we find ourselves preparing a second edition of the book and recognizing that the 2000 census has already redefined the reality of Hispanics in the United States, simply through its initial numbers. Hispanics will soon be the largest minority group in the United States. The census data not only show the dramatic growth of this population, but also document its increasing diversity. We did not want the book to go into a second printing without acknowledging these results. Additionally, the sheer numbers alone mean that all sectors of American society must recognize the Hispanic population as an integral part of American society and culture—a part that will increasingly shape the economic and political life of this nation.

We are constrained by the fact that the census results will not be available in their entirety until later in the year 2001; only after this availability can we ask our colleagues to revise their analyses of the reality of Hispanic lives and produce a volume that addresses the facts as we know them from the 2000 census. We therefore faced a conflict: The book sold out its first run in twelve months, so a second printing was in order, but a second printing could not be accomplished in time to keep the book in stock if we edited the book to take into account the 2000 census. Given the significance of the Hispanic population, and realizing that sales of this volume seem to offer proof that it fills a need for knowledge about Hispanics, we decided that it was important to keep the book in print. Hence, we offer this edition as a compromise solution to that dilemma.

We have addressed the preliminary facts garnered from the 2000 census in the introduction. Thus, we provide a new numerical context in which to read the chapters that follow. We do so believing that, although the book was intended to draw a portrait of the Hispanic population, all of us who contributed to the volume were mindful of the limitations of the data. We now have newer data, but they are still incomplete and problematically continue to obscure the great diversity among Hispanic groups. The authors discussed the facts as they knew them, but also raised questions for the twenty-first century. We believe that the focus of their analyses and the questions those analyses pose are not made obsolete, but rather more relevant, given the initial 2000 census data. If anything, the numbers make the discussions in the chapters that follow even more compelling. Facts are only used to define the questions; as important as facts may be, it is the *implications* of what we know that we as editors and authors believe to be crucial. It is the questions that are important. The answers will continue to change.

PASTORA SAN JUAN CAFFERTY
DAVID W. ENGSTROM
San Diego, 2001

Introduction

Pastora San Juan Cafferty and David W. Engstrom

We began this book by outlining questions that we believe must be addressed if one is to understand the role of Hispanics in American society. This role has been shown to be dramatically more important by the growth of the Hispanic population in the United States over the past decade, as documented by the United States Census of 2000. The chapters in this book, written before the 2000 census data were available, are intended not only to offer a comprehensive portrait of Hispanics in the United States, but also to raise questions about the role of the individual and the role of public and private institutions in creating a society that enables its people to meet their fullest potential. The questions posed in this book are only made more relevant, and the need to address them more immediate, in light of the Hispanic population growth.

More than 200 years ago, the United States began as an experiment in democracy. It quickly became a magnet that drew people from many lands, and our nation has successfully and continuously incorporated many generations of immigrants into the bold American experiment in capitalism and democracy. At the beginning of the twenty-first century, though, perhaps due in part to that successful incorporation, we sometimes have difficulty seeing our country as a place of refuge and opportunity for those who continue to come. Many problems have proven difficult to solve and new ones have arisen. At the end of the nineteenth century, we worried about the implications of the closing of the frontier for the health and well-being of the nation. At the end of the twentieth century, we worried about the effects of technology and globalization, about full employment, about maintaining quality of life for our children, and about safety and security. Perhaps most of all, we worried about what American society—experiencing new growth from immigrants who mostly do not call European countries home—would become in the twenty-first century. These worries are intensified at the beginning of the twenty-first century by an awareness that the American economy, which saw unprecedented expansion in the last decade of the preceding century, may be growing at a slower pace and that the economies of other countries may be increasingly constrained.

Those who immigrated at the end of the century just past found a society very different from that encountered by earlier European immigrants. The new immigrants have to contend with a bureaucracy designed to improve the quality of life of the American people but increasingly difficult to navigate. They come to a nation concerned about the limits of resources available to its people, where newcomers are often unwelcome. Many of those who came before have forgotten their immigrant roots or have transmuted the memory of their immigrant past to one of easy assimilation into an idealized American society. This changed national context in which newcomers find themselves, as well as the changed nature of the immigrant population, gives rise to the questions that must be asked and the new public policy agendas that must be created. Because of the numbers of Hispanic immigrants, their heterogeneity, and the proximity of their migration, we believe that Hispanics—and the way American society incorporates this growing population—will largely define America in the twenty-first century.

Hispanics constitute a diverse population, part of which settled more than 400 years ago in what is now the United States of America. Now, at the beginning of the twenty-first century, they are making their influence felt in new and commanding ways throughout American society. The Hispanic population grew by more than 50 percent in the 1980s and then increased by about 58 percent in the 1990s. By the year 2000, 35.3 million Hispanics resided in the United States, constituting more than 12 percent of the total population, and this overarching group is projected to grow to nearly a quarter of the U.S. population by the middle of the twenty-first century. This growth is caused by immigration as well as by natural increase. The census figures, used in the redrawing of congressional districts, show the Hispanic population pulling into a rough parity with Blacks. Indeed, Hispanics now outnumber Blacks in large states such as California, Florida, and Texas, and within several years will do so in the national population. Along with increasing numbers of Asians, the expanding population of Hispanics is forcing the reexamination of a historic tendency to view the racial and ethnic makeup of America in terms of "black" and "white."

This racial diversity is reflected in the 2000 census, which for the first time gave respondents the option of identifying themselves as belonging to more than one race. Nearly 7 million people, or slightly more than 2 percent of the population, identified themselves as multi-racial. It is too soon to know how this now-acknowledged racial diversity will redefine traditional social and political concepts of race relations in America. However, the very terms "majority" and "minority" become suspect in cities where non-Hispanic whites do not make up the vast percentage of the population. Editorial writers, among the first to respond to the numbers in the 2000 census, ponder the implications of Hispanics being "the largest minority." Politicians and policy makers cannot be far behind.

The new census data confirm that the growth in the Hispanic population has made the United States more racially and ethnically complex. They also document demographic shifts among Hispanic populations. Mexican-Americans, who have long been the largest group in the Hispanic population, now account for a little less than 60 percent of all Hispanics in the United States, a slight decrease from the previous census. Census data not broken down by Hispanic groups disproportionately reflect only Mexican-American socioeconomic reality, distorting differences among the Hispanic groups. Even though the population of Cuban-Americans and Puerto Ricans increased during the 1990s, proportionally those groups make up a smaller percentage of the total Hispanic population in 2000. Hispanics originally from Central and South America now represent about 9 percent of all Hispanics. Although more detailed information about the sociodemographic composition of the Hispanic population is not yet available from the 2000 census, data from the Census Bureau's 2000 *Current Population Report* (CPR) are likely to anticipate many of the findings from the latest census.

Though found throughout the United States, Hispanics are concentrated, and thus increasingly visible, in the western and southern regions of the country. They continue to migrate to a few "gateway" cities in Florida, Texas, and California, the Midwest, and along the East Coast. However, although the majority of Hispanics live in a handful of states, secondary internal migration is resulting in greater dispersal. Indeed, the states with the fastest growing Hispanic populations during the 1990s were Arkansas, North Carolina, Nevada, Georgia, and Tennessee.

Hispanics are also highly concentrated in major American cities. According to the 2000 CPR, more than nine out of ten Hispanics live in a metropolitan area, compared to less than seven in ten non-Hispanic Whites. Indeed, more than twice as many Hispanics (47 percent) reside in a central city, as opposed to non-Hispanic Whites (21 percent). Hispanics have transformed cities such as Miami, where Spanish is now the language of the marketplace, and also cities such as Chicago, where (after years of continuing non-Hispanic White migration to the suburbs) there has been an urban population increase largely due to the growth of the Hispanic population.

The newcomers, many from countries south of the United States borders and from the Caribbean, are changing the complexion of urban America. Hispanics are a young population with relatively high fertility rates. Indeed, high fertility rates more than immigration account for the dramatic increase in the Hispanic population during the last decade of the twentieth century. Also, because Hispanics are a young population, questions involving education are especially germane. In certain areas Hispanic children are becoming the majority population in the public schools. Hispanics, like other Americans before them, migrate to metropolitan areas and thus to those areas' overcrowded and ineffective school systems. The large influx of Hispanic students may cause society and its leaders to perceive that Hispanics are creating the problem, rather than (like other Americans) struggling with antiquated institutions that are often ill-suited to serve American society in the twenty-first century. Hispanics' very numbers at the end of the twentieth century, and their projected growth throughout the twenty-first century, make this population of great importance to American society as a whole, as well as to policy makers and service providers. One could argue that addressing the issues raised by this heterogeneous population will define how Americans in general deal with issues of class, race, and ethnic identity during the twenty-first century.

Hispanics explored and first settled what was to become United States territory long before the English established permanent settlements on the East Coast. Conquest and diplomatic treaty brought the first populations of Hispanics into the United States during the nineteenth century. Despite this history, many regard Hispanics as recent arrivals. According to the 2000 CPR, 39 percent of the Hispanic population in the United States was foreign-born, with nearly half (43 percent) arriving in the 1990s. Despite the importance of understanding the socioeconomic conditions of Hispanics, policy makers are greatly limited by poor and often nonexistent data. Until relatively recently, areas such as health care, education, criminal justice, and social welfare had no national data sets using the identifier "Hispanic." Such paucity of data has made analysis of important long-term trends for Hispanics nearly impossible. Today, policy makers and scholars are more likely to have access to data that classify people by their Hispanic origins.

However, in many cases the term *Hispanic* confuses our understanding of this population. It denotes as homogeneous a pan-ethnic population that is in fact highly heterogeneous. For example, data often fail to break Hispanics into important national-origin groups, such as Mexican or Cuban. Additionally, few sources of data make it possible to track immigration status, clearly an important consideration for Hispanics.

The term *Hispanic* is used to describe people in the United States who are descended or have migrated from countries in which Spanish is spoken. Because the term is rooted in the use of language rather than in race, *Hispanic* encompasses White; Black; and *mestizo/mulato*, the mixture of African, Native American, and European races that often leads both Hispanic spokespersons and other Americans to refer to Hispanics as a *brown* race. The terms *Hispanic*, *Black*, and *non-Hispanic White* are U.S. Census terms that are used for consistency in this book as well. However, these terms do not even begin to capture the diversity that is American society and that is the population we identify as Hispanic. Nor do these terms reflect the richness of racial identity that is the reality of the lands that were colonized by the Spanish conquistadors.

Also, because the term denotes a common linguistic heritage, it includes those who are recent immigrants as well as those who have been in the United States for generations. The very fact that the primary group identity of Hispanics is rooted in language also leads to the misconception that Hispanics do not (and do not wish to) speak English. In fact, Hispanics, like most other Americans, speak English; however, unlike most other Americans, they also are likely to speak another language. Hispanics retain the Spanish language—and some would argue Spanish culture—long after the first generation that comes to the United States. There are many reasons for this, but the most obvious is proximity: Hispanics, who come from south of what is essentially one long contiguous land mass, travel freely to visit family and friends in Spanish-language societies, and Spanish language use is constantly renewed and reinforced by the migration stream. Here again we find that language becomes the visible proxy for culture; in the context of American society, the issue becomes the retention of Spanish. Spanish speaking is seen as problematic and threatening to the assumed pattern of assimilation in a society that historically has both expected linguistic assimilation of each successive immigrant group and demanded abandonment of native languages and ways as the price for immigrants' becoming recognized as American.

Thus, identification of Hispanics in the United States is often based on an assumed shared native language. Although Hispanics share a common heritage of originally being from areas that were home to or colonized by the Spanish, so that they once shared a common Spanish language, they are a highly heterogeneous population that defy easy classification. They include the descendants of settlers in the southwestern United States and what is now Florida, Georgia, and Alabama, as well as the most recent immigrants. They do not all share common ethnic memories, common myths and symbols, or even the Spanish language. Thus, identification as a Hispanic is more than the condition of a common racial or ethnic origin, or of shared language, traditions, sentiments, or cultural networks. It can be a form of self-conceptualization by the individual or an identity that society assigns to the individual, creating a Hispanic pan-ethnicity that is impossible to define and that, indeed, may be of little real consequence.

The majority of persons who are identified as Hispanic, either by themselves or by society, are further identified not only as an ethnic group but also as a minority. The fact that this "minority" will soon be the largest minority group in the United States has important social and political implications in a post-civil-rights-era America.

There is no guarantee that a shared ethnic or cultural heritage produces homogeneity of thought, feeling, or behavior, or even group loyalty. In the case of Hispanics, this supposedly shared ethnic heritage may be so diverse as to have little weight and be of little use in understanding Hispanic ethnicity. Even the same Hispanic ethnic identity may have different meanings to its different bearers. Certain features of ethnic identity may be deeply embedded in an individual and persist even when shown to be dysfunctional in the individual's adopted society; other aspects of ethnic identity may be discarded or changed over time. The strength of an individual's identification with an ethnic group varies over time and differs with circumstances. All these voluntary and involuntary aspects of ethnicity, as well as the huge diversity in the Hispanic population, make it very difficult to discuss "Hispanic culture" in the United States.

The socioeconomic status of Hispanics is more problematic and more predictable: Hispanics are more likely to be poor than almost any other group in American society. However, recent poverty data show that the economic boom of the mid- to late 1990s reduced the percentage of the Hispanic population living below the poverty line from a high of nearly 31 percent in 1994 to a twenty-year low of about 23 percent in 1999. Because of their low economic status, many Hispanics find themselves relying on inadequately funded and antiquated social welfare programs. Recent changes in federal policy have made hundreds of thousands of Hispanic immigrants ineligible for social welfare and health care benefits, further contributing to their social and economic isolation. Many Hispanics are best described as *working poor*. Hispanics are overrepresented in blue-collar, service, and seasonal jobs. Because many Hispanics have lower educational levels than the general population, better-paying and more secure jobs are often out of reach, though Hispanics who attend college seem to have earnings similar to those of other groups. Increasingly, Hispanics are overrepresented in the criminal justice system. However, their health is better and their mortality is lower than their socioeconomic position might suggest.

Changing Context of Society

Certainly American society changed drastically during the twentieth century. The nineteenth century ended with the declared closing of the frontier and the excitement of an age that had discovered the marvels of technology, the beginning of mass production, and the dawning of the age of telecommunications. The twentieth century saw two world wars, initial explorations of space, the expansion of mass communications, the development of the computer age, new frontiers of science and biotechnology, and an expansion in the frontiers of human knowledge that has created new ethical dilemmas.

In this American society, education is critical for those who wish to enter and succeed in the labor market. Hispanics continue to have the lowest educational attainment. According to the 2000 CPR, the Hispanic population aged 25 years and older was less likely to have graduated from high school than non-Hispanic Whites (57 percent and 88 percent, respectively). More than one-quarter of all Hispanics had less than a ninth-grade education (27 percent), compared to 4 percent of non-Hispanic Whites. Whereas one in ten adult Hispanics had a bachelor's degree or more, almost three in ten non-Hispanic Whites had at least a bachelor's degree. Hispanic groups continue to show considerable difference in educational attainment. Nearly three-quarters of adult Cuban-Americans completed high school, compared with about one-half of Mexican-Americans.

This society also demands English-language skills of those who would participate in its economic promise. Unlike those who labored on the farms and in the factories of nineteenth- and early twentieth-century America, who needed little English and less education, persons who aspire to any but the lowest-paying jobs need at least a high school diploma and English verbal and written skills. Hispanics' generally low levels of education route them into low-paying service occupations. Hispanics, more than non-Hispanic Whites, are concentrated in service occupations (19 percent and 12 percent, respectively) and as operators and laborers (22 percent and 12 percent, respectively). In contrast, twice as many non-Hispanic Whites than Hispanics are in managerial or professional occupations (33 percent and 14 percent respectively). The demise of manufacturing has greatly limited the availability of semi-skilled jobs for Hispanics. This concentration of Hispanics in low-level service and manufacturing jobs results in low wages for this population. While nearly half of non-Hispanic White full-time, year-round workers earned $35,000 or more in 1999, less than a quarter of Hispanics did so. Within Hispanic groups, Cuban-Americans continue to report the highest annual earnings and Mexican-Americans the lowest. The concentration of so many Hispanics in poorly paid jobs means that few receive health care benefits through work and few are covered by private pension plans. Despite occupational barriers, a growing Hispanic middle class is emerging. Economists have demonstrated the importance of parents' passing on skills, values, and resources that affect their children's performance in the labor market. The growth of a Hispanic middle class suggests that Hispanics may become increasingly divided between those who possess backgrounds that translate into economic gain and those who do not.

Although civil rights efforts have reduced many social, economic, and educational barriers, Hispanics still remain the targets of discrimination and prejudice. Current discrimination and prejudice are different in form than they were thirty to forty years ago. Hispanics live in a nation that has enacted important civil rights laws that, for the most part, ended de jure discrimination. Nevertheless, though there are greater protections from obvious discriminatory behavior, de facto discrimination persists. In their daily lives, many Hispanics encounter poorly funded school systems, punitive and biased encounters with law enforcement officials, and insensitive social welfare agencies, all of which contribute to the marginalization of the Hispanic population as a whole. Even today, discrimination is manifest in policy. Employer sanctions regarding undocumented immigrants have led to widespread employment discrimination against Hispanics. Paradoxically, many Americans resent what are seen as privileges granted to members of disadvantaged populations. Affirmative action and other policies designed to expand economic and educational opportunities for "minorities" are under increasing legislative and judicial assault. Clearly, the growing numbers of Hispanics play a role in the increasing opposition to affirmative action. It is not surprising that California, with its large Hispanic population, has led the effort to end affirmative action programs. The diversity of the Hispanic population also raises questions as to which among them should benefit from policies aimed at remedying historical social injustices.

There is concern about the lack of education, employment, mobility, and wealth formation in the Hispanic population. There is also recognition of cultural traditions long valued by American society. Hispanics show evidence of a strong, extended family culture; they are well represented in the labor market; they have strong religious affiliations; and their political participation evidences a traditional civic culture.

In many ways, Hispanic immigrants have been particularly and adversely affected by changing notions of civil rights and the rights of immigrants in the United States. Recent immigration reforms have greatly reduced the due process rights to which immigrants—whether documented or undocumented—are entitled during their interactions with immigration and law enforcement authorities. The changes in immigration law have redefined the idea of citizenship by making greater distinctions between the civil and economic rights of citizens and immigrants.

Partly as a consequence of changing attitudes toward citizenship, greater numbers of Hispanic immigrants are becoming naturalized United States citizens. As these new Hispanic citizens join with native-born Hispanics, existing political alignments will be altered, which may define new policy initiatives responsive to twenty-first-century American society. The ethnic and socioeconomic diversity of Hispanics suggests that they will not have a uniform political voice. Nevertheless, it is clear that Hispanic voters already play a key role in influencing the electoral outcomes in major states such as California, Florida, and Texas, and they are taking on an increasingly important role in shaping the outcomes of national elections.

The relative youthfulness of the Hispanic population raises intergenerational and inter-ethnic issues about the social contract. As the baby boomers age and begin to retire, Social Security and other retirement programs will be financed by the payroll and income taxes from a workforce largely consisting of Hispanics and other groups that have traditionally been disadvantaged in American society. As the descendants of European ethnic groups age, it is Hispanics, Blacks, and Asians who will contribute to the welfare of non-Hispanic Whites. Presently, these minority populations often find that the public programs they rely on for education, health care, and social welfare are underfunded and neglected.

Clearly, all this calls for understanding of the role that is being played—and, more importantly, that could be played—by the fastest growing population group in our society. Because of their size, their heterogeneity, and their projected growth, Hispanics may be the most important population group in American society in the twenty-first century. Society must create mechanisms that enable them to become an integral part of the nation. Effective policies and programs must recognize Hispanic diversity, needs, and contributions to the developing culture of twenty-first-century America that Hispanics will have such a primary role in making.

The writings in this book address the issues raised by this growing Hispanic population and draw a portrait of the complexity of the Hispanic population. Each chapter not only discusses things as they are, but also raises questions for the twenty-first century. The discussions of present and future issues are carried out in the context of the history, politics, and society of the United States at the end of the twentieth century. Although facts are used to define the questions, the numbers employed have already changed and will continue to change. The first census of the twenty-first century only underscores the fact that the reality defined by the numbers will constantly change. It is the implications of what is known that are crucial. It is the questions that are important. The numbers—and the answers to the questions—will continue to change.

The book is organized into two sections. The first establishes the historical, demographic, cultural, and religious context of Hispanics in the United States. The second describes the major issues facing this population in the context of contemporary American society and institutions: specifically, the educational system, labor market participation, the health care and social welfare systems, and the criminal justice system. The book concludes with a discussion of Hispanics' political participation in American society, for it is this participation that perhaps best shows Hispanics' current role in American society and that will help define the public policy agenda for the twenty-first century.

The demographic portrait drawn by Teresa Sullivan both defines the population and raises questions about the meaning of its size and heterogeneity. The 2000 census shows the numbers she used to have grown in dramatic proportions. However, her analysis continues to provide a framework to understand issues that have only become more immediate. Hispanics are not only the most rapidly growing minority group, but also will become the largest minority group in American society in the twenty-first century. Hispanic children soon will be the majority of school children in California, and they are an important and growing presence in a number of school systems in major metropolitan areas in other states as well. The disadvantages that Hispanics suffer because of their low levels of education are addressed by Barry Chiswick and Michael Hurst, who point out that the low educational skills and limited English skills of Hispanics help explain their concentration in lower-paying jobs. Recent census data offer a solid foundation for and further proof of their analysis.

The lowest labor market and language skills are, predictably, those of first-generation immigrants. David Engstrom discusses Hispanic immigration in the context of historic trends and offers explanations for why so many Hispanic immigrants come to the United States. He reviews the unintended consequences of recent immigration policies and argues that withdrawing public assistance for immigrants is, in the long run, counterproductive.

The need to craft policy and design programs that adequately address the needs of Hispanics are raised by Melissa Roderick, Zulema Suárez, Katie McDonough, and Alvin Korte. Roderick raises questions about the best way to address the educational needs of Hispanic children; she argues that it cannot be done without a combination of broad-based efforts to support education and efforts targeted to the special needs of Hispanic youth and the school systems that serve them. McDonough and Korte document the strong family and community orientation of Hispanics and call for community-based social welfare practice to better meet their needs. They confirm the findings, supported by the data analyzed in other chapters, that although Hispanics are often characterized as lacking human capital of education and language, they are rich in social capital and contribute to the strengthening of traditional family and community values in this society. It is not only the strong family culture but also the youth of the Hispanic population that defines many of the questions raised by Zulema Suárez's discussion of Hispanic health care needs. Suárez argues that far too many Hispanics face barriers in accessing medical care. Her analysis addresses policy issues, such as the high number of Hispanics who lack health insurance, and raises concerns about the ability of the health care system to provide care to those covered by private and public insurance programs. In her discussion of traditional belief systems such as *curanderismo*, she highlights specific strengths of Hispanic culture.

The importance of culture, as well as the need to understand and respect culture when crafting policy solutions, is a *leitmotif* throughout these chapters. Pastora San Juan Cafferty discusses the persistence of Hispanic cultural traditions and the continuing retention of the Spanish language and Spanish language identity across many generations. This analysis attempts not only to understand the meaning of language to the Hispanic communities, but also, equally importantly, to examine the problems that native culture and native language retention are perceived to present to American society and to the assimilation of Hispanics into mainstream America. David Maldonado, Jr., explores another important aspect of Hispanic culture: the Catholic religious tradition. In documenting the growing shift among Hispanics to Protestant churches (and in particular to Protestant evangelical sects), he questions whether Hispanic culture itself will be impacted by Protestant religious values and practice.

In perhaps in no other aspect does society better define itself than in questions of social justice. Increasing involvement of Hispanics in the American criminal justice system raises important questions, both about Hispanics and about American society's commitment to social justice and equal treatment under the law. Cruz Reynoso notes that while Hispanics are increasingly being arrested and incarcerated, they are underrepresented in law enforcement and judicial positions. The dramatic population increases documented by the 2000 census made these imbalances more pronounced. Reynoso points out that in all too many instances, Hispanics encounter abuse of power by law enforcement personnel.

The very growth of the Hispanic population and its increasing political participation suggests that Hispanics themselves will have a strong voice in defining the agenda for the twenty-first century. From local to national arenas, politicians and the media have focused considerable attention on Hispanic voters, reflecting the growing electoral importance of this group. However, its youthfulness, its relatively low economic standing, and the sizeable proportion of immigrants who are not citizens circumscribe its political strength. Christine Sierra raises important questions about building a common agenda across the heterogeneity of Hispanic ethnic groups, and calls for better understanding of the contributions Hispanics can make to the American political process. She concludes that the response by the political system of the United States to Hispanic demands for political inclusion will determine the role Hispanics play in defining American public policies and, ultimately, American society in this century.

In trying to answer some of these questions, we were troubled not only by the paucity of the data, but also by the limits of social science analysis. We realize the importance of the contributions made by demographers, economists, political scientists, legal scholars, and historians in defining problems, and by social workers, health care professionals, educators, attorneys, public officials, and ordinary citizens in addressing them. Nevertheless, we believe that to understand the soul of a people, one must go well beyond descriptive data to the literature that voices the reality of their being. This book raises more questions about Hispanics than we can answer, based on what is known; our hope is that the questions raised in these chapters will stimulate discussion and continued scholarship that will raise further questions. The answers will define twenty-first century American society.

Acknowledgments

We continue to be grateful to all those whose ideas over the years have led to our editing this volume. We are most indebted to our colleagues who so generously contributed their knowledge and wisdom in the writing of the book. We have learned much from each author of each chapter. We have immensely enjoyed working with them in producing this volume and we are most profoundly in their debt.

We are also most grateful to Irving Louis Horowitz and Mary Curtis at Transaction Press, who suggested we develop a book about Hispanics in the United States at the end of the twentieth century and then enthusiastically supported our proposal to develop an agenda for the twenty-first century. Their encouragement to bring out a second edition and acknowledge the dramatic findings of the 2000 census is further proof that working with them is always a rewarding as well as a pleasant experience.

We are most grateful to Brooke Graves of Graves Editorial Service, whose intelligent and careful editing continues to make the information clearer and the analyses more persuasive. We also thank Andrea Batista Schlessinger, who initially read and raised questions about the manuscript. Each of them has made valuable contributions. All of us have been kept organized and been repeatedly encouraged by Betty Bradley. Her attention to detail, her organizational skills, and her enthusiastic support contributed greatly to each phase of writing and publishing this volume.

We are each deeply indebted to colleagues in our respective institutions, the University of Chicago and San Diego State University. At the University of Chicago, all those who, over the years, have taken the time to discuss social problems and issues raised by the diversity and complexity of society have educated us and have contributed to the thinking that shaped this book. The creation of this book began with encouragement from the Dean at the School of Social Service Administration, Jeanne Marsh. Dr. Marsh, together with the Associate Dean, Tina Rzepnicki, not only encouraged thinking about diversity in American society but also allowed the development of graduate seminars on the subject, which thus made it possible to develop the outline for this book. Two former deans, Margaret Rosenheim and Laurence Lynn, encouraged our creation of courses on immigration and on the development of communities, which provided the intellectual capital for this collaboration. Edward Lawlor, the current Dean of the School, provided the valued support of time to be spent writing.

San Diego State University has provided a rich atmosphere to explore the importance of Hispanics to the United States and to understand the strengths they possess and the difficulties they encounter. A sabbatical at New Mexico Highlands University greatly facilitated the writing and editing of the first edition of this book. Alvin O. Korte and Katie McDonough provided a wonderful sounding board for ideas and countless hours of discussion about issues of diversity and cultural change. Maurice Rodriquez and Valerie Pacini, two recent alumni of NMHU, richly gave of their expertise and knowledge of issues facing Hispanics in the United States. Anna Walton provided much-needed encouragement and timely editorial assistance throughout the writing of this book.

We are grateful to all our friends and colleagues and to our students who, with many others too numerous to mention, have generously shared their ideas and debated ours. It is from them that we learn and it is with them that we share our concerns and our hopes for a future American society that is better designed to enable all citizens to realize their fullest potential.

History is prologue but does not necessarily define the future. It is the questions we raise in the present and how we answer them to define the public agenda that will create the America of the twenty-first century.

1

A Demographic Portrait

Teresa A. Sullivan

More than 500 years ago, a Hispanic influence was first felt in the New World of the Americas. The Spanish Empire spread the language and culture of Spain to nearly all of South America, most of Central America, and the southern third of North America. Today, at the brink of the twenty-first century, Hispanic influence is being felt in the United States in a new and vibrant way. This influence comes about primarily through the demographic impact of Hispanics—that is, the number and composition of their population, their migration, and their growth. This chapter presents a demographic portrait of the Hispanic population.

The Hispanic population of the United States comprises more than 29 million people, about 11 percent of the national population; they are the fastest growing minority group in the United States. Table 1.1 shows the fraction of the United States population that is Hispanic, and it also shows the increase from 1990 to 2000 in the proportion of the population that is Hispanic. For reasons of size and rapid growth alone, the Hispanic population would deserve the attention of policy makers and analysts. The Hispanic population grew by 53 percent during the 1980s and then by another 27 percent between 1990 and 1996.[1] If Census Bureau projections are correct (see table 1.1), by 2020 Hispanics will number 52 million persons and 16.3 percent of the population, and by 2050 they will number 97 million persons and constitute 24.5 percent of the United States population.[2]

As this chapter explains, the Hispanic population is growing both through immigration (movement across national boundaries) and through natural increase (the number of births in excess of the number

Table 1.1
Resident Population of the United States, 1990 and 2000
(percentages)

Group	1990	2000
Non-Hispanic White	75.7	71.7
Black	11.8	12.2
American Indian, Eskimo, Aleut	0.7	0.7
Asian, Pacific Islander	2.8	3.9
Hispanic origin[a]	9.0	11.4

[a] Persons of Hispanic origin may be of any race.

Source: United States Bureau of the Census, *Statistical Abstract of the United States*, 116th ed. (Washington, D.C.: GPO, 1996).

of deaths). About one-third of the population growth can be attributed to immigration; the remaining two-thirds is due to natural increase. Contrary to many myths about Hispanics, the Hispanic population is relatively young, urban, and very diverse. These myths are discussed and compared with the facts later in this chapter. First, though, we need to discuss the term *Hispanic,* which is itself somewhat controversial.

Who Are the Hispanics?

The term *Hispanic* is used by government agencies and others to describe persons who themselves or whose ancestors were born into a Spanish-speaking community. The statisticians' intention was to develop a nonpejorative term that could include persons born in the United States but descended from Spanish-speaking peoples, as well as immigrants from Spain, Mexico, countries in the Caribbean and Central America, and South America except for Brazil. (Brazil and Portugal are technically not included because the people in those countries speak Portuguese rather than Spanish.)

Because the Hispanic term is rooted in the use of a language rather than in race, persons of Hispanic origin have varied skin color. Some Hispanics consider themselves White, and they may have blue eyes and blonde or red hair. Other Hispanics are descended from ancestors who were brought from Africa as slaves; they are dark-skinned and may identify their race as Black. Still other Hispanics, descended from the original peoples of North and South America, may be brown-skinned.

Moreover, although the Hispanic term is based on language use, persons from Spanish-speaking countries may speak other languages instead of or in addition to Spanish. Many immigrants from Central America, for example, speak an Indian language instead of Spanish, but they are still considered Hispanic. Thus, this single term describes a diverse group of individuals.

Other terms are also in common use within the Hispanic community. Some Southwestern Hispanics, especially those whose families have lived there since Spanish colonial times, prefer the terms *Spanish, Spanish-American,* or *Hispano.* Many persons of Mexican origin prefer the term *Mexican-American,* and some younger Mexican-Americans prefer the terms *Chicano, Xicano,* or *Mexicano.* People who come from other Latin American countries may prefer terms that refer to their country of origin, such as *Cuban-American, Cubano,* or *Dominican.* The term *Puertorrequeño* is sometimes used to refer to persons from Puerto Rico. Finally, some commentators prefer the term *Latino* to refer generally to persons who are from or descended from peoples in Spanish-speaking countries of the Americas.

The nationality of the Hispanic population differs quite a bit by region of residence within the United States, and thus there also are some differences in the terms used in various regions. In the Western states, where 45 percent of the Hispanic-origin population lives (and 58 percent of the Mexican-origin population), the terms *Latino* and *Chicano* have gained some currency. The second largest Hispanic region is the South (especially Florida), where 30 percent of all Hispanics and 71 percent of Cubans live. Here the terms that define the specific nationality are often used. The Northeast accounts for about 17 percent of the Hispanic population and 69 percent of the Puerto Rican population. Here the term *Puertorrequeño* is common, although other nationalities are also identified. Only 7 percent of the Hispanic population lives in the Midwest, and no single nationality group is concentrated there, so the term *Hispanic* is most often used.

Use of the term *Hispanic* may create an emergent ethnic identity among persons who might otherwise have thought of themselves as Mexican or Puerto Rican or Cuban.[3] This identity, which is constructed through the statistics and official rhetoric, may nevertheless be adopted by persons who bear the label in the general society. A similar process occurred among Italian immigrants in the last century, and it might be happening among Asian-Americans today: persons who had identified themselves by smaller places of origin (nation, province, city) become identified by the larger society in terms of a larger place of origin and thereafter adopt that identity developed by others.

In government data, such as the 1990 census and subsequent population surveys, individuals designate themselves in terms of both race and Hispanic origin. This self-identification ensures that persons are classified in the way that they themselves prefer. In some earlier censuses, the government also tried other techniques, including classifying persons as Hispanic if they had Spanish surnames. This latter procedure is now rarely used by statistical agencies. Intermarriage may lead Hispanic women to take non-Hispanic surnames, and some surnames are shared by Hispanics and by other nationalities (for example, the surname Martin). Some Hispanic immigrants change their names or anglicize them: for example, substituting the name "King" for the Hispanic "Rey," which means *king*. Self-identification is preferred to the surname identifier as a more accurate means of measurement. For vital statistics data, such as birth certificates and death certificates, members of the family provide information on whether a person is Hispanic. Thus, a baby who is classified as Hispanic has been so identified by her mother. On death certificates, a funeral director sometimes provides ethnic identification, but may be mistaken about the identity the decedent preferred.

Hispanic origin is not considered to be a racial category, although the term "Mexican" was once used as a racial category (in the census of 1930). The U.S. Census and most other government surveys today provide both a racial identifier and a Hispanic-origin identifier for each individual. Persons who call themselves Hispanic may be from any racial group. Use of the racial category "other" has been increasing among Hispanics, perhaps because they do not feel comfortable with existing racial categories.

A 1997 government report discussed in some detail the advantages and disadvantages of various terms for accurate collection of statistics.[4] This report and many similar studies indicate the significance of heterogeneity within the Hispanic population. This heterogeneity should not be overlooked; use of the broad term *Hispanic* conceals much of the internal diversity within the Hispanic population.

This chapter uses the word *Hispanic*, the term most often used in demographic studies. However, readers should remember that other researchers may use different terms to refer to the same population. This chapter compares data for Hispanics with data for non-Hispanic Whites and Blacks. Readers should remember that the data for Hispanics come from the self-report question on Hispanic origin, and the data on Whites and Blacks come from the self-report question on race. These comparisons, then, do not involve mutually exclusive categories of the population. Some people report themselves as *both* White and Hispanic, and others report themselves as *both* Black and Hispanic.

A Thumbnail Sketch

Four major groupings of Hispanics are commonly discussed in the literature: Mexican-Americans, Puerto Ricans, Cuban-Americans, and Central and South Americans. In this section, each of these groups is briefly highlighted and described. There is also a group of "other Hispanics" that includes Dominicans (who are sometimes counted with Central America or with South America), Spaniards from Spain, and a variety of persons who report themselves as "Spanish" or "Spanish-American." These "other Hispanics" are not separately discussed. As previously mentioned, Brazilians and Portuguese are excluded from these tabulations because they use the Portuguese language rather than Spanish.

Mexican-Americans

The Hispanic population in the United States originated from many different countries, but Mexico is the most important country of origin. A little more than 61 percent of Hispanics are of Mexican origin. In the early nineteenth century, most of what are now the southwestern states were part of Mexico. Through war, annexation, and purchase, these portions of Mexico became part of the United States. Some of the Hispanic population of states such as California, Arizona, New Mexico, and Texas dates from these colonial times.

By 1990, about 13.4 million Americans identified themselves as Mexican-American, and 4.3 million of them were actually born in Mexico.[5] The remaining 9.1 million are the children of persons who were born in Mexico. Mexican-Americans who were born in the United States are U.S. citizens by birth. Almost 1 million Mexican-Americans who were born in Mexico are citizens by naturalization.

Although Mexican-Americans have been in the Southwest since colonial times, there is a significant recent immigration flow from Mexico. Nearly one-third of all the Mexican immigrants who were counted in the 1990 census had entered the United States since 1985. Mexico's significance as a country of origin remained strong in the 1990s as well.

In 1994, Mexico was the largest sending country of immigrants, with 111,400 Mexicans legally admitted to the United States.[6] Mexicans were also believed to be the largest single group of undocumented immigrants, with the INS estimating that 2.7 million Mexicans were undocumented in 1996.[7]

Mexican-Americans live all over the United States, but the largest concentrations are found in California, Texas, and other southwestern states; Illinois also has a large Mexican-origin population. Several of the fastest-growing states between 1990 and 1995, including Texas, New Mexico, Arizona, Colorado, Utah, and Nevada, are states with relatively large populations of Mexican-Americans. Because many Mexicans enter the United States periodically to harvest crops, the stereotype persists that Mexican-Americans are mostly rural residents. This is not true, however; the Mexican-American population is heavily urbanized.

Puerto Ricans

As a result of the Spanish-American War, the island of Puerto Rico became a possession of the United States instead of Spain. Puerto Rico is termed a "commonwealth" and its people are U.S. citizens by birth. Because of their U.S. citizenship, Puerto Ricans are not considered immigrants. They may be considered migrants, just as any citizen who moves may be considered a migrant. Puerto Ricans may move freely between the U.S. mainland and the island, and some may periodically move between an East Coast city and Puerto Rico. The issue of statehood for the island of Puerto Rico is frequently raised, but in 1998 the island's voters narrowly rejected statehood in a referendum.

About 2.7 million Puerto Ricans were enumerated on the mainland in the 1990 census, and they account for 12.1 percent of all Hispanics, making them the second largest group of Hispanics. On the mainland, Puerto Ricans are most likely to live in eastern seaboard cities, especially in the New York City–New Jersey metropolitan complex. Another 3.5 million people were enumerated on the island of Puerto Rico. In this chapter, references to Puerto Ricans are references to persons within the fifty U.S. states, not to the population of the island.

Cuban-Americans

Some Cuban-Americans immigrated to the United States through the early years of the twentieth century, but the largest group of Cubans entered in the early 1960s, after Fidel Castro came to power in Cuba. In 1990, Cubans were the third largest group of Hispanics, with a little more than 1 million persons. Of this number, about 72 percent were foreign born.[8] Since 1960, most immigrant Cubans have been considered political refugees from Fidel Castro's communist regime. Large concentrations of Cubans settled in the New York City–New Jersey metropolitan area and in Florida, especially in Miami. In fact, a part of Miami has come to be called "Little Cuba," and many Cuban refugees and their children have become important business and civic leaders. A second but smaller refugee flow from Cuba came to the United States, often in small boats, in the so-called Mariel boatlift that occurred in 1980. Although travel restrictions between the United States and Cuba have recently been somewhat relaxed, the flow of additional Cubans to the United States has been relatively small during the 1990s. Not quite 15,000 Cubans entered the United States in 1994, a small fraction of the 269,000 Hispanic immigrants who entered in that year.

Central and South Americans

Political upheavals, rapid population growth, and poverty are among factors that have promoted a large migration stream from the countries of Central America to the United States. Central Americans comprise about 6 percent of the Hispanic population. There are about 1.3 million Central Americans in the United States, of whom 79 percent are foreign born. The leading country of origin is El Salvador. More than 565,000 Salvadorans lived in the United States in 1990; another 117,000 entered the United States between 1991 and 1994. The next leading country of origin is Guatemala, with more than 269,000 Guatemalans living in the United States in 1990 and another 54,000 entering the United States between 1991 and 1994.[9]

There are also smaller numbers of Nicaraguans, Hondurans, Panamanians, and Costa Ricans. Some of these Central Americans have sought refugee status in the United States because of violence and persecution in their home countries. Most of these immigrants have entered the United States since 1985. Others are economic immigrants, and some of them are undocumented. Cities that already have Spanish-speaking populations are attractive destinations for them.[10]

More than 1 million persons from the diverse countries of South America live in the United States. The largest groups come from Colombia, Ecuador, and Peru. South Americans enter the United States for many reasons, but this group includes a large number of well-educated economic immigrants who hold professional jobs in the United States. These are essentially the only Hispanic groups who have used the skilled-worker provisions of immigration laws to enter the United States.

Besides the Central and South Americans, there are other groups that indicate Hispanic origin. Some of them are from Spain, but the largest groups are from the Caribbean islands that formerly were colonies of Spain. Numerically most important among them are some 520,000 from the Dominican Republic, largely concentrated in the New York City area with smaller numbers in Florida. The Dominican flow is composed mostly of economic migrants. The Dominican Republic shares the island of Hispaniola with Haiti, a French-speaking republic from which 270,000 persons have come to the United States, some of them claiming refugee status. Some observers do not count the Haitian immigrant flow as Hispanic, but others do.

Diversity

As the preceding account indicates, among the Hispanic population of the United States there exists a wide variety of home countries, and many different historical influences have led these people to the United States.[11] Some Hispanics have lived in the Southwest since Spanish colonial times; others have arrived within the last few months from the Caribbean or Central America. Some are U.S. citizens by birth, whereas others come as economic immigrants or refugees. This diversity has led some observers to criticize the term *Hispanic* as too broad to indicate any underlying economic or political commonality. Almost certainly, the internal diversity of Hispanics has defied generalization. For this reason, many common assertions about Hispanics are only partially true. The following section reviews a series of myths about Hispanics and presents more recent data to correct the underlying stereotypes.

Myths About Hispanics

A *stereotype* is an incorrect generalization about a group of people based on the characteristics or behavior of some of those people. Stereotypes are potentially harmful if they lead to prejudice about a group or to discrimination, which can be defined as harmful differential treatment of a group. It is important to correct stereotypes about Hispanics because there has been a legacy of discrimination against some Hispanics (especially Mexican-Americans and Puerto Ricans). Moreover, stereotypes often hinder efforts to craft legitimate and effective public policy in areas that affect all groups, such as education and public health. Because stereotypes are misleading, they often give rise to myths about a group. Although *myth* has a number of definitions, in this chapter the term refers to false beliefs that are used to justify action or inaction.

Myth #1: Hispanics Are Primarily Rural People

This myth arose because many Hispanics, especially Mexican-Americans, worked on farms and ranches earlier in the twentieth century. In the Southwest, some of these people were farm or ranch owners, and they and their families lived on their land. Migrant farm workers, who followed the harvests northward through the Midwest or along the Pacific coast, were often Spanish speakers from Mexico. On the East Coast, migrant farm workers also came from the Caribbean. The farm workers were housed in rural areas close to the fields or orchards in which they worked. During World War II, when agricultural labor was scarce because of the mobilization of millions of soldiers, the United States and Mexico agreed to the Braceros Program, which brought single Mexican males to the United States under specified work contracts, primarily as agricultural workers.

It is probably because of such circumstance that the myth of Hispanic rural living arose. It is true that there are still migrant farm workers of Hispanic origin, and their welfare and the schooling of their children remain important policy issues in many states. Like most other Americans, however, Hispanics are primarily urban people. In 1990, more than 90 percent of Hispanics lived in metropolitan areas, compared with 75 percent of the non-Hispanic White population and 84 percent of the Black population.[12] Only about 6 percent of Hispanic workers are now employed in forestry, fishing, and agriculture, compared with 3 percent of the general population. In contrast, of all the workers in forestry, fishing, and agriculture, Hispanics constitute a fraction (18 percent) larger than their fraction of the national population.[13]

Not only are most Hispanics urban, but they are also highly concentrated in relatively few metropolitan areas. Los Angeles alone contains 21 percent of the Hispanic population, and gained 2 million Hispanic residents during the 1980s.[14] Today there are nearly 5 million Hispanics in Los Angeles, nearly 3 million in New York City, and more than 1 million in Miami. Los Angeles is an important destination city for Mexican-Americans and Central Americans. Puerto Ricans on the mainland are more likely to reside in New York City and the New Jersey suburbs; however, the movement of Puerto Ricans between the mainland and the island makes the accuracy of these counts questionable. Hispanics in Miami are most likely to be Cubans or Central or South Americans. When Hispanics move among cities in the United States, they are likely to move to metropolitan areas relatively close to other Hispanic concentrations, such as San Diego and Sacramento in California. The 1990 census showed 29 metropolitan areas with populations of 100,000 Hispanics or more. Some of these metropolitan areas are located in the Midwest (such as Chicago), but a great number of them are in the southwestern states.

Myth #2: Hispanics Are Mostly Immigrants

Although many Hispanics are immigrants, it is not true that most Hispanics have immigrated. Many of them have been born in the United States. Somewhat more than one-third of all the Hispanics in the United States are immigrants from another country. About 38 percent of the 21.9 million Hispanics enumerated in 1990 were born in another country; the remainder were born in the United States and are U.S. citizens. (All Puerto Ricans, about 2.6 million, are born U.S. citizens.) Another 30 percent are the second generation—that is, they are native born with at least one foreign-born parent, or they are foreign born with at least one native-born parent. The remaining 32 percent are the third generation, native born of native-born parents.[15]

In absolute numbers, the largest single group of immigrants to the United States is Mexican; 33 percent of the Mexican-origin population in the United States (about 4.4 million persons) was born abroad. Many of them are recent arrivals. In 1994, more than 111,000 Mexicans legally entered the United States as immigrants. Almost 3 million Mexicans immigrated to the United States between 1981 and 1993.[16] The *proportion* of the group who are immigrants is highest among Central Americans, of whom 79 percent were born in another country; it is lowest among those of "other Hispanic origin," of whom 32 percent were born in another country. This latter group includes persons who report themselves as Spaniards, Spanish, and Spanish-American.

The perception that most Hispanics are immigrants is fueled by media attention to immigration, by the ease of travel, and by the fact that many native-born Hispanics continue to use the Spanish language both at home and in their communities. As immigration became an important policy issue, newspapers and electronic media developed stories about immigration and immigrants. These stories often focus on Hispanic immigrants, perhaps giving rise to the false belief that most immigrants are Hispanic—and, conversely, that most Hispanics are immigrants. In some areas where immigration is particularly controversial, there is also an especially large proportion of Hispanic immigrants. In California, for example, where the largest number of immigrants live, about half of the immigrants are Hispanic, mostly Mexican-American and Central American.[17] In total, more than a third of all foreign-born Americans are Hispanic, and something less than half of the Hispanics are immigrants.

There are also many visitors between the United States and Latin American countries. Although most of these visitors do not intend to remain as immigrants, others may perceive them as immigrants rather than as visitors and guests. Unlike the earlier waves of European immigrants, who could not afford to return to Europe to visit, the proximity of Latin American countries and relatively inexpensive air travel make frequent travel possible for both U.S. citizens and Latin American citizens.[18] Travelers frequently move between the United States and the Dominican Republic, Mexico, and other Latin American countries to visit relatives and conduct business. About 47,000 Latin American students study at American colleges and universities.[19] In addition, recent economic initiatives such as the NAFTA treaty have greatly increased commerce among the United States and Mexico, Central America, and South America.

Hispanic immigrants, like other immigrant groups, continue to use their native language and to pass it on to their children. Many in the native-born Hispanic population speak Spanish as either a first or a second language. Where there are large Hispanic communities, Spanish-language advertisements, radio, and television are often available. Church services may be conducted in Spanish, and bilingual signs may be common. In some states, ballots and state notices are translated into Spanish, in compliance with the Voting Rights Act. These indicators are sometimes interpreted as proof that the Hispanic community is made up mostly of immigrants who cannot yet speak English. A more correct interpretation is that many Hispanic citizens continue to use Spanish for some aspects of daily life.

Immigration is an important contemporary policy topic in the United States. Although Hispanics are among the oldest population groups in the country, Hispanics are also among the newest immigration streams. The proximity of Mexico to the United States has made it possible for undocumented persons to enter the United States as illegal immigrants. But it would be erroneous to define the immigration "problem" as a Hispanic problem.

It is nevertheless important to observe the interaction of immigration with other population characteristics. Immigration from Mexico has enlarged the proportion of all Hispanics who are of Mexican origin, whereas the proportion of Hispanics who are Puerto Rican has shrunk.

Myth #3: Hispanics Have Large Families with Many Children

About two-thirds of the increase in the Hispanic population may be attributed to the balance of births and deaths within the population. The Hispanic population is relatively young, and thus has a larger proportion of young adults in their prime childbearing years. The median age is a simple summary measure of age structure. Half of all people are older than the median age and half are younger. In the United States in 1995, the median age for the whole population was 34.3 years; for Hispanics it was 26.2 years. Children under the age of 5 constitute about 7 percent of the whole population, but a little more than 11 percent of the Hispanic population.[20]

At the other end of the age structure, there are fewer seniors among the Hispanic population. The White population has about 12.9 percent over the age of 65; in the Black population, the proportion over the age of 65 is 7.6 percent. Among Hispanics, only 5.2 percent were over the age of 65, but this figure conceals a great deal of heterogeneity. Among Cubans, 17.9 percent are over the age of 65, but among Mexican-Americans and Central and South Americans only 4.3 percent are over the age of 65.[21] Thus, by three measures the Hispanic population is younger than either the non-Hispanic White or the Black populations of the United States.

A young population is said to have a great deal of growth momentum. Young persons marry and have children who keep the population youthful. If the young persons also have a fairly large number of children, the age structure grows still more youthful. Three variables can accentuate this trend: relatively youthful childbearing; close spacing of children; and having a relatively large number of children. The aggregate statistics for Hispanics are heavily affected by the large fraction of the Hispanic population that is Mexican-American. Although there are variations among the different Hispanic groups, each of these three variables comes into play for at least some portions of the Hispanic population.

In terms of early childbearing, Hispanic teenagers bear 17.1 births per 1,000 women, compared with 22.7 for Black teenagers and 10.9 for White teenagers. Puerto Rican women are even more likely to begin childbearing as teenagers; their teenage birth rate is 21.4, and for Mexican-Americans it is 18.0. For Cubans the rate is 7.1 and for Central and South Americans it is 9.6. Hispanic women tend to space their babies somewhat closer together than White women. Between the ages of 25 to 29 years, Hispanic women have had on average 1,493 babies for every 1,000 women, whereas non-Hispanic White women have had only 1,077 babies.[22]

In every age group, Hispanic women have more children than White women, and in most age groups they also have more children than Black women. The total fertility rate for Hispanic women is 2,977. This figure means that if the current birth rates at every age were to continue indefinitely into the future, 1,000 Hispanic women now aged 15 years old would have given birth to 2,977 babies by the time they reached the end of their biological childbearing years. For Black women, the number is 2,427, and for White women the number is 1,984.[23] When asked how many babies they expect to have, Hispanic women expect more babies (2,331 per thousand) than Black women (2,136 babies) or White women (2,098).[24] Only 5.7 percent of Hispanic women expect to have no births during their lifetimes, compared with 9.3 percent of both Black and White women.

The claim that Hispanics have large families has some statistical support. Almost two-thirds of Hispanic families have two parents in the home, compared with 75 percent of White families and 36 percent of Black families. Besides the presence of two parents, Hispanic families are more likely to have children in the home than either Black or White families. Nineteen percent of Hispanic families have three or more children in the home. By comparison, only 14 percent of Black families and only 9 percent of White families have three or more children at home. Notably, though, the prevalence of the three-child family is declining, even among Hispanics. In 1970, 31 percent of Hispanic families had 3 or more children in the home.

Each of these indicators—young childbearing, close spacing of children, higher number of births—points to a population that can grow rapidly through natural increase. The young age structure of the Hispanic population is also associated with higher fertility. Moreover, because many recent immigrants have come from countries in which fertility is usually higher than in the United States, they may bring with them the expectation for a larger family. Hispanic culture also values good relationships with family members, including care for older and younger relatives. Thus, this myth has some factual basis.

Nevertheless, the reality behind the myth may be changing with time. Hispanic fertility is expected to decline by 2010 to a total fertility rate of 2,777. The expected lifetime births of Hispanic women are also lower than the current fertility rates, which suggests that fertility may fall if the women have access to medical care and contraception. The number of families with three or more children has been declining. Moreover, Hispanics are similar to other population groups in beginning to post-pone marriage or to end marriage through divorce. A larger proportion of Hispanic adults in 1995, compared with 1970, had never married (28.6 percent) or had been divorced (7.9 percent).[25] Most observers believe that the trend in Hispanic fertility is converging with the fertility trends of other groups in the United States. In general, as groups become more prosperous, their fertility declines. It might be that as more Hispanics achieve economic success, they will choose to have fewer children. Over time, the Hispanic population will probably come to resemble the rest of the U.S. population in terms of fertility.

Myth #4: Hispanics Do Not Value Education

Among the major ethnic groups in the United States, Hispanics as a group have a relatively low level of educational attainment. This does not indicate, however, that Hispanic families do not value education. As the following discussion shows, it is more probable that the availability of educational opportunity plays a crucial role in Hispanic educational attainment.

Table 1.2 shows the educational attainment of Hispanics and non-Hispanics aged 25 and older in 1990 and 1994. The data show a substantial gap between the two groups. By 1996, when 86 percent of White adults and 75 percent of Black adults were high school graduates, only 53 percent of Hispanic adults were high school gradu-ates. This was an improvement over the 1994 figure, but there is still a large gap.

Table 1.2
Educational Attainment: March 1990 and 1994
(percent 25 years old and over)

	Hispanic		Non-Hispanic	
	1990	1994	1990	1994
High school diploma or higher	51	53	80	83
Bachelor's degree or higher	9	9	22	23

Source: United States Bureau of the Census, Statistical Abstract of the United States, 116th ed. (Washington, D.C.: GPO, 1996).

The attainment rate of high school graduation is reduced further by the low educational level of the largest Hispanic group, Mexican-Americans. Among Mexican-American adults, only 47 percent were high school graduates; the proportion among the other origin groups was 60 percent or higher, ranging from 60 percent for Puerto Ricans to 64 percent for Cubans.[26]

In similar fashion, Hispanics are much less likely than other groups to hold a bachelor's degree or more advanced college degree. In contrast to 26 percent of Whites, 14 percent of Blacks, and 37 percent of "other non-Hispanics" (a category that includes American Indians and Asian-Americans), only 9 percent of Hispanics held a college degree. Within Hispanic origin groups, there is again a good deal of heterogeneity, with 7 percent of Mexican-Americans and 19 percent of Cuban-Americans holding college degrees.[27] However, Hispanic high school graduates are about as likely as graduates from other groups to attend college.[28]

These data do not indicate, therefore, that Hispanics do not value education. Instead, they indicate a distribution of previous opportunity. Many immigrants from Latin America, for example, had little opportunity as children to gain a formal education. Among the foreign born, 42 percent are high school graduates and only 8 percent are college graduates. For Hispanics born in the United States, by contrast, 70 percent are high school graduates and 12 percent are college graduates. Hispanic children born in the United States have access to free public education and they are likely to take advantage of that access.

There is also an indication that the renewed American concern with educational opportunity (which gained momentum in the late 1960s) has benefited Hispanics. Before then, it was common for Hispanic youth to attend segregated schools that often had poorer facilities and less well paid teachers. A combination of legislation and litigation began to change this pattern. Younger Hispanic adults are better educated than older Hispanics, indicating that more recently Hispanics have been able to take greater advantage of schooling. Among Hispanics older than 35 in 1995, only 49 percent have a high school diploma, but among those aged 25 to 34 years the proportion rises to 61 percent.[29]

Nevertheless, there is reason for policy makers to remain concerned about the educational opportunities and chances for achievement offered to Hispanic children. Parental financial resources have a positive impact on children's achievement, and Hispanic families have fewer financial resources, on average, than most other Americans. Nurseries, kindergartens, and other preschools help to prepare children for school, but such experiences are not always provided by the local public schools. Hispanic children are historically less likely to attend any preschools, and the gap in preschool attendance between Hispanic children and other children has been increasing.[30] Moreover, Hispanic parents may not have the financial resources to provide other educational benefits, such as tutors, special after-school lessons, or summer camps.

Language use certainly complicates Hispanic children's achievement in school. Although in the long run it is beneficial to be bilingual, students whose primary language is Spanish may experience difficulty in school, and teachers may erroneously classify such students as less able or even retarded. Bilingual education is one method that school districts use to help Spanish-speaking children learn English and the other subjects at the same time. Some bilingual programs also seek to maintain and improve the Spanish the children speak. In a 1998 survey, a majority of Hispanic parents said that learning to read, write, and speak English was the most important goal of their children's education.[31] Spanish-speaking parents may have difficulty communicating with teachers or understanding the letters that school authorities send home. Children may also be encouraged to speak Spanish at home to communicate with other family members, especially grandparents.

That this is so is suggested by patterns of language use. Next to English, Spanish is the language most likely to be spoken in American homes, with more than 17 million persons 5 years of age and older speaking Spanish at home. (French was third, with only 1.7 million speaking French at home.) In 1990, 4.1 million school-aged children (ages 5 to 17) spoke Spanish at home, and 39 percent of them reported that they did *not* speak English "very well." For adults aged 18 to 64,

12.1 million spoke Spanish at home and almost one-half thought that they did *not* speak English "very well." Among senior citizens aged 65 or older, 1 million spoke Spanish at home, and of these 62 percent did not speak English "very well."[32] So, although the youngest Hispanics had the best English-language ability, their parents and grandparents on average had much less ability to speak English well, a fact that might affect ability to understand teachers and principals and to help children with schoolwork.

In their study of Hispanic youth in high school, Romo and Falbo[33] noted that although dropout rates declined from 1971 to 1991 for both majority Whites and Blacks, the dropout rate for Hispanics aged 16 to 24 remained about 35.5 percent. In other words, more than a third of young Hispanic adults are not enrolled in high school and have not received a high school diploma. In their study, Romo and Falbo noted that many factors affect Hispanic teenagers' dropping out, including the adult culture of the schools, the student culture of the schools, and home cultures. Romo and Falbo stated that poorly educated parents are not in a good position either to monitor their children or to understand the school's communications. Children who were successful in graduating, however, were likely to have parents who offered inspiration and encouragement. One mother said, "I use myself as an example, and I'll say things like, 'OK, you know there's two different kinds of people in this world—those that give orders, those that take. What do you want to be?'"[34]

Improvements in educational achievement are important for occupational attainment, as this mother knew. Individual students from all groups are capable of excelling in school. To improve the educational attainment of an entire group, however, requires the concerted work of the community, the schools, and the group itself, and it may well take more than a generation for the benefits to be manifest. Thus, the low achievement of Hispanics as a group is likely to result from a number of causes, including recent immigration, the historic effects of segregation and discrimination, Spanish language use, and the relatively long time needed for generational improvements to appear.

Myth #5: Hispanics Prefer Blue-Collar Work

Partly because of their historic association with agriculture, and partly because of their relatively low levels of formal education, many Hispanics have held blue-collar or service occupations. New immigrants often find work in such fields, and so the large number of immigrants within the Hispanic community also increases the number of blue-collar and service workers. Hispanics make up about 8.9 percent of the labor force, but they are overrepresented in service occupations (13 percent Hispanic); in precision production, craft, and repair occupations (10.6 percent); and as operators, fabricators, and laborers (14.3 percent).

Some occupational groups are even more heavily Hispanic. More than one-quarter of sewing machine operators (26.9 percent) and almost one-third of pressing machine operators (31.9 percent) are Hispanic. One reason for this overrepresentation is the traditional hiring of immigrants in the needle trades, and also the concentration of clothing manufacturers in cities with many Hispanics (e.g., New York City, Los Angeles, El Paso). Even today, more than 40 percent of farm workers are Hispanic.

In the service industries, almost one-quarter of private household employees (24.8 percent) are Hispanic. These workers include nannies, cleaners, and household cooks. More than one-fifth of waiters' and waitresses' assistants (20.1 percent)—workers who might be called "busboys"—are Hispanic. A similar proportion of maids, cleaners, and janitors are Hispanic. Hispanics are also overrepresented in some of the skilled construction trades, such as glazing and tilesetting.

By contrast, Hispanics are much less likely to be employed in higher-paying, white-collar jobs. Only 4.4 percent of managers and professional specialty workers are Hispanic. Hispanics make up less than 3 percent of engineers, natural scientists, dentists, pharmacists, and speech therapists. About 3 to 4 percent of physicians, lawyers, and teachers are Hispanic. Hispanics are also generally underrepresented among technical workers, sales workers, and administrative workers.[35]

Hispanics are less likely than other workers to use computers on the job; about 29 percent of Hispanics use computers in the workplace, compared with 36 percent of Black workers and 49 percent of White workers. Although computers are used in many types of industries, their use is more frequent among those with higher levels of education, and computer use may be consistent with higher productivity workplaces.[36] Computers are now strongly associated with many types of white-collar work.

These patterns of work do not necessarily indicate a preference for blue-collar work, however. Younger Hispanic workers, especially those with strong educational backgrounds, have found many opportunities in all industries. Hispanic entrepreneurs have opened businesses of all types, especially in urban areas with large Hispanic populations.[37] In 1994, there were 5,459 Hispanic elected officials, a 73 percent increase over the number of Hispanic elected officials only 9 years earlier. This number includes 2,400 school board members and 199 state executives and legislators.[38] In 1997, 17 voting and 2 nonvoting members of Congress were Hispanic.

One consequence of the Hispanic overrepresentation in service and blue-collar jobs has been that Hispanic families' income levels are usually lower, and their poverty rates higher, than those of other groups. This is true despite high rates of participation in the labor force. More than 79 percent of Hispanic men were in the labor force in 1995, compared with 75 percent of all men. Among Mexican-origin men, the rate was even higher, almost 81 percent; among Cuban men (who are the oldest group and most likely to be retired) it was lower, at 69.9 percent. Hispanic women participated at lower levels than all women: 57.6 percent versus 58.9 percent. "Other Hispanic" women had the highest participation, 57.5 percent among Hispanic women, and Puerto Rican women had the lowest at 47.4 percent.[39]

The lower incomes of Hispanic families can be traced to several causes, each of which is in turn linked to low levels of education: unemployment, jobs with low earnings, and the numbers of earners per household. Unemployment is higher among Hispanics than among other groups. In 1995, when the overall unemployment rate was 4.8 percent, the Hispanic rate was nearly twice as high, at 8.0 percent. For those without a high school education, the rate was even higher, almost 11 percent. But for Hispanics with a college degree, the unemployment rate was only 3.7 percent, a rate that is low enough to be frictional unemployment.[40] *Frictional unemployment* is the temporary loss of work that occurs when moving between one job and another. Unemployment was highest for Puerto Ricans and lowest for Cubans.[41]

An important source of unemployment is displacement. In 1994 there were 361,000 displaced Hispanic workers—that is, workers who had been employed by the same employer for three years or more and who had lost a job because of plant closure, reduction in the availability of work (slack work), or the elimination of their positions. Hispanic displaced workers were more likely than the general work force to have lost their jobs because of plant closure or transfer and because of slack work.[42] The rate of unemployment for these displaced workers was especially high, with about 30 percent still looking for work at the time of the survey. As the economy generally improved, however, the displacement rates of Hispanic workers also improved, so that by 1994 there were about 150,000 fewer displaced Hispanic workers than there had been in 1992.

Hispanic workers on average are more likely to be in jobs with low hourly earnings. The median hourly earnings for Hispanic workers in 1995 was $7.00, compared with $8.17 for all workers, $8.32 for White workers, and $7.66 for Black workers.[43] Not all workers receive hourly wages; some receive salaries, and so it is important also to examine other measures of earnings. These measures corroborate the finding that Hispanics have lower earnings. Median weekly earnings for Hispanic workers in 1993 were $505, compared with $707 for all families. Median annual income for Hispanic families was $23,670, compared with $41,110 for non-Hispanic families. Since 1972, when the figures became available, the median income of Hispanic families has been below that of Whites but above that of Blacks.

Increasing the number of earners per family is one way that a low-income family can increase its monetary resources. In married-couple families with only one earner, the median weekly earnings for Hispanics are only $334—lower than for either Blacks or Whites. With two or more earners, however, the Hispanic weekly income goes up to $744. Unlike White families, however, where nearly 64 percent of married couples have 2 or more earners in the family, in Hispanic families only 41 percent have 2 or more earners.[44]

As these indicators of labor market disadvantage suggest, Hispanics are more likely than other groups to have family incomes below the poverty line. The poverty line, a measure used by the federal government, was developed by pricing a market basket of basic foods that provide basic nutrition. Because surveys of poor families showed that they spent about one-third of their income on food, the price of the basic food basket was multiplied by three to yield a total budget figure. This figure, which is graduated by family size and by the age of the householder, is also adjusted each year for inflation. The poverty line for a family of four is commonly used as a benchmark. In 1997, that figure was $16,400.

In 1994, Hispanics were very likely to be below the poverty line. In the United States as a whole, 14.5 percent of the total population was below the poverty level, but 30.7 percent of Hispanics—or 8.4 million persons—were below the poverty line. This included 4.0 million Hispanic children, or 41.1 percent of all Hispanic children; and 323,000 Hispanic persons over the age of 65, or 22.6 percent of the total.[45] A month-to-month study of poverty, which adjusted for the fact that earnings may vary from month to month, showed that 12.2 percent of Hispanics were in poverty for all 24 months of the 2-year survey, and 29.8 percent were poor in an average month. This figure also varied by education, with 38 percent of householders without a high school diploma below the poverty level; 20.7 percent of those with a high school diploma but no college were below the poverty level.[46] Puerto Rican and Mexican-origin families are most likely to be poor, and Cubans are the least likely among Hispanic groups to be poor.

The most recent poverty data, from 1997, show that 24.7 percent of Hispanic families, nearly one-quarter of the total, received incomes below the poverty level. A similar proportion of Black families was below poverty (23.6 percent), compared with 10.2 percent of Asian-American families and 8.4 percent of White families. The proportion of Hispanic families in poverty has declined during the 1990s, with a 1.7 percent drop between 1996 and 1997 alone.[47] The cause of this decline was a 4.5 percent increase in the real (that is, inflation-adjusted) household median income for Hispanics, from $25,477 to $26,628. A generally low unemployment rate is often cited as the reason for this improvement.

To return to the myth with which this discussion began, however, there is no indicator of preference for blue-collar work. Lower levels of education, less familiarity with the American labor market (for immigrants), and concentration in lower-paying occupations and industries appear to be more likely reasons for the labor force status of Hispanics. Native-born Hispanics who attend college appear to enjoy socioeconomic achievement at levels similar to those of other groups.

Other Demographic Aspects

The health of Hispanics is better, and their mortality is lower, than their socioeconomic position might otherwise suggest. Despite their high fertility and poverty levels, Hispanics have relatively low levels of low birthweight and infant mortality. Only about 6 percent of Hispanic babies are low birthweight, compared with 7.1 percent for the total population and 13.3 percent for Blacks. Mexican-origin babies are even less likely to be low birthweight: only about 5.6 percent. Puerto Rican babies are most likely to be low birthweight, about 9.2 percent.[48] What is even more remarkable is that Hispanic women are twice as likely as White women (a little more than 9 percent, versus 4.2 percent) not to seek prenatal care at all or to wait for prenatal care until the third trimester. The proportion of Black women who do not get prenatal care or who wait to get care is about the same as of Hispanics.

The reasons for such healthy babies, despite predictors of high infant mortality, are not well understood. Hispanic mothers have traditionally followed good health practices, such as emphasizing good nutrition and not smoking, drinking, or using drugs during pregnancy. In general, Hispanics are less likely than others to be heavy drinkers or to smoke cigarettes, although they are less likely to follow some other recommended health practices such as eating breakfast, rarely snacking, and exercising regularly.[49]

Adult mortality for Hispanics is not unusually high, especially considering their likelihood of poverty. Some researchers believe that Hispanics' continuing use of a traditional Mexican diet, which emphasizes grains, beans, and fresh vegetables, may help explain the lower rates of some types of disease in the Hispanic population. Modern medical advances do not appear to be a substantial part of the explanation, because Hispanics are somewhat less likely than other population groups to have adequate health care. One-third of Hispanics are not currently covered by health insurance. Medicaid covers about 22.5 percent of the Hispanic population, including 48 percent of those who are below the poverty line.[50]

Some causes of death appear to be more significant for Hispanics than for other population groups. Diabetes is much more prevalent in the Hispanic community. It is a significant cause of death among Hispanic women, and public health authorities have tried to target advertising to the Hispanic community to encourage more preventive and diagnostic care. Hispanic women are frequently checked for gestational diabetes during pregnancy, because the development of temporary diabetes during pregnancy is sometimes a precursor of adult-onset diabetes later in life. This is one reason that public health authorities encourage prenatal care in the Hispanic community.

As the Hispanic population grows, so does the effort to target them in advertising and in retail sales.[51] Public health advertising is only one example of efforts to find and inform Hispanics. As the Hispanic market increases, even with relatively low income in the average household, more businesses will seek to offer goods and services to them.

Within the Hispanic community, a growing population creates niches for local entrepreneurs, who in turn can provide employment for others from the group. This phenomenon, which has been well documented in the Cuban community, may well be replicated in other Hispanic communities.[52]

The political presence of the Hispanic population is expected to grow as the size of the population increases. In the 1990s, there has been increased interest in naturalization among the immigrant Hispanic population. Voter registration and voting are increasing among the Hispanic citizenry, but the proportions remain substantially below those for Whites. With increasing education, however, the gap in voting behavior appears to diminish. The geographic concentration of Hispanics should intensify their political impact. Hispanics have served as mayors, members of Congress, Cabinet officers, and as U.S. Ambassador to the United Nations.

Policy Issues Affecting Hispanics

Earlier in this chapter, the methods for counting Hispanics in the United States were mentioned. One of the most important policy issues affecting Hispanics in the United States is the extent to which government statistics undercount Hispanics. For the 1990 census, the U.S. Census Bureau estimated that 5 percent of the Hispanic population was not counted.[53] By comparison, the undercount for Blacks was 4.4 percent and for non-Hispanic Whites it was only 0.7 percent. An undercount is significant because it translates into lower political representation and lower levels of funding for local communities. To the extent that the missed Hispanics were concentrated in particular geographic areas, the negative policy effects are exacerbated.

Many of the demographic characteristics of Hispanics are consistent with an undercount. Children are more likely than adults to be undercounted, and the Hispanic community has relatively more children.[54] Immigrants are more likely to be undercounted,[55] in part because of language difficulties. People with low levels of education are more likely to be undercounted, partly because they may not understand the purpose of the questionnaire and partly because they may not know how to answer the questions. Finally, undocumented persons are likely to try to avoid the census because they fear and avoid *any* encounter with the government. Moreover, many Americans appear to be confused about the concept of "Hispanic origin." In 1990, the question on Hispanic origin had the highest rate of nonresponse of any of the questions asked of 100 percent of the population.

An important policy issue for the year 2000—and beyond—will be improving the count of Hispanics and other undercounted groups. A number of proposals have been made, including provisions for more Spanish-language materials and greater use of telephone and other more convenient response methods.[56] Perhaps the most controversial suggestion, however, has been deploying a sample survey nearly simultaneously with the census itself to permit immediate identification of and adjustment for the undercount.

A postenumeration survey has been used for many years and is one means currently used for estimating the undercount. The basic postenumeration survey asks respondents whether they did or did not participate in the census. From these data, and taking into account the sampling error, it is possible to extrapolate both the number of persons who were missed by the census and their characteristics. The proposed survey would happen at the same time as the census so that ordinary migration of the population would not confuse the results.

The controversy about the sampling technique is closely tied to partisan beliefs about which political party would benefit from an adjusted count, as well as concern that sampling does not represent the "actual enumeration" called for by the Constitution. The Supreme Court has decided that the use of sampling to adjust census counts for congressional reapportionment is unconstitutional. The U.S. Census Bureau will seek to encourage all of the Hispanic population to participate in the census, through increased advertising, by provision of informational materials in Hispanic community organizations, and by making the census questionnaire more readily available.

The Census Bureau's reliance on self-enumeration, however, may mean that some persons in similar situations will report themselves differently. Take, for example, the case of Hispanic women who marry non-Hispanic men. There are some indications that the rate of out-marriage between Hispanics and non-Hispanics is rising. One Hispanic woman who adopts a husband's non-Hispanic surname may hesitate to report herself as Hispanic on the census questionnaire; a different woman, also married to a non-Hispanic man, may choose to report not only herself but also her children as Hispanic. The government, for strong policy reasons, does not tell respondents how to identify themselves in such situations, but rather relies on each individual's own interpretation of his or her ethnic background. Thus, the accuracy of the total count will reflect hundreds of thousands of individual interpretations of ethnic identity.

Other important policy issues that affect Hispanics arise from the age structure of the group. Because of the large number of Hispanic children, education policy is an important area of interest. Some education issues include concerns about bilingual education in schools, segregation of Hispanic children, and adequate education for children whose parents do not have a high level of education. For higher education, there are the issues of increasing the numbers of Hispanic students and producing Hispanic teachers and professionals who can work in Hispanic communities. Several states have recently eliminated affirmative action in education, and the issue of adequate access to higher education for Hispanic children inevitably arises in such states.

The youthful age structure of the Hispanic population also raises issues of health care, particularly for children and mothers. Hispanic communities need access to prenatal care, vaccinations against disease, and pediatric care for children, and in settings in which many potential clients are not covered by health insurance. Moreover, general issues that affect poverty and health care, jobs and job security, and occupational health and safety may be of special concern to Hispanics, because of their low incomes and jobs in lower-skilled occupations. Many of these policy issues are discussed in greater detail in subsequent chapters.

The policy issue of greatest significance to Hispanics, however, is probably the immigration policy of the United States. Who is legally allowed into the United States, and what measures are taken to prevent and prosecute illegal immigration, are issues with which the Hispanic community is vitally concerned. Political and economic upheavals in Central and South America, and even natural disasters (such as Hurricane Mitch, which struck Honduras, Nicaragua, and Guatemala) often are not anticipated by policy makers. Thus, immigration policy must frequently be revised or improvised.

Conclusion

America's Hispanic population is its most rapidly growing minority group, and in the next century it will become the largest minority group. In California, Hispanic children are about to become a majority of the school children, and in many other metropolitan areas, the Hispanic community is growing rapidly. Young, hard-working, and family-oriented, Hispanics bring much to their communities. Many of the disadvantages suffered by this large ethnic group are currently attributable to their low levels of education and to the effect that poor education has on unemployment, occupation, income, and the acquisition of wealth. Recent economic prosperity appears to benefit the Hispanic community, as incomes have begun to rise and poverty rates to fall. It is a sign of the times and the influence of this important group that salsa has replaced ketchup as the most popular condiment at the same time that salsa music is heard over more and more radio stations.

Notes

1. William H. Frey, "The New Geography of Population Shifts," in *State of the Union: America in the 1990s*, ed. Reynolds Farley, vol. 2 (New York: Russell Sage Foundation, 1995), 271–336; Jorge del Pinal and Audrey Singer, "Generations of Diversity: Latinos in the United States," *Population Bulletin* 52, no. 3 (October 1997): 1–48.
2. United States Bureau of the Census, *Statistical Abstract of the United States*, 116th ed. (Washington, D.C.: Government Printing Office, 1996), Table 19 [middle projection].
3. Alejandro Portes and Ruben Rumbaut, *Immigrant America: A Portrait* (Berkeley, Cal.: University of California Press, 1990).
4. United States Office of Management and Budget, "Recommendations from the Interagency Committee for the Review of the Racial and Ethnic Standards: Notice," *Federal Register* 62, no. 131 (July 9, 1997): 36930–31.
5. Barry R. Chiswick and Teresa A. Sullivan, "The New Immigrants," in *State of the Union: America in the 1990s*, ed. Reynolds Farley, vol. 2 (New York: Russell Sage Foundation, 1995), 211–70.
6. United States Bureau of the Census, *Statistical Abstract of the United States* (1996), 11.
7. Del Pinal and Singer, "Generations of Diversity," 20.
8. Ibid., 10.
9. United States Bureau of the Census, *Statistical Abstract of the United States*, 116th ed. (Washington, D.C.: Government Printing Office, 1996), 11.
10. Jacqueline Maria Hagan, *Deciding to Be Legal: A Maya Community in Houston* (Philadelphia: Temple University Press, 1994).
11. Frank D. Bean and Marta Tienda, *The Hispanic Population of the United States* (New York: Russell Sage Foundation, 1987).
12. Roderick J. Harrison and Claudette E. Bennett, "Racial and Ethnic Diversity," in *State of the Union: America in the 1990s*, ed. Reynolds Farley, vol. 2 (New York: Russell Sage Foundation, 1995), 206–7.
13. United States Bureau of the Census, *Statistical Abstract of the United States* (1996), 405–7.
14. Frey, "The New Geography of Population Shifts," 290.
15. Del Pinal and Singer, "Generations of Diversity."
16. United States Bureau of the Census, *Statistical Abstract of the United States* (1996), 11.
17. Kevin McCarthy and Georges Vernez, *Immigration in a Changing Economy: California's Experience* (Santa Monica, Cal.: RAND Corporation, 1997).

18. Douglas S. Massey, Rafael Alarcon, Jorge Durand, and Humberto Gonzalez, *Return to Aztlan: The Social Process of International Migration* (Berkeley, Cal.: University of California Press, 1987).
19. United States Bureau of the Census, *Statistical Abstract of the United States* (1996), 297.
20. Ibid., 22–23.
21. Ibid., 49–51.
22. Ibid., 82–83.
23. Ibid., 77.
24. Ibid., 83.
25. Ibid., 54–58.
26. Del Pinal and Singer, "Generations of Diversity," 32.
27. Ibid.
28. Population Reference Bureau, "Diverse Hispanic Population to Become Largest U.S. Minority," *Population Today* 25, no. 11 (November 1997): 1–2.
29. Del Pinal and Singer, "Generations of Diversity."
30. Ibid.
31. Michael Barone, "How Hispanics Are Americanizing," *Wall Street Journal*, February 6, 1998, section A, at 22.
32. United States Bureau of the Census, *Statistical Abstract of the United States* (1996), 53.
33. Harriett D. Romo and Toni Falbo, *Latino High School Graduation: Defying the Odds* (Austin, Tex.: University of Texas Press, 1997).
34. Ibid., 207.
35. United States Bureau of the Census, *Statistical Abstract of the United States* (1996), 405–7.
36. Ibid., 423.
37. Barone, "How Hispanics Are Americanizing"; Alejandro Portes and Robert L. Bach, *Latin Journey: Cuban and Mexican Immigrants in the United States* (Berkeley, Cal.: University of California Press, 1985).
38. United States Bureau of the Census, *Statistical Abstract of the United States* (1996), 283.
39. Ibid., 397–98.
40. Ibid., 415.
41. United States Bureau of the Census, "The Nation's Hispanic Population—1994," Statistical Brief SB/95-25 (September 1995).
42. United States Bureau of the Census, *Statistical Abstract of the United States* (1996), 635.
43. Ibid., 429.
44. Ibid., 427.
45. Ibid., 472–73.
46. Ibid., 475–76.
47. United States Bureau of the Census, *March 1997 Current Population Survey.* Internet posting; United States Bureau of the Census, "Poverty Level of Hispanic Population Drops, Income Improves," *Census Bureau Reports*, September 24, 1998.
48. United States Bureau of the Census, *Statistical Abstract of the United States* (1996), 78.
49. Ibid., 146.
50. Ibid., 118–21.
51. Brad Edmondson, "Hispanic Americans in 2001," *American Demographics* 19, no. 1 (January 1997): 16–17.

52. Portes and Bach, *Latin Journey*.
53. United States Bureau of the Census, *Report to Congress—The Plan for Census 2000* (Washington, D.C.: Author, August 1997), 4.
54. Ibid., 3.
55. National Research Council, *Modernizing the U.S. Census* (Washington, D.C.: National Academy Press, 1995), 34.
56. National Research Council, *Counting People in the Information Age* (Washington, D.C.: National Academy Press, 1994).

Bibliography

Barone, Michael. "How Hispanics Are Americanizing." *Wall Street Journal*, February 6, 1998, section A, at 22.

Bean, Frank D., and Marta Tienda. *The Hispanic Population of the United States*. New York: Russell Sage Foundation, 1987.

Binder, Norman E., J. L. Polinard, and Robert D. Wrinkle. "Mexican American and Anglo Attitudes Toward Immigration Reform: A View from the Border." *Social Science Quarterly* 78, no. 2 (June 1997): 324–37.

Chavez, Linda. *Out of the Barrio: Toward a New Politics of Hispanic Assimilation*. New York: Basic Books, 119.

Chiswick, Barry R., and Teresa A. Sullivan. "The New Immigrants." In *State of the Union: America in the 1990s*, edited by Reynolds Farley, vol. 2, 211–70. New York: Russell Sage Foundation, 1995.

del Pinal, Jorge, and Audrey Singer. "Generations of Diversity: Latinos in the United States." *Population Bulletin* 52, no. 3 (October 1997): 1–48.

Edmondson, Brad. "Hispanic Americans in 2001." *American Demographics* 19, no. 1 (January 1997): 16–17.

Farley, Reynolds, ed. *State of the Union: America in the 1990s*. New York: Russell Sage Foundation, 1995.

Frey, William H. "The New Geography of Population Shifts." In *State of the Union: America in the 1990s*, edited by Reynolds Farley, vol. 2, 271–336. New York: Russell Sage Foundation, 1995.

Hagan, Jacqueline Maria. *Deciding to Be Legal: A Maya Community in Houston*. Philadelphia: Temple University Press, 1994.

Harrison, Roderick J., and Claudette E. Bennett. "Racial and Ethnic Diversity." In *State of the Union: America in the 1990s*, edited by Reynolds Farley, vol. 2, 141–210. New York: Russell Sage Foundation, 1995.

Lieberson, Stanley, and Mary C. Waters. *From Many Strands: Ethnic and Racial Groups in Contemporary America*. New York: Russell Sage Foundation, 1990.

Massey, Douglas S., Rafael Alarcon, Jorge Durand, and Humberto Gonzalez. *Return to Aztlan: The Social Process of International Migration*. Berkeley, Cal.: University of California Press, 1987.

McCarthy, Kevin, and Georges Vernez. *Immigration in a Changing Economy: California's Experience*. Santa Monica, Cal.: RAND Corporation, 1997.

National Research Council. *Counting People in the Information Age*. Washington, D.C.: National Academy Press, 1994.

———. *Modernizing the U.S. Census*. Washington, D.C.: National Academy Press, 1995.

Pedraza, Silvia, and Ruben G. Rumbaut, eds. *Origins and Destinies: Immigration, Race, and Ethnicity in America*. Belmont, Cal.: Wadsworth, 1996.

Population Reference Bureau. "Diverse Hispanic Population to Become Largest U.S. Minority." *Population Today* 25, no. 11 (November 1997): 1–2.

Portes, Alejandro, and Robert L. Bach. *Latin Journey: Cuban and Mexican Immigrants in the United States*. Berkeley, Cal.: University of California Press, 1985.

Portes, Alejandro, and Ruben Rumbaut. *Immigrant America: A Portrait*. Berkeley, Cal.: University of California Press, 1990.

Romo, Harriett D., and Toni Falbo. *Latino High School Graduation: Defying the Odds*. Austin, Tex.: University of Texas Press, 1997.

United States Bureau of the Census. *March 1997 Current Population Survey*. Internet posting: http://www.census.gov/hhes/poverty/poverty96/pv96estl.html

———. "The Nation's Hispanic Population—1994." Statistical Brief SB/95-25 (September 1995).

———. "Poverty Level of Hispanic Population Drops, Income Improves." *Census Bureau Reports*, September 24, 1998.

———. *Report to Congress—The Plan for Census 2000*. Washington, D.C.: Author, August 1997.

———. *Statistical Abstract of the United States*, 116th ed. Washington, D.C.: Government Printing Office, 1996.

United States Office of Management and Budget. "Recommendations from the Interagency Committee for the Review of the Racial and Ethnic Standards: Notice." *Federal Register* 62, no. 131 (July 9, 1997): 36874–946.

2

Hispanic Immigration at the New Millennium

David W. Engstrom

Hispanics were among the first immigrants to the United States. More than twenty years before the Pilgrims established a foothold near Plymouth Rock, the Spanish had already created settlements in New Mexico. Yet Hispanics are also among the most recent immigrants. For the past thirty years, well over one-third of foreign nationals emigrating to the United States have come from Latin American and Spanish-speaking Caribbean countries. Like all immigrants, Hispanics have encountered in their adopted country a host of conflicting perceptions and government policies about immigrants. At times, United States policy has encouraged Hispanic immigration, in order to meet labor shortages and serve foreign policy objectives. At other times, the United States has tried to close the gate to Hispanic immigration and even forcibly returned not only legal residents, but also Hispanic citizens to their countries of origin. Some Americans view Hispanic immigrants as hard workers who add to the diversity of the country. Others perceive Hispanic immigrants as a population that drains the public coffers and contributes to the Balkanization of the United States.[1]

Scholars have developed various theories to explain the flow of immigration and the mechanisms for maintaining it. This chapter reviews Hispanic immigration in the context of current immigration theory, making comparisons between historic and present-day immigration to the United States. The history of United States policies to screen and channel immigration flows is examined, as are instances in which those policies have produced unanticipated results.

To aid comprehension of the vast terrain of Hispanic immigration and the issues it raises, this chapter also briefly discusses the recent volume of immigration, the provisions by which immigrants enter the United States, where immigrants settle, and the problems inherent in immigration statistics.

The chapter concludes by exploring several contentious issues surrounding Hispanic immigration, including border enforcement, fiscal effects, and the backlash against immigrants (particularly Hispanic immigrants) that has resurfaced as the twentieth century draws to a close. Efforts to restrict immigrant use of social services, welfare programs, and other public services are examples of that backlash.

The Importance of Hispanic Immigration to the United States

In 1990, Congress authorized the creation of a commission to study immigration and to make recommendations to reform United States immigration policy. The United States Commission on Immigration Reform asked the distinguished National Research Council (NRC) to convene a panel of demographers to study the demographic implications of immigration for the population of the United States and to estimate what the population will look like at the year 2050. Employing a sophisticated model for examining population change, the NRC predicted that if the current volume of immigration continues in the future, the United States can expect to have a population of 387 million residents by 2050.[2] Fertility and mortality changes partially explain the 120-million-person growth in population, but the NRC identified immigration—and specifically Hispanic immigration—as the major factor. Whereas one in eleven Americans in 1995 claimed Hispanic ancestry, in 2050 about one in four Americans will identify themselves as Hispanic. Clearly, Hispanic immigration is transforming the United States.

What Has Created and Maintained the Flow of Hispanic Immigration

The classic model of immigration is referred to as *push-pull*. Conditions in country "A" push people to emigrate, while conditions in country "B" pull them to immigrate. Put another way, people leave their country of origin because they believe that their lives will be improved by settling in another country. Jorge Castaneda wrote, "The 'push-pull' effect is truly the decisive determinant of the intensity, size, and evolution of migratory flows."[3] The model seems wonderfully simple. However, the model masks the tremendous complexity of the forces that create the push-pull dynamic.

Historically, immigration to the United States has been caused in part by economic transformation or economic development in sending countries. However contradictory this may seem, much of nineteenth- and early twentieth-century immigration from Europe actually occurred when countries such as England, Germany, and Italy industrialized. This weakened the social and economic importance of agriculture and created large-scale population movements to urban areas. But not every urban migrant found employment, so many emigrated. Improvements in communication and transportation facilitated emigration.

Not surprisingly, Hispanic immigration has been moved by similar currents. Economic development and political instability (often, the two go hand-in-hand) have been the major push factors behind Hispanic emigration.[4] The intrusion of worldwide markets into rural areas, the introduction of more efficient agricultural techniques, the development of transportation facilities, the rapid growth and improvement of communications, and population increases are among the contributing factors in the exodus from rural Latin American communities. The growth of urban areas in Latin America and the economic opportunities found there have held some Hispanics to their homeland. However, like their European counterparts 100 years ago, tens of thousands have chosen to emigrate. As Douglas Massey reminded us, "In the short run ... [economic] development does not reduce the impetus for migration, but only increases it."[5]

Nevertheless, even in the era of unrestricted immigration to the United States, most people chose to stay in their homelands rather than leave them. The same is true today. The overwhelming majority of Latin Americans never attempt to immigrate—legally or illegally—to the United States. As Portes and Rumbaut observed, "The questions can thus be reversed to ask not why many come, but why so few have decided to undertake the journey, especially with difficult economic and political conditions in many sending countries."[6]

The United States has been, and continues to be, the major magnet of Hispanic immigration. American policies have triggered immigration through labor recruitment, military intervention, and foreign policy.

Additionally, higher wages, better employment and educational opportunities, regional economic development, political freedom, family reunification, and the lure of the "good life" have all contributed to pull Hispanic immigrants to the United States.

Changes in economic and political institutions create incentives to immigrate, but the act of emigrating remains an individual or family decision. Immigrants have been and continue to be self-selected. People do not leave their homeland if they are content and satisfied with their lives. Generally, it is not the advantaged or the poor of a society who decide to leave. Blocked opportunity often provides the classic reason to emigrate. Portes and Rumbaut wrote:

> The basic reason [to emigrate] is the gap between life aspirations and expectations and the means to fulfill them in the sending countries. Different groups feel this gap with varying intensity, but it clearly becomes a strong motive for action among the most ambitious and resourceful. Because *relative*, not absolute deprivation lies at the core of most contemporary immigration, its composition tends to be positively selected in terms of both human capital and motivation.[7]

It is clear that relative deprivation plays a role in Hispanic immigration. Describing the interaction of poor economic prospects and political instability on Central American emigration, Sergio Diaz-Briquets wrote:

> These changes result in rising individual aspirations not likely to be satisfied in countries of origin, given limited domestic opportunities that stand in stark contrast to what emigrants can hope for in the far more tranquil and prosperous United States.[8]

Arguing a similar point, de la Garza and Szekely contended that Mexican immigrants leave to use their talent and energy in the United States because they are frustrated by their inability to advance economically, politically, and socially in their native country.[9] It takes initiative, resources, willingness to take risks, and skill to immigrate.

Several facts, however, differentiate recent Hispanic immigration from the European and Asian immigration streams of the nineteenth and early twentieth centuries. First, present-day Hispanic immigrants arrive in areas already long settled by Spanish descendants. It was through the Texas War for Independence, the Mexican-American War, and the subsequent Treaty of Guadalupe Hidalgo that the United States took possession of the present-day Southwest; indeed, military conquest and diplomatic treaty brought more Hispanics into the United States than did immigration during the nineteenth century. Prior settlement has contributed to a sense among many Hispanics, particularly in the Southwest, that the southern border is an artificial and arbitrary line. That sentiment is best characterized by the saying: "We didn't cross the border, the border crossed us."

Proximity also is fact. Mexico shares a 2,000-mile-long border with the United States, which makes it a relatively easy entry point for Mexicans and other Hispanic immigrants. The 90 miles of ocean that separate Cuba from the United States have proven too short a distance to dissuade Cubans from sailing to southern Florida. Second, modern transportation has made travel easy for those living further from the United States. Virtually all Hispanic sending countries have regular air service to the United States, placing those immigrants mere hours from their destination. This is in stark contrast to the weeks, if not months, it took nineteenth-century immigrants to leave their countries of origin and reach the shores of the United States. Distance and time are no longer the serious considerations they were a century ago.

Geographic proximity and the transportation revolution affect emigration in added ways. To emigrate from Europe or Asia 100 years ago meant separation from family and friends for years, if not a lifetime. Oscar Handlin's classic book, *The Uprooted*, eloquently spoke of the difficulty of severing links to the old country and starting life over in a far-off land.[10] An American mythology grew which held that every immigrant who came to the United States stayed permanently—the benefit of America more than outweighed the pain of separation. In fact, difficult as it was to make the journey back, as many as one-third of the European immigrants eventually returned to their homelands, although repatriation usually took years.

In contrast, contemporary Hispanic immigrants do not encounter the same circumstances. As Jorge Castaneda wrote, "Emigrating from next door produces sharply different effects on the mind-set and lifestyle of the migrant than does embarking on a long, once-in-a-lifetime voyage with no return."[11] Ties to family, friends, and community are presently much easier to maintain. Cyclical or temporary immigration occurs more frequently now than in the past. Studies of sending communities in Mexico consistently report that immigrants make multiple trips to and from the United States.[12] Proximity is an especially important factor in explaining the cyclical dynamics of undocumented immigrants who travel with relative ease between their homelands and the United States.

Social networks are important to the process of immigration. Networks start when immigrants permanently settle in an area and use their knowledge of local opportunities to help relatives, friends, and acquaintances from back home emigrate. As more people join the network, ethnic enclaves form and extend the network. Hispanic immigration to the United States is sustained by rich migration networks that have developed over several decades. Writing about certain migration networks, Massey observed that

> networks consist of kin and friendship relations that link Mexican sending communities to particular destinations in the United States. People from the same family or town are enmeshed in a web of reciprocal obligations. New migrants draw upon these obligations in order to enter and find work in the United States. As these networks develop and mature, they dramatically reduce the costs of migration, inducing others to enter the migrant work force. The entry of additional migrants, in turn, leads to more extensive networks, which encourages still more migration.[13]

Individuals connected to networks are more likely to immigrate than those who have no such connection. Tapping into immigrant networks reduces the psychological, social, and economic costs of immigrating.[14] Many pressing questions are answered before the emigrant starts out: How will I get to my destination? Where will I live? Who do I know there? Where will I work? As Carlos Rico stated, "The existence of old and complex social networks gives a truly social character to the phenomenon of migration. ... This breeds increased familiarity and very well established 'connections' for many Mexican sending communities."[15]

Once established, migrant networks facilitate and promote further immigration. Examples of this abound. The presence of Cuban enclaves in Florida and New Jersey has encouraged Cuban refugee flows for nearly four decades. Observing Guatemalan networks in Houston, Texas, Hagan and Gonzalez-Baker discovered the importance networks play in transmitting information about U.S. immigration policy.[16] Central American immigration during the 1980s was facilitated by existing networks used by Mexicans to gain entry into the United States.[17] Relatives of Central Americans already living in the United States played a role in fostering immigration. Commenting on Nicaraguan immigration, Lars Schoultz noted that "nearly two-thirds of the tickets from Managua to Mexico City are purchased in the United States by friends or relatives of the traveler, who picks up the ticket at a Managua travel agent or airline office."[18] A rich body of Mexican community studies has documented the importance of migration networks in the movement of Mexicans, particularly undocumented ones, into the United States.[19]

The existence of migration networks also explains why Hispanic immigrants, both legal and illegal, settle in so few states. Established in certain states, the extensive networks effectively guide immigrants to these areas. Settlement is generally not a random process. As Portes and Rumbaut noted, "Migration is a network-driven process, and the operation of kin and friendship ties is nowhere more effective than in guiding new arrivals toward preestablished ethnic communities."[20]

Migration networks are central to understanding immigration. Once established, networks create a self-sustaining dynamic. Community studies show that

> the migration decision became increasingly disconnected from the social and economic conditions in the sending community and determined more by the accumulation of migration-related human capital and social capital in the form of network conditions.[21]

In effect, the "push" part of the migration equation becomes less important as networks mature and expand. U.S. immigration policy has actually aided the creation of migrant networks by emphasizing family reunification (most recently) and temporary worker programs (in the past). Significantly, migrant networks have made it increasingly difficult for U.S. immigration policy to control the flow of persons coming to the United States. Research examining efforts to reduce undocumented immigration, by enhancing border enforcement and denying job opportunities through employer sanctions, has largely concluded that such policies have scarcely made a dent in the immigration flow. Donato, Duran, and Massey found that migration networks effectively countered attempts by the United States to clamp down on illegal immigration.[22]

Hispanic Immigration and U.S. Immigration Policy

Economic, political, and social conditions and immigration networks trigger and maintain immigration, but the movement of people across international boundaries is shaped, to some extent, by the immigration policies of nation states. During its first 100 years, the United States federal government, which has jurisdiction over immigration, allowed unrestricted immigration. Starting in 1875, the federal government began to screen out immigrants for various reasons, including lewd and immoral character and later on the basis of race. By the turn of the century, Congress had greatly increased the number of exclusion categories used to screen immigrants—yet such actions did little to stem the flow of the millions of immigrants who came to the United States.

Not until 1921, and then with the Immigration Act of 1924 (commonly referred to as the National Origins Act), did the United States effectively restrict the total number of immigrants it would accept annually and allocate immigration visas on the basis of country of origin.

The National Origins Act exempted Western Hemisphere immigration from the quotas. The exemption meant that the United States placed no restrictions on Hispanic immigration, which had begun in earnest during the first three decades of the new century. Fueled by the instability created by the Mexican Revolution and encouraged by U.S. labor recruiters, more than 660,000 Mexicans streamed to the industrial Midwest and the rapidly developing Southwest. The United States encouraged this immigration in the 1910s and 1920s to meet industrial and agricultural labor shortages created by the diminished flow from Europe. However, U.S. immigration authorities deported hundreds of thousands of Mexicans during the Great Depression, in the first instance of a practice that would be followed time and time again.[23] During years of prosperity, the United States encourages Mexican immigration; during economic recessions, the United States attempts to limit Mexican immigration.[24] Interestingly, despite these fluctuations in policy and treatment, the social and economic networks developed by the initial Mexican immigrants survived.

The Start of Large-Scale Hispanic Immigration

Faced with growing labor shortages brought about by World War II, the United States and Mexico negotiated the Braceros Program in 1942, which allowed Mexicans to work temporarily in the United States. Between 1942 to 1964, the United States issued more than 4.5 million temporary work visas to Mexicans.[25] The Braceros Program had several unintended consequences. Because the terms of the bilateral agreement required U.S. employers to provide Braceros workers the same benefits and amenities as were provided to U.S. workers, U.S. employers had economic incentives to hire the cheaper, undocumented workers who found it easier to work illegally than wait for their applications for Bracero visas to be processed. Additionally, some Braceros workers overstayed their work visas and became illegal immigrants.[26] Perhaps most important, as Freeman and Bean noted, the Braceros Program "re-established the practice of seasonal agricultural work that had declined significantly during the depression."[27] The Braceros Program exposed tens of thousands of Mexican workers to employment and social networks in the United States. Not surprisingly, those networks facilitated immigration to the United States well after the Braceros Program ended in 1964.

During the 1950s and early 1960s, unforeseen consequences of immigration policy, coupled with the politics of the Cold War, had a profound impact on Hispanic immigration. In 1952 Congress passed the McCarren-Walters Act, which prohibited the entry of Communists into the United States, emphasized labor market criteria in allocating immigration visas, and codified existing immigration law. Two aspects of the law had direct bearing on Hispanic immigration. First, the McCarren-Walters Act included the "Texas Proviso," which made it perfectly legal to knowingly hire someone who had violated immigration law by entering the country illegally. In effect, the Texas Proviso acknowledged the dependence of Southwest agricultural interests on undocumented workers. The Texas Proviso greatly contributed to enlarging the stream of undocumented immigration in the following decades. Second, a little-known and little-discussed provision in the act granted the Attorney General the authority to parole foreign nationals into the United States. Parole allowed the Attorney General to admit foreign nationals without having to fit them into existing immigration categories. Congress clearly intended parole to be exercised only on an individual basis, but subsequent administrations used it as a means to admit hundreds of thousands of refugees. Parole ended up serving as the de facto refugee policy for several decades.

Among the prime beneficiaries of the parole provision were Cubans, who began to flee the Cuban Revolution in 1959. The postrevolutionary exodus settled in small, preexisting Cuban enclaves, primarily in south Florida and New Jersey. Like Mexican immigrants, Cuban refugees established social and economic networks that encouraged further immigration. Unlike Mexican immigrants, the United States rolled out the welcome mat for the Cubans. The United States encouraged immigration from the island because the Cubans were fleeing from a Communist government; Cuban immigration thus served the larger goals of U.S. foreign policy. From 1960 until 1980, the United States granted parole to hundreds of thousands of Cubans.[28]

Cold War concerns also played a major role in the creation of immigration from the Dominican Republic. Fearing the possibility of a leftist takeover of the Dominican Republic following the assassination of Trujillo in 1961, the United States freely granted both temporary and permanent immigration visas to middle-class Dominicans.[29] United

States policy makers viewed immigration as a safety valve, reducing political instability and discontent.[30]

The 1965 Immigration Act

Social and political changes in the 1960s forced policy makers to reexamine immigration policy. Intense civil rights efforts and the containment of Communism made untenable a policy that banned or greatly limited the immigration opportunities of entire regions of the world. In 1965, Congress, at the urging of the Johnson administration, fundamentally altered policy by stressing the equality of all nations in the allocation of immigration slots. The Immigration Act of 1965 struck down the national origins quotas; ended the almost absolute ban on Asian immigration; and imposed, for the first time, numeric restrictions on immigration from the Western Hemisphere (120,000 visas per year). Although the 1965 reforms permitted no country in the Eastern Hemisphere to receive more than 20,000 restricted visas, it placed no limit on the number available to specific Western Hemisphere countries. Equally important, the law changed the criteria for selecting immigrants. Whereas the McCarren-Walters Act of 1952 had emphasized occupational skill as the primary selection criterion, the 1965 Act shifted the selection emphasis to family reunification.

Proponents of immigration reform had argued that the 1965 Immigration Act would not significantly increase immigration. Such predictions were wrong. Numbers of immigrants during the 1970s increased by more than one-third over the immigration flows of the 1960s. Switching to a kinship-based preference system meant that as families immigrated to the United States, they could sponsor more family members from "the old country." By encouraging families to immigrate, the United States created a dynamic that fostered more immigration. A little more than ten years after the 1965 Act, family reunification accounted for three-quarters of all immigrants.

The 1965 immigration reform addressed problems associated with previous policy, but it created a new set of problems. By placing a numeric ceiling on Western Hemisphere immigration, the United States restricted immigration from Latin American countries just when the pressure to immigrate had increased. Not surprisingly, applicants for immigration visas outstripped supply, and long waiting lists resulted. To deal with the fact that Mexican immigration dominated the 120,000 restricted visas awarded annually, Congress approved a measure in 1978 to impose a 20,000-visa limit for countries in the Western Hemisphere. Although this "freed up" more visas for countries like the Dominican Republic, the reform "had the effect of exacerbating the backlog of Mexican visa applications that had prompted the concern in the first place."[31] Additionally, the abrupt termination of the Braceros Program in 1964 withdrew the means by which Mexican workers could legally enter the United States—but it changed neither the supply of workers nor the demand for workers. Ultimately, U.S. immigration policy could not address the continuing demand for legal immigration. Immigrants continued to come, with or without visas, and created a growing illegal immigration flow.

Refugee Policy

The 1965 Immigration Act included, for the first time, statutory language creating an annual refugee admissions quota. However, refugee admissions were limited to the Eastern Hemisphere. Even before President Johnson signed the 1965 Immigration Act into law, these narrow refugee provisions were tested and found wanting. That year the Cuban government allowed Cuban exiles to sail to Cuba to pick up friends and relatives. The United States quickly negotiated an end to the boatlift from the village of Camarioca and established an immigration accord. The "Freedom Flights" brought almost 200,000 Cubans to the United States between 1965 and 1973.[32] Because of the 1965 Immigration Act, though, refugee slots were reserved solely for Eastern Hemisphere refugees, so the Johnson and Nixon administrations used the parole authority of the Attorney General to admit the Cubans.

Refugee flows from Cuba, and later the need to admit large numbers of Indochinese refugees following the fall of South Vietnam, pointed up the necessity for a more comprehensive refugee policy. In response, Congress passed the 1980 Refugee Act, which increased the number of refugee slots from 17,400 a year to 50,000 and removed the geographic restriction on admission. More importantly, the 1980 act altered the definition of *refugee* from one who is fleeing from Communism to anyone with a well-founded fear of persecution (political, racial, ethnic, religious) who is residing in a country of first asylum. The act created, for the first time, asylum provisions that allowed individuals to enter the United States and request asylum. Finally, it also provided an extensive array of resettlement benefits fully funded by the federal government.

As had happened fifteen years earlier with the 1965 Immigration Act, a large, uncoordinated boatlift from Cuba presented the first test to the newly passed Refugee Act. In 1980, boats chartered by Cuban exiles were again allowed to pick up Cuban nationals, this time at the port of Mariel. Approximately 125,000 Cubans were brought to the shores of the United States. The Carter administration fumbled and threatened in an effort to gain control over the massive human exodus, to no effect.[33] Unable to stop the flow of refugees, policy makers looked for means to legally admit them. Although members of Congress encouraged the Carter administration to use the newly created Refugee Act to handle the problem, the Carter administration rejected congressional advice and opted to parole the Cubans. The administration further angered policy makers in areas (such as south Florida) heavily impacted by the boatlift, by refusing to pay full federal reimbursement for the costs of resettling the Cubans, as had been done under the earlier Cuban Refugee Program.

Central American refugee flows to the United States further tested the Refugee Act. Sparked by economies unable to absorb growing numbers of workers, and social and political instability created by civil wars, immigration to the United States began in earnest from Central America in the late 1970s. The active involvement of the United States in suppressing leftist insurgency movements played a central role in creating a large-scale exodus. Many Nicaraguans, Salvadorans, and Guatemalans left their homelands seeking refuge in neighboring states. Over the years, well over a million Central Americans journeyed to the United States and entered the country as undocumented workers.[34] Once in the United States, growing numbers of Central Americans petitioned for asylum. By any standard, the number of asylum seekers was large: between 1985 and 1990, the Immigration and Naturalization Service (INS) received more than 225,000 asylum requests from Central Americans.

Policy makers had envisioned that the asylum provisions, included as almost an afterthought in the Refugee Act, would be used only occasionally. The arrival of so many Central Americans stirred considerable public debate. Human rights groups advocated for granting asylum to a majority of Central American applicants, while the Reagan and Bush administrations argued that most applicants were illegal immigrants who should be returned home. Asylum application was a useful survival strategy for extending their stay in the United States. Because the initial asylum provisions had strong due process guarantees, asylees could stay in the United States while the immigration bureaucracy decided their cases.[35] The large number of asylum applicants completely overwhelmed the capacity of the INS and State Department to process and decide the validity of each case. It took years for cases to be finally decided.

Although the pace of processing worked to the advantage of many asylees, the decisions, once made, often did not. Advocates for reforming U.S. refugee policy had hoped that the new definition of *refugee/ asylee* in the Refugee Act would depoliticize the determination of who was a refugee or asylee. In fact, ideology and politics played a huge role in asylum decisions regarding Central American applicants in the 1980s. Because the United States supported the governments of El Salvador and Guatemala, it seldom found in favor of asylum applicants from those countries. For example, only 5 percent of Salvadoran and 4 percent of Guatemalan asylum cases decided in 1987 granted asylum. In contrast, applicants from Nicaragua, whose government the United States opposed, fared well. Of Nicaraguan asylum cases decided in 1987, 86 percent were awarded asylum.

Central American refugee flows have remained high throughout the 1990s. Continued conflict in the region, coupled with changes in asylum policy, has contributed to the growing numbers of asylum seekers.[36] So, too, have the expanding enclaves of Central Americans that aid in the exodus. From 1990 to 1996, the INS received 441,305 applications for asylum from Central Americans. To deal with the continuing legal and asylum issues involving Central Americans, Congress passed the Nicaraguan Adjustment and Central American Relief Act in late 1997. The act established procedures to legalize the status of tens of thousands of Central Americans.

Illegal Immigration and the Immigration Reform and Control Act of 1986

Illegal immigration emerged as the dominant immigration issue in the late 1970s and 1980s.[37] By then, the consequences of restricting legal immigration had become obvious. More foreign nationals were illegally entering the United States. At the same time, many in the United States expressed concern over the perceived negative effects of illegal immigration. Undocumented workers were blamed for undercutting wages and taking jobs away from U.S. citizens, increasing crime, and fostering cultural divisions. In times of economic prosperity such charges would have had little resonance, but during a period characterized by economic recessions, high unemployment, and stagnant wages, arguments linking illegal immigration to the economic woes of the United States were powerful. As Espenshade and Calhoun noted, "Illegal immigrants are convenient scapegoats for a wide variety of societal ills."[38]

Several key themes surfaced in the discussion of what to do about illegal immigration. First, attention focused almost entirely on the southern border as the source of or entry point for undocumented immigration. Illegal immigration became synonymous with Mexico. Seldom did illegal immigration at the northern border enter into the debate. Second, policy making and debate were hampered by the absence of quality data on the size and characteristics of undocumented immigration. No official count of population, such as the census, measured illegal immigration. Lacking reliable data, the INS records of apprehension of undocumented immigrants became the proxy measure for illegal immigration, despite the inherent weakness of those statistics. Third, proponents of a tough stance on illegal immigration used the lack of solid estimates to make exaggerated claims about the size of the undocumented population. In particular, the INS and its supporters framed illegal immigration as a law enforcement issue and used concern over the problem to argue for a larger budget and more personnel.

Acknowledging illegal immigration as an issue proved far easier than developing a consensus on what to do about it. The Ford and Carter administrations formed interagency task forces to examine the problem. In 1978, Congress authorized the creation of the Select Commission on Immigration and Refugee Policy (SCIRP) to study immigration issues and make recommendations to Congress. In its 1981 final report to Congress, SCIRP recommended both restrictive and progressive measures to deal with illegal immigration, most notably employer sanctions and amnesty. After five years of failed attempts by advocates for immigration reform to secure legislation adopting SCIRP recommendations, the Immigration Reform and Control Act of 1986 (IRCA) cleared both the House and the Senate and was signed into law by President Reagan.

The IRCA adopted a law enforcement policy focused on creating disincentives to immigrate illegally. The law overturned the Texas Proviso by making it illegal for employers knowingly to hire undocumented workers. Employer sanctions operated on the premise that if the United States could cut off the employment opportunities for undocumented workers, there would be less incentive to immigrate illegally. The IRCA required that employers verify the work eligibility of all workers or face civil and criminal penalties. Additionally, the law authorized a sizable increase in the budget and personnel of the INS Border Patrol. Lawmakers reasoned that more border enforcement would make it more difficult to enter the country illegally. Virtually all the additional Border Patrol agents were assigned to police the southern border.

To garner enough votes to pass Congress, the IRCA created two amnesty, or legalization, programs that permitted eligible undocumented workers to apply for and receive legal immigration status. The Legally Authorized Workers (LAWs) program granted those undocumented workers with long-standing ties to the United States the opportunity to legalize their immigration status. Unlike the basic provisions of the LAWs program, which had existed in earlier immigration reform efforts, the Special Agricultural Workers (SAWs) program found its way into the IRCA relatively late in the congressional debate.[39] With its more liberal eligibility criteria, the SAWs program allowed agricultural workers to apply for legalization after working in the country for only one year. Both programs granted qualified applicants temporary legal status and outlined procedures for attaining permanent resident status and, ultimately, naturalization.

Despite initial difficulty and controversy in implementing the amnesty programs, the INS eventually developed extensive outreach efforts. The majority of applicants were processed within several years of the program's creation. Exceeding earlier estimates of the number of eligible undocumented workers, the INS legalized approximately 1.7 million LAWs and 1 million SAWs.[40] Although undocumented workers of any nationality could apply for amnesty, the legalization programs were used mostly by undocumented Hispanic immigrants. One study of the LAWs program found that Mexican and Central Americans accounted for 70 percent and 13 percent, respectively, of all applicants.[41]

The amnesty programs succeeded in legalizing the status of millions of undocumented workers, but the IRCA's attempt to regulate illegal immigration did not go according to script. Initially, the INS did report a drop in apprehensions along the Mexican borders. Some scholars attribute the decline to the legalization of several million undocumented workers who no longer had to cross the border illegally. Others suggest that many undocumented workers waited for a while to see how the INS would implement the law. Regardless, almost every long-term assessment of the IRCA has concluded that there is little evidence to suggest that employer sanctions and increased border enforcement substantially reduced the flow of undocumented workers. To begin with, the INS lacked sufficient personnel to enforce the employer sanctions. Too few inspectors meant that only a handful of the millions of U.S. businesses could anticipate having their employment records scrutinized. A preexisting market for fraudulent documents, such as Social Security cards, quickly expanded. Additionally, employers wishing to comply with the law had no way of determining the authenticity of documents. Researchers could not "uncover statistically reliable evidence that [the] IRCA had a significant effect in deterring undocumented migration from Mexico."[42]

Opponents of the IRCA feared that employer sanctions would create job discrimination. They reasoned that many employers would avoid the possibility of violating the law by hiring no foreign-born or minority workers. To address those concerns, lawmakers included a sunset provision in the IRCA, which would terminate employer sanctions if a "widespread" pattern of discrimination could be linked to the law. In its 1990 report to Congress, the General Accounting Office (GAO) estimated that 10 percent of employers engaged in "one or more practices that represent national origin discrimination."[43] The GAO concluded that "it is more reasonable to conclude that a substantial amount of discriminatory practices resulted from [the] IRCA rather than not."[44] Not surprisingly, given the perception that illegal immigrants are predominantly Hispanic, employment discrimination based on national origin frequently affected Hispanics. However, despite evidence pointing to widespread discrimination, Congress decided to keep the employer sanctions and instead make incremental improvements to the process of employment verification.

1990 Immigration Act and Current Immigration Policy

Once Congress had dealt with illegal immigration through the IRCA in 1986, it turned to the task of overhauling the system of legal immigration. The 1965 Immigration Act had created a number of problem areas for legal immigration. Long queues existed for family-based immigrant visas. The amnesty provisions of the IRCA meant that the waiting lists would only lengthen as greater numbers of legalized immigrants sponsored their family members. Some members of Congress raised the concern that legal immigration from Asia and Latin America had effectively "choked off" European immigration. Advocates for diversity wanted to continue efforts started in 1988 to encourage immigration from "traditional" sending countries. Also, concern over productivity and economic growth in the United States led some to advocate that U.S. immigration move to labor market criteria in awarding immigration visas, and away from family reunification criteria.

Congress eventually passed the Immigration Act of 1990, which, for the first time in twenty-five years, substantively altered legal immigration policy. Despite little public support for increasing the number of immigrants, the 1990 Immigration Act created a new, permanent ceiling of 675,000 per year. During the first two years of its implementation, Congress authorized higher ceilings to shorten the backlog of immigrant visas. To deal further with the effects of the IRCA, policy makers granted 55,000 additional visas from 1992 to 1994 for immediate family members of IRCA-legalized immigrants. The Immigration Act increased the per-country quota immigrants from 20,000 to 28,000. Addressing concerns that the United States should admit more skilled immigrants, the act narrowed the type of categories available for family reunification and greatly expanded employment-based immigrant visas. Finally, the act reserved 55,000 diversity slots for immigrants coming from "unrepresented countries."

It is too soon to assess the overall impact of the 1990 Immigration Act. It is clear that family-based preferences continue to be the primary basis on which immigrants enter the country. In 1996, approximately two out of every three immigrants were family sponsored. Immigrants coming to the United States by means of employment-based preferences make up around one-eighth of all immigrants. Contrary to the intention of the 1990 Immigration Act, waiting queues for immigration visas remain high. In 1996, the Visa Office at the State Department reported a worldwide waiting list of 3,692,506 persons.[45]

Finally, responding to continuing concern over illegal immigration and prompted by the findings of the U.S. Commission on Immigration Reforms, Congress passed the Illegal Immigration Reform and Immigrant Responsibility Act of 1996 (IIRIRA).[46] The return of Congress to the issue of undocumented immigration signified that its previous efforts at reform had not solved the problem. The IIRIRA framed undocumented immigration almost solely as a law enforcement problem. It gave the INS more resources and personnel for law enforcement, expanded the agency's authority to remove "illegal aliens," weakened the role of the courts in reviewing enforcement decisions, and increased the civil and criminal penalties associated with illegal immigration (such as smuggling and creating and using fraudulent documents).[47] In a move away from amnesty, the IIRIRA required that undocumented immigrants leave the United States to adjust their immigration status. The act further barred undocumented immigrants from returning to the United States for periods of three to ten years, depending on how long they had lived illegally in the country.

Recent Hispanic Immigration

Legal Immigration

Since the late 1960s, the United States has experienced a surge in immigration. From 1971 to 1996, approximately 18 million persons have come to the United States as immigrants.[48] The legal immigration numbers come close to matching the peak years of immigration to the United States, at the turn of the twentieth century. At that time, from 1890 to 1915, slightly more than 21 million persons, mostly from Europe, immigrated to the United States. That large European immigration had a proportionately greater effect on the peopling of the United States than the most recent immigration wave. In 1910, nearly one in seven United States residents was foreign born, compared with one in thirteen in 1990.

Of the 18 million immigrants from 1971 to 1996, nearly 7 million have been Hispanics. Thus, roughly 39 percent of all immigrants in the past 25 years have been Hispanic. The large number of Hispanic immigrants is not an aberration in the annals of American immigration. Throughout the history of the United States, immigration has been dominated for periods of time by certain countries or regions. For example, from 1841 to 1850, the Irish constituted nearly half of all immigrants. During the immigration at the turn of the century, immigrants from Southern and Central Europe accounted for more than 60 percent of all immigrants.

Between 1986 and 1996, more than 2,969,000 Mexicans, 195,000 Cubans, 405,000 Dominicans, 678,000 Central Americans, and 604,000 South Americans legally immigrated to the United States. Immigration from Mexico dwarfs that from all other countries. In 1996, 18 percent of immigrants to the United States came from Mexico. In 1996, three of the top ten immigrant-sending countries to the United States were Hispanic.

Although immigration policy is almost exclusively the domain of the federal government, it has very real effects locally. Throughout the history of the United States, immigrants have concentrated in certain areas.[49] For example, Scandinavians settled almost exclusively in the upper Midwest. The Irish tended to settle in large urban areas such as New York, Boston, and Chicago. Immigrants from Poland and Croatia settled in the industrial areas of Illinois, Indiana, Ohio, and Pennsylvania. Like their immigrant predecessors, Hispanic immigrants also concentrate in certain states or regions. Cubans have stayed mostly in south Florida and northern New Jersey. The Dominicans have settled almost exclusively in the New York metropolitan area. Mexican immigrants are widely dispersed, but the majority of them can be found in a handful of states: California, Texas, Illinois, and, now, New York. In fact, 70 percent of all immigrants now settle in only 6 states: California, New York, Texas, Florida, Illinois, and New Jersey.[50]

Family reunification provisions are the most available and most-used means by which foreign nationals legally immigrate to the United States; certainly, family reunification is the dominant route for legal Hispanic immigration. In 1996, 65 percent of all immigrants and 85 percent of Hispanic immigrants were admitted under family reunification provisions. In the largest source country for immigrants, Mexicans overwhelmingly use family reunification to gain admission to the United States; approximately 95 percent of Mexican immigrants were sponsored by a family member. Dominican immigrants rely even more on family reunification: 99 percent immigrated to the United States using family reunification provisions.

Employment-based visas represent the other major method by which people may immigrate to the United States.[51] In 1996, approximately 13 percent of all immigrants, compared to 7 percent of all Hispanic immigrants, entered under employment-based visas. Within Hispanic sending countries, great variation exists. Of the top three Hispanic sources of immigration (Mexico, Cuba, and the Dominican Republic), employment preference provisions account for 2 percent or less of immigrant visas. A greater percentage of immigrants from countries such as El Salvador (15 percent), Argentina (39 percent), Bolivia (33 percent), Chile (21 percent), and Venezuela (21 percent) rely on employment-based preferences to gain entry into the United States.

It is important to note that immigration data are often portrayed as measuring the yearly addition of foreign nationals living in the United States. When the statistic is presented that 915,900 foreign nationals were admitted to the United States in 1996, many people assume that the country's population just increased by that same number. Immigration statistics do not account for emigration *from* the United States. On average, approximately one-third of all immigrants eventually leave the United States to return to their homelands or to live in another country.[52] Emigration is even more of a factor with undocumented immigrants than with legal immigrants. Studies of sending communities in Mexico consistently find that a majority of Mexican undocumented immigrants living in the United States eventually return home.[53]

Additionally, immigration data are often used to suggest that the statistics are measuring new arrivals, when in fact they do not. Of the 915,900 immigrants admitted to the United States in 1996, only 46 percent were new arrivals. The rest were already residing in the United States—legally or illegally—prior to having their immigration status changed to that of "immigrant." The distinction between "adjustments" and "new arrivals" is particularly important in understanding immigration data from the years 1989 to 1994. Data from that five-year span imply an enormous jump in overall levels of immigration, especially from Mexico. Yet almost half of the 6 million persons classified as permanent resident aliens or immigrants during those years were already living in the United States as undocumented foreign nationals. As noted earlier, the provisions in the 1986 Immigration Reform and Control Act gave millions of undocumented workers the means to legalize their immigration status.

Undocumented Immigration

The issue of undocumented immigration adds to the complexity of any study of Hispanic immigration. Legal immigrants have permission from the federal government to enter and live in the United States. Undocumented or illegal immigrants do not. Generally, there are three ways for foreign nationals to enter the United States and remain as undocumented immigrants. First, a foreign national may slip across the border of the United States undetected by the Border Patrol of the INS. In immigration jargon, such persons are *EWIs* (enters without inspection). Second, a foreign national may have temporary permission to enter the United States, for example, as a student or tourist, but then not return to the country of origin once his or her entry visa has expired. That group is called *visa overstayers*. Third, a foreign national may violate the terms of the entry visa. For example, tourists who take jobs violate the conditions of their visas and become illegal immigrants.[54] Visa overstayers and visa violators are a significant proportion of the undocumented immigrants, representing slightly more than 40 percent of that population.[55]

Undocumented immigrants are a difficult population to count. Thomas Espenshade wrote:

> For numerous reasons, illegal immigration is a difficult issue to study. Not the least of the obstacles is the fact that the number of unauthorized immigrants entering the United States is unobserved and therefore not precisely known. In addition, no census or other federally sponsored survey asks respondents about their legal status, so the impact of undocumented immigration is often inferred from other indicators.[56]

Over time, demographers have developed more precise methods to estimate the size of the undocumented population. Research by demographers from the Census Bureau and the INS have produced estimates that consistently place the size of the undocumented immigrant population as between 3 to 5 million persons. This is considerably less than estimates in the 1970s and 1980s, which reported this population as 8 to 12 million.

According to the most recent estimates, Hispanics make up more than two-thirds of the undocumented immigrant population. Representing more than 50 percent, Mexico is far and away the single largest source of undocumented immigrants, followed by El Salvador (6.7 percent) and Guatemala (3.3 percent). The NRC estimated that between 200,000 and 300,000 undocumented immigrants settle in the United States each year.[57] Based on available data, it is estimated that between 138,000 to 207,000 Latin Americans yearly enter the United States as undocumented immigrants.

Undocumented immigrants tend to concentrate in the same handful of states that legal immigrants do. The only difference between the two groups is that undocumented immigrants are even more likely to reside in California, New York, Texas, Florida, Illinois, and New Jersey than are legal immigrants. Roughly 70 percent of legal immigrants are found in those states, compared to 80 percent of undocumented immigrants.[58] The concentration of both types of immigrants in so few states goes a long way toward explaining why the issue is so important to California but not to Maine.

Current Issues with Hispanic Immigration

NAFTA and Emigration Policy

In studies of Hispanic immigration, the emigration policies of sending countries are often ignored as a factor in shaping the characteristics and volume of immigration. Virtually all nation-states place some restrictions on the ability of their citizens to travel to foreign states. Christopher Mitchell noted that until the overthrow of the Trujillo regime in the Dominican Republic in 1961, it was almost impossible for any but very wealthy Dominicans to obtain exit permits to leave the island.[59] The difficulty of securing exit visas from Cuba and the absence of normal immigration channels from Cuba to the United States effectively blocked large-scale immigration for years.[60]

Emigration policy, however, is more than just granting or withholding permission to leave. Through domestic policy, states can intentionally or unintentionally develop incentives for people to emigrate. For example, civil war and persecution in states such as El Salvador, Guatemala, and Nicaragua during the 1980s created the impetus for tens of thousands to leave. Rodolfo O. de la Garza and Gabriel Szekely argued that the domestic policies of the Mexican government have played a direct role in promoting emigration.[61] One could argue that the most significant emigration policy in recent years is the North American Free Trade Agreement (NAFTA) among Mexico, the United States, and Canada.

One of the selling points of NAFTA for Mexico and the United States was that it would reduce undocumented immigration. For Mexico, NAFTA represented a clear emigration policy. Mexican President Salinas stated, "Without the free-trade agreement you will witness millions of Mexicans crossing the border and looking for work."[62] The link between NAFTA and emigration is based on the assumption that free trade will create economic growth and economic growth will create enough jobs to employ the growing number of Mexicans now entering their working years. NAFTA is meant to keep more Mexicans in Mexico.

The long-term impact of NAFTA on Mexican immigration is the subject of much speculation. Cornelius and Martin argued, "In the long term ... economic dynamism in Mexico stemming from a free trade agreement could deter substantial future emigration." Others have argued that the free-trade agreement will produce large-scale emigration.[63] There is general consensus, however, that economic development policies such as NAFTA will produce short-term increases in immigration. NAFTA has removed many of the trade protections for sheltered areas of the Mexican economy, such as small business and agriculture. International competition in those areas is likely to create, at best, temporary economic dislocations resulting in greater underemployment and unemployment. Such economic problems will increase migratory pressures.

United States policy makers have not used immigration policy to soften the economic transitions within Mexico resulting from NAFTA. Massey argued, "If it is in the U.S. interest to promote rapid economic development in Mexico, then it is also in the U.S. interest to accept relatively large numbers of Mexican immigrants."[64] But in the four years since the passage of NAFTA, the opposite has occurred. The Clinton administration never pushed Congress for a short-term increase in the number of immigration visas available for Mexico. In fact, the administration implemented the toughest policies in recent memory to deter illegal immigration (discussed later in this section) from Mexico. There is evidence that since NAFTA was approved in 1994, efforts to legally and illegally immigrate to the United States from Mexico have increased. In its most recent report, the Visa Office noted a backlog for immigration visas from Mexico of more than 1 million.[65] The most recent INS apprehension data reveal that the Border Patrol apprehended nearly 1.6 million Mexicans in 1996, a 46 percent increase since 1994.

Border Enforcement

Just as demand for immigration opportunities has increased in Mexico, the United States has engaged in a series of policy initiatives designed to curtail undocumented immigration. Since entering office in 1992, the Clinton administration has devoted more attention to, and directed more resources at, law enforcement along the southern border than have prior administrations. Congress has authorized a 5,000-person increase in the number of Border Patrol agents over a 5-year period, making the INS the largest federal law enforcement agency. The 1996 Illegal Immigration Reform and Immigrant Responsibility Act gave the INS added legal means to deter illegal immigration. High-profile initiatives, such as Hold-the-Line (El Paso) and Gatekeeper (San Diego), have attempted to stem the flow of undocumented immigration by making it more difficult to illegally enter the United States.

Increased border enforcement along the southern border perpetuates the perception and bias that only Mexico supplies the U.S. with undocumented immigrants.[66] For example, Canada shares a longer border with the United States than does Mexico, yet Canadians accounted for less than 1 percent of all apprehensions in 1996. According to INS data, the INS apprehends 500 Mexicans for every 1 Canadian. That Mexico has approximately three times the population of Canada may account for some of the difference in this ratio. That the economic and social incentives to immigrate illegally are fewer in Canada than in Mexico may also explain the ratio. However, it is telling that the United States positions 82 percent of its Border Patrol officers on the Mexican border, compared with 7 percent at the Canadian border.[67] This is despite estimates suggesting that more than 120,000 Canadians live in the United States illegally, making Canada the fourth largest source country for undocumented immigrants. It is a rare day when the media or policy makers focus on the northern border as a source of undocumented immigration. Nor does the press acknowledge that several million "undocumented immigrants" did not sneak across the southern border, but are, in fact, visa overstayers.

Welfare and Fiscal Impact

One of the ongoing assumptions Americans have about immigrants is that they come to the United States to use welfare programs.[68] Indeed, one of the first categories created to screen immigrants was the provision barring the entry of immigrants "likely to become a public charge." That provision was established in 1882, long before the existence of modern entitlement programs. A recent Gallup poll reported that 60 percent of those surveyed thought that Latin American immigrants ended up on welfare.[69] Despite the tenacity of this perception, there is little evidence that immigrants disproportionately rely on welfare programs. For example, major welfare entitlement programs have excluded undocumented workers from receiving benefits. Even when legal immigrants were eligible for welfare services and benefits, prior to 1996, relatively few immigrants used them.

Of all types of immigrants, refugees rely the most on welfare programs, because the conditions under which they flee their countries of origin usually leave them with few resources. Using data from the 1990 census, Fix and Passel reported that once refugees are factored out, only 2.8 percent of recent adult immigrants received welfare, compared to 4.2 percent of native-born adults. Including refugees, all foreign-born adults have a welfare rate of 4.7 percent, only slightly higher than native born.[70] Research points to the immigrant elderly as the one subgroup with relatively high rates of welfare use. Van Hook and Bean found that 31 percent of immigrant elderly relied on Supplemental Security Income (SSI), compared to only 5.9 of native-born elderly.[71]

Because many immigrant elders have not worked in the United States long enough to qualify for Social Security retirement, they rely on SSI in relatively large numbers.

Hispanic immigrant use of welfare programs is hard to determine, because many studies do not account for the ethnicity of immigrant welfare recipients. Examining census data, researchers from the University of Texas found that a greater number of Mexican, Guatemalan, and Salvadoran immigrant households relied on public assistance in 1990 than in 1980. Most of the increase was attributed to "the increasing size of the sub-group rather than to changes in sub-group rates." Immigrants from those Latin American countries had higher welfare rates than all other immigrant households. Interestingly, in 1990, native-born Mexican households (13.9 percent) reported greater use of welfare than Mexican and Central American immigrant households (11.7 percent). The researchers concluded that "Mexican/Central American immigrants ... are not pronouncedly welfare-prone and do not manifest increases during the 1980s in either AFDC [Aid to Families with Dependent Children] or SSI recipiency."[72]

Despite the lack of compelling evidence of widespread welfare abuse by immigrants, Congress passed legislation in 1996 to restrict immigrant use of welfare. The Illegal Immigration Reform and Immigrant Responsibility Act required that all family-based immigrants have an "affidavit of support" from a sponsor before they enter the United States. The affidavit of support means that sponsors commit to supporting each petitioned immigrant at 125 percent of the poverty level. If individuals cannot meet this financial commitment, they are prevented from sponsoring family members as immigrants. The law assigned public welfare agencies the responsibility of enforcing the affidavit of support requirement, which went into effect in 1997. Given the generally low income levels of Hispanic households, it is likely that the affidavit of support will prevent many Hispanics, immigrant and citizen alike, from sponsoring the immigration of their relatives.[73]

The Personal Responsibility and Work Opportunity Reconciliation Act (PROWA) is one of the best known of the recent immigrant welfare reforms. PROWA made immigrants ineligible for SSI and food stamps and allowed states to restrict eligibility to Medicaid and TANF (the replacement program for AFDC). Immediately after signing the welfare bill into law, President Clinton said he would work to reverse the prohibition against immigrants qualifying for welfare benefits. Clinton was not alone in arguing for repealing the provisions denying immigrants use of welfare. In 1997, the U.S. Commission on Immigration Reform, created to advise Congress on immigration, voiced its opposition to the recent legislation. The commission wrote that "the denial of safety net programs to immigrants solely because they are noncitizens is not in the national interests."[74] Soon after passage of that legislation, some of the most restrictive elements were repealed. In addition, many states continue to provide welfare to immigrants.[75]

Welfare use by immigrants is part of a larger debate on the overall fiscal impact of immigrants on the United States. Assessments of this impact vary greatly according to the models used, the sources of revenue attributed to immigrants, and the cost associated with providing public services to them. Passel estimated that immigrants bring in a net $25–30 billion in revenue; Huddle contended that immigrants cost the United States slightly more than $42 billion per annum.[76] Despite the differences in estimates, most research acknowledges that immigration has different effects locally and nationally. As Fix and Passel noted, "While most of the taxes paid by immigrants go to federal coffers, the costs of providing social services fall to state and local governments."[77]

The National Research Council has explored the local fiscal effects of immigration. Using two states with large numbers of immigrants as case studies, the NRC found that the fiscal burden on native-headed households in New Jersey was $232 and in California $1,178 per year (in 1996 dollars). The NRC attributed these results to three primary reasons:

> (1) immigrant-headed households include more school-age children than native households on average, and they currently consume more educational services; (2) immigrant-headed households are poorer than native households on average, and therefore receive more state and locally funded income transfers; and (3) immigrant-headed households have lower incomes and own less property than native households on average, and thus pay lower state and local taxes.[78]

The NRC found that immigrants make a small but positive contribution to the federal government. Studying the long-term fiscal implications of immigration, the NRC stated, "Under most scenarios, the long-run fiscal impact is strongly positive at the federal level, but substantially negative at the state and local levels."[79]

Few research studies exist that focus on the fiscal impact of Hispanic immigration. In their comprehensive review of research on the topic, Gonzales-Baker and her colleagues noted, "None of the studies provide detailed information on the fiscal impact of specific national-origins populations."[80] Studies have concluded that undocumented workers "generate more expenses than revenues across all levels of government."[81] Given that Hispanics make up a large percentage of undocumented immigrants, it can be concluded that that particular subgroup of Hispanic immigrants creates fiscal costs largely in the areas of law enforcement, education, and health services. The NRC study mentioned earlier did examine the fiscal impact of immigrants from Europe/Canada, Asia, Latin America, and other regions. It estimated that Latin American immigrant households in New Jersey and California used, respectively, $3,396 and $4,977 per year more in public services than they paid in taxes.[82] The negative fiscal impact of Latin American immigrants is largely explained by the fact that their low household income means they pay less in taxes. However, it must be pointed out that Hispanic immigrants contribute to the local economy by buying housing, food, and other goods and services.

Attempts to measure the fiscal impact of immigration serve political agendas. Immigrants have been easy targets on which to pin the blame for federal and state budget deficits.[83] Findings that associate negative costs with immigrants are used to bolster assertions that too many immigrants enter the country and use too many public services; the country, it is said, cannot afford immigrants. The fiscal impact of immigration is of particular concern to the handful of states that receive large numbers of legal and illegal immigrants. There is nothing new about that concern. In the 1960s, Florida successfully lobbied Washington to reimburse it for the costs of resettling Cuban refugees. In recent years, California has claimed that it is bearing almost the entire fiscal burden for the consequences of federal immigration policy. In 1994, Californians approved Proposition 187, which sought to save revenue by denying almost all public services to undocumented workers. A court challenge eventually overturned Proposition 187, but the sentiment remains. At the national level, efforts to restrict welfare benefits to immigrants are often justified as one way to reduce the federal deficit.

Conclusions and Policy Recommendations

The United States can anticipate strong immigration flows from Latin America and the Spanish-speaking Caribbean well into the twenty-first century. Wage differentials, employment opportunities, and political stability will continue to attract Hispanic immigrants to the United States. Underemployment, unemployment, low wages, and political and economic instability will continue to foster emigration. Recent efforts to promote a Western-Hemisphere equivalent of NAFTA will create economic transformations in Latin America and will increase immigration pressure on the United States. Already established and extensive Hispanic migration networks will continue to facilitate Hispanic immigration.

The reality is that immigration policy can only partially control and shape Hispanic immigration. The United States can choose between making the immigration flow mostly legal or retaining policies that legalize only parts of it. Suggestions to construct hundreds of miles of walls along the Mexican border and to deploy military personnel to patrol the border are likely to run into strong political resistance and legal challenges. Moreover, there is strong evidence that while enhanced border enforcement may make entry more difficult, it will not prevent undocumented immigration. It is difficult to imagine that a country that so effectively used the image of the Berlin Wall to combat Communism will create a wall of its own to keep people out. Reducing the incentives to immigrate illegally have proven difficult to implement. So far, the federal government seems unwilling to put enough resources into the enforcement of employer sanctions to give the policy much credibility, let alone effectiveness. Employers who rely on undocumented workers find ways around the law, and those who wish to comply with the law do not have the expertise to identify fraudulent identification papers. A national identification card might aid the latter group, but thus far Americans have resisted instituting such a system of identification.

It must first be recognized that there are no easy answers to immigration problems. However, the United States can choose options that reflect American values and interests. Through its immigration policies, the United States could reaffirm the special relationship it has with Latin America and Spanish-speaking countries of the Caribbean. For countries such as Mexico, where there is great emigration pressure, the per-country ceiling on immigration creates tremendous backlogs in visa requests. Long waits for immigration visas force families to make difficult choices by obeying the law and being apart or disobeying the law and being together. Periodically passing time-limited legislation to clear up visa backlogs would help ensure that people who have the opportunity to legally immigrate do so. It is equally clear that placing even greater emphasis on labor market criteria, at the expense of family reunification, will reduce the opportunity for many Hispanics to immigrate. Devaluing family reunification will turn legal immigrants into illegal immigrants.

A country that so values the rule of law must develop policies that establish incentives for prospective immigrants to immigrate legally. The issue of illegal immigration obviously defies simple policy remedies. The continuing stream of undocumented workers to the United States demonstrates strong demand for their labor.

One controversial policy that recognizes this symbiotic relationship would be for the United States to reinstitute a guestworker program that would permit short-term immigration. Learning from problems with the Braceros and guestworker programs in Europe, a U.S. version could provide temporary legal status for most undocumented immigrants. Any guestworker program should contain strong incentives to reward those who eventually return home. For example, once workers have returned to their countries of origin, their contributions to the Social Security system could be refunded. The issue in such a policy would be withholding enough to encourage return but not too much to make the program unattractive to would-be participants. A guestworker program has other benefits as well. It would greatly reduce discrimination based on national origin, because workers would have work authorization. Also, a guestworker program would provide some administrative review of participants before they enter the United States. A guestworker program will reduce but not eliminate illegal immigration. It is clear that some recipients of guestworker visas will overstay their visas and permanently settle in the United States. That dynamic is really no different from the one that now characterizes illegal immigration.

In recent years, through legislation and court decisions, the United States has created a growing distinction between citizen and immigrant. Until recently, citizenship primarily conferred the right to participate in the political dimension of American life. Citizenship now confers greater economic, social, and legal rights. It is too soon to assess the long-term implications of these changes. The increasing advantage of citizenship may prompt more and more immigrants, particularly Hispanic immigrants who have low naturalization rates, to petition for naturalization. The emphasis on citizenship may add to the marginalization of immigrants and increase the difficulty of adjusting to American life and institutions.

One of the key needs regarding immigration in the next millennium is to better address the local effects of immigration. The nation as a whole benefits from immigration, while states and localities incur very real costs. One way to reduce the divisions and tensions that produced Proposition 187 is for the federal government to offer more economic aid to areas heavily settled by immigrants. In the past, the United States has offered impact aid to communities that resettle refugees; the same can be done for immigrants. It is counterproductive to ignore the reality that localities seldom have the resources to provide adequate educational and social services to immigrants. How well immigrants and their children do in their communities will ultimately determine the health and well-being of the United States. Assuring that immigrants become incorporated into the fabric of American life at the local level is an investment in America's future.

Notes

1. David M. Kennedy, "The Price of Immigration," *Atlantic Monthly* 278, no. 3 (November 1996): 51–68.
2. James P. Smith and Barry Edmonston, eds., *The New Americans: Economic, Demographic, and Fiscal Effects of Immigration* (Washington, D.C.: National Academy Press, 1997).
3. Jorge Castaneda, *The Mexican Shock: Its Meaning for the United States* (New York: New York Press, 1995), 16–17.
4. Scholars looking at Mexican immigration have noted that economic changes created by the Mexican Revolution ushered in the first wave of large-scale Mexican immigration to the United States.
5. Douglas Massey, "Economic Development and International Migration in Comparative Perspective," in *Determinants of Emigration from Mexico, Central America, and the Caribbean,* ed. Sergio Diaz-Briquets and Sidney Weintraub (Boulder, Colo.: Westview Press, 1991), 15.
6. Alejandro Portes and Ruben G. Rumbaut, *Immigrant America: A Portrait* (Los Angeles, Cal.: University of California Press, 1990), 8–9.
7. Ibid., 12.
8. Sergio Diaz-Briquets, "The Central American Demographic Situation: Trends and Implications," in *Mexican and Central American Population and U.S. Immigration Policy*, ed. Frank D. Bean, Jurgen Schmandt, and Sidney Weintraub, 34 (Austin, Tex.: University of Texas Press, 1989).
9. Rodolfo O. de la Garza and Gabriel Szekely, "Policy, Politics and Emigration: Reexamining the Mexican Experience," in *At the Crossroads: Mexican Migration and U.S. Policy*, ed. Frank D. Bean, Rodolfo O. de la Garza, Bryan R. Roberts, and Sidney Weintraub (Lanham, Md.: Rowman & Littlefield, 1997).
10. Oscar Handlin, *The Uprooted* (Boston: Little, Brown, 1951).
11. Casteneda, *The Mexican Shock*, 19.
12. Katharine M. Donato, "U.S. Policy and Mexican Migration to the United States: 1942–92," *Social Science Quarterly* 75, no. 4 (December 1994): 707–29; Douglas Massey, Rafael Alarcon, Jorge Durand, and Humberto Gonzalez, *Return to Aztlan: The Social Process of International Migration from Western Mexico* (Berkeley, Cal.: University of California Press, 1987),
13. Douglas Massey, "The Social Organization of Mexican Migration to the United States," *Annals* 487 (September 1986): 103.
14. Douglas Massey, Joaquin Arango, Graeme Hugo, Adela Pellegrino, and J. Ed-

ward Taylor, "An Evaluation of International Migration," *Population and Development Review* 20, no. 4 (December 1994): 728.

15. Carlos Rico, "Migration and U.S.-Mexican Relations, 1966–1986," in *Western Hemisphere Immigration and United States Foreign Policy*, ed. Christopher Mitchell (University Park, Pa.: Pennsylvania State University Press, 1992), 236.

16. Jacqueline Maria Hagan and Susan Gonzalez-Baker, "Implementing the U.S. Legalization Program: The Influence of Immigrant Communities and Local Agencies on Implementing Policy Reform," *International Migration Review* 27, no. 3 (Fall 1993): 513–36.

17. Lars Schoultz, "Central America and the Politicization of U.S. Immigration Policy," in Mitchell, *Western Hemisphere Immigration and United States Foreign Policy*, 182.

18. Ibid., 185.

19. For a review of studies documenting the importance of networks to Mexican migration, see Massey et al., "An Evaluation of International Migration."

20. Portes and Rumbaut, *Immigrant America*.

21. Massey et al., "An Evaluation of International Migration," 729.

22. Katherine M. Donato, Jorge Durand, and Douglas Massey, "Stemming the Tide? Assessing the Deterrent Effects of the Immigration Reform and Control Act," *Demography* 29 (May 1992): 155.

23. George C. Kiser and Martha Woody Kiser, eds., *Mexican Workers in the United States* (Albuquerque, N.M.: University of New Mexico Press, 1979).

24. One can argue that the recent efforts to counter illegal Mexican immigration during prosperous times contradicts the historic norm. It must be remembered that California's recent and influential role in lobbying for tighter border enforcement occurred when the state—but not the nation—was recovering from the effects of economic recession.

25. Larry C. Morgan and Bruce L. Gardner, "Potential for a U.S. Guest-Worker Program in Agriculture: Lessons from the Braceros," in *The Gateway: U.S. Immigration Issues and Policies*, ed. Barry R. Chiswick (Washington, D.C.: American Enterprise Institute, 1982).

26. Frank D. Bean, George Vernez, and Charles Keely, *Opening and Closing the Doors: Evaluating Immigration Reform and Control* (Washington, D.C.: Urban Institute Press, 1989), 7.

27. Gary P. Freeman and Frank D. Bean, "Mexico and U.S. Worldwide Immigration Policy," in Bean, de la Garza, Roberts, and Weintraub, *At the Crossroads*, 25.

28. David W. Engstrom, *Presidential Decision Making Adrift: The Carter Administration and the Mariel Boatlift* (Lanham, Md.: Rowman & Littlefield, 1997).

29. Christopher Mitchell, "U.S. Foreign Policy and Dominican Migration to the United States," in Mitchell, *Western Hemisphere Immigration and United States Foreign Policy*, 100.

30. Massey et al., "An Evaluation of International Migration," 728.

31. Freeman and Bean, "Mexico and U.S. Worldwide Immigration Policy," 27.

32. For an excellent history of Cuban immigration, see Felix Roberto Masud-Piloto, *From Welcome Exiles to Illegal Immigrants: Cuban Migration to the U.S.* (Lanham, Md.: Rowman & Littlefield, 1996).

33. Engstrom, *Presidential Decision Making Adrift*.

34. Schoultz noted that the emigration represented up to 6 percent of the region's population. Schoultz, "Central America and the Politicization of U.S. Immigration Policy," 168.

35. Norman L. Zucker and Naomi Flink Zucker, *The Guarded Gate: The Reality of American Refugee Policy* (New York: Harcourt, Brace, Jovanovich, 1987).

36. Class-action lawsuits, such as *American Baptist Churches v. Thornburgh*, and congressional action granting temporary protected status have allowed hundreds of thousands of Central Americans to remain in the United States. Growing concern over the volume of asylum applications has led Congress to streamline asylum provisions and increase the number of officers, to speed up processing asylum claims.

37. Illegal immigration has existed since the United States began imposing restrictions on immigration. The predecessor to the Border Patrol was established in 1906, to patrol the border of the southwest to prevent the illegal entry of Chinese immigrants. The first large-scale effort to deal with illegal immigration occurred during the recession of the early 1950s. The Immigration and Naturalization Service (INS) tightened its enforcement at the southern (but not northern) border; this campaign culminated in the implementation of Operation Wetback in 1954. That year the INS apprehended more than 1 million undocumented immigrants.

38. Thomas J. Espenshade and Charles A. Calhoun, "An Analysis of Public Opinion Toward Undocumented Immigration," *Population Research and Policy Review* 12 (1993): 191–92.

39. Susan Gonzalez-Baker, "The 'Amnesty' Aftermath: Current Policy Issues Stemming from the Legalization Programs of the 1986 Immigration Reform and Control Act," *International Migration Review* 31, no. 1 (Spring 1997): 5–27.

40. United States Department of Justice, *Immigration Reform and Control Act: Report on the Legalized Alien Population* (Washington, D.C.: Government Printing Office, 1992).

41. Gonzalez-Baker, "The 'Amnesty' Aftermath."

42. Donato, Durand, and Massey, "Stemming the Tide?," 155. Other immigration scholars reached similar conclusions. Jeffrey S. Passel, Frank D. Bean, and Barry Edmonston, "Assessing the Impact of Employer Sanctions on Undocumented Immigration to the United States," in *The Paper Curtain: Employer Sanctions' Implementation, Impact, and Reform*, ed. Michael Fix (Washington, D.C.: Urban Institute Press, 1991).

43. United States Congress, Senate Committee on the Judiciary, *The Implementation of Employer Sanctions: Hearings before the Subcommittee on Immigration and Refugee Affairs*, 102d Cong., 2d sess, April 3–10, 1992.

44. Quote from Lindsay B. Lowell, Jay Teachman, and Zhongren Jing, "Unintended Consequences of Immigration Reform: Discrimination and Hispanic Employment," *Demography* 32 (November 1995): 618.

45. United States Department of State, *Report of the Visa Office 1996* (Washington, D.C.: Government Printing Office, 1998).

46. United States Commission on Immigration Reform, *U.S. Immigration Policy: Restoring Credibility* (Washington, D.C.: Government Printing Office, 1994).

47. Peter Schuck argued that the 1990 and 1996 immigration legislation "radically limited the procedural and substantive rights that aliens had come to enjoy." See Peter H. Schuck, *Citizens, Strangers, and In-Between* (Boulder, Colo.: Westview Press, 1998), 14.

48. These numbers do not reflect undocumented or illegal immigration. Unless otherwise indicated, all immigration data are drawn from the United States Department of Justice, *1996 Statistical Yearbook of the Immigration and Naturalization Service* (Washington, D.C.: Government Printing Office, 1998).

49. Portes and Rumbaut, *Immigrant America*.

50. U.S. Commission on Immigration Reform, *Becoming an American: Immigration and Immigrant Policy* (Washington, D.C.: Government Printing Office, 1997).

51. For an analysis of employment-based preferences, see Demetrios G. Papademetriou

and Stephen Yale-Loehr, *Balancing Interests: Rethinking U.S. Selection of Skilled Immigrants* (Washington, D.C.: Brookings Institution, 1996).

52. Bean, Vernez, and Keely, *Opening and Closing the Doors*, 19; Smith and Edmonston, *The New Americans*, 39–40.
53. Massey et al., *Return to Aztlan*; Donato, "U.S. Policy and Mexican Migration."
54. For example, Christopher Mitchell wrote: "A good many Dominicans entered the United States on visitor's visas and remained to work, violating the terms of those visas. Although it is not possible to measure this 'undocumented' migrant flow precisely, it may have totaled between one-third and one-half the size of the legal immigrant stream from the Dominican republic." Mitchell, "U.S. Foreign Policy and Dominican Migration," 93–94.
55. Jeffrey S. Passel, "Undocumented Immigration," in *The Debate in the United States over Immigration*, ed. Peter Duignan and Lewis H. Gann (Stanford, Cal.: Hoover Institution Press, 1998).
56. Thomas J. Espenshade, "Unauthorized Immigration to the United States," *Annual Review of Sociology* 21 (1995): 196.
57. Smith and Edmonston, *The New Americans*, 51.
58. United States Commission on Immigration Reform, *Becoming an American*, 35.
59. Mitchell, "U.S. Foreign Policy and Dominican Migration."
60. Block migration opportunities did result in three dramatic boatlifts from Cuba to the United States in 1965, 1980, and 1994. For a discussion of the boatlifts, see Engstrom, *Presidential Decision Making Adrift*.
61. They noted that most commentators on Mexican immigration "have ignored or dismissed the role politics and policy have played in shaping emigration policy." De la Garza and Szekely, "Policy, Politics and Emigration."
62. Quoted in Wayne A. Cornelius and Philip L. Martin, "The Uncertain Connection: Free Trade and Rural Mexican Migration to the United States," *International Migration Review* 27, no. 3 (Fall 1993): 485.
63. For a balanced discussion of NAFTA and Mexican immigration, see Peter H. Smith, "NAFTA and Mexican Migration," in Bean, de la Garza, Roberts, and Weintraub, *At the Crossroads*, 263–82.
64. Massey, "Economic Development and International Migration in Comparative Perspective," 15.
65. United States Department of State, *Report of the Visa Office 1996*.
66. Jeffrey S. Passel and Michael Fix, "Myths about Immigrants," *Foreign Policy*, no. 95 (Summer 1994): 154.
67. The remaining 11 percent of INS Border Patrol agents are assigned to patrolling the coastal areas. United States General Accounting Office, *Border Patrol: Staffing and Enforcement Activities*, Report to Congressional Committees, GAO/GGD-96-65 (Washington, DC: Government Printing Office, 1996).
68. Michael Katz noted that immigrants were blamed for rising taxes when taxes were used to fund poor relief in the early nineteenth century. Michael Katz, *In the Shadow of the Poorhouse* (New York: Basic Books, 1996).
69. As reported in Thomas J. Espenshade and Maryann Belenger, "U.S. Public Perceptions and Reaction to Mexican Migration," in Bean, de la Garza, Roberts, and Weintraub, *At the Crossroads*, 227–62.
70. Michael Fix and Jeffrey S. Passel, "Setting the Record Straight," *Public Welfare* 52, no. 2 (Spring 1994): 10.
71. Jennifer V. W. van Hook and Frank Bean, "The Growth in Non-Citizen SSI Caseloads During the 1980s: Immigration versus Aging Effects," Texas Population Research Center Papers No. 96-97-12 (Austin, Tex.: Texas Population Research Center, 1996–97).

72. Frank D. Bean, Jennifer V. W. van Hook, and Jennifer E. Glick, "Mode-of-Entry, Type of Public Assistance and Patterns of Welfare Recipiency Among U.S. Immigrants and Natives," Texas Population Research Center Papers No. 94-95-17 (Austin, Tex.: Texas Population Research Center, 1994–95), 20.
73. An individual sponsoring the immigration of three family members must have a total yearly income of $20,050. Many individuals and families will lack the financial resources to be sponsors. For example, data from Chiswick and Hurst (see chapter 6) indicate that the average yearly earnings of many Hispanic male subgroups are insufficient to meet the $20,050 sponsorship threshold; male Mexican immigrants average only $15,994 in yearly wages.
74. United States Commission on Immigration Reform, *Becoming an American*, 22.
75. Congress gave states the discretion on whether to allow legal immigrants the opportunity to continue participating in various programs such as TANF, food stamps, and Medicaid. Some observers argued that states would disenroll immigrants from welfare programs to save revenue. A recent GAO study found that most states have continued to provide welfare benefits to immigrants who entered the United States before August 22, 1996. The GAO found that "about a third of the states provide state-funded temporary assistance to needy families, medical assistance, or both to new immigrants during their 5-year bar from federal programs." United States General Accounting Office, *Welfare Reform: Many States Continue Some Federal or State Benefits for Immigrants*, Report to the Ranking Minority Member, Subcommittee on Children and Families, Senate Committee on Labor and Human Resources, GAO/HEHS-98-132 (July 1998), 8.
76. Cited in Susan Gonzales-Baker, Robert G. Cushing, and Charles W. Haynes, "Fiscal Impacts of Mexican Migration to the United States," in Bean, de la Garza, Roberts, and Weintraub, *At the Crossroads*, 145–76.
77. Michael Fix and Jeffrey S. Passel, "Setting the Record Straight," 8.
78. Smith and Edmonston, *The New Americans*, 293.
79. Ibid., 12.
80. Gonzales-Baker, Cushing, and Haynes, "Fiscal Impacts of Mexican Migration to the United States," 146.
81. Passel and Fix, "Myths about Immigrants," 158; Gonzales-Baker, Cushing, and Haynes, "Fiscal Impacts of Mexican Migration to the United States."
82. Smith and Edmonston, *The New Americans*.
83. Papademetriou and Yale-Loehr, *Balancing Interests*.

Bibliography

Bean, Frank D., Rodolfo O. de la Garza, Bryan R. Roberts, and Sidney Weintraub, eds. *At the Crossroads: Mexican Migration and U.S. Policy.* Lanham, Md.: Rowman & Littlefield, 1997.

Bean, Frank D., Jurgen Schmandt, and Sidney Weintraub, eds. *Mexican and Central American Population and U.S. Immigration Policy.* Austin, Tex.: University of Texas Press, 1989.

Bean, Frank D., Jennifer V. W. van Hook, and Jennifer E. Glick. "Mode of-Entry, Type of Public Assistance and Patterns of Welfare Recipiency Among U.S. Immigrants and Natives." Texas Population Research Center Papers, No. 94-95-17. Austin, Tex.: Texas Population Research Center, 1994–95.

Bean, Frank D., George Vernez, and Charles Keely. *Opening and Closing the Doors: Evaluating Immigration Reform and Control.* Washington, D.C.: Urban Institute Press, 1989.

Castaneda, Jorge. *The Mexican Shock: Its Meaning for the United States.* New York: New York Press, 1995.

Chiswick, Barry R., ed. *The Gateway: U.S. Immigration Issues and Policies.* Washington, D.C.: American Enterprise Institute, 1982.

Cornelius, Wayne A., and Philip L. Martin. "The Uncertain Connection: Free Trade and Rural Mexican Migration to the United States." *International Migration Review* 27, no. 3 (Fall 1993): 484–512.

de la Garza, Rodolfo O., and Gabriel Szekely. "Policy, Politics and Emigration: Reexamining the Mexican Experience." In *At the Crossroads: Mexican Migration and U.S. Policy*, edited by Frank D. Bean, Rodolfo O. de la Garza, Bryan R. Roberts, and Sidney Weintraub. Lanham, Md.: Rowman & Littlefield, 1997.

Diaz-Briquets, Sergio. "The Central American Demographic Situation: Trends and Implications." In *Mexican and Central American Population and U.S. Immigration Policy*, edited by Frank D. Bean, Jurgen Schmandt, and Sidney Weintraub. Austin, Tex.: University of Texas Press, 1989.

Diaz-Briquets, Sergio, and Sidney Weintraub, eds. *Determinants of Emigration from Mexico, Central America, and the Caribbean.* Boulder, Colo.: Westview Press, 1991.

Donato, Katharine M. "U.S. Policy and Mexican Migration to the United States: 1942–92." *Social Science Quarterly* 75, no. 4 (December 1994): 707–29.

Donato, Katherine M., Jorge Durand, and Douglas Massey. "Stemming the Tide? Assessing the Deterrent Effects of the Immigration Reform and Control Act." *Demography* 29 (May 1992): 139–57.

Duignan, Peter, and Lewis H. Gann, eds. *The Debate in the United States over Immigration.* Stanford, Cal.: Hoover Institution Press, 1998.

Engstrom, David W. *Presidential Decision Making Adrift: The Carter Administration and the Mariel Boatlift.* Lanham, Md.: Rowman & Littlefield, 1997.

Espenshade, Thomas J. "Unauthorized Immigration to the United States." *Annual Review of Sociology* 21 (1995): 195–216.

Espenshade, Thomas J., and Maryann Belenger. "U.S. Public Perceptions and Reaction to Mexican Migration." In *At the Crossroads: Mexican Migration and U.S. Policy*, edited by Frank D. Bean, Rodolfo O. de la Garza, Bryan R. Roberts, and Sidney Weintraub, 227–62. Lanham, Md.: Rowman & Littlefield, 1997.

Espenshade, Thomas J., and Charles A. Calhoun. "An Analysis of Public Opinion Toward Undocumented Immigration." *Population Research and Policy Review* 12 (1993): 189–224.

Fix, Michael, ed. *The Paper Curtain: Employer Sanctions' Implementation, Impact, and Reform.* Washington, D.C.: Urban Institute Press, 1991.

Fix, Michael, and Jeffrey S. Passel. "Setting the Record Straight." *Public Welfare* 52, no. 2 (Spring 1994): 6–15.

Freeman, Gary P., and Frank D. Bean. "Mexico and U.S. Worldwide Immigration Policy." In *At the Crossroads: Mexican Migration and U.S. Policy*, edited by Frank D. Bean, Rodolfo O. de la Garza, Bryan R. Roberts, and Sidney Weintraub. Lanham, Md.: Rowman & Littlefield, 1997.

Gonzales-Baker, Susan. "The 'Amnesty' Aftermath: Current Policy Issues Stemming from the Legalization Programs of the 1986 Immigration Reform and Control Act." *International Migration Review* 31, no.1 (Spring 1997): 5–27.

Gonzalez-Baker, Susan, Robert G. Cushing, and Charles W. Haynes. "Fiscal Impacts of Mexican Migration to the United States." In *At the Crossroads: Mexican Migration and U.S. Policy*, edited by Frank D. Bean, Rodolfo O. de la Garza, Bryan R. Roberts, and Sidney Weintraub, 145–76. Lanham, Md.: Rowman & Littlefield, 1997.

Hagan, Jacqueline Maria, and Susan Gonzalez-Baker. "Implementing the U.S. Legalization Program: The Influence of Immigrant Communities and Local Agencies on Implementing Policy Reform." *International Migration Review* 27, no. 3 (Fall 1993): 513–36.

Handlin, Oscar. *The Uprooted*. Boston: Little, Brown, 1951.

Katz, Michael. *In the Shadow of the Poorhouse*. New York: Basic Books, 1996.

Kennedy, David M. "The Price of Immigration." *Atlantic Monthly* 278, no. 3 (November 1996): 51–68.

Kiser, George C., and Martha Woody Kiser, eds. *Mexican Workers in the United States*. Albuquerque, N.M.: University of New Mexico Press, 1979.

Lowell, Lindsay B., Jay Teachman, and Zhongren Jing. "Unintended Consequences of Immigration Reform: Discrimination and Hispanic Employment." *Demography* 32 (November 1995): 617–28.

Massey, Douglas. "Economic Development and International Migration in Comparative Perspective." In *Determinants of Emigration from Mexico, Central America, and the Caribbean*, edited by Sergio Diaz-Briquets and Sidney Weintraub. Boulder, Colo.: Westview Press, 1991.

———. "The Social Organization of Mexican Migration to the United States." *Annals* 487 (September 1986): 102–13.

Massey, Douglas, Rafael Alarcon, Jorge Durand, and Humberto Gonzalez. *Return to Aztlan: The Social Process of International Migration from Western Mexico*. Berkeley, Cal.: University of California Press, 1987.

Massey, Douglas, Joaquin Arango, Graeme Hugo, Adela Pellegrino, and J. Edward Taylor. "An Evaluation of International Migration." *Population and Development Review* 20, no. 4 (December 1994): 699–751.

Masud Piloto, Felix Roberto. *From Welcome Exiles to Illegal Immigrants: Cuban Migration to the U.S.* Lanham, Md.: Rowman & Littlefield, 1996.

Mitchell, Christopher. "U.S. Foreign Policy and Dominican Migration to the United States." In *Western Hemisphere Immigration and United States Foreign Policy*, edited by Christopher Mitchell. University Park, Pa.: Pennsylvania State University Press, 1992.

Mitchell, Christopher, ed. *Western Hemisphere Immigration and United States Foreign Policy*. University Park, Pa.: Pennsylvania State University Press, 1992.

Morgan, Larry C., and Bruce L. Gardner. "Potential for a U.S. Guest-Worker Program in Agriculture: Lessons from the Braceros." In *The Gateway: U.S. Immigration Issues and Policies*, edited by Barry R. Chiswick. Washington, D.C.: American Enterprise Institute, 1982.

Papademetriou, Demetrios G., and Stephen Yale-Loehr. *Balancing Interests: Rethinking U.S. Selection of Skilled Immigrants*. Washington, D.C.: Brookings Institution Press, 1996.

Passel, Jeffrey S. "Undocumented Immigration." In *The Debate in the United States over Immigration*, edited by Peter Duignan and Lewis H. Gann. Stanford, Cal.: Hoover Institution Press, 1998.

Passel, Jeffrey S., Frank D. Bean, and Barry Edmonston. "Assessing the Impact of Employer Sanctions on Undocumented Immigration to the United States." In *The Paper Curtain: Employer Sanctions' Implementation, Impact, and Reform*, edited by Michael Fix. Washington, D.C.: Urban Institute Press, 1991.

Passel, Jeffrey S., and Michael Fix. "Myths about Immigrants." *Foreign Policy*, no. 95 (Summer 1994): 151–60.

Portes, Alejandro, and Ruben G. Rumbaut. *Immigrant America: A Portrait*. Los Angeles, Cal.: University of California Press, 1990.

Rico, Carlos. "Migration and U.S.-Mexican Relations, 1966–1986." In *Western Hemisphere Immigration and United States Foreign Policy*, edited by Christopher Mitchell. University Park, Pa.: Pennsylvania State University Press, 1992.

Schoultz, Lars. "Central America and the Politicization of U.S. Immigration Policy." In *Western Hemisphere Immigration and United States Foreign Policy*, edited by Christopher Mitchell. University Park, Pa.: Pennsylvania State University Press, 1992.

Schuck, Peter H. *Citizens, Strangers, and In-Between*. Boulder, Colo.: Westview Press, 1998.

Smith, James P., and Barry Edmonston, eds. *The New Americans: Economic, Demographic, and Fiscal Effects of Immigration*. Washington, D.C.: National Academy Press, 1997.

Smith, Peter H. "NAFTA and Mexican Migration." In *At the Crossroads: Mexican Migration and U.S. Policy*, edited by Frank D. Bean, Rodolfo O. de la Garza, Bryan R. Roberts, and Sidney Weintraub, 263–82. Lanham, Md.: Rowman & Littlefield, 1997.

United States Commission on Immigration Reform. *Becoming an American: Immigration and Immigrant Policy.* Washington, D.C.: Government Printing Office, 1997.

United States Commission on Immigration Reform. *U.S. Immigration Policy: Restoring Credibility.* Washington, D.C.: Government Printing Office, 1994.

United States Congress. Senate Committee on the Judiciary. *The Implementation of Employer Sanctions: Hearings before the Subcommittee on Immigration and Refugee Affairs.* 102d Cong., 2d sess., April 3–10, 1992.

United States Department of Justice. *Immigration Reform and Control Act: Report on the Legalized Alien Population.* Washington, D.C.: Government Printing Office, 1992.

United States Department of Justice. *1996 Statistical Yearbook of the Immigration and Naturalization Service.* Washington, D.C.: Government Printing Office, 1998.

United States Department of State. *Report of the Visa Office 1996.* Washington, D.C.: Government Printing Office, 1998.

United States General Accounting Office. *Border Patrol: Staffing and Enforcement Activities.* Report to Congressional Committees. GAO/GGD-96-65. 1996.

United States General Accounting Office. *Welfare Reform: Many States Continue Some Federal or State Benefits for Immigrants.* Report to the Ranking Minority Member, Subcommittee on Children and Families, Senate Committee on Labor and Human Resources. GAO/HEHS-98-132. July 1998.

van Hook, Jennifer V. W., and Frank Bean. "The Growth in Non-Citizen SSI Caseloads During the 1980s: Immigration versus Aging Effects." Texas Population Research Center Papers No. 96-97-12. Austin, Tex.: Texas Population Research Center, 1996–97.

Zucker, Norman L., and Naomi Flink Zucker. *The Guarded Gate: The Reality of American Refugee Policy.* New York: Harcourt Brace Jovanovich, 1987.

3

The Language Question

Pastora San Juan Cafferty

Language as a means of preserving culture is the history of every society. The history of organized language consciousness, language loyalty, and language maintenance is also the history of the formation of the large nation-states. Assimilation of successive generations of immigrants into American society has also meant assimilation into speaking the English language.

Although culture and language are inextricably entwined, there is little public discussion about the retention of native group culture among Hispanics. There is, however, an ongoing national public debate about retention of the Spanish language. In the United States, historically, acquiring the language of the majority of society has come to mean relinquishing the native culture in favor of the culture of majority society. Linguistic assimilation has been assumed to be a proxy for cultural and political assimilation. The issue of language is an easy and tangible benchmark to represent the less easily defined but more visceral issue of culture.

To understand the concern with the retention of Spanish language and culture among Hispanics in the United States, it is important: (1) to understand the historical desire of Americans to have all who live in the United States use English as a common language; (2) to understand the history of native-language retention among European immigrants; and (3) to discuss how and if Hispanics differ from other language communities in this country. Only then can one address the public policy concerns regarding cultural and linguistic assimilation and retention among Hispanics.

Linguists and anthropologists disagree on whether retention of native language is intrinsic to the retention of native culture. Nevertheless, the political debate, emotional and compelling, has considered this connection as truth. This debate centers on the questions of whether Hispanics should retain their native language; and, if so, to what extent it is society's responsibility to facilitate that retention. Conversely, it also considers to what extent it is the responsibility of Hispanic individuals to learn and use the language of majority society. Understanding answers to those questions and their social and political implications would inform the true policy choices, which may be different and not necessarily the same as the debate engaged in by policy makers in the context of larger political questions. The political debate centers practically around this question: Should the United States be, in law and practice, a country in which only English is the language of official business, public life, schools, and other institutions? Or should it officially acknowledge the multiplicity of languages spoken by those who live in it?

The predominance of conversations on how best to educate and acculturate the Hispanic population into American group culture will only increase as the Hispanic population continues to make its presence dramatically felt in the United States. According to the U.S. Census Bureau, as of March 1996, 9.3 percent of the U.S. population was foreign born. Of that group, more than 40 percent are of Hispanic origin. The fact that only 7.4 percent of natives are Hispanic indicates that the next decades will witness a huge growth of a native Hispanic generation, as the foreign born have native children.[1] From 1990 to 1994, the Hispanic population grew to 27 million. In 2050, one in four Americans are projected to be Hispanic.[2]

Culture and Language

The data on Hispanics in the United States are inconclusive at best. The census began identifying Hispanic-surnamed persons in 1970, and through the end of the century has struggled to identify the complexity and multiplicity of the Hispanic population. The presence of a large number of undocumented immigrants and the increasing number of intermarriages makes it even harder to get an accurate portrait of the Hispanic population. Certain factors, such as religious affiliation, are changing rapidly. Hispanics, known as predominantly Catholic, are increasingly becoming Protestant.

The other major factor that prevents us from being able to speak of Hispanic culture definitively is our lack of a definition of *culture*. The term *culture* speaks to a complexity of factors that make it difficult to define: it encompasses a shared group consciousness, a common history, and common oral and written traditions. *Culture, ethnicity*, and *identity* all capture different but similar phenomena, making the concepts difficult to define. *Hispanic*, as an ethnic group, becomes defined only in contrast to another group of people. That is what allowed Greeley to say: "Ethnicity is a way of being American. Immigrants did not arrive as ethnics; they became such on the shores of their new country."[3] As Yinger similarly described, there is a "thickness of ethnicity" that is defined by how society views an individual and his group. Discrimination toward a racial or ethnic group "thickens" or strengthens ethnic consciousness. Thus, the retention of ethnic and racial identity may be increased by isolation and its loss may be accelerated by economic and social integration into the majority group.[4]

Greeley defined an *ethnic group* as a pool of individuals with "the presence of cultural heritage that influences attitude, values, personality, and behavior, even if the people influenced are unconscious of the impact of the past on the present."[5] Stephen Steinberg, in *The Ethnic Myth*, argued that ethnic identity persists beyond immigration because of the new country's inability to let the immigrant forget her ethnicity, as a result of continual discrimination and societal rejection.[6] Steinberg, Yinger, and Greeley all suggested that an "ethnicity" does not exist until it is defined as such by another ethnic group.

Fishman has argued that because the United States socioeconomic system is based on competition, ethnic identification is used as a means of coping with inequality.[7] Ethnic group boundaries become recognized in society to define status and social organization.[8] This classification of individuals by their ethnic group can raise group consciousness and create attachments to cultural elements, such as language, specific to the identity of the ethnic group. Fishman argued that heightened ethnic consciousness "can produce heightened language consciousness and language loyalty."[9] Use of the ethnic group's language, such as Spanish by Hispanics in the United States, is viewed by both members and non-members of that ethnic group as a sign of membership and loyalty to the minority ethnic group.[10] Language becomes a unifying symbol, providing individuals with a sense of identity and membership, and serves as a symbol of the group's reality to members of that group as well as to those outside the group. Thus, language becomes a proxy for shared group culture and language loyalty comes to be equated with loyalty to the group.

This relationship among language, culture, and group identity defines a shared social reality for the group and for its individual members. Language both symbolizes and expresses the group's and the individual's position in society. Language is not simply words used to convey meaning, but "a system of symbols with a coherent set of rules of reference and transformation by means of which a social group finds it possible to communicate."[11]

Language has been used as an indicator of assimilation since the inception of the United States as a nation. America realized the importance of language in forging national identity early in its history, learning from the various European nation-states which had painfully recognized the relationship between linguistic and political and economic dominance. In the nineteenth century, as successive waves of immigrants came to American shores, the importance of English in forging a national identity was affirmed. By the middle of the century, speaking English had come to be recognized as one of the most important attributes of being an American. As this was the most easily identified characteristic separating the native born from the newly arrived foreigner, it became increasingly important. America's geographic isolation in the nineteenth century—and its political and economic dominance in the twentieth—have reinforced English as the only national language.

The notion of assimilation itself is a complicated one. Much of the rhetoric offered in the English-only or bilingual education debates assumes that there is an arrow from immigration to assimilation that is linear and discrete—but assimilation is not a linear process. Because of the continuing and cyclical migration patterns of Hispanics, the process may be much more complicated than for other immigrant groups. The linear assimilation model was built on a combination of the myth and the fact that successive generations of immigrants learned the American language and American ways and often forgot or gave up their own. The Hispanics in the United States learn English, but often retain their native Spanish language and teach it to their U.S.-born children. The nature of their migration is very different from that of others who came and those who continue to come from other continents.

Immigration and Assimilation

Those who created the government of the young nation briefly debated the wisdom of having both English and French as its official languages. After considering that many linguistic and cultural identities could potentially be a threat to the formation of a single political entity, in 1786 Congress chose English as the language in which to conduct its official business. However, it decided that there would be no official American language. The new nation had strong linguistic constituencies who spoke languages other than English. Although debates on the notion that group identification precludes allegiance to the nation continue, English monolingualism has never really been challenged. Waves of immigrants have initially posed a threat to English-language dominance, but their successive linguistic assimilation has ultimately reinforced it.

The process of accepting English as the common language, given the presence of immigrants whose native language was not English, has not been easy. Strains of ethnocentrism and nativism at different periods in American history reflect derision and fear of foreign languages and foreign accents. Immigrants unable to speak and write English have been classified as illiterate and often as ignorant, and have been subjected to social and economic sanctions. Employers often advertised for English-speaking workers in eighteenth-century broadsides. Papers and etiquette books published in the early nineteenth century stressed the importance of speaking English correctly to be accepted in polite society.

There is no evidence that bilingualism was ever welcomed by the majority of Americans. Rather, efforts at maintaining a bilingual community were always met with resistance. Despite this, bilingual programs were offered in public schools between 1840 and 1880. The initial state support came from the desire to promote assimilation of ethnic communities. There were German bilingual education schools in the Midwest, French-English schools in Louisiana, and Spanish-English schools in New Mexico. Bilingual programs existed in public schools mainly due to political pressure exerted by ethnic communities; they were merely tolerated by the English-speaking. After 1880, only one group successfully maintained bilingual programs in the public schools: the Germans did so until 1917.[12]

Following World War I, all bilingual education efforts ceased in public schools, although such programs continued in parochial schools. Having fought a war to save democracy and end all future wars, Americans asserted the uniqueness of their democratic experience and of all things American, including English. The political rhetoric expressed in mass media denounced all things foreign. There was little interest in foreign languages during the 1920s, 1930s, and 1940s. After 1945, foreign-language efforts were focused on teaching English as a second language—to assimilate the immigrants who continued to cling stubbornly to their native tongues.[13]

Much of the stress on English monolingualism was based on the assumption that immigrants, who came to live in a land promising economic opportunity as well as political and religious freedom, would become citizens and raise a new generation of Americans. Although the majority of American immigrants have arrived with the intention of settling permanently, there has always been a pattern of immigration and emigration such that for every major stream, a counterstream developed.[14] Existing studies indicate that the decision to return or stay is directly related to the degree to which the immigrant adapts to American society.

The process of becoming an American is not easily understood. There is little knowledge of the factors that make for successful adaptation and assimilation. The reasons for immigration are not so easily understood either. From the earliest days, Europeans have migrated to America for a variety of reasons. There is a mythology defining America as a nation whose founders came in pursuit of religious and political freedom. The patriotism of those idealistic colonists was mythologized by their descendants into a distinction between themselves and the newer immigrants, whom they saw as coming for economic motives. Yet, despite even the colonists' claims that more recent settlers would threaten national solidarity, in the long term their assimilation only affirmed it. Each group of immigrants that has proven itself to be "American"—historically measured almost entirely by learning to speak English—has reinforced the model of American assimilation. This model was built on a combination of the myth and the fact that generations of immigrants learned the American language and ways and often forgot their own.

The Hispanic population learns English but often retains its native language. The nature of their immigration is very different from that of other groups. Immigrants in the nineteenth century found the journey long and arduous and the return trip difficult, if not impossible. Today's immigrants find it much easier to return. Hispanics migrating within continental boundaries have always returned. This cyclical migration pattern differentiates Hispanics from other ethnic groups. This pattern also affects language retention. Hispanics come to the United States, but frequent trips back to their homelands force Hispanics to continue speaking Spanish as well.

Puerto Ricans, who are United States citizens by birth, travel between a Spanish-speaking society on the island and an English-speaking society on the mainland, and present a new and important question to an American society that has traditionally been monolingual.[15] This question, yet to be addressed, will have to be faced as the issue of statehood for Puerto Rico continues to be debated.

Clearly, many of those who speak Spanish at home use English in the workplace. Research conducted on second-generation immigrants shows that children of immigrants who consider themselves fully bilingual also believe themselves to be dominant in the English language.[16]

There has always been language retention among immigrant groups in the United States, but the Spanish-speaking have retained their native language more than has any other group.[17] There are a number of reasons for this phenomenon:

1. The proximity of the Mexican border and the relative ease of travel for Mexican nationals (and others from Spanish-speaking nations to the south), resulting in a continuing migration stream that constantly renews the linguistic tradition;
2. The pervasiveness of the Hispanic heritage;
3. The long and continuing isolation of the Spanish-speaking in the Southwest; and
4. Segregation patterns in American society that have often kept Hispanics isolated in a social and economic ghetto.

Of these, only the renewal of the linguistic tradition by a constant migration stream has been successfully documented as being different from the experience of any other national group that came to America.

Native-born Americans who are not Hispanics are most likely to speak only English; less than 3.5 percent speak a language other than English, and of those, the majority claim to speak English "very well." Hispanics, in contrast, retain their native language well into the second generation and beyond. Of those native-born Hispanics who reported speaking English "very well," nearly 47 percent reported speaking Spanish as well; only 37 percent of native-born Hispanics reported speaking only English. Among the foreign born, only a little more than 5 percent reported speaking "only English," whereas almost 30 percent of the non-Hispanic foreign born reported speaking "only English." Of perhaps greater importance is that 35 percent of non-Hispanic foreign born and 30 percent of Hispanic foreign born reported speaking English "very well," which seems to indicate that about a third of all immigrants claim to speak English very well, whether or not they also speak Spanish or other native languages. However, only 35 percent of non-Hispanic foreign born, as opposed to nearly 65 percent of the Hispanic foreign born, reported speaking "limited English."[18]

Regardless, any doubts about the primacy of English in the United States should be answered easily. Only a small percentage of the general population speaks Spanish. Among those Hispanics, it is only the older members of a population that is generally very young who do so exclusively. There is strong evidence that among bilinguals, English language usage increases with age. English is the language of the majority society, and Hispanics—like other immigrants before them—speak English as they become part of that society.

Why, then, are Hispanics at the forefront of a debate on the relationship between language and culture? And why does the official-English movement capture the attention of so many Americans? The complexity of the answers to those questions is manifested in the debates on bilingual education and official-English policies. Official-English policies are not just about English; bilingual education is not just about teaching Spanish. The history of organized language consciousness, language loyalty, and language maintenance by different groups is a political history. The struggle for linguistic independence is closely allied to the struggle for political and economic independence. For those who struggle to maintain linguistic dominance, the threat of political and economic challenges is not far behind.

The English-Only Movement

The English-only movement, which gained political momentum during the 1980s, resulted in a series of legislative campaigns to give English official status and to restrict the use of other languages. As of 1997, 27 states had made English their official language, either by statute, constitutional amendment, or resolution. All but three of those states made that decision since 1980. In 1996, the House approved a bill designating English as the federal government's only official language. Two years later, the bill had yet to pass in the Senate.

Many of the individuals who led the English-only campaigns were from groups that were also proponents of restricted immigration.[19] However, the movement has been widely supported by individuals ranging from Nobel-Prize-winning novelist Saul Bellow, former Senator Eugene McCarthy, and the late President Richard Nixon to a diversity of other public figures, including the popular actress, Whoopi Goldberg, and respected news commentator, Walter Cronkite.

Public opinion polls show that proposals to declare English the official language receive continuing approval from the American public. The answers seem to depend on how the question is phrased: U.S. English, a leading English-only organization, highly publicizes its marketers' findings that 86 percent of 1,209 "likely voters" believe that English should be made the official language of the United States. However, in a Time/CNN poll of 1,000 Americans, 65 percent believed that there should be a law making English the official language; another survey of 1,618 persons showed that 60 percent of those surveyed believed that in parts of the country where many people speak a language other than English, state and local governments should conduct business in that language as well as in English. Thus, although many Americans apparently feel that English should be made the official language, they do not necessarily believe in the rest of the official-English platform. Though Hispanics are more likely to oppose such measures, their support for English-only measures has been increasing.[20]

In 1998, Proposition 227, an initiative on the California ballot designed to end native-language teaching for children with limited English ability in the public schools, received support from 61 percent of those voting, in spite of a national campaign that included opposition from the President of the United States. However, exit polls showed that a majority of Hispanics and Black voters opposed it.[21] This opposition by Blacks as well as Hispanics suggests that this was seen as a civil rights as well as a language issue.

The English-only movement is driven by the belief that English has been the language used by most Americans but that today's immigrants "refuse to learn English." This opinion is demonstrated by one of the latest and most popular antibilingual-education/pro-American identity books, *One Nation Indivisible* by Judge Harvie Wilkinson.[22] The latter contention has no basis in fact. Though the number of speakers of immigrant languages is on the increase, reflecting the high immigration levels at the end of this century, immigrants continue to learn English. This knowledge is often accompanied by loss of the native language; immigrants have typically lost their native language by the third generation.[23] A study led by Alejandro Portes showed Hispanics to be English-language dominant by the second generation, even in communities such as south Florida where Spanish is widely spoken. Even Cuban second-generation immigrants attending private bilingual schools in south Florida were found to be English-language dominant. It is interesting, however, that in these studies bilingualism showed a definite correlation with high cognitive skills. The authors concluded that although language assimilation to English monolingualism will vary in the second generation, "the passage of time will lead inexorably toward greater English proficiency and English preference and gradual abandonment of the immigrants' tongues."[24] In the political debate, however, English-only advocates seem to confuse those who do not speak English with those who speak English as well as another language. The 1990 census reported that more than 94 percent of minority-language speakers speak English as well. Less than 1 percent of U.S. residents reported speaking no English at all.[25]

The Issue of Education

Assuring American children an equal educational opportunity was the guiding principle for the United States Supreme Court in *Brown v. Board of Education*.[26] In *Brown*, the Court concluded that segregated schools were inherently unequal and that any state laws segregating Black and White students in the school system were therefore unconstitutional. Civil rights leaders in the Black community repeatedly underscored the inequality of educational opportunity in segregated school systems, which led to economic inequality. Since the 1960s, the Spanish-speaking community has also focused its civil rights efforts on the public schools. Its leaders have decried the lack of equal access to education for the Spanish-speaking in public schools.

The Bilingual Education Act of 1967 established programs that teach the language and culture of minority students as well as the native (majority) language and culture.[27] Since then, there have been more than thirty years of controversy and political activism by proponents and opponents of bilingualism and bilingual education. The argument is easily made that Hispanics, like other immigrants, should learn the American language and assimilate into the mainstream of American society. But Hispanics argue that their experience is different: they were in the Southwest as established Spanish-speaking communities long before those territories became part of the United States; and, as circular migrants, large numbers of Hispanics are traveling between two monolingual societies. English and Spanish are thus of equal value to the individual. In the case of Puerto Ricans, this migration is being undertaken by individuals who are American citizens, traveling between the island of Puerto Rico and the mainland United States.

The difficulty in creating policy to deal with this tension is related to several issues. First is the American notion, despite no official policies in the first two centuries making it so, that English is the official language of the nation. Second, the public school system has almost always succeeded in teaching English to successive waves of immigrants. In spite of the experience of bilingual programs in public and parochial schools for more than a century, public funding of bilingual education essentially ended early in the twentieth century; it was not until 1968 that public funds were again authorized for use in bilingual education programs.

The concept of what constitutes sufficient education is not only a pedagogical concept but also a pragmatic social judgment that varies with time and place. Earlier immigrants to America needed to understand and speak English but often had little need for other educational skills to participate in the labor market. In today's highly technological service economy, a high school diploma is often a minimum requisite for entry-level jobs.

According to the National Center for Education Statistics, 80 percent of Hispanic 16- through 24-year-olds in the United States reported speaking Spanish in their homes. Of those, 22 percent had never attended U.S. schools; 96 percent of the Hispanic youth whose homes were English monolingual attended school. The dropout rates of those attending school in the United States, regardless of which language was spoken in the home, were similar.[28]

Seventy-six percent of Hispanic 16- through 24-year-olds who spoke Spanish at home also spoke English "well" or "very well." Ninety-four percent of that population attended American schools. The dropout rate is similar to those Hispanics who speak only English at home, though still high (19.2 percent). Those who reported as limited in their ability to speak English did not fare as well. Only 25 percent were in school in the United States, and of those in school, one-third dropped out. Eighty-one percent of those who did not speak English well, or at all, never enrolled in U.S. schools and did not have a high school education in their native country.[29]

Bilingual Education Legislation

The Bilingual Education Act of 1974, which superseded the 1968 act, was more explicit in intent and design. Children no longer needed to be from low-income families, a criterion that had previously prevented the law from meeting the needs of large numbers of children. The 1974 act also provided a definition of a bilingual education program:

> Instruction given in, and study of, English and to the extent necessary to allow a child to progress effectively through the educational system, the native language of the children of limited English-speaking ability, and such instruction is given with appreciation for the cultural heritage of such children, and, with respect to elementary school instruction, such instruction shall, to the extent necessary, be in all courses or subjects of study which will allow a child to progress effectively through the education system.[30]

In another legislative action related to bilingual education, the Equal Education Opportunity Act of 1974 listed six actions that Congress defined as denials of equal educational opportunity. Among them is the failure of an educational agency to take appropriate action to overcome language barriers that impede equal participation by its students in an instructional program. This act allowed the initiation of civil lawsuits by individuals who had been denied equal education opportunity. Thus, for the first time a direct statutory right of action was available to non-English-speaking persons seeking equal educational opportunity through the institution of effective bilingual programs in public schools.[31]

In 1974, the Supreme Court ruled that Chinese students who did not know English well enough to be instructed in that language were not receiving an appropriate education. Justice Douglas delivered the opinion of the court:

> Under these state-imposed standards there is no equality of treatment merely by providing students with the same facilities, text books, teachers, and curriculum; for students who do not understand English are effectively foreclosed from any meaningful education.
> Basic English skills are at the very core of what these public schools teach. Imposition of a requirement that, before a child can effectively participate in the educational program, he must already have acquired those basic skills is to make a mockery of public education. We know that those who do not understand English are certain to find their classroom experiences wholly incomprehensible and in no way meaningful.[32]

In spite of legislative activity reflecting continuing concern with English-limited students, between 1980 and 1996 the budget for bilingual education programs dropped 51 percent, from $262.4 million to $128 million. Given the increase in Spanish-speaking students, the per capita expenditure decreased even more dramatically. Of the eight program areas in the United States Department of Education, the Office of Bilingual Education and Minority Affairs is appropriated the fewest dollars.[33]

Educational Approaches

Several types of education approaches attempt to address the concerns of language-minority students. The first, English as a Second Language (ESL), attempts to make non-English-speaking children proficient in English by providing supplementary instructional sessions in English for a specified time. Instruction in all other classes is in English. ESL differs from foreign-language instruction in that it is designed to meet the immediate communication needs of students by providing them with the skills needed to communicate with teachers and peers in the classroom. The ESL approach seems to work best in communities where children receive enough exposure to English outside of school to achieve proficiency in a relatively short time.

Another strategy is bilingual education, which offers instruction in both languages in varying degrees: (1) transitional bilingualism, in which the child is moved out of the program after gaining basic mastery of the English language; (2) monoliterate bilingualism, in which aural-oral skills in both languages are taught, but reading and writing are taught in English only, as is done with some Native American languages; (3) partial bilingualism, in which fluency and literacy are offered in both languages, but the native language is restricted to certain subject areas, such as music and gym; (4) a full bilingual program, in which both languages are used equally as media of instruction for all subjects.

The premises behind ESL and bilingual education programs are drastically different. Bilingual programs are designed to build on and enhance a child's existing native-language skills to develop English-language skills. Generally, classes requiring cognitive development are taught in the native language until the child has mastered the English language. Afterward, both languages are used as the media of instruction. ESL programs are designed solely to teach English-language skills so that the student can function in an English-monolingual school system. There is no effort to maintain native language.

Opponents of bilingual education argue that such programs will not provide enough incentives for the student involved to learn English quickly. They also cite a lack of evidence that these programs will be successful. These contentions are difficult to address because most attempts to evaluate bilingual education have been very poor. The majority of the research has been done by commissioned government bodies intent on measuring fiscal accountability and providing a cost-benefit analysis of programs designed to teach limited-English students. The resulting data on the efficacy of the various programs are seemingly contradictory.

Critics of bilingual education, such as Rosalie Pedalino Porter,[34] rightly assert that there is no clear evidence that any particular pedagogy among the various methods—maintenance bilingual, bicultural programs, transitional bilingual education, ESL, structural immersion— is superior. Yet examination of their critiques demonstrates the seemingly inevitable trap of drawing conclusions from limited and often conflicting information.

In 1994, the General Accounting Office (GAO), at the request of the Senate Committee on Labor and Education, published *Limited English Proficiency: A Growing and Costly Educational Challenge Facing Many School Districts*, asserting that immigrant students are almost 100 percent non-English-speaking on arrival in the United States and that such students are often poor. More interestingly, only 43 percent of limited-English students in the study were immigrants.[35] The 57 percent who were native born may well be the children who speak English but do not write and read it well enough to perform well in school. The study may indeed be including many native-born children, far removed from the immigrant experience, whose only language is English but who are illiterate and unable to perform at grade level. The report's tone, however, is unmistakably alarmist in its suggestion that the cost of educating such children is very high to American local school districts throughout the United States and, thus, to the American taxpayer.

The financial cost of bilingual education was the subject of a report issued by the American Legislative Council (ALEC) as a supplement to its *Report on the Condition of American Education, 1994*. The often-quoted ALEC report, while admitting the difficulty of gathering data, did offer evidence that there are more limited-English students (an estimated 2.3 million) enrolled in American public schools than there are enrolled in only special-language programs (an estimated 1.9 million). Thus, approximately half a million limited-English students are left without the benefit of any special education.[36]

Studies cited by the advocates of bilingual education are as limited in scope as those cited by its opponents. In the 1960s, a number of studies provided evidence that bilingual education not only was *not* detrimental to the acquisition of English, but that it actually increased cognitive skills. Studies in Canada (notably those by Lambert and Tucker)[37] and in the United States (notably by Natalie T. Darcy)[38] showed bilingual education to have a positive effect on learning.

A number of early studies showed that Hispanic students in a bilingual curriculum can progress faster than those in an English-only curriculum, and recent analysis of the research on second-language learning seems to indicate that bilingualism has a positive effect on cognitive functioning. A study of the San Antonio Independent School District, examining the schools in 1995 and 1996, concluded that the children receiving instruction in both English and Spanish made gains in English vocabulary and grammar superior to those made by children in the English-only program. A similar result was obtained in a program operating in the El Paso public school system between 1966 and 1967.[39] In an Illinois experiment, children enrolled in a bilingual education program were compared to students in an ESL program. The results challenged the theory that children learn more English in a monolingual program.[40]

Other studies, notably the longitudinal study conducted in New York City between 1990 and 1994, show that students in ESL programs are more quickly integrated into mainstream classrooms than those in bilingual education programs.[41] Studies such as those in New York, Texas and California,[42] and Massachusetts[43] lead to the conclusion that the speedy acquisition of English in ESL programs is more conducive to school success than gradual learning of English.

However, a small study conducted by the University of Rhode Island found otherwise. The highest dropout rate in the 1991–92 school year was that of Hispanics (40 percent as compared to 29 percent of Blacks and 27 percent of non-Hispanic Whites). The study concluded, though, that

[a] high level of English proficiency and longevity in the country indicate a likelihood of dropping out rather than of academic success. Assimilation into the American mainstream seems to correlate with dropping out, while Spanish language preference and recent immigration correlate with staying in school and even recommending stricter school regulations.[44]

Bilingual programs "did not seem to be a determining factor in students' decision to stay in school or drop out." Of the fifteen dropouts interviewed, half had been in bilingual programs and half had not.[45] The sample in the study is too small to draw any widespread conclusions about the relationship between English-language proficiency, native-language retention, and academic success.

Evaluation of the effectiveness of bilingual education programs offers contradictory and inconclusive evidence. The premise that the best medium of instruction for a child is in his native tongue has been shown to be valid by several studies. An early UNESCO report[46] was influential in shaping congressional support for bilingual education.[47] However, as Joshua Fishman noted early in the debate over bilingual education that ensued after institution of the bilingual education program in the 1960s, "few behavioral science fields have been studied as frequently and with such contradictory results as bilingualism, intelligence and learning."[48] The debate has only become more acrimonious at the end of the century, and good evaluation of nearly a half-century of bilingual education programs in the United States is just as difficult.

The issue of creating and implementing bilingual education policy for Hispanics is complicated by the fact that, in a society committed to equality for all, it is difficult to distinguish among different types of immigrants who may have different needs. The permanent immigrant may need bilingual education only as a transition to English-language skills, whereas the cyclical migrant may need maintenance programs.

The Private Sector

Concerned less with politics and more with profit, the private sector has developed an approach that sheds new light on the language and culture debate. Reacting to the buying power of Hispanics, industries from health care to advertising have given special attention to the needs of this population. They have successfully tapped the market by considering the subtleties of the relationship between language and culture, and how that relationship makes Hispanics more amenable to product messages and to purchasing.

For example, in the highly competitive health care industry, the Clinica Asociación Cubana (CAC), created in the 1960s to serve Cuban refugees in Miami and now called CAC Ramsay, has become a publicly traded company listed by *Fortune* magazine as one of the 100 fastest-growing companies. Of CAC's almost 250,000 members in south and central Florida, 75 percent are Hispanic. CAC has succeeded in part because of the extensive bilingual services it offers. However, there is an element of culture as well as language: CAC has done things such as building its waiting and examining rooms much larger than usual clinics, allowing Hispanic patients to comfortably bring their families.[49]

Some businesses have turned to marketing firms that specialize in the Hispanic population. Such firms are able to prescribe the same approaches as taken by CAC Ramsay, incorporating concerns about communicating to Hispanics in both the right language and the right way. Henry Adams-Esquivel, vice-president of Market Development, Inc., believes that Hispanics can be acculturated without actually speaking English:

> The objective of advertising in Spanish is to create the unique learning environment needed to pointedly and relevantly reinforce new attitudes about product/service categories which would, otherwise, take many years to learn about due to the English-language barrier.[50]

Thus, though communicated in Spanish, the content of the message promotes American marketing values. One could perhaps draw the parallel that the Spanish-speaking can learn about American values and attitudes, as they would with regard to American products and services, in Spanish and, in so doing, adopt those values and attitudes. Adams-Esquivel would agree that acculturation is therefore enhanced by communication in Spanish. Language becomes a means of transgressing cultural borders, not of reinforcing those boundaries. Such an argument directly contrasts with those of the English-only movement, which consider English to be integral to that which is American.

In some ways, the avenues of communication for Hispanics, such as Spanish-language radio and television, are developed; but in other ways Hispanics are not fully equipped to enter the twenty-first century. As reported by *Hispanic* magazine in 1996, Hispanics lag behind non-Hispanic Whites in their use of computers and access to the World Wide Web. Whereas almost half of non-Hispanic Whites use a computer in the workplace, less than a third of Hispanics do. Only one in eight Hispanics owns a home computer; that rate is double for non-Hispanic Whites. The study concluded that the disparity was not about class: when controlling for income, Hispanics were still less likely to own a home computer. According to Harry Pachon, president of the Tomas Rivera Center, this adds up to a half-billion-dollar market that is not being tapped by the computer industry.[51] For Hispanics, the implications are greater: they lack access to what may be the primary information source of the next century.

Hispanics are, however, in tune with the more traditional media of radio and television (in descending order of preference). Hispanics who speak Spanish spend about 5 hours a day (1.4 in English) watching television and 36 minutes a day reading newspapers. Those who speak primarily English watch 4.4 hours (3.4 in English) and also spend 36 minutes a day reading newspapers. Bilingual Hispanics prefer reading newspapers and watching television in English.[52]

The Political Context

Language usage in public institutions became a volatile political issue as Hispanic communities demanded a range of actions that would recognize Spanish as a semiofficial language. This has included requesting federally funded language training programs for federal, state, and local civil servants; translation into Spanish of all government forms, brochures, and manuals intended for the general public; simultaneous translation for Hispanic persons in the criminal justice system; and translation of all legislation, significant public speeches, and other government documents. As Hispanic community leaders made these demands, society reacted with varying degrees of concern.

There have been a number of successful efforts by Hispanics, as well as by other language communities (notably Asian), to increase political participation by having bilingual (and in some cases multilingual) ballots and election literature required by law. However, these are transitional efforts in that they are designed to bring immigrants into the mainstream by encouraging political participation. Although much is made of the "new linguistic militancy," these efforts are not new. English literacy was not universally required for either voting or citizenship until the twentieth century. It was not until 1926 that the last state denied the franchise to lawful residents who did not write or speak English, and not until 1950 that Congress required English literacy as a condition for citizenship.

Hispanic civil rights organizations, both at the grassroots and national levels, emphasize the importance of Spanish language use to facilitate access to programs and ensure equity of participation. The Mexican American Legal Defense and Education Fund (MALDEF), founded in 1968 in Denver, sponsors a community education program to let grassroots groups know how they can use the nation's institutions to obtain services. The Puerto Rican Legal Defense and Education Fund (PRLDEF), founded in New York in 1972, has frequently joined MALDEF in demanding publicly funded bilingual services. The courts have mandated bilingual election materials in New York City, Philadelphia, and Chicago, as well as in parts of New Jersey and in a number of localities in the Southwest. Connecticut welfare offices provide bilingual written matter and bilingual social workers as a result of a PRLDEF suit.

The Questions to Be Raised

There are three possibilities for the speakers of a minority language in any society: (1) give up the native language and thus reduce, if not eliminate, the ethnic identity it articulates; (2) organize to influence changes in the educational system and mandate adoption of minority language for certain public processes; or (3) abandon the society by emigration or revolution. Thus, bilingualism can be a permanent characteristic of a society, resulting from sustained multilingual contact, or an intermediate stage for members of minority-language communities in transition from linguistic pluralism to monolingualism.

Historically in the United States, bilingualism has been an intermediate step for the immigrant. First- and second-generation immigrants may continue to speak the native language among themselves, but they find that English is the only means of communicating with majority society. Eisenstadt[53] defined two stages of assimilation: *cultural assimilation*, which is the adaptation to values, norms, patterns of behavior, and expectations without which the individual is unable to function in society; and *social assimilation*, which is the absorption of the newcomers into the host society as accepted members of social groups ranging from club memberships to marriage. The classic research of Gordon,[54] Greeley,[55] and Glazer and Moynihan[56] indicated that assimilation takes place in incremental stages; the ethnic culture may subsist for several generations even though social assimilation is well under way. The very concept of assimilation continues to be challenged, notably by the work of Andrew Greeley, whose sociological studies continue to document its complexity.[57] However, there is continuing evidence that the most recent immigrants continue to adopt the American language—and there are indications that they also adopt American political values, indicating that the process of becoming an American continues. The difficulty is in defining how this assimilation into American society takes place.

The question of linguistic assimilation becomes central to that of cultural assimilation, because a common language can support both maintaining relationships within the ethnic group and maintaining a group identity separate from majority society. Lieberson[58] contended that in the United States, maintaining a distinct native language is more closely linked to ethnic differences than is religion.

It is valuable to distinguish between linguistic retention, which depends on literary, cultural, and emotional values; and linguistic assimilation, which depends on political and economic values. Richard Rodriguez,[59] in his moving autobiography, made the distinction between private language (used with one's family) and public language (used in social activities). He argued that although Spanish may remain the private language of Hispanics, it is necessary to learn English, the public language, to achieve social assimilation and economic success. His book, a poignant autobiography of the immigrant experience that is far from a pedagogical work of evaluation, was lauded by opponents of bilingual education.

The reality is that the United States is not a bilingual society; the majority of Americans have no need to be bilingual. One can certainly argue the cultural and educational advantages of learning a second language, but for the majority of Americans such knowledge is not an absolute need. For native speakers of a language other than English, learning English is necessary to function fully in American society. For most immigrants to America, this may require a transitional bilingual program. These individuals will learn English through their native languages.

The debates over bilingual education and official English are closely connected. The former asks: Should public institutions play a role in fostering bilingualism, though that could mean both supporting language and indirectly promoting the celebration of another culture? The latter asks: Should public institutions be a place where only English monolingualism is allowed?

If bilingualism is to be encouraged, one must ask whether it is the individual or the nation that is to be bilingual. American society as a whole is strongly monolingual. There are historical, economic, and political reasons for monolingualism, and there is no evidence that this is changing. There is some evidence of strong native-language retention among a number of ethnic groups, but there is no greater incidence of this retention now than there was at the beginning of the century.

Thus, there is little serious possibility that America will become a bilingual nation. English will continue to be the language of the marketplace except in the few places where large communities of Hispanics make it economically attractive and politically possible to foster a bilingual community. The American economy continues to demand English-language skills of those who wish to participate in it. The majority of immigrants came to America for economic reasons and will learn English to enjoy its economic benefits. The question is not whether America will become a bilingual society, but whether society should encourage the existence and maintenance of the Spanish language in the Hispanic community and, if so, in what context. A related question is whether Spanish-language retention is detrimental to assimilation for the individual—and for the group—in an essentially English-monolingual society.

Carmen Judith Nine-Curt, a professor in the College of Education in the University of Puerto Rico, wrote in a 1980s conference paper of her realizations about language and culture: "Language seems to be just one third of culture. The rest is nonverbal communication." Much of the difficulty in communication between Hispanics and non-Hispanic Whites results from misunderstandings of nonverbal signals. For example, she says that a Puerto Rican gesture of friendliness is interpreted by non-Hispanic Whites as "a sign of mental retardation."[60] It could be the potential for miscommunication that drives the English-only movement, or rather an issue of Spanish- or English-language use. It could also be an issue of color and race rather than culture and language.

Although the debate about language clearly influences public policy that affects all Americans' lives, answers to the following questions are necessary before effective public policies can be enacted:

* What does history tell us about the relative values of assimilation, acculturation, bilingualism, and biculturalism? What does the American experience tell us in particular?
* What is the social responsibility and benefit in maintaining native language and culture? What may be the dangers in doing so?
* What is the role of educational institutions in social assimilation and acculturation?
* What are the benefits of present bilingual institutions (schools, social service agencies, churches) to the Hispanic community? To society as a whole? What are their disadvantages?

- To what degree is native-language retention beneficial or detrimental to the Hispanic individual? To the Hispanic community? To American society?
- What is the relationship between language and culture? What is the role of language and culture in defining individual identity?
- What other factors, besides language, make cross-cultural communication difficult?

To address these issues, empirical research must be done. Equally important, the thinking of philosophers, historians, linguists, and educators must be brought to bear on the questions. The most evocative and articulate voices in the debate over linguistic and cultural assimilation of Hispanics in the United States may be those of the new generation of writers, such as Richard Rodriguez and Christina Garcia.

Notes

1. Kristen A. Hansen and Carol S. Faber, "The Foreign-Born Population," in *Current Population Reports* (United States Census Bureau, 1996), Internet posting.
2. Data from table 1.1 in chapter 1 of this book.
3. Andrew M. Greeley, "Why Study Ethnicity?," in *The Diverse Society*, ed. Pastora San Juan Cafferty and Leon Chestang (Washington, D.C.: National Association of Social Workers, Inc., 1976), 8.
4. J. Milton Yinger, "Intersecting Strands of Race and Ethnic Relations," in *Racial and Cultural Minorities: An Analysis of Prejudice and Discrimination*, ed. George Eaton Simpon and J. Milton Yinger (New York: Harper & Row, 1965), 20–40.
5. Greeley, "Why Study Ethnicity?," 9.
6. Stephen Steinberg, *The Ethnic Myth: Race, Ethnicity in America* (New York: Athaneum, 1981), 92.
7. Joshua Fishman, *Language and Ethnicity in Minority Sociolinguistic Perspective* (Cleveland, Ohio: Multilingual Matters, 1989), 40.
8. J. De Press, "Ethnicity: What Data and Theory Portend for Plural Societies," in *The Prospects for Plural Societies*, ed. David Maybury Lewis (Washington, D.C.: American Ethnological Society, 1984), 14.
9. Joshua Fishman, *Language Loyalty in the United States* (London: Mouton & Co., 1966), 41.
10. Fishman, *Language and Ethnicity in Minority Sociolinguistic Perspective*, 190.
11. Fishman, *Language Loyalty in the United States*, 300.
12. Theodore Andersen, "Bilingual Education: The American Experience," *Modern Language Journal* 55 (November 1971): 427.
13. Ibid.
14. Ernest G. Ravenstein, "The Laws of Migration," *Journal of the Royal Statistical Society* 48 (June 1985): 167–235.
15. Pastora San Juan Cafferty and Carmen Rivera-Martinez, *The Politics of Language: The Dilemma of Bilingual Education for Puerto Ricans* (Boulder, Colo.: Westview Press, 1981), 113–19.
16. Alejandro Portes and Richard Schauffler, "Language and the Second Generation," in *The Second Generation*, ed. Alejandro Portes (New York: Russell Sage Foundation, 1996), 8–29.

17. Leobordo F. Estrada, "Language and Political Consciousness Among the Spanish-Speaking in the United States: A Demographic Study," in *Politics and Language: Spanish and English in the United States*, ed. D. J. R. Bruckner (Chicago: University of Chicago Press, 1980), 16–19.

18. Data from table 6.2 in chapter 6 of this book.

19. James Crawford, *Anatomy of the English-Only Movement: Social and Ideological Sources of Language Restrictionism in the United States* (1996), Internet posting: http://ourworld.compuserve.com/homepages/JWCRAWFORD/anatomy.htm

20. Carol Schmidt, "The English-Only Movement: Social Bases of Support and Opposition among Anglos and Latinos," in *Language Loyalties: A Source Book on the Official English Controversy*, ed. James Crawford (Chicago: University of Chicago Press, 1991) , 126–52.

21. Ramon G. McLeod and Maria Alicia Gaura, "Prop. 227 Got Few Latino Votes," *San Francisco Chronicle*, June 5, 1998, at 3.

22. J. Harvie Wilkinson, III, *One Nation Indivisible: How Ethnic Separatism Threatens America* (Reading, Mass.: Addison-Wesley, 1997), 151–71.

23. Einai Eaugen, "The Ecology of Language," in *The Ecology of Language: Essays by Einai Haugen*, ed. Anwar S. Dil (Stanford, Cal.: Stanford University Press, 1971), 37.

24. Portes and Schauffler, "Language and the Second Generation."

25. Data from table 6.2 in chapter 6 of this book.

26. 347 U.S. 483 (1954).

27. 20 U.S.C. § 880b (1970).

28. Marilyn McMillen, *Dropout Rates in the United States 1995* (Washington, D.C.: United States Department of Education, July 1, 1997), 34.

29. Ibid.

30. 20 U.S.C.A. § 880 *et seq.* (Supp. 1975).

31. 20 U.S.C.A. § 1701 *et seq.* (Supp. 1975).

32. *Lau v. Nichols*, 414 U.S. 563, 566 (1977).

33. James Crawford, *Babel in the Schools* (1977), Internet posting.

34. Rosalie Pedalino Porter, *Forked Tongue: The Politics of Bilingual Education*, 2d ed. (New Brunswick, N.J.: Transaction Press, 1996).

35. Ruth Ann Heck and Jill F. Norwood, *Limited English Proficiency: A Growing and Costly Educational Challenge Facing Many School Districts* (Washington, D.C.: General Accounting Office, January 1994).

36. American Legislative Exchange Council, *The Report Card on American Education 1994* (Washington, D.C.: Author, September 9, 1994), 56–57.

37. Wallace Z. Lambert and Richard Tucker, *Bilingual Education of Children* (Rowley, Mass.: Newberry, 1972).

38. Natalie T. Darcy, "Bilingualism and the Measurement of Intelligence: Review of a Decade's Research," *Journal of Genetic Psychology* 103 (December 1963): 259–82.

39. "Bilingual Early Childhood Programs," in *Model Programs: Childhood and Education* (San Antonio, Tex.: United States Office of Education, 1970).

40. H. Ned Seelye, Rafaela Elizondo de Weefer, and K. Balasubramonian, "Do Bilingual Education Programs Inhibit Language Achievement? A Report on an Illinois Experiment," paper presented at the 7th Annual Convening Teachers of English to Speakers of Other Languages, San Juan, Puerto Rico, May 9–13, 1973.

41. Division of Assessment and Accountability, *Educational Progress in Bilingual and ESL Programs: A Longitudinal Study 1990–94* (New York: Board of Education, City of New York, 1994).

42. Jay Chambers and Tom Parrish, "Cost of Programs and Services for LEP Stu-

dents," in *Meeting the Challenge of Diversity: An Evaluation of Programs for Pupils with Limited Proficiency in English IV* (Boston: Pioneer Institute, 1996).

43. Christine H. Rossell and Keith Baker, *Bilingual Education in Massachusetts: The Emperor Has No Clothes* (Boston, Mass.: Pioneer Institute, 1996).
44. "Hispanic Students and Their Teachers Assess the Needs of Local Hispanic Students" (Providence, R.I.: University of Rhode Island, Urban Field Center, September 1993), 1.
45. Ibid., 5.
46. UNESCO, *The Use of the Vernacular Languages in Education* (Paris: Author, 1953).
47. United States Congress, Senate Special Subcommittee on Bilingual Education, *Hearings on S. 428*, 90th Cong., 1st Sess. 52–53 (1967).
48. Joshua Fishman, "The Status and Prospects of Bilingualism in the United States," *Modern Language Journal* 49 (March 1965): 227.
49. Maria Zate, "Bicultural Bedside Manners," *Hispanic Business* (April 1995): 14–18.
50. Henry F. Adams-Esquivel, *How Advertisers Help Acculturate Hispanics Through Spanish-Language Advertising* (Los Angeles, Cal.: Market Development, Inc.), 2–3.
51. Federico Cura, "Latinos Lag in Computer Use," *Hispanic* 9 (April 1996): 10–11.
52. Maria Magelonsky, "First Language Comes First," *American Demographics* (October 1995): 21.
53. S. N. Eisenstadt, *The Absorption of Immigrants* (Glenco, Ill.: Free Press, 1955), 72–75.
54. Milton M. Gordon, *Assimilation in American Life* (New York: Oxford University Press, 1964).
55. Andrew M. Greeley, *Ethnicity in the United States* (New York: John Wiley & Sons, 1974).
56. Nathan Glazer and Daniel Patrick Moynihan, *Beyond the Melting Pot* (Cambridge, Mass.: MIT Press, 1970).
57. Andrew M. Greeley has written extensively on the subject since his *Ethnicity in the United States*. A good compendium of his writings is *The Sociology of Andrew Greeley* (Atlanta, Ga.: Scholars Press, 1994).
58. Stanley Lieberson, *Language and Ethnic Relations in Canada* (Toronto: John Wiley & Sons, 1970).
59. Richard Rodriguez, *Hunger of Memory: The Education of Richard Rodriguez* (New York: Bantam Books, 1982).
60. Carmen Judith Nine-Curt, "Hispanic-Anglo Conflicts in Nonverbal Communication," paper presented at 2d Annual Conference at the Institute of Nonverbal Research, Teachers College, Columbia University, New York, 1980, at 4.

Bibliography

Adams-Esquivel, Henry F. *How Advertisers Help Acculturate Hispanics Through Spanish-Language Advertising.* Los Angeles, Cal.: Market Development, Inc.

American Legislative Exchange Council. *The Report Card on American Education 1994.* Washington, D.C.: Author, September 9, 1994.

Andersen, Theodore. "Bilingual Education: The American Experience." *Modern Language Journal* 55 (November 1971): 427.

"Bilingual Early Childhood Programs." In *Model Programs: Childhood and Education.* San Antonio, Tex.: United States Office of Education, 1970.

Bruckner, D. J. R., ed. *Politics and Language: Spanish and English in the United States.* Chicago: University of Chicago Press, 1980.

Cafferty, Pastora San Juan, and Leon Chestang, eds. *The Diverse Society.* Washington, D.C.: National Association of Social Workers, Inc., 1976.

Cafferty, Pastora San Juan, and Carmen Rivera-Martinez. *The Politics of Language: The Dilemma of Bilingual Education for Puerto Ricans.* Boulder, Colo.: Westview Press, 1981.

Chambers, Jay, and Tom Parrish. "Cost of Programs and Services for LEP Students." In *Meeting the Challenge of Diversity: An Evaluation of Programs for Pupils with Limited Proficiency in English IV.* Boston: Pioneer Institute, 1996.

Crawford, James. *Anatomy of the English-Only Movement: Social and Ideological Sources of Language Restrictionism in the United States* (1996). Internet posting: http://ourworld.compuserve.com/homepages/JWCRAWFORD/anatomy.htm

———. *Babel in the Schools.* 1977. Internet posting: http://ourworld.compuserve.com/homepages/jwcrawford/can-bil.htm

Crawford, James, ed. *Language Loyalties: A Source Book on the Official English Controversy.* Chicago: University of Chicago Press, 1991.

Cura, Federico. "Latinos Lag in Computer Use." *Hispanic* 9 (April 1996): 10–11.

Darcy, Natalie T. "Bilingualism and the Measurement of Intelligence: Review of a Decade's Research." *Journal of Genetic Psychology* 103 (December 1963): 259–82.

De Press, J. "Ethnicity: What Data and Theory Portend for Plural Societies." In *The Prospects for Plural Societies,* edited by David Maybury Lewis. Washington, D.C.: American Ethnological Society, 1984.

Division of Assessment and Accountability. *Educational Progress in Bilingual and ESL Programs: A Longitudinal Study 1990–94.* New York: Board of Education, City of New York, 1994.

Eaugen, Einai. "The Ecology of Language." In *The Ecology of Language: Essays by Einai Haugen,* edited by Anwar S. Dil. Stanford, Cal.: Stanford University Press, 1971.

Eisenstadt, S. N. *The Absorption of Immigrants*. Glenco, Ill.: Free Press, 1955.

Estrada, Leobordo F. "Language and Political Consciousness Among the Spanish-Speaking in the United States: A Demographic Study." In *Politics and Language: Spanish and English in the United States*, edited by D. J. R. Bruckner, 16–19. Chicago: University of Chicago Press, 1980.

Fishman, Joshua. *Language and Ethnicity in Minority Sociolinguistic Perspective*. Cleveland, Ohio: Multilingual Matters, 1989.

———. *Language Loyalty in the United States*. London: Mouton & Co., 1966.

———. "The Status and Prospects of Bilingualism in the United States." *Modern Language Journal* 49 (March 1965): 227.

Glazer, Nathan, and Daniel Patrick Moynihan. *Beyond the Melting Pot*. Cambridge, Mass.: MIT Press, 1970.

Gordon, Milton M. *Assimilation in American Life*. New York: Oxford University Press, 1964.

Greeley, Andrew M. *Ethnicity in the United States*. New York: John Wiley & Sons, 1974.

———. *The Sociology of Andrew Greeley*. Atlanta, Ga.: Scholars Press, 1994.

———. "Why Study Ethnicity?" In *The Diverse Society*, edited by Pastora San Juan Cafferty and Leon Chestang. Washington, D.C.: National Association of Social Workers, Inc., 1976.

Hansen, Kristen A., and Carol S. Faber. "The Foreign-Born Population." In *Current Population Reports*. United States Census Bureau, 1996. Internet posting: http://www.census.gov:80/prod/2/pop/p20/p20-494pdf

Heck, Ruth Ann, and Jill F. Norwood. *Limited English Proficiency: A Growing and Costly Educational Challenge Facing Many School Districts*. Washington, D.C.: General Accounting Office, January 1994.

"Hispanic Students and Their Teachers Assess the Needs of Local Hispanic Students." Providence, R.I.: University of Rhode Island, Urban Field Center, September 1993.

Lambert, Wallace Z., and Richard Tucker. *Bilingual Education of Children*. Rowley, Mass.: Newberry, 1972.

Lewis, David Maybury, ed. *The Prospects for Plural Societies*. Washington, D.C.: American Ethnological Society, 1984.

Lieberson, Stanley. *Language and Ethnic Relations in Canada*. Toronto: John Wiley & Sons, 1970.

Magelonsky, Maria. "First Language Comes First." *American Demographics* (October 1995): 21.

McLeod, Ramon G., and Maria Alicia Gaura. "Prop. 227 Got Few Latino Votes." *San Francisco Chronicle*, June 5, 1998, at 3.

McMillen, Marilyn. *Dropout Rates in the United States 1995*. Washington, D.C.: United States Department of Education, July 1, 1997.

Nine-Curt, Carmen Judith. "Hispanic-Anglo Conflicts in Nonverbal Communication." Paper presented at 2d Annual Conference at the Institute of Nonverbal Research. Teachers College, Columbia University, New York, 1980.

Porter, Rosalie Pedalino. *Forked Tongue: The Politics of Bilingual Education*, 2d ed. New Brunswick, N.J.: Transaction Press, 1996.

Portes, Alejandro, ed. *The Second Generation*. New York: Russell Sage Foundation, 1996.

Portes, Alejandro, and Richard Schauffler. "Language and the Second Generation." In *The Second Generation*, edited by Alejandro Portes, 8–29. New York: Russell Sage Foundation, 1996.

Ravenstein, Ernest G. "The Laws of Migration." *Journal of the Royal Statistical Society* 48 (June 1985): 167–235.

Rodriguez, Richard. *Hunger of Memory: The Education of Richard Rodriguez*. New York: Bantam Books, 1982.

Rossell, Christine H., and Keith Baker. *Bilingual Education in Massachusetts: The Emperor Has No Clothes*. Boston, Mass.: Pioneer Institute, 1996.

Schmidt, Carol. "The English-Only Movement: Social Bases of Support and Opposition among Anglos and Latinos." In *Language Loyalties: A Source Book on the Official English Controversy*, edited by James Crawford, 126–52. Chicago: University of Chicago Press, 1991.

Seelye, H. Ned, Rafaela Elizondo de Weefer, and K. Balasubramonian. "Do Bilingual Education Programs Inhibit Language Achievement? A Report on an Illinois Experiment." Paper presented at the 7th Annual Convening Teachers of English to Speakers of Other Languages. San Juan, Puerto Rico, May 9–13, 1973.

Simpon, George Eaton, and J. Milton Yinger, eds. *Racial and Cultural Minorities: An Analysis of Prejudice and Discrimination*. New York: Harper & Row, 1965.

Steinberg, Stephen. *The Ethnic Myth: Race, Ethnicity in America*. New York: Athaneum, 1981.

UNESCO. *The Use of the Vernacular Languages in Education*. Paris: Author, 1953.

United States Congress, Senate Special Subcommittee on Bilingual Education, *Hearings on S. 428*, 90th Cong., 1st Sess. 52–53 (1967).

Wilkinson, III, J. Harvie. *One Nation Indivisible: How Ethnic Separatism Threatens America*. Reading, Mass.: Addison-Wesley, 1997.

Yinger, J. Milton. "Intersecting Strands of Race and Ethnic Relations." In *Racial and Cultural Minorities: An Analysis of Prejudice and Discrimination*, edited by George Eaton Simpon and J. Milton Yinger, 20–40. New York: Harper & Row, 1965.

Zate, Maria. "Bicultural Bedside Manners." *Hispanic Business* (April 1995): 14–18.

4

The Changing Religious Practice of Hispanics

David Maldonado, Jr.

One can argue that no issue or aspect of life is more central to the history and experience of Hispanics than religion. No other aspect of Hispanic life reflects that group's formative history, current trends, and questions for the future as well as religion. Religion is a sensitive issue because it is so personal and private—yet it is an important part of culture and cultural identity. Religion is at the core of the human experience at the individual, familial, and community levels. Nonetheless, it is avoided, overlooked, or ignored by many social sciences, ethnic studies, and mainstream academics in the study of Hispanics.

At the individual level, religion reflects self-understanding within the context of the universe, and is experienced at the innermost sanctuary of the spirit; it is highly private and personal. Yet religion is also a familial heritage. It is learned within the intimate context of parents and family. It represents a familial bond and treasure. Children are nurtured in the spirituality of mothers, as well as in their arms. Religion connects us with ancestors and previous generations.

Religion is also a community matter. People belong to communities of faith that share religious symbols, rituals, events, beliefs, ethics, values, and memory. It also allows identification with a larger faith group and religious tradition. Despite its undeniably private aspects, religion is very much a public matter, and is celebrated with others. It imbues individuals with a larger sense of belonging, being, and history.

Religion can be a vehicle of cultural identity as well. Ethnic identity and religious identity have merged in many populations. Among Hispanics, religion and cultural identity have blended over centuries to produce a context in which ethnic and Catholic identities are dramatically and intimately connected. However, even for those who are not Catholic, the connection between ethnicity and religious identity has important consequences.

Religion, religious movements, and religious motivation have shaped world history, and have been root causes of the birth of nations and societies. Religions have also provided core values and worldviews that shape cultures and guide human action. For the Hispanic population, religion has played a major role in its birth, history, culture, social life, and social institutions. Major historical events, such as the Spanish Inquisition and the Spanish conquest of the indigenous populations of the New World in the name of religion, have shaped the Hispanic population and its experience. Hispanic history and cultures are deeply rooted in religious dynamics and reflect the central role that religion has played in their development.

Today, religion still plays an important role in the cultural and social histories of Hispanics in the United States. Because of the leading role that the Catholic Church played in the Spanish conquests, the church as an institution and cultural Catholicism have been central to traditional Hispanic societies and the core of historic Hispanic identity. However, current Hispanic religious life also reflects modern complexities and challenges in a multicultural and increasingly religiously diverse society. Hispanics have begun to examine and claim other religious options, raising questions not only about Hispanic religious identity and religious life, but also about Hispanic ethnic identity and culture. If religion is at the core of culture and identity, and provides foundational social and ethical values, religious faith and practice will deeply affect what happens among Hispanics today and what lies ahead for Hispanics in the United States.

Mestizo Religion

The Hispanic populations have often been described as *mestizo* or *mulatto* populations. This refers to the biological and cultural blending of Spanish and indigenous or African populations. *Mestizaje* refers primarily to blending of Spanish with indigenous cultures on the mainland, whereas *mulatez* refers to blending with African populations that were brought as slaves to the Caribbean area.[1] However, mulattos are also found in various Latin American countries, such as Mexico, Columbia, and some Central American nations. Although blending sounds like a natural process of coming together, the *mestizaje* and *mulatez* experienced in the Americas was not. Blending with the native populations occurred after military conquest that resulted in the forced imposition of Spanish culture, language, and religion upon native populations. In addition, physical imposition resulted in the birth of a new people. The Spanish conquest involved much brutality and painful consequences for the conquered indigenous populations. The imposition of that which was Spanish was systematic, forceful, and as thorough as possible.[2]

In addition to geopolitical and economic interests, the Spanish were clearly interested in transporting their culture to the New World and in the conversion of native peoples to Spanish Catholicism. Religious motivation must be understood in the historical context of the Spanish Inquisition, when religious intolerance was the rule. Religious beliefs and practices outside of the Catholic Church were not permitted. On the contrary, drastic measures were taken to rid Spanish territories of non-Catholic religious practices; hence the destruction of native religious symbols and the mass conversion of native populations. The church was interested in the evangelization of the indigenous population and in assuring that they were baptized in the Christian faith. The outcome has been a diversity of Latin American cultures with the common thread of Catholicism at the core of national and cultural identities. Catholic religious practices, events, and symbols emerged as central to Latin American cultures. In addition, the Catholic Church as an institution, and Catholic priests as religious leaders, played central roles in the daily lives of Hispanics. Hispanic cultural, religious, and personal identities were shaped in thoroughly Catholic societies. It is not surprising that over the years, to be Hispanic was to be Catholic.

However, debate has emerged with regard to the success of the transposition of Spanish Catholicism and the conversion of native populations. Some have argued that the Spanish themselves kept an orthodox religious faith and truly evangelized the native peoples. This argument suggests that the Catholic faith that emerged in Mexico and other Latin societies was a true continuation of the faith learned in Spain.[3] On the other side are those who suggest that the Spanish were not totally successful in their conversion and evangelization of native peoples. Several scenarios are suggested.[4] The first is that the native populations submitted to their conquerors and outwardly accepted the Spanish religion, while privately maintaining their native religions. This is especially true of the *mulatez* experience in the Caribbean among the descendants of African slaves.

Another view holds that religious syncretism occurred, through which native and Spanish Christian traditions merged to create a new form of *mestizo* religion. This suggests that Hispanic Catholicism incorporated religious symbols, beliefs, and rituals from both the Spanish and indigenous heritages.[5] Thus, there was no true conversion, but rather a shallow submission to a new religious order accompanied by a creative integration of religious traditions that allowed natives to maintain some form of continuity through a syncretic religion. Nonetheless, religious *mestizaje* implies that two deeply held religious traditions were joined at the very point of the birth of the *mestizo* peoples, and thus were at the core of identity from the very beginning.[6]

Catholic Religious Identity

Whether or not conversion was sincere and complete, Hispanic countries emerged as Catholic societies and cultures. In some nations, such as Mexico, non-Catholic religious expressions were not allowed for many years. The Catholic Church and Catholic religious practices played dominant roles in the peoples' daily lives, in their cultural formation, and in the formation of their self-identities. From birth to death, the religious calendar of the church, with annual celebrations of religious events such as Christmas, Lent, Easter, and the various saints' days, guided the lives of communities. Key religious rituals or sacraments, such as baptism, catechism, first communion, *quincenieras*, marriage, and funerals, marked personal life journeys. Marriage and baptism shaped social relations. Religious values, teachings, and rituals shaped personal worldviews and individual and social behavior. The family, community, and society were all Catholic, thus providing a unified socioreligious cultural system. In essence, the culture and social formation for Hispanics in their nations of origin or in the period before American westward expansion was thoroughly Catholic.[7]

Hispanics in the United States have historically mirrored their cultures of origin with a strong sense of identity with Catholicism. Being Hispanic has meant being Catholic. Surveys have historically shown that the majority of Hispanics in the United States identify themselves as Catholic. Notably, though, Catholic identity seems to be somewhat independent of active participation in the church. Catholic identity among Hispanics is more a sense of self-identity than actual membership or even church participation. Catholic baptism at infancy initiates Catholic formation and identity. Even if some individuals do not return to church after baptism, they still share a sense of identity with the faith. This suggests that the Hispanic family and community play important roles in Catholic identity formation and in the maintenance of that identity. Such formation develops a strong sense of loyalty to the faith of the family and of the ancestors. It also involves bonding and solidarity with the broader Hispanic community.

Religious Diversity

In spite of the strong Catholic cultural history and traditional religious identity, religious life and identity among the Hispanic population in the United States have become increasingly diverse. The Hispanic population is no longer a monolithic Catholic population. It has come to mirror much of the religious diversity found in the broader culture and society. The trend is away from traditional Catholicism, and even beyond mainline Protestant denominations such as Methodists, Baptists, Presbyterians, Disciples, and Lutherans, who have been active in Hispanic communities for more than a century. Hispanic religious life also includes such religious groups as Seventh Day Adventists, Mormons, and Jehovah's Witnesses. In addition, some Hispanics claim religious identity with Jewish, Buddhist, and Islamic traditions. However, the fastest growing Hispanic religious group has been the Pentecostal and evangelical denominations.[8]

Along with this growing diversity, there has been a gradual decline of Hispanic Catholic identity. In a review of recent reports on Hispanic religious affiliations, Diaz-Stevens and Stevens-Arroyo presented findings from various studies indicative of the changing religious profile of U.S. Hispanics. It is also interesting to note that religious diversity varies among the different Hispanic populations. For example, Mexican-Americans and Cubans have the highest Catholic profile, whereas the Puerto Rican profile reflects a higher proportion of Protestants. In the Latino Voices study report, Catholic identity ranges from 74.8 percent among Cuban-Americans to 65.1 percent among Puerto Ricans. The Kosmin study found that 67 percent of U.S. Hispanics identified themselves as Catholic, 26 percent as Protestant, and 3 percent as other or none. These reports confirm that Hispanic populations in the United States are no longer monolithic Catholic populations, and also that

Hispanic religious identity covers a wide spectrum of religious traditions. Nonetheless, the majority of Hispanics still are Catholic.[9]

Religion in the Margins

Hispanic Catholics

Historically, and even today, Hispanic religious life has been lived on the margins of U.S. society. For both Hispanic Catholics and Hispanic Protestants, religious identity and ethnic identity have resulted in marginalized religious experiences. For example, Hispanic Catholics live within a broader dominant culture that has a deeply rooted Protestant history and culture. Although the United States proclaims religious freedom and tolerance, its history exposes abundant anti-Catholic sentiment and action. This was especially true during the western expansion period, when the doctrine of manifest destiny guided large numbers of non-Hispanic Whites toward the frontier. As the expansionist settlers confronted the Mexicans, anti-Catholic and anti-Mexican language and ideology became the rule of the day. It was then that Hispanics first experienced prejudice against their religious faith and their culture.[10] Mexicans were viewed as racially inferior, especially the *mestizos*. Non-Hispanic Whites saw the Catholic faith as superstitious and inferior to the Protestant faith.

At the turn of the century, religion within the Hispanic context was judged through the immigrant assimilation model, which suggested that the ideal for all immigrants was acculturation and eventually assimilation. *Acculturation* involves taking on the total culture of the host society; in this case, it included Protestantism. The expectation was that immigrants and minority populations would convert to Protestantism and thus blend into the dominant Protestant population. The bulk of the Hispanic population did not convert. Thus, for Hispanic Catholics, loyalty to their religious faith, identity, and traditions were perceived as obstacles to full acculturation and assimilation. To the majority Protestant culture, Hispanic Catholic traditions were negative, problematic, and inferior. In fact, Hispanic Catholicism was seen as detrimental to the advancement of Hispanics in the United States, because to maintain religious and cultural traditions was to resist acculturation and Americanization.[11] This in turn resulted in continued prejudice; in essence, Hispanics were marginalized both because of their ethnicity and because of their religious faith and practices. Non-Protestants, such as

Jews and Catholics, were religious minorities and thus on the edge of the social fabric of society; on occasion, these religious groups were subject to violence from extremists.

The experience of Hispanics, however, is also related to race, ethnicity, and cultural prejudice. Manifest destiny introduced the notion of Hispanic inferiority, and this racial and ethnic prejudice has never quite disappeared. Hispanic Catholics have had to face a complex social reality in which they are both a religious and an ethnic minority in a White Protestant culture.

In addition to the challenges of minority status within the larger social context, Hispanic Catholics have also had to battle marginalization within the institution and culture of the Catholic Church. As an ethnic minority within the Catholic Church in the United States, Hispanics have long struggled to get the Catholic Church hierarchy to recognize their presence, significance, and loyalty. Hispanic Catholics have fought for church acceptance of Hispanic religious practices and leadership since Catholic work was transferred from Mexican authorities to those in the United States.

Marginal status and cultural alienation were especially severe prior to the Second Vatican Council and the civil rights movement. As discussed later in this chapter, Hispanic Catholics have done a great deal of organizing within the church because of their sense of exclusion and their need for recognition from the church.

Hispanic Protestants

With the arrival of non-Hispanic White settlers in Texas during the Mexican Period (1821–1836), Protestantism also arrived in the Hispanic Southwest. Although welcomed to Texas with the understanding that they were to become Mexican citizens and accept Catholicism as their official religion, American settlers retained their Protestant faith. No public Protestant services were permitted, but in secret, away from the eyes of Mexican authorities, the newcomers continued their Protestant religious practices. The initial Protestant activity was aimed at serving settlers from the United States, and was often ignored by Tejano officials in the interest of peace and good relations. However, public Protestant activity such as Bible distribution caused tension. Protestant outreach to Tejanos and Mexicans during the Mexican Period was not the primary mission of Protestant activity. However, with the Texas War of Independence in 1836, the political and religious situations dramatically changed for Tejanos. The new Texas Republic was no longer Mexican nor officially Catholic. The doors were opened wide for the entry of Protestant missionaries from many denominations. Slowly Tejanos and Mexicans were exposed to Protestant material: preaching, singing, and especially the Bible.[12] By 1859, organized Protestant efforts specifically developed for Mexicans in Texas emerged. In New Mexico, the first Hispanic Presbyterian appeared in 1869.[13]

Hispanic Protestantism developed from the Protestantism practiced by those who had come from the United States and the Protestant missionary work that specifically targeted the Hispanic population in the Southwest during the late nineteenth century. Hispanics quickly became involved in missionary and evangelistic work and were instrumental in expanding Protestantism within the Hispanic population. Denominational structures for Hispanic work arose, especially in the West and Southwest. For example, the Methodist Church established missionary conference structures along the United States-Mexican border that eventually became the Rio Grande Conference in Texas and New Mexico, and another conference in California.[14] The Baptists developed special Conventions for Hispanic Work and Presbyterians also created regional structures to administer their Hispanic work. In addition, Protestant churches established schools, such as the Presbyterian schools in New Mexico, the Methodist Lydia Paterson Institute in El Paso, and the Holding Institute in Laredo.[15] Many community centers were also established throughout the Southwest; the Wesley Community Centers of the Methodist Church are probably the best known.

Like their Hispanic Catholic neighbors, Hispanic Protestants also have experienced marginalization of their religious lives. Within the Hispanic community, Hispanic Protestants are a religious minority and practice their faith outside the Catholic religious tradition of the broader Hispanic community. Protestants do not participate in most Hispanic events, festivals, or activities that are perceived to be Catholic. They do not share many of the traditional Catholic religious symbols or practices, such as the crucifix, the veneration of saints, or devotion to the Virgin of Guadalupe. They also do not participate in the many Catholic sacraments or festivals, such as *Posadas* and pilgrimages. Protestant lifestyles based on religious beliefs keep many Hispanic Protestants from other community events, such as dances. As a result, Hispanic Protestants are perceived as different and outside the mainstream religious life of the Hispanic community. They are at the religious margins within their own community.

In addition, like their Catholic counterparts, Hispanic Protestants are also marginalized within their Protestant denominations. Historically, because of their culture and ethnicity, Hispanics have been treated as missional and not part of the main structure of the denomination. Thus, they lack denominational and decision-making power. Only within recent decades have Hispanics begun to serve on national boards and agencies or been elected to positions of authority. Most Hispanic ministers are appointed to Hispanic congregations or work, and thus earn less than most ministers serving larger non-Hispanic churches. Although occurring more often, it is still unusual for Hispanic ministers to be appointed to non-Hispanic churches. A two-track system seems to prevail. In addition, Hispanic Protestants have long struggled with the task of incorporating Hispanic culture into their religious practices. Most mainline Protestant congregations offer only Spanish translations of non-Hispanic religious practices. Pentecostal denominations and churches are probably the most successful at integrating Hispanic culture into their religious expression.

Hispanic Immigration and Religion

Probably the most significant factor in Hispanic religious life in the United States in recent years has been the immigration of Hispanics from various Latin American nations. There has always been immigration, especially from Mexico. Likewise, the migration flow between Puerto Rico and the mainland has long been a part of Hispanic social dynamics. In addition, political crises, such as the Cuban revolution and political unrest in Central America, have resulted in related sharp increases in immigration. At this point in history, immigration from Central American countries and the increased flow from Mexico for economic reasons have been the most significant.

However, it is not simply the numbers or the motivation that are important for Hispanic religious life in the United States. What is significant is that many recent immigrants have a Protestant background, especially a Pentecostal background. The rapid rise of Pentecostalism in Latin America has been the religious phenomenon of recent decades, and seems likely to continue its momentum for a considerable time into the future. It has begun to change the religious picture in Latin America;

immigration brings those dynamics to this country and thus affects Hispanic religious life here. As a result, many Hispanic immigrants seek Protestant churches upon arrival, especially of the denominational traditions they knew back home.

Another phenomenon is Hispanic immigrants' exposure to and contact with Protestant and Pentecostal churches after arriving in the United States. As new immigrants, many Hispanics are introduced to Protestant churches through immigration services, social services, or evangelistic outreach by churches and religious organizations. Although many Protestant churches offer assistance simply for humanitarian reasons, some also include a religious message or invitation to religious activities. Such contact has led to religious conversions and denominational switches from Catholicism to Pentecostalism or Protestantism.

The movement from Catholic to Protestant is probably of greatest interest to students of Hispanic religion and of greatest concern to Catholic Church leaders. Not surprisingly, the Catholic-to-Protestant movement has initiated a debate not only between Protestants and Catholics, but also within the Catholic Church. The Catholic Church is quite concerned about such changes in religious identity and denominational loyalty. There has been increased attention to evangelization within the Catholic Church, illustrated by promotional material inviting Catholics back home to the Catholic Church. Important questions have been raised,[16] including the question of "why?" and the ethical questions involved in evangelizing Catholics for the purpose of membership in Protestant churches. Ecumenical relations among some denominations have been adversely affected.

Denominational Hispanic Programs

The sharp rise in the Hispanic population has caught the attention of the Catholic Church and most Protestant denominations. For years, the Catholic Church and most mainline denominations have had special national staff and offices to address the Hispanic presence. For example, the Catholic Church established the Office for the Spanish Speaking and held regional and national *Encuentros*. The Division for the Spanish Speaking, later known as the Secretariat for the Spanish Speaking, has long represented Hispanic concerns within the structures of the church.[17] Among Protestants, the United Methodists, Presbyterians, and Disciples also have national staff to address Hispanic interests. Another popular denominational response to recent Hispanic population increases and issues has been the development of national strategies or plans for Hispanic ministries among major denominations. A good example is the National Hispanic Plan of the United Methodist Church. Now in its second four-year phase, the United Methodists established this plan to provide funds and incentives for developing new Hispanic congregations, community services, and the revitalization of Hispanic congregations. A major component of this plan is the training of laypersons for volunteer involvement in Hispanic ministries. This program has a national staff and offices.

These programs indicate that religious work among the Hispanic population has become a concern and interest among most denominations. Hispanic work has increasingly gotten the attention and financial support of denominational structures, and Hispanic outreach has taken on a more thoughtful and intentional perspective. It is also interesting that these programs are national in scope and reflect the presence of Hispanics in most parts of the country. From New York to California and from Florida to the state of Washington, denominational structures are developing Hispanic programs to engage the Hispanic populations residing in their communities. That most denominations are actively involved in some type of Hispanic ministry further suggests that Protestant denominations no longer see Hispanics as the sole responsibility of the Catholic Church, but rather perceive Hispanics as part of their mission and ministry.

Hispanic Organizational Activity

An important trend within Hispanic religion is the emergence of religious organizations developed by Hispanics to address religious issues, interests, and needs of the Hispanic population. Most are internal to denominational groups and are intended to advocate for Hispanic issues within denominations. Others are ecumenical and their interests, though reflecting denominational problems, transcend denominational structures.

Within the Catholic Church, a series of Hispanic organizations give witness to Hispanic efforts to impact their denomination. Three are selected here to illustrate Hispanic Catholic activity. The first Hispanic Catholic organizational effort was among the clergy: in 1970, Padres Asociados para Derechos Educativos, Religiosos, y Sociales (PADRES) was created to advocate for social justice on behalf of Hispanics within the Catholic Church, especially in the Southwest. PADRES had an initial membership of Chicano priests; efforts to create a national membership organization did not materialize until 1990, when the Asociación Nacional de Sacerdotes Hispanos, EE.UU (ANSH) was established. ANSH is a clergy membership organization and is concerned primarily with ecclesiastical issues.[18] The Academy of Catholic Hispanics in the United States (ACTHUS) is another Hispanic organization composed primarily of theologians and academics whose interests appear to be theology and the promotion of intellectual discourse.[19]

Yet another important Hispanic Catholic organization is Las Hermanas. This organization was initiated in Texas in 1971, with a membership of both lay and religious women. Its concerns have been to promote the interests of Hispanic Catholic women within the church, provide mutual support, advocate for social justice, and take positions on issues such as the ordination of women. Like PADRES and ANSH, Las Hermanas reflects organizational efforts of Hispanic Catholics to influence their church on behalf of Hispanic concerns.[20]

An example of a Protestant Hispanic organization is Metodistas Asociados Representando la Causa Hispana Americana (MARCHA). This organization is a Hispanic caucus within the United Methodist Church, created to advocate for Hispanic interests in denominational structures, policy, and programs. Its membership is both clergy and laity, and the group is national in scope. It is active mostly at the national church level.

The existence of such organizational efforts within denominations indicates that Hispanics, both Catholic and Protestant, perceive the need to organize to address denominational structures on behalf of Hispanics. This suggests that Hispanic interests would otherwise be forgotten or marginal to normal denominational life. It further shows a degree of tension between Hispanics and church structures within most denominations as a result of Hispanic activity.

Hispanic Religion and Theological Education

An important trend during the last twenty-five years is the emergence of Hispanic studies within theological education and religious studies. Several schools of theology have established special programs or concentrations of study related to religion and religious life within the Hispanic populations. For example, Perkins School of Theology at Southern Methodist University has had a Mexican American Program for more than twenty years. This program is particularly interested in

Hispanic Protestantism and especially the United Methodist Church. It provides training for lay and clergy preparing for Hispanic ministries.

This and other Hispanic Protestant programs remind us that Hispanics have not developed independent institutions of higher education in the United States. This is also true of theological education. Hispanic programs tend to exist within or in association with established schools of theology. The one exception is the Seminario Evangelico de Puerto Rico, an ecumenical Protestant seminary in Puerto Rico. Many of its graduates serve in the mainland United States. It provides theological education for and by Hispanics in a Hispanic context.

The Mexican American Cultural Center, on the campus of Oblate Seminary in San Antonio, Texas, is a leader within the Catholic community. It serves as an educational and training center for theological, pastoral, and language studies. Although on the campus of Oblate, the Center reflects efforts by Hispanic Catholics to create a space for Hispanics to address issues of interest to their community.

During the last decade, an ecumenical group of more than twenty-five seminaries, schools of theology, and universities have pooled resources to establish the Hispanic Summer Program. The purpose of this program is to provide a setting in which Hispanic students can study under the leadership of Hispanic Protestant and Catholic faculty. Most of the students are Hispanic Protestant and Catholic seminarians, and the courses address Hispanic topics and interests. Courses are offered in Spanish and in English, and are eligible for credit at the students' home institutions.

Despite these programs, a major question remains: Will Hispanic theological and religious interests continue to be marginal within the life and work of established seminaries and university religious studies programs? How can universities and schools of theology appropriately incorporate Hispanic topics into their curricula and programs?

At the doctoral level, the Pew Charitable Trusts funded the Hispanic Theological Initiative in 1996 to recruit and facilitate the enrollment of Hispanics in doctoral programs in theology and religion. After only a few years, the Hispanic Theological Initiative has successfully placed Hispanics in various doctoral programs around the country. It has also funded dissertation work and sabbaticals for young Hispanic scholars. This project is another indication of the attention Hispanics have drawn within the religious field and the support this area draws from foundations and other institutions.

Hispanic Theological and Religious Scholarship and Research

One of the most promising aspects of religion within the Hispanic context is the emergence of Hispanic scholarly work. As in most other areas of study, scholarship in religion and theology requires a doctorate or related degree, membership in the academic community, and publishers willing to publish Hispanic religious material. Hispanics have long struggled to get accepted in graduate theological schools and for a long time only a handful of Hispanics were able to do so. Among the pioneer scholars in this field were Justo Gonzalez, Virgilio Elizondo, Eldin Villafane, Ada Maria Isasi-Diaz, Allan Figueroa Deck, Orlando Espin, and Fernando Segovia. A second generation of Hispanic scholars includes people such as Ana Maria Diaz-Stevens, Ana Maria Pineda, Samuel Solivan, Harold Recino, Roberto Goizueta, and Anthony Stevens-Arroyo. Most recently, a third generation of younger Hispanic scholars is emerging from graduate schools and initiating academic careers. These include Luis Pedraja, Edwin Aponte, Daisy Machado, and Lara Medina. Yet, in the area of religion and theological studies, Latinos still struggle to be accepted into graduate study programs and to get academic institutions to incorporate Hispanic studies into the mainstream. In such a context, it is significant that a small but energetic number of Hispanic scholars are opening doors and breaking new ground.

Of importance to Hispanic religious studies and theological education is the emergence of journals that address and facilitate Hispanic publication and discourse. Established journals of religion have long ignored Hispanic topics and writers; thus, the creation of two key Hispanic journals. *Apuntes: Reflexiones desde el Margen Hispano*, a journal sponsored by the Mexican American Program at Perkins School of Theology, SMU, is the first journal established for the purpose of facilitating publications on Hispanic topics. Of special interest was the need to address issues of Hispanic ministry and to encourage discourse between Hispanic scholars and clergy in the field. Justo Gonzales has edited this journal for nearly twenty years. The audience of *Apuntes* is primarily Protestant. The second such Hispanic journal to be established was *The Journal of Hispanic/Latino Theology*. Its audience is primarily academic and Catholic, although Protestants publish in it. This journal was established in 1993 by the Academy of Catholic Hispanic Theologians in the United States, and has achieved high marks for its scholarly content.

The emergence of these two Hispanic journals reflects the new energy in Hispanic religious scholarship. Hispanics are increasingly producing scholarly work within this field and have created a demand for scholarly outlets. In addition, these journals suggest that there is a viable market for Hispanic religious scholarship. There is a demand for Hispanic material among the clergy, among students in theology and religious studies programs, and among faculty who wish to use this material in their teaching. It is uncertain, however, whether and when mainstream journals of religion will recognize Hispanic scholarship. Hispanic topics and authors have always been on the fringe. Will the establishment of *Apuntes* and the *Journal of Hispanic/Latino Theology* further marginalize Hispanic religious scholarship? Will academic institutions accept these two journals as appropriate in their evaluation of Hispanic scholars?

Hispanic Ecumenical Realities

Ecumenical activity within the Hispanic religious community is a unique situation. Although some aspects mirror the broader ecumenical reality in the United States, there are some important differences. For example, the Catholic-Protestant gap within the Hispanic community has been a dramatic and painful historical experience, especially before the Second Vatican Council. The division was not simply a theological or even doctrinal matter, as important as these may be. The split cut deeply into cultural, social, and familial relationships. Strong anti-Protestant and anti-Catholic sentiments divided Hispanic families, friendships, and the Hispanic community in general. There was much misrepresentation, and biases grew to the extent that antagonism, suspicion, and ignorance made relations between the two religious traditions very difficult, if not impossible. With Pentecostal and evangelical churches growing rapidly, at the expense of Catholic membership, the tension between Catholics and Pentecostals increased. In the meantime, relations between Catholics and mainstream denominations improved to the point of tolerance and even conversation.

Ecumenical activity at the local level has usually been successful among mainline Protestant churches such as the United Methodist, Presbyterian, Lutheran, and Disciple, with the Baptists and Pentecostals/evangelicals usually maintaining a discreet and independent distance. These activities include the organization of Hispanic ministerial alliances and joint religious services (especially during Lent and Easter).

At the national level, the most promising example of ecumenical spirit is the organization of La Asociación para la Educación Teológica Hispana (AETH). This organization is composed of individuals from mainline and Pentecostal traditions who share interests in theological education and ministerial training. Although it is an organization of individual members and not of denominations, it is a sign of a more open spirit.

At a more ecumenical level is the Hispanic Summer Program. As described earlier, this program is sponsored by seminaries and schools of theology from Catholic and Protestant traditions. However, participation includes students from Pentecostal backgrounds as well as Catholic and mainstream Protestant churches. This is probably the only situation in which Catholics, Protestants, and Pentecostals share time and space addressing mutual Hispanic religious issues. Part of the program experience is joint worship and sharing about each other's traditions.

Issues of Transition

This brief review of historical roots and of current dynamics suggests that Hispanic religion is going through several transitions after painful beginnings, a rich Catholic history, and difficult religious conflicts between Protestant and Catholic traditions within the Hispanic community. In addition, Hispanics have struggled within their denominations for recognition, justice, and dignity. Hispanics have now come of age with regard to theological sophistication, leadership, and organizational skills. They desire to express and celebrate their religious faiths and spirituality within the context of their cultures, visions, and realities. How they address these transitions and the extent to which they are able to claim both ethnic identity and religious identity within diverse contexts will determine success.

Issues of Religious Diversity

The first transition refers to the Hispanic community moving toward greater religious diversity. Hispanics are traditionally Catholic, but now they also follow Protestant, Pentecostal, and evangelical, as well as Jewish, Mormon, and many other religious traditions. The Hispanic community is now challenged to overcome past divisions such as the painful Protestant–Catholic gap that split Hispanic friendships, families, and communities. These divisions include doctrinal, ritual, symbolic, and sacramental issues, but also social, cultural, and attitudinal issues as well. Doctrine, sacrament, and ritual are issues for the denominations to address. However, Hispanics need to ask whether religious doctrine and such issues justify the deep divisions and pain they have caused within Hispanic families and communities. The question is religious tolerance and the acceptance of religious diversity within the Hispanic community. To some extent, institutional self-interest has influenced relations between individuals. Will Protestant and Catholic clergy, church leadership, and laity of all traditions respect the others? At what point will religion stop being an internal barrier?

Related to the question of diversity is the current issue of conversion and denominational switching. As Hispanics explore other religious traditions, tension and suspicion have arisen among Catholic, Pentecostal, and evangelical traditions. Protestants are perceived as targeting Catholics for evangelistic outreach, with the intention of converting these persons to a Pentecostal, evangelical, or other Protestant tradition. Protestants claim that they are reaching out to unchurched persons; Catholics claim that these denominations are trying to proselytize their flock. Very little is known about conversion and denominational switching within the Hispanic community. Much research is needed on this topic, but equally necessary is dialogue among the various denominations, especially between Catholic and Protestants, including the Pentecostals and evangelicals. How denominational leadership deals with this issue will have important consequences for the Hispanic community.

Issues of Religion and Cultural Diversity

The second transition refers to the increasing diversity of Hispanic cultures in the United States, including the nature of the recent immigrant population. The traditional assumption that Hispanics are Mexican-American, Puerto Rican, or Cuban is outdated. Recent immigration from Central and South America, as well as other Caribbean nations, has changed the Hispanic population in this country. Implications for the religious picture have also become more complex. For example, immigrants from the Caribbean have strengthened the presence of *santería* and other African-influenced religious practices among Hispanics. How these practices will be integrated into the Hispanic religious fiber remains to be seen.

As the Hispanic population becomes culturally more diverse, the parallel question of religious diversity arises. Even within Hispanic Catholicism there is diversity. For example, the Virgin of Guadalupe is a central religious symbol for Mexicans and Mexican-Americans; she is also a national and cultural icon for this population. However, among Hispanics with Caribbean roots, the Virgin of Guadalupe is not very important. For them, other manifestations of the Virgin Mary take precedence. To what extent will Mexican-American Catholics acknowledge other Hispanic religious icons? To what extent will other Hispanics accept the Virgin of Guadalupe as the icon for all the Americas? Will Catholic Hispanics eventually come together around one icon? Will this become a divisive issue?

Among Hispanic Protestants, cultural diversity is also an issue. Among some Hispanic cultures, such as the Puerto Rican and Cuban, worship styles can be quite expressive and outgoing, with the use of drums and other musical instruments, especially among the Pentecostals and evangelicals. Among Mexican-Americans in mainline traditions, worship is much more subdued. There is also the question of Hispanic integration. Will Hispanic Protestant churches become culturally inclusive, or will they develop as ethnic-specific churches, with Cuban, Puerto Rican, or Mexican congregations? How will an inclusive Hispanic church operate and carry out its religious life and ministries?

Immigration and Religion

In addition to the issue of diversity discussed earlier in this chapter, immigration raises other important questions for Hispanic religious life. Immigrants bring with them religious experiences, perceptions, and attitudes from their nations of origin. For example, recent Central and South American immigration has brought Latin American contextual religious dynamics to the United States. They come from a religious background in which the Protestant–Catholic dynamic is much more conflictual than in the United States. When such experiences and perceptions are brought into United States society, they affect the religious situation here by reinforcing or renewing old tensions. For example, in Latin America Pentecostalism is a dynamic religious phenomenon with great success in evangelistic outreach. The Catholic response has not been favorable. How will the Hispanic religious community in the United States respond when Pentecostal and Catholic immigrants bring such dynamics with them? Will they accept, reject, or tolerate such tensions? Will it perpetuate old Catholic–Protestant divisions?

Another question is how to integrate immigrants into Hispanic churches. This is especially acute with regard to undocumented, poor, and limited-English Hispanic immigrants. Many Hispanic churches are located in older Hispanic barrios, but are composed of Hispanics of the second generation and beyond. Many of these Hispanics speak limited Spanish, are somewhat acculturated, may be middle class and professional, and do not live in the Hispanic area. Some of these congregations have become bilingual or English-dominant. As a result, when recent immigrants visit the church, they may not feel comfortable or even understand what is happening. They may feel alienated, confused, and unwelcome. The congregation may also be uncomfortable and at a loss as to how to communicate with persons they do not quite understand.

Each congregation is used to a certain form of worship, including language, and is reluctant to give it up. How will Hispanic churches respond to immigrants? Will Hispanic churches develop special immigrant ministries? Will they integrate immigrants into their life? Are Hispanic churches willing to change to incorporate the needs of immigrants? Or will Hispanic immigrants be left outside the walls of Hispanic congregations? Will Hispanic immigrant churches emerge?

Acculturation and Religion

The third transition refers to the mutual impact of acculturation and Hispanic religious life. *Acculturation* is defined as the process of taking on the culture of another population or society at the expense of one's own culture. A successful acculturation involves losing the old culture in exchange for the new culture. This process normally takes two to three generations, with varying degrees of change within each generation. Acculturation is complete when there is no cultural difference between the acculturated person and others from the culture to which the person acculturated. For Hispanics, the issue of acculturation seems to be a matter of degree.

The issue of acculturation and religion flows from the notion that religion is a central element in culture. For Hispanics, culture and Catholicism have been intimately intertwined, to the extent that they are virtually inseparable. As a result, the relationship between acculturation and religious identity has been hotly debated. The idea that to be Hispanic was also to be Catholic led to the suggestion that as Hispanics acculturate, they become Protestant, or that they become Protestant in order to acculturate. This theory assumed that Hispanics intentionally became Protestants for cultural, social, or even economic reasons. Likewise, such a position suggests that it is not possible to acculturate and continue to be Catholic. Thus, is Hispanic Protestantism connected to acculturation? Does Hispanic Catholicism prevent acculturation?

The social reforms of the 1960s and the subsequent rise of the Hispanic middle class suggests that acculturation may be more a function of education, social mobility, and economic status (as well as environment and peer pressure) than of religion. Acculturation is much more complex than affiliation with a Protestant church. Both Hispanic Catholics and Hispanic Protestants experience acculturation. Middle-class and professional Hispanics are loyal Catholics; many of them are quite acculturated. In contrast, many Hispanic Protestants possess a strong sense of ethnic identity and enjoy their cultural roots. It is also important to recognize that there are many Protestant Hispanics who are poor.

Nevertheless, the question of acculturation and religion within the Hispanic community persists, though it is now a different sort of question. If Hispanics are acculturating within both Catholic and Protestant traditions, what does this say about the role of religion—and especially about cultural Catholicism—in the Hispanic community? Does this mean that the Catholic faith and cultural Catholicism will no longer be the formative forces they once were? Can Protestantism serve the same function? What modern formative forces will shape values, identity, and community? If cultural Catholicism provided a sense of identity and community within the Hispanic population, what will do so in the future? Is religion playing a lesser role? How do immigration and its cultural forces affect this question?

Power and Self-Determination

A fourth trend is the movement toward more organizational activity and greater participation in denominational structures. Hispanic Protestants and Catholics have become active in the organization and promotion of Hispanic issues and interests within their denominations. Some have achieved status and even power. For example, in both Catholic and Protestant traditions, Hispanics have been elected bishop or serve in high church office. Similarly, Hispanic organizations have gained recognition and influence. How will Hispanics use these achievements and the power that comes with their new status? Will this make any difference to denominational policy, priorities, and philosophies? How will organizational achievement and power benefit Hispanic congregations and the Hispanic community?

Will the development of Hispanic offices and programs within denominations empower Hispanics, or continue the separation of Hispanic interests from the primary concerns of denominations? In other words, will Hispanic concerns continue to be marginal and simply delegated to Hispanic offices? Have these offices and programs been effective? Are these good models?

It remains to be seen whether Hispanic organizational achievement and the development of religious leadership will facilitate networking and joint ventures with Hispanic secular organizations and leadership. Will Hispanic religious leadership work exclusively within the religious realm and limit their energy to the religious agenda? Or will they reach out to other centers of Hispanic organizational activity and leadership? Will Hispanic religious leadership tackle social issues such as social justice, poverty, discrimination, and immigration?

Religion, Culture, and Identity

The Hispanic population is rapidly becoming even more complex. Its cultural base has expanded from the traditional Mexican-American, Puerto Rican, and Cuban profile to include a significant presence from every Latin American country. The acculturation of the younger Hispanic generations and the continuing immigration of Hispanic newcomers further expand and complicate the cultural profile. In addition, the socioeconomic profile has also broadened to include professional and middle classes, including a growing entrepreneurial and wealthy class. Furthermore, religious diversity has emerged within this population; it is no longer a monolithic Catholic population. Given these complexities, what does it mean to be Hispanic? Does the term refer simply to Spanish surname? Language use? Place of birth? Parental heritage? Religion?

The answer to these questions is probably no. To be Hispanic will not be limited to immigrants, the Spanish-speaking, or the Spanish-surnamed. It certainly will not be limited to those who are Catholic. Ethnicity is a matter of individual and group identity; it refers to a sense of peoplehood and identification with a people. However, when that "people" becomes increasingly more complex and different from the traditional group, the determination of identity becomes more challenging. To be Hispanic no longer means to be Mexican and Catholic; it also means to be Mexican and Mormon, Honduran and Pentecostal, Puerto Rican and Seventh Day Adventist, Guatemalan and evangelical. A core issue is how Hispanics will define the new Hispanicity. How inclusive will the community be of the emerging cultural and religious diversity within this population? How will the new Hispanicity incorporate the acculturated, the immigrant, the poor, the wealthy, the Catholic, and the Protestant?

Will Hispanics be able to come together, affirm each other, and identify with each other? This would mean that Hispanic Catholics would affirm Hispanic Protestants, and that Hispanic Protestants would affirm and identify with Hispanic Catholics. Can the Hispanic Protestants respect Catholic traditions and practices? Can Catholics respect Pentecostal religious style and practices?

Catholic–Protestant *Mestizaje*

Hispanics stand at a cultural and religious intersection in their history. The many Hispanic cultures and the broad variety of Hispanic religious expressions are at a crossroads in today's urban areas and barrios in this country. There is some curiosity and suspicion. Past experiences, prejudices, and pain linger in many memories. Religious biases are difficult to overcome. But there are also rays of hope and possibilities. They all identify as Hispanic. The majority believe in the same God. Ecumenical activity in academic circles has been positive and mutually helpful. This intersection could very well be a point of cultural and religious convergence—the beginning of a new sense of peoplehood and a new sense of religious expression within the Hispanic context. It could be the point where Hispanics overcome cultural differences in defining the new Hispanicity. It could also be the birth of a new religious *mestizaje*—the coming together of Catholics and Protestants to celebrate their faiths and their Hispanic culture. Will they overcome historical prejudices and institutional forces? Can they work together? How would this affect their denominations and religious institutions? What would a new Hispanic religious *mestizaje* look like? Will it happen?

Religion is central to the human experience and has played a critical role in Hispanic history. Hispanic religious life reflects key aspects and issues in the Hispanic reality, such as immigration, culture, acculturation, organizational assertion, leadership development, and identity. But religion also carries the potential to unify a community that has a long history of religious division. If Hispanic religious leaders and members of the various religious traditions within the Hispanic community reach out to each other, the promise of a new *mestizaje* is possible.

Notes

1. See Virgilio Elizondo, *Galilean Journey* (Maryknoll, N.Y.: Orbis Books, 1983), 7–18; Arturo Bañuelos, *Mestizo Christianity* (Maryknoll, N.Y.: Orbis Books, 1995).
2. Luis N. Pagan, *A Violent Evangelism* (Louisville, Ky.: Westminster/John Knox Press, 1992), 89–234.
3. E. C. Orozco, *Republican Protestantism in Aztlan* (n.p.: Petereins Press, 1980), 1–30.
4. See discussion in ibid.
5. David Carrasco, *Religions of Mesoamerica* (New York: Harper & Row, 1990), 124–27.
6. Elizondo, *Galilean Journey*, 7–18.
7. Timothy M. Matovina, *Tejano Religion and Ethnicity, 1821-1860* (Austin, Tex.: University of Texas Press, 1995), 7–23.
8. See Ana Maria Diaz-Stevens and Anthony Stevens-Arroyo, *The Latino Resurgence in U.S. Religion* (Boulder, Colo.: Westview Press, 1998), 34–38; Barry Kosmin and Seymour P. Lachman, *One Nation Under God: Religion in Contemporary American Society* (New York: Harmony Books, 1993), 137–42.
9. Diaz-Stevens and Stevens-Arroyo, *The Latino Resurgence in U.S. Religion*, 34–38.
10. Ed Sylvest, "The Protestant Presence," in *Fronteras*, ed. Moises Sandoval (San Antonio, Tex.: Mexican American Cultural Center, 1983), 277–338.
11. See David Maldonado, Jr., "Hispanic Protestantism: Historical Reflections," *Apuntes* 11, no. 1 (Spring 1991): 3–16.
12. Matovina, *Tejano Religion and Ethnicity*, 24–81.
13. Douglas Brackenridge and Francisco O. Garcia-Treto, *Iglesia Presbiteriana: A History of Presbyterians and Mexican Americans in the Southwest* (San Antonio, Tex.: Trinity University Press, 1974), 37.
14. Paul Barton, "Inter-ethnic Relations Between Mexican American and Anglo American Methodists in the U.S. Southwest, 1836-1938," in *Protestantes/Protestants*, ed. David Maldonado, Jr. (Nashville, Tenn.: Abingdon Press, 1999), 60–84.
15. Brackenridge and Garcia-Treto, *Iglesia Presbiteriana*, 33–62.
16. Allan Figueroa Deck, "The Challenge of Evangelical/Pentecostal Christianity to Hispanic Catholicism," in *Hispanic Catholic Culture in the U.S.*, ed. Jay P. Dolan and Allan Figueroa Deck (Notre Dame, Ind.: Notre Dame Press, 1994), 409–39.
17. Moises Sandoval, "The Organization of a Hispanic Church," in Dolan and Deck, *Hispanic Catholic Culture in the U.S.*, 131–65.
18. Ibid.
19. Diaz-Stevens and Stevens-Arroyo, *The Latino Resurgence in U.S. Religion*, 199.
20. Ana Maria Diaz-Stevens, "Latinas and the Church," in Dolan and Deck, *Hispanic Catholic Culture in the U.S.*, 240–278.

Bibliography

Bañuelos, Arturo. *Mestizo Christianity*. Maryknoll, N.Y.: Orbis Books, 1995.

Barton, Paul. "Inter-ethnic Relations Between Mexican American and Anglo American Methodists in the U.S. Southwest, 1836-1938." In *Protestantes/Protestants*, edited by David Maldonado, Jr., 60–84. Nashville, Tenn.: Abingdon Press, 1999.

Barton, Paul, and David Maldonado, Jr., eds. *Hispanic Christianity Within Mainline Protestant Traditions: A Bibliography*. Decatur, Ga.: Asociación para la Educación Teológica Hispana, 1998.

Brackenridge, Douglas, and Francisco O. Garcia-Treto. *Iglesia Presbiteriana: A History of Presbyterians and Mexican Americans in the Southwest*. San Antonio, Tex.: Trinity University Press, 1974.

Carrasco, David. *Religions of Mesoamerica*. New York: Harper & Row, 1990.

Deck, Allan Figueroa. "The Challenge of Evangelical/Pentecostal Christianity to Hispanic Catholicism." In *Hispanic Catholic Culture in the U.S.*, edited by Jay P. Dolan and Allan Figueroa Deck, 409–39. Notre Dame, Ind.: Notre Dame Press, 1994.

———. *The Second Wave*. New York: Paulist Press, 1989.

Diaz-Stevens, Ana Maria. "Latinas and the Church." In *Hispanic Catholic Culture in the U.S.*, edited by Jay P. Dolan and Allan Figueroa Deck, 240–78. Notre Dame, Ind.: Notre Dame Press, 1994.

Diaz-Stevens, Ana Maria, and Anthony Stevens-Arroyo. *The Latino Resurgence in U.S. Religion*. Boulder, Colo.: Westview Press, 1998.

Dolan, Jay P., and Allan Figueroa Deck, eds. *Hispanic Catholic Culture in the U.S.* Notre Dame, Ind.: Notre Dame Press, 1994.

Dolan, Jay P., and Jaime Vidal, eds. *Puerto Rican and Cuban Catholics in the U.S. 1900-1965*. Notre Dame, Ind.: Notre Dame University Press, 1994.

Elizondo, Virgilio. *Galilean Journey*. Maryknoll, N.Y.: Orbis Books, 1983.

Gonzalez, Justo. *Mañana*. Nashville, Tenn.: Abingdon Press, 1990.

Isasi-Diaz, Ada Maria, and Fernando Segovia, eds. *Hispanic/Latino Theology*. Minneapolis, Minn.: Fortress Press, 1996.

Kosmin, Barry, and Seymour P. Lachman. *One Nation Under God: Religion in Contemporary American Society*. New York: Harmony Books, 1993.

Maldonado, David Jr. "Hispanic Protestantism: Historical Reflections." *Apuntes* 11, no. 1 (Spring 1991): 3–16.

———. *Protestantes/Protestants*. Nashville, Tenn.: Abingdon Press, 1999.

Matovina, Timothy M. *Tejano Religion and Ethnicity, 1821-1860*. Austin, Tex.: University of Texas Press, 1995.

Orozco, E. C. *Republican Protestantism in Aztlan*. N.p.: Petereins Press, 1980.

Pagan, Luis N. *A Violent Evangelism*. Louisville, Ky.: Westminster/John Knox Press, 1992.

Sandoval, Moises, ed. *Fronteras*. San Antonio, Tex.: Mexican American Cultural Center, 1983.

———. "The Organization of a Hispanic Church." In *Hispanic Catholic Culture in the U.S.*, edited by Jay P. Dolan and Allan Figueroa Deck, 131–65. Notre Dame, Ind.: Notre Dame Press, 1994.

Sylvest, Ed. "The Protestant Presence." In *Fronteras*, edited by Moises Sandoval, 277–338. San Antonio, Tex.: Mexican American Cultural Center, 1983.

Stevens-Arroyo, Anthony. *Discovering Latino Religion: A Comprehensive Social Science Bibliography*. New York: Bildner Center Books, 1995.

Villafane, Eldin. *The Liberating Spirit*. New York: University Press of America, 1992.

5

Hispanics and Education

Melissa Roderick

Introduction

Hispanic-Americans—Mexicans, Puerto Ricans, and Central Americans in particular—are currently the most educationally disadvantaged group in America. Whether one looks at students' skill levels, years of school completed, or performance in school, Hispanic students fare worse than any other racial or ethnic group. The educational attainment and achievement of Hispanics has also not been improving as rapidly as other groups.

For immigrants and nonimmigrants alike, education has always been a means to upward mobility in America. Through education, young adults gain access to better jobs and economic mobility. Through education, groups gain access to the political process. Through education, groups enhance their ability to make important cultural and intellectual contributions to American society.

The ability of the Hispanic community to address the poor educational performance and experiences of its youth will shape the future of this community—and the ability of the education system to address the disadvantaged status of Hispanic youth will shape the future of America. Economists and public policy makers agree that America must raise the skill level and educational attainment of its workers if it is to compete in a changing global economy and meet the challenge of technological change. Changes in the payoffs for skills are at the center of the most pressing social problem in America: the widening of income distribution.[1] The skills that Hispanic students obtain and their educational attainment will in large part shape the skills distribution of the future workforce. Hispanic children may experience their education as one that limits and frustrates their potential, or as one that offers opportunity and a sense of citizenship; this also will shape America far beyond economic measures.

This chapter focuses on trends and challenges in education facing the Hispanic community in the context of three important developments in education: (1) changes in the nature of early childhood education and increases in preschool participation; (2) an emphasis on increased standards and achievement in elementary and secondary schools; and (3) the need for increased educational attainment. The conclusion outlines five policy strategies for improving educational outcomes among Hispanic youth. Hispanic-Americans are a diverse group, and the educational challenges facing Puerto Ricans, Central and South Americans, Cubans, and other Hispanic national-origin groups often differ. Thus, whenever possible, this chapter reports differences in trends across national-origin groups within the Hispanic community.

Setting the Context: New Tasks and New Costs for Immigrants and Education

The 1980s and 1990s have seen the most immigration to the United States since the beginning of this century. Hispanics (in particular, immigrants from Mexico and Central America) make up the largest proportion of these new immigrants.[2] In 1996, more than 47 percent of the foreign-born population who were recent immigrants had immigrated from Mexico, Central America, or South America.[3] Immigration from Mexico alone accounts for more than 25 percent of new immigration since 1980.

Like immigrants at the beginning of this century, these new immigrants look to education as a means of helping their children become assimilated and gain economic mobility. Also like earlier immigrants, these new immigrants face similar barriers: unfamiliarity with the American educational system, language barriers, overcrowding in urban schools, poverty, familial and social disruption, and discrimination by schools and teachers who are unfamiliar with the new group's culture and norms.[4]

This, however, is where the similarity ends. Recent changes in the American educational system and economy have altered what we expect children to do to be successful in school and what level of education is required to enable access to economic progress. This in turn has dramatically changed what schools and families must do to ensure students' success.

At the beginning of this century, school policy toward urban students (in both the public and private sectors) focused on increasing enrollment to provide assimilation, allow socialization, instill good habits, and attain minimal literacy, particularly for the burgeoning immigrant populations in American cities.[5] Neither immigrant nor nonimmigrant students attended school for very long. The majority of students did not graduate from the eighth grade. In 1910, for example, only 14.5 percent of adolescents aged 14 to 17 made it to high school.[6] Even as late as 1940, the median years of school completed by workers aged 25 and older was 8.6 years. Among Blacks, median attainment was less than six years.[7] Despite these low levels of attainment, the expansion of school enrollment that occurred at the beginning of this century was considered an important success because the goal was not to produce a highly skilled or credentialed student but rather to ensure socialization, language skills, and good work habits. Low levels of education for the average student did not preclude success in the workforce.[8] As Patricia A. Graham noted, "the proportion of students who needed to succeed academically was small while the proportion who needed to move smoothly into the workforce was great."[9]

Whereas most immigrant groups in the early 1900s looked to public, and often private Catholic, schools[10] for socialization and acclimation to American society, Hispanic families and school-age immigrants at the turn of this century need very different things from their schools. The American education system in the 1990s is one of rapidly rising expectations for higher and more equitable distributions of academic achievement.[11] Students are expected to enter school earlier and stay in school longer. Schools and families are faced with heightened expectations of what children should be able to do at all levels of education. This is true of all children. In the next three sections, this chapter examines how Hispanic children and families are faring in this changing educational context.

Rising Payoffs for Skills and College

The reasons why we are seeing changes in educational expectations are varied and reflect broader developments in policy, the economy, and American society. The entry of women into the workforce means that more and more children are beginning school at earlier ages. Declines in family size mean that more resources and attention are devoted to individual children within families. In the early 1980s, the declining competitiveness of the U.S. economy led to the claim that American students simply could not compete with their international counterparts, which spurred a focus on standards and achievement. Although all of these (as well as other) factors are important, a central theme driving policy debates in education comes from changes in the payoffs for skills.

If there is one clear trend in the American economy, it is one of rising payoffs for skills and dramatic declines in the economic status of the noncollege-bound. This trend will continue in the decades ahead. From 1980 to 1995, the median earnings of 25- to 34-year-old Hispanic male high school dropouts declined by 36 percent.[12] The median earnings of Hispanic male young adults who graduated from high school but did not attend college also declined by 24 percent during this period. Similar trends are observed among Hispanic women, though declines in earnings have not been as large. Between 1980 and 1995, the median earnings of Hispanic female young adults aged 25 to 35 who had not graduated from high school or attained a high school equivalency degree declined by 23 percent.

During the 1980s and 1990s, the only group that was able to maintain earning power was college graduates. Between 1980 and 1990, the median earnings of young adult Hispanic males with four years of college or more remained stable; earnings for young adult Hispanic female college graduates increased by 12 percent. Obviously, the payoff for completing college has increased significantly for Hispanic young adults. In 1980, the median earnings of Hispanic young adult male college graduates were 40 percent higher than those of Hispanic male high school dropouts. By 1995, the median earnings of Hispanic young adult male college graduates were more than twice as high (payoff = 2.08) as those of Hispanic male high school dropouts, and were 60 percent higher (payoff = 1.62) than those of Hispanic males in this age group who had not gone on to college. Among Hispanic females in 1995, the median earnings of young adult college graduates were more than three times those of Hispanic females who had not attained a high school diploma or equivalent.

The payoff for completing four years of college is particularly high for Hispanics. In 1995, the median earnings of Hispanic males aged 25 to 34 with a bachelor's degree or higher were almost 50 percent higher than those of Hispanic males who had had some college study but had not completed a four-year degree. The comparable figure for all male workers regardless of race was 1.36. Thus, the payoff for postsecondary training that does not result in a bachelor's degree is lower for Hispanics than for other racial and ethnic groups. As we will see later in this chapter, part of this lower return for college study among Hispanics may be because of their choice of two-year programs.

Although the payoffs for education have increased dramatically among Hispanics, it is important to recognize that education does not reduce the ethnic gap in earnings among men. In 1996, the earnings of Hispanic male young adults who had four years of college was 81 percent of those of non-Hispanic White college graduates. This earnings gap was comparable across education levels. Among women, in contrast, there is less earnings disparity by ethnicity.

One of the most striking aspects of these trends is that changes in the payoffs for skills have been color- and ethnic-blind. Every race and ethnic group has been affected. For example, from 1980 to 1990, the median earnings of non-Hispanic White male young adults who did not have a high school diploma or equivalent declined by 23 percent, while those of non-Hispanic White college graduates remained stable. Hispanics have been disproportionately affected because they have the lowest level of educational attainment of any ethnic or racial group. Thus, although education has always been a key to economic mobility for immigrant groups, there is an urgent need to raise educational attainment in the Hispanic community, because changes in the economy have made skills a primary key to economic viability.

Educational Attainment among Hispanics: A Crisis

The rising value of skills has dramatically increased the costs of low educational attainment, for both Hispanics and non-Hispanics. Unlike in other groups, though, progress in improving high school completion rates among Hispanics has been slow. Table 5.1 shows trends in educational attainment of twenty-five- to twenty-nine-year-olds from 1971 to 1996 by race and Hispanic origin.

In 1996, approximately 40 percent of Hispanic 25- to 29-year-olds had not graduated from high school or obtained a high school equivalency degree, compared to only 7.4 percent of non-Hispanic Whites and 14 percent of non-Hispanic Black young adults. This educational

Table 5.1
Educational Level of 25- to 29-Year-Olds, by Race and Ethnicity, 1971 to 1996
(percentages)

		White Non-Hispanic	Black Non-Hispanic	Hispanic
High school	1971	81.7	58.8	48.3
diploma or	1980	89.2	76.7	57.9
equivalent	1990	90.1	81.8	58.2
	1996	92.6	86.0	61.1
	Change	10.9	27.2	12.8
Some college	1971	44.0	30.9	30.6
	1980	53.8	42.3	39.9
	1990	53.6	44.1	40.1
	1996	67.0	55.9	50.9
	Change	22.1	25.0	20.3
Four or more years	1971	23.1	11.5	10.5
of college	1980	28.0	15.0	13.2
	1990	29.3	16.4	14.0
	1996	34.1	17.0	16.4
	Change	11.0	5.5	5.9

Source: United States Department of Education, National Center for Education Statistics, Condition of Education: Supplemental and Standard Error Tables, 1996 (Washington, D.C.: United States Department of Education, 1997) (NCES 97-998).

picture differs across national-origin groups in the Hispanic community. Mexicans are the largest and fastest-growing group within the Hispanic population in the United States, followed by Puerto Ricans, Central and South Americans, and Cubans. Both immigrant and native-born adults of Mexican descent have much lower levels of educational attainment than do adults of Central and South American and Cuban descent.[13] In 1993, for example, approximately half (47 percent) of Mexican-origin young adults aged 25 to 34 had not graduated from high school or obtained a high school equivalency degree, compared to 26 percent of Puerto Ricans residing on the U.S. mainland, 16 percent of young adults of Cuban descent, and 32 percent of young adults of

Central and South American origin.[14] Cuban and Central- and South-American-origin Hispanics also have higher rates of college completion. In 1993, more than one-quarter of Cuban-American young adults had graduated from college, compared to 13.5 percent of young adults of Central and South American origin, 10.4 percent of Puerto Rican young adults residing on the U.S. mainland, and less than 6 percent of young adults of Mexican origin.[15]

As seen in table 5.1, throughout the past two decades, Blacks substantially increased their rate of high school graduation, closing the racial gap in high school attainment. Hispanics have not made similar gains. From 1971 to 1996, the proportion of Blacks aged 25 to 29 who graduated from high school or obtained an equivalency degree increased from 59 to 86 percent. In comparison, the proportion of Hispanics in this age group who graduated from high school increased from 48 to only 61 percent.

Trends in educational aspiration among high school seniors suggest, however, that Hispanic young adults are increasingly aware of the benefits of postsecondary education. Two national surveys conducted by the U.S. Department of Education show that while educational aspirations have increased among all high school seniors, they have increased the most among Hispanics.[16] In 1982, only 60 percent of Hispanic seniors in the "High School and Beyond" survey stated that they hoped to attend college at some point, compared to 71 percent of Whites. Ten years later, in the National Educational Longitudinal Survey, the proportion of Hispanic seniors who stated that they hoped to attend college was equal to that of Whites, approximately 91 percent. The proportion of Hispanic seniors who stated that they would like to go to college immediately after graduation also increased, from 45.6 percent in 1982 to 75 percent in 1992.

Despite these increased aspirations, neither Hispanics nor Blacks are making progress at closing the gap in four-year college completion. Although the proportion of Hispanic young adults with at least some college increased from 30.6 percent in 1971 to 51 percent in 1996, the proportion of Hispanics who completed a four-year college degree increased from 10.5 to only 16.4 percent. A combination of factors explains why Hispanics are not closing the gap in college completion, despite increases in college enrollment. Hispanic high school seniors are less likely to enroll in college, are more likely to delay enrollment, and are more likely to work while in school. All these factors are associated with lower rates of four-year college completion.[17] One of the

most important factors shaping lower rates of four-year college completion among Hispanics, however, is that Hispanic students are much more
likely to attend two-year colleges and proprietary schools than non-
Hispanic Whites. This is particularly true for Mexican-Americans. Two-
thirds (65 percent) of Mexican-origin undergraduates in 1989–1990 were
enrolled in two-year colleges, compared to 24 percent of Puerto Ricans
and 49 percent of students of Cuban descent.[18] According to a U.S.
Department of Education survey of undergraduates, Hispanic college
students are also more likely to enroll in private, for-profit institutions
that "typically offer programs of short duration leading to a vocational
certificate in fields such as cosmetology, administrative and secretarial
programs, health related programs, or trade and industry programs."[19]
Fifteen percent of Hispanic undergraduates in 1989–1990 were enrolled
in private, for-profit, two-year institutions, compared to 6.4 percent of
non-Hispanic White undergraduates. Students who enter two-year colleges, even if their stated objective is obtaining a four-year degree, are
much less likely to attain that goal.[20] The result of lower high school
completion rates, lower transition rates between high school and college, and differential college choice is that Hispanics are less than half
as likely as non-Hispanic Whites to complete four years of college.

  Although many factors influence college choice and enrollment, one
of the most important is rising college costs combined with stagnant
and—in the case of Hispanics—falling real family incomes.[21] Between
1980 and 1994, the costs of tuition at public two-year colleges rose by
70 percent in real terms.[22] The costs of attending a public four-year
college increased by 86 percent. At the same time, the real value of the
maximum Pell grant fell by more than 25 percent.[23] The economic cost
of college is a significant factor in the choice of two- over four-year
institutions.[24] Thus, rising college costs have constrained the ability of
students to respond to increases in the payoffs for skills.[25] For example,
the U.S. Department of Education estimated that although college attendance rates for Hispanic seniors from high-socioeconomic-status
(high-SES) families have increased dramatically, college attendance
rates of Hispanic students from families in the low to middle socioeconomic quartiles have been relatively stagnant.[26] From 1972 to 1989, the
percentage of high-SES Hispanic seniors attending a postsecondary
institution within two years following high school graduation increased
from 68 to 93 percent, an attendance rate comparable to that of
high-SES non-Hispanic Whites. In comparison, in 1972, the U.S.
Department of Education estimated that 53 percent of low-SES

Hispanic seniors attended college within two years of graduation; in 1989, that figure was 56 percent. Hispanic students, however, are not the only group for which college cost has constrained access. College attendance rates among low-SES non-Hispanic Whites and non-Hispanic Blacks have also been stagnant.

Another factor shaping the poorer educational attainment of Hispanic young adults is immigration. Because of high rates of immigration, many Hispanic young adults are immigrants who never attended U.S. schools; this proportion has clearly risen throughout the past two decades. About one in five Hispanic young adults never attended U.S. schools.[27] These late-age immigrants have lower educational attainment than Hispanics who attended U.S. schools. Even excluding these later-age immigrants, however, the dropout rate among Hispanics is still more than twice as high as among non-Hispanic Whites and 60 percent higher than among Blacks.[28]

In summation, trends in educational attainment suggest that Hispanics as a group show less capacity to respond to the declining economic status of the noncollege-bound. The question this data raises is: How can we explain the poorer educational performance of Hispanics vis-à-vis their counterparts and the lack of progress of Hispanics, despite rising educational aspirations? Part of this explanation lies in differences in the resources available to Hispanic students in their families and schools, differences that begin even before elementary school.

Kindergarten and Early Preschool: Changing Expectations and Enrollment

One of the most important developments in education over the past twenty years is the expansion of years of formal schooling to include kindergarten. In 1950, only about a third of first-graders had attended kindergarten the year before.[29] Kindergarten enrollment increased throughout the postwar years. From 1950 to 1960, the estimated proportion of first-graders who attended kindergarten increased from 32 to 52 percent, and by 1970 it had reached 72 percent. Since 1970, kindergarten has become an almost universal experience for children. In 1980, more than 92 percent of first-graders had participated in kindergarten. In 1990, the attendance rate reached 99.6 percent.

The growth of kindergarten attendance both reflects and has contributed to three significant developments in early childhood education:

1. an increase in preschool enrollment;
2. a change in the focus of early childhood education from social development to academic skills; and
3. rising expectations as to what constitutes readiness for school.[30]

As kindergarten enrollment increased, so too did the proportion of children in child care and pre-primary programs. For example, in 1965 only 4.9 percent of 3-year-olds and 16 percent of 4-year-olds were enrolled in some kind of formal education setting that could be called a pre-primary program. These proportions increased to more than one-third (36 percent) in 1985; by 1995, 62 percent of 4-year-olds were enrolled in a pre-primary or early school program.

The most famous of these pre-primary programs is Head Start, the federal program to prepare disadvantaged children for school. But, as seen in table 5.2, growth in preschool enrollment has been concentrated among children from more highly educated and more financially well-off families. Table 5.2 shows trends in the preschool participation rates of three-, four-, and five-year-olds based on analysis of the National Household Education Survey. In 1995, 61 percent of 3-year-olds and 81 percent of 4-year-olds from upper-income families (families with incomes of $50,000 or more) were enrolled in some form of center-based or pre-primary program. In comparison, only 24 percent of 3-year-olds and 52 percent of 4-year-olds from poor families participated in formal preschool education.

Hispanic children, particularly children from families in which the mother's first language is Spanish, are the least likely to participate in early childhood programs.[31] Hispanic three-year-olds were only about half as likely to be enrolled in an early childhood program as non-Hispanic White or Black three-year-olds. However, reflecting the expansion of public school kindergarten, Hispanic children were no less likely to be enrolled in kindergarten.

The gap in preschool participation of Hispanics, non-Hispanic Whites, and Blacks is also widening. In just the short period between 1991 and 1995, the proportion of non-Hispanic White three-year-olds enrolled in pre-primary or other programs increased by 20 percentage points, whereas preschool participation rates changed little among Hispanics. Indeed, the number of Hispanics in preschool has increased only slightly since the early 1970s.[32]

Preschool is important because it promotes early school success among children, improves health and behavioral outcomes, reduces the likelihood of grade retention, and promotes literacy environments in

Table 5.2
Three-, Four-, and Five-Year-Olds Enrolled in Nursery, Prekindergarten,
Kindergarten, and Head Start Programs, 1991 and 1995
(percentages)

	Three-year-olds		Four-year-olds		Five-year-olds	
	1991	1995	1991	1995	1991	1995
Total	31.4	37.4	52.7	60.9	86.4	90.3
Race						
White	33.4	40.2	52.4	60.8	85.7	88.6
Black	31.6	41.1	57.4	68.2	92.3	93.7
Hispanic	19.8	21.2	47.5	49.0	85.3	93.4
Household income						
10,000 or less	25.4	26.2	43.3	54.3	86.1	90.9
10,000–20,000	23.2	27.0	45.0	52.3	84.6	89.7
20,001–35,000	21.3	27.7	48.0	49.7	85.1	90.7
35,001–50,000	33.4	38.1	52.3	59.5	87.3	88.5
50,001 or more	52.9	61.2	74.8	80.7	89.0	90.9
Parental education						
Less than high school	17.3	16.0	33.1	42.4	85.5	92.5
High school or GED	23.0	26.3	40.8	51.1	84.8	89.2
Some college	31.0	35.6	56.3	63.3	87.7	90.2
Four years college	41.5	51.7	67.2	70.7	88.1	91.6
Graduate school	53.0	60.8	72.0	77.9	87.0	89.8
Mother's language						
English	32.3	39.5	53.0	62.2	86.5	89.9
Spanish	12.3	18.9	45.0	47.3	88.6	93.0
Other	37.1	43.2	50.0	61.5	84.1	88.8

Source: United States Department of Education, National Center for Education Statistics, "Condition of Education 1996," from United States Department of Education, *National Household Education Survey (NHES) 1991 and 1995 Early Childhood Participation File.*

the home.[33] The lower preschool participation rate of Hispanic children means that many Hispanic children will enter kindergarten without the behavioral experience of being in formal school and without a chance to develop the skills that lay the basis for early school success. Nonparticipation in preschool is particularly problematic for Hispanic children because they are also less likely to come from home environments where mothers actively teach children reading and numeracy skills in preparation for school.[34] The result is that Hispanic children are much less likely than non-Hispanic White and Black children to enter kindergarten displaying skills that denote readiness for school. For example, 61 percent of Hispanic mothers of preschoolers in the National Household Education Survey reported that their children could identify the primary colors, versus 73 percent of Black and 91 percent of non-Hispanic White mothers. Hispanic mothers were only half as likely as non-Hispanic Whites to report that their preschoolers could recognize letters (31 versus 61 percent) and count to 20 (39 versus 66 percent).[35]

These and other indicators of early numeracy and literacy, along with studies of IQ development, suggest that Hispanic children are in a "catch-up" position even before they enter kindergarten.[36] The widening gap between Hispanic and non-Hispanic White children, in both preschool participation and entering skills, also suggests that Hispanic children are at higher risk of being retained in grade, one of the greatest risk factors for leaving school early.[37]

Ongoing School Attainment: Rising Standards and Skills

Growth in educational expectations for students at early ages reflects a national trend toward increased expectations of student performance at all levels of education. Beginning in the 1980s, America entered a two-decade courtship with higher standards, in the quest to improve test scores. Much of the initial emphasis of local and state efforts was on areas such as increasing requirements for high school graduation.[38] More recent reform efforts, often called "systemic reform initiatives," have moved to a focus on curriculum and instruction, by setting standards for what students should know, assessing performance through standardized tests, and holding students and schools accountable for performance outcomes.[39] As these reforms evolved, they reflected a growing consensus about three common themes:

1. improved standardized test scores are the primary measure of success;
2. schools are responsible for student performance and must do more for the students they serve; and
3. all students need to reach higher standards and begin to develop the problem-solving, thinking, and analytic skills previously reserved for only the top students if they are to succeed in the changing American labor market.

As Fuhrman, Elmore, and Massell noted:

> The reforms of the 1980's focused educational policy on a very important goal: academic learning for all students, regardless of race, social class or cultural background. It is now increasingly common to hear elected officials, members of the business community, and educators alike voice the expectation that all students will need a higher level of understanding of academic subjects, a capacity for problem solving, and an ability to apply knowledge to concrete situations to function effectively in an increasingly demanding economy and society.[40]

Sample Reforms

Recent reforms in Chicago, Illinois, one of the largest gateway cities for immigrants, best illustrate these national trends. In a step heralded by President Clinton in his 1998 State of the Union address, Chicago enacted a range of measures to improve student performance and focus attention on poorly performing schools.[41] The centerpiece of these reforms is the threat of retention for students and reconstitution for schools as a means of spurring improvement in basic skills and test scores. Beginning in the 1995–1996 school year, the Chicago public schools linked promotion in grade to performance on standardized tests and implemented more rigorous academic requirements for high school students. Students in the third, sixth, eighth, and ninth grades now must attain a minimum score on achievement tests in reading and mathematics to progress to the next grade level. Students who do not meet the standards are required to participate in summer school and are given a chance to retake the test at the end of the summer. In 1997, one in ten Chicago students in the third, sixth, eighth, and tenth grades attended summer school. At the end of the summer 32,000 student retook the test; 57 percent of sixth-graders, 44 percent of third-graders, and 65 percent of eighth-graders passed.[42]

These tough promotional policies are accompanied by equally tough policies for schools. Schools that are not improving or that have consistently low performance are placed on probation with the threat of reconstitution (a measure in which the staff is fired and the school is reorganized) if the school does not improve. In 1997, Chicago reconstituted seven schools, all of them high schools, and placed more than forty schools on academic probation.

Trends in Achievement of Hispanic Youth Nationally

Since the early 1970s, the U.S. Department of Education, through the National Assessment of Educational Progress (NAEP), has conducted regular assessments of the proficiency of children, via a national sample of nine-, thirteen-, and seventeen-year-old students who are tested in mathematics, reading, science, writing, history, and geography. This national assessment allows us to assess trends in skill levels across racial and ethnic groups and to examine the extent to which Hispanic youths are making progress in meeting higher standards.

Over the past twenty years, the predominant trend in education across all racial and ethnic groups has been one of rising mathematics achievement and of relatively flat scores in reading.[43] An equally important trend in the NAEP is a decreasing gap in achievement between Whites and Blacks and between Whites and Hispanics.[44] Progress has been particularly marked for Blacks. Between 1973 and 1994, the average gap in mathematics between the scale score of Whites and Blacks decreased by 28 percent among 9-year-olds and by more than one-third among 13-year-olds. During this period, the gap in mathematics scores between White and Hispanic students increased slightly among 9-year-olds and declined by 28 percent among 13-year-olds.

Progress has been most marked, in both mathematics and reading, among minority seventeen-year-olds. Between 1975 and 1994, the average scale score of Black 17-year-olds increased from 241 to 255 in reading and from 270 to 286 in mathematics, thus decreasing the racial gap in reading and mathematics by 22 and 14 points respectively. Among Hispanics, the average scale score increased from 252 to 263 in reading and from 277 to 291 in mathematics, decreasing the gap in scores between Hispanic and White 17-year-olds by 8 points in reading and 12 points in mathematics.

Table 5.3 takes a closer look at trends in math proficiency by the proportion of students whose measured achievement meets various levels of proficiency for their grade. This table illustrates two major points. First, at each grade level, progress in increasing Hispanic test scores has been achieved largely by improving the proportion of students who reach the most basic level of skills for their grade. This trend in raising the bottom rather than the top partly reflects the predominant policy focus, in urban schools, on basic skills—a focus that began in the 1970s and has continued over the past two decades.[45] More recent reform

Table 5.3
Students Meeting Basic, Proficient, or Advanced Levels for Their Grade in Mathematics, 1990 and 1996
(percentages)

	White 1990	White 1996	Black 1990	Black 1996	Hispanic 1990	Hispanic 1996	Asian/Pacific Islander 1990	Asian/Pacific Islander 1996
Grade 4								
Basic or above	59	76	19	32	31	41	65	73
Proficient or above	16	28	1	5	5	8	23	26
Advanced	2	3	0	0	0	0	3	5
Grade 8								
Basic or above	61	74	22	28	32	39	not	not
Proficient or above	19	31	5	4	5	9	reported	reported
Advanced	3	5	0	0	0	1		
Grade 12								
Basic or above	66	79	27	38	36	50	75	81
Proficient or above	14	20	2	4	4	6	23	33
Advanced	2	2	0	0	0	0	5	7

Note: At grade 4, students at basic level should be able to estimate and use basic facts to perform simple computations with whole numbers; show some understanding of fractions and decimals; and solve simple real-world problems. Fourth-graders performing at the proficient level should be able to use whole numbers to estimate, compute, and determine whether results are reasonable, and should have a conceptual understanding of fractions and decimals.

Source: United States Department of Education, Office of Educational Research and Improvement, National Center for Education Statistics, *NAEP 1996 Mathematics Report Card* (Washington, D.C.: National Center for Education Statistics, 1997).

standards, such as those being pursued in Chicago, similarly focus on the bottom. At the same time, a consistent criticism of the American education system is that although public schools do a good job of providing basic skills for students, they fail to move students on to more complex problem-solving, analytical, and communication skills. Trends in Hispanic achievement test scores support this criticism. As seen in table 5.3, few Hispanic students demonstrate mathematics proficiency that is considered adequate to above average for their grade. Little progress has been made in increasing the proportion of Hispanic students with high achievement. For example, in the 1996 NAEP assessment, White eighth-graders were three times more likely than Hispanic students to have mathematics test scores demonstrating proficiency for their grade—a level of proficiency that suggests they are ready to move on to high-school-level math. Similarly, in the 1994 reading assessment, Hispanic 13-year-olds were half as likely (38 percent versus 68 percent) as Whites to reach level 250 in reading (an achievement level indicating that students are ready to move beyond "learning to read" to "reading to learn").[46] Thus, Hispanic students are substantially less likely to enter high school with a foundation that enables them to move on to high-school-level work; again they will be playing catch-up in gaining the skills and high school grades that permit entrance to postsecondary institutions.

A second important trend illustrated in table 5.3 is that Hispanic students do better as they progress through school than at earlier ages. This is true in both reading and mathematics. The greater relative improvements in achievement among high-school-aged youth may be because Hispanic students are pursuing much more academically oriented high school programs. Between 1982 and 1994, the proportion of Hispanic high school graduates who had taken algebra at some point during high school increased from 42.4 to 70.7 percent, a rate comparable to algebra course taking among Whites.[47] During this time period, the proportion of Hispanic seniors who had taken geometry in high school doubled. By 1994, Hispanic seniors were only slightly less likely than Whites to have taken geometry (69.4 percent versus 72.7 percent). These rates of course taking do not indicate whether teachers are presenting similar material to students, even within courses with the same title. Nevertheless, these data do suggest that Hispanic high school students are currently pursuing more rigorous programs of study in high school than they were in the early 1980s.

What Shapes Trends in Hispanic School Achievement
and Attainment?

Researchers studying Hispanic educational performance tend to focus on three areas when attempting to explain the trends described in the preceding sections, and particularly the poorer performance of Hispanic students vis-à-vis their counterparts:

1. differences in the educational resources available to children and adolescents in Hispanic families,
2. differences in the quality of schools, and
3. cultural differences in views of childrearing and education.

Differences in Family Resources for Education

The degree to which children receive home support for their education, at all points in their school careers, is associated with better school performance. Simply, children do better in school and stay in school longer when their parents and families (1) provide educational resources in the home; (2) interact with children about education and provide day-to-day monitoring and support of schoolwork; (3) set high expectations and educational aspirations; and (4) use parenting strategies that promote problem-solving and thinking skills.[48]

Unfortunately, Hispanic children are less likely to come from homes that provide these resources and supports for education. For example, research finds that Hispanic parents are much less likely to provide preschoolers with activities linked to the development of early numeracy and reading skills, such as having literacy materials in the home, having adults read to children, or having parents actively teach skills to their children.[49] Similar differences in Hispanic parents' home involvement, involvement in their children's schools, and in educational aspirations are observed throughout students' school careers.[50]

The central question is this: To what extent do the demographic and socioeconomic characteristics that distinguish Hispanic families from other racial and ethnic groups make it more difficult for families to create home environments that provide these supports? Hispanic adults have, on average, the lowest level of education of any racial or ethnic group in America, and the educational attainment of Hispanics has not improved as rapidly as that of other racial and ethnic groups. This is particularly true for Mexican-Americans and recent immigrants.

Hispanic families are also poorer. In 1996, the median income of Hispanic households was $24,906, compared to $38,787 for non-Hispanic Whites.[51] The median income of Hispanic households in 1996 was slightly higher than for Blacks, but Hispanic children in America are the most likely to live in poverty because Hispanic families are larger.[52] In 1996, more than half of Hispanic children lived below 1.5 times the poverty level. Puerto Rican children are particularly disadvantaged. Puerto Rican children, who are also much more likely to live in single-parent homes, have the highest poverty rates. In 1993, the latest report in which the Census Bureau reported poverty statistics by national origin within the Hispanic population, 52 percent of Puerto Rican children and 40 percent of children of Mexican origin lived below the poverty line, compared to 25 percent of children of Central and South American origin, 18 percent of children in Cuban-origin households, and 19 percent of Whites.[53]

There are three important mechanisms by which low family income, low parental education, and language barriers shape the capacity of Hispanic families to support their children's education: (1) by limiting the resources the family can provide to children; (2) by limiting the family's ability to use those resources to support their children's schooling; and (3) by constraining knowledge of what educational activities and supports promote school success.

Resource Constraints Caused by Low Family Income

Families that are poor simply have less money to buy educational materials. They also have fewer resources to purchase formal education for their children, such as preschool, or to buy better schools through residential choice or private schooling. The impact of low family income is particularly important in shaping the ability of families to respond to the trends outlined in this chapter. Early childhood education in the home, formal preschooling before public school, and college and postsecondary education all require more private resources. Low family income also limits families' ability to provide educational resources in the home if parents with low income work more or experience more stress. Poor parents, particularly in working-poor families, may be less able to spend time with their children, and are less likely to have work schedules that permit visits to school or regular contact with teachers.[54] This is particularly true in larger families where resources are spread across children.

Resource Constraints Caused by Low Human Capital Within Families

Parental education, language ability, and familiarity with the U.S. education system are also critical educational resources for children, often called *social capital*. They largely control the extent to which families can provide educational experiences and supports. Parents with low education have a harder time helping their children with schoolwork, interacting with their children in literacy and numeracy activities, and creating home environments in which children see adults reading and engaging in educational activities. Language barriers and a lack of literacy skills in English further exacerbate barriers that parents face when engaging in educational activities. Research finds that despite efforts to support their children's education, many Hispanic families are consistently frustrated by inability and feelings of inadequacy when helping their children with schoolwork.[55] A study of Black, Hispanic, and White families of elementary-school-aged children in Chicago found that Hispanic mothers felt significantly less able to support their children's education.[56] Only 77 percent of Hispanic mothers in the Chicago study, versus all of the Black and White mothers of elementary school children, believed that they could help their children in reading. Stevenson, Chen, and Uttal concluded: "Hispanic mothers were eager to be helpful to their children but believed that they were less capable of helping their children and that their help was less likely to contribute to their child's achievement." All of these familial supports for education are just as critical during middle childhood and adolescence as in the earlier years.[57] Any barriers parents face in supporting their children's education are exacerbated during adolescence; in particular, as children move into high school. As students enter high school, they experience an increase in academic demands and begin to take classes in algebra, science, and advanced subjects that only parents who had attended college might have taken. Indeed, as standards and requirements for high school graduation increase, the extent to which parents provide day-to-day monitoring becomes even more important, even as their capacity to do so becomes less. A recent longitudinal study of adolescents in three high schools in the Chicago public schools asked Mexican-American and Black parents of ninth-graders whether they felt capable of helping their children with schoolwork.[58] In this largely working-poor sample (n = 73), the average years of education for Mexican-American parents was only 5 years, compared to 13 years for Blacks. Fully 92 percent of Mexican-American parents of ninth-graders, versus 8 percent of Black parents, stated that they felt unable to help their adolescents with schoolwork on a day-to-day basis.

Lack of Knowledge and Barriers to Support

Lack of knowledge and access to knowledge of what is expected of children in school and what home activities most benefit school performance is also an important factor limiting the educational environments of Hispanic homes, despite strong support for education. Helping with and monitoring homework, getting extra help, and supporting and guiding a child's education require that parents understand what children should be doing and accomplishing each day to be successful. This is easier for parents who have experience with the U.S. education system, have access to social networks that provide links to education, and can communicate with teachers in finding out what children should be doing. Research finds that many Hispanic parents try to support their children's schooling, but how they do so (e.g., what specific activities occur in the home) is determined by the parent's knowledge of academic requirements and the kinds of information and resources provided by schools.[59] Lack of information on what is expected of children is particularly problematic for parents who are recent immigrants, because knowledge of how children learn may not translate across cultures. Guadalupe Valdes, in his ethnographic study of ten Mexican families, offered an example of how cultural differences create confusion for many immigrant parents about what is expected by schools:

> [W]hen Mrs. Lockley [a teacher] complained that Velma Soto had not taught Saul his ABCs she did not consider that the teaching and the learning of the alphabet might not be equally valued in all school contexts. She could not possibly imagine that there might be very valid reasons why parents might not have prepared their children for school by teaching them the alphabet and it was difficult for her to consider that parents might not understand, even when told, why learning the ABCs was important. Indeed, the learning of the alphabet by children is an example of how parents' experience did not help them make sense of their new world. In Mexico, the ability to recite the alphabet per se is not considered particularly important. Instead recognition of syllables containing a consonant and a vowel is considered fundamental to reading. ... What is important (in Spanish) is the sound of the letter combinations and not their names.[60]

Again, communication with schools and understanding what students need to do to be successful become increasingly difficult as students enter high school. Urban high schools are large, complex environments that pose special barriers to parents who are not empowered or who cannot communicate with the school to obtain information regarding their children's performance, identify their educational needs, and become involved in resolving problems. Parents who themselves have not attended high school have a more difficult time understanding what children do in school and what they need to be do to succeed. This is particularly true for children who aspire to college. In addition, adolescence adds another task for parents, who often struggle with issues of how best to raise their children in America, where peer group pressures and identity development are increasingly important. These difficulties are reflected in what Hispanic parents would like from schools. When asked what kinds of programs they would be interested in, Hispanic parents of ninth-graders were significantly more likely than Black parents to say they would be very interested in programs about how to raise teenagers (76 percent versus 46 percent); programs that introduced parents to the education system (76 percent versus 43 percent); and programs that helped parents understand the work their children do in school (80 percent versus 64 percent).[61] Hispanic mothers were as likely as Black mothers to state that they were very interested in programs that taught parents what students need for success and that showed parents how to help with homework.

The Impact of Low Family Income and Home Educational Resources on Educational Outcomes

The previous section looked at what qualitative or survey studies tell us about how differences in the educational and income characteristics of Hispanic families shape parents' capacity to provide educational supports for children. How important are these characteristics in explaining the poorer relative educational performance of Hispanic children? Quantitative studies generally find that the combination of low parental education, low family income, and family language status explains much of the poorer school performance and lower educational attainment of Hispanics vis-à-vis Blacks and non-Hispanic Whites.[62] Parental educational attainment and income also explain differences in educational performance within the Hispanic community. Among Hispanics, adolescents whose parents graduated from high school, those who come from smaller families, and those who have higher family income have significantly higher achievement than their counterparts.[63] Although differences in family structure explain a higher proportion of poor educational outcomes among Blacks, differences in parental education are central in explaining variation in outcomes within the Hispanic community and among Hispanics, Blacks, and non-Hispanic Whites.[64]

Most importantly, the slower relative improvement of educational attainment and achievement of Hispanics vis-à-vis Blacks and non-Hispanic Whites can be attributed in part to a similar lack of progress in the income and educational characteristics that are linked to better school performance. The average level of parents' education in both Black and non-Hispanic White families increased over the past two decades, whereas family size in these racial groups has declined and family income remained stable. Despite an increase in female-headed households and slight declines in the average age of mothers, the net resources available to children in Black and non-Hispanic White households have increased since the early 1970s. In an analysis of the National Assessment of Educational Progress and test scores in other national surveys, Grissmer, Kirby, Berends, and Williamson found that these trends in non-Hispanic White and Black family characteristics help explain increases in test scores throughout the 1970s and 1980s.[65] Changes in family demographics in the Hispanic community have not been as positive. Between 1975 and 1990, Hispanic maternal education improved only slightly. Resources within Hispanic families for individual children also declined, because of declines in family income and only slight reductions in family size. As Grissmer and his colleagues noted, "Although both black and non-Hispanic white families registered large gains in parental education, reduced family size, and stable real family income, Hispanic families showed much smaller gains in parents' educational attainment, smaller reductions in family size, and declines in family incomes."[66] The gains made by Hispanic students in the NAEP, then, are particularly important, because actual gains for both Black and Hispanic students far exceeded the gains that would have been predicted from family characteristics alone.

In summary, research on family characteristics as an explanation for the poorer performance of Hispanic students suggests that without improvements in Hispanic family income and investments in education, Hispanic families will continue to face barriers to responding to the changes in educational expectations outlined in this chapter. In this respect, the picture is daunting. There is little evidence that parental education is increasing among Hispanics; more importantly, poverty rates among Hispanic children have been increasing. The percent of Hispanic children under the age of 18 living in poverty increased from 33.2 percent in 1980 to 40 percent in 1996.[67] The new welfare reform legislature is particularly troubling in light of these trends, because recent welfare changes substantially reduce the availability of food stamps, disability assistance, and Medicare to low-income Hispanic children from immigrant families. Puerto Rican families will be the hardest hit by time limits and welfare benefit reduction for children receiving Aid to Families with Dependent Children, because this community is distinguished by previously high rates of welfare participation.[68]

Schooling Resources as an Explanation of Differences in Student Performance

Historically, schools have played a vital role in providing social capital for children and in helping families overcome resource and information gaps. Families can do much to try to support their children's education. However, if children are not attending schools that give them opportunities to learn and educational environments that push them to develop high aspirations and a positive sense of school attachment, then parents are trying to support an inadequate education system that provides little for their children and will ultimately undermine their efforts.

Research on parenting helps us understand what aspects of home environment tend to promote learning and school achievement. Likewise, research on effective schools has sought to understand what school environments tend to be beneficial to students. This research finds that effective schools often combine four essential supports that produce higher achievement among students from diverse backgrounds.[69] First, these schools set high expectations, develop a core mission of the school centered around learning, and provide instruction that continually exposes students to new content and skills so that students develop higher levels of competence. Second, these schools create a web of support that includes individual attention; opportunities for students to develop relationships with adults; and a safe, responsive, and orderly learning environment that communicates consistent expectations for student behavior. Third, these schools work to develop a positive sense of school membership and identity among students, through a focus on developing self-esteem, instilling a sense of future orientation, and placing high value on students' language and culture. Fourth, effective schools work to engage parents in developing common goals and strategies for reaching those goals.

Hispanic Students' Schools: Urban and Increasingly Segregated

Research on effective schools has documented that even within high-poverty, immigrant neighborhoods, schools can develop effective educational environments if they have quality teachers, strong leadership, high academic standards, and personal supports for their students. Unfortunately, Hispanic children, particularly immigrant children, are much less likely to attend schools that provide these experiences and supports.

Although the education of Hispanic students is a national issue, Hispanics and the growth of the Hispanic population are concentrated in several states and in the largest urban school districts within them. Fifteen states account for 90 percent of the Hispanic population. The largest group of Hispanics lives in California, followed by Texas, New York, Florida, and Illinois. As segregation has decreased for Blacks, high rates of immigration, poverty, and fertility in the Hispanic community lead to increasing segregation of Hispanic children in predominantly minority schools—usually the largest and most troubled school systems within these states.[70] Between 1968 and 1995, the proportion of Hispanic students who attended schools in which most students were minority increased from 54.8 to 74.0 percent.[71] The proportion of Hispanic students who attended all-minority schools, in which 90–100 percent of the students in the school were Hispanic, increased from 23.1 to 34.8 percent.[72] Of the states in which Hispanics predominantly reside, segregation is highest in New York, where the Hispanic population is predominantly Puerto Rican; and in the West, where the Hispanic population is predominantly of Mexican and Central American origin.

There is nothing wrong, in and of itself, with segregated schools, if those schools and communities provide safe and resource-rich environments for children. But this is seldom the case. Segregation and concentration in poor neighborhoods are a concern because too often segregation by race indicates segregation by poverty and student achievement.[73] There are several reasons why the concentration of Hispanic children in poor neighborhoods and schools constrains educational resources. First, segregation by ethnicity and socioeconomic status limits the net amount of educational resources available to help overcome resource and knowledge constraints within families. Segregation by class is particularly deleterious for Hispanics because overall low educational attainment in the Hispanic community limits community information and networking resources available to families.[74]

Second, children are also resources for each other. Poor neighborhoods and schools are often plagued by high rates of social disruption and negative peer influences, which further undermine families' efforts to support education and create significant pressure on youths. When low-achieving children are exposed to higher-performing peers, they work harder in their classrooms, are less likely to misbehave, and are more likely to have higher educational aspirations.[75] Studies have also found that the socioeconomic characteristics of a school's student body have independent effects on students' dropout rates, behavior in school, attitudes toward school, and absenteeism, over and above the effect of individual characteristics.[76] What this means is that when poor students attend more advantaged schools, they are more likely to have higher educational aspirations, to not drop out, to attend school regularly, and to be more positive regarding their school and teachers—in short, they conform to positive expectations. In contrast, the concentration of Hispanics in poorly performing schools means that to do well is to be nonconformist, a role that is difficult for all but the most resilient students.

Finally, and most importantly, segregation of Hispanic students in high-poverty and urban schools is important because low-income urban schools are less likely to provide the social supports and academic environments that have been linked to higher performance and greater student engagement.[77] For example, a study of instruction in Chicago compared the skills on which students were being tested (by standardized tests) to what teachers reported they taught. Even within the same school district, opportunity to learn was significantly greater in mixed- and middle-income schools. In these schools, as students progressed through grades, teachers introduced new content and moved students on to new material. Teachers in poor schools, on average, cycled through the same material year after year, so that many students were not exposed to the content and skill levels expected for standardized tests.[78] Low educational challenge and low teacher efficacy are often combined, in urban schools, with chaotic school environments that do not provide personal supports and monitoring. Urban schools are often larger, and have larger class sizes and higher pupil-teacher ratios.[79] This is particularly true for heavily Hispanic schools. Studies have consistently found that larger schools are associated with more negative student outcomes, less personal support and monitoring for students, lower academic orientation among teachers and students, and less professional community among teachers—all critical to the development of effective schools.

Student Disengagement During the Early Years of High School: A Critical Period

Adolescence introduces new stresses and challenges for Hispanic families. Adolescence is a particularly critical period in the formation of school attachment and identity, and is a time when the quality of school and community environments play an important role. Researchers studying ghettos and barrios, for example, most often focus on the negative effects that living in such neighborhoods have on adolescents; at this age, peer influences, lack of safety, lack of access to role models, negative social norms, and lack of opportunities to work and be involved in productive extracurricular activities have the greatest negative influence.[80] For many students, schools and teachers play an important role in counteracting negative influences by offering students challenge, a sense of the future, a positive sense of school membership, and relationships with adults who can foster resilience.[81] In addition, at a time when more and more students need to be graduating from high school and going on to college, high schools are being called upon to play a new role: increasing educational attainment and exposing all students to more rigorous coursework and analytical and conceptual skills. Yet there is an increasing body of evidence that high schools are the weakest link and most troubled educational institutions in large urban school systems, particularly for Hispanic students.

Research consistently finds that urban adolescents' school performance, involvement, and perception of the quality of their school environments and relationships with teachers decline markedly as they move to high school. These declines are linked to school dropout.[82] In Chicago, for example, more than 40 percent of entering ninth-graders fail a major subject in the first semester (English, math, history, or science); 20 percent fail 2 or more. Hispanics, in particular Hispanic males, are at the most risk of course failure, even after accounting for differences in Hispanic and non-Hispanic students' prior achievement, early high school attendance patterns, bilingual education status, age, and prior school mobility.

The reasons why Hispanic students may experience greater difficulty than others during the transition to high school include all of the family and community factors discussed in previous sections. The quality of Hispanic high schools and school policy also play a role. Hispanic students are concentrated in large, often overcrowded, urban high schools that are plagued by low standards, high rates of student and teacher disengagement, and poor performance. For example, when the Chicago public schools moved to place poorly performing schools on "academic probation," more than half of the city's high schools met the criteria (less than 15 percent of their students were doing math or reading at grade level on national norms). All but one of the predominantly

Hispanic high schools in the city were placed on academic probation. Hispanic high schools are characterized by both low performance and less positive environments that provide less support for Hispanic students and their families. A recent study in Chicago found that teachers in predominantly Hispanic high schools reported the lowest levels of communication with and academic support for parents.[83] Importantly, these poor family-school relationships in majority-Hispanic high schools stand in marked contrast to those in Hispanic elementary schools. Elementary school teachers in schools that serve mostly Hispanic families reported greater levels of communication with parents and more positive relationships with parents than teachers in either majority-Black or mixed Black and Hispanic high schools. This means that Hispanic parents whose children attend majority-Hispanic schools experience the largest changes in their relationships with and supports from school as their children move to high school.

Even within more diverse schools, many policy and practices of high schools make it particularly difficult for Hispanic students to find the supports they need. Ann Locke Davidson, in her research in California high schools, highlighted four aspects of high school environments that give Hispanic youth fewer challenges and supports and send the message that their education is not as valuable as that of other groups. These messages strongly influence Hispanic youths' identity, school attachment, and behavior. Negative messages include:

1. track placement where students are often unchallenged by their coursework;
2. ethnically targeted policies, such as rules against certain modes of dress or discipline rules that single out Hispanic youths and their peer culture;
3. low expectations of minority adolescents, which put Hispanics at odds with teacher attitudes about students' intelligence, value of education, and gang membership; and
4. bureaucratic relationships and barriers to information that place Hispanic adolescents, particularly those from language-minority backgrounds, behind their more advantaged peers with regard to pathways to college and full participation in the schools.[84]

Cultural Differences in Shaping Educational Practices and School Attachment

The previous descriptions of how family characteristics and schools shape educational outcomes among Hispanic youths could be characterized as structural interpretations. These structural interpretations suggest that both the socioeconomic characteristics of Hispanic families and the characteristics of the schools Hispanic children attend create barriers to family support of children's education and to successful school engagement among Hispanic youths. The implication of structural explanations is that if Hispanic families had higher incomes and higher parental education, they would be more involved in their children's education and would make decisions regarding their children's education as do other racial and ethnic groups. Structural explanations also predict that if schools provided Hispanic students with the same opportunities and supports that non-Hispanics receive, Hispanics adolescents would be more likely to stay in school. Yet up until recently, most researchers studying Hispanics and education attempted to explain the poorer relative educational performance of Hispanic children on the basis of cultural differences in childrearing practices and the value placed on educational attainment in Hispanic households. Much of this initial work was criticized for ignoring structural issues. However, a focus on structural explanations alone may miss cultural issues that help explain why parents who are immigrants may strongly emphasize education but not endorse the family processes that accompany these expectations. An important example of cultural mismatch is research on optimal home environments.

One of the most important studies of early literacy development was Reginald Clark's work on successful home environments for Black children.[85] Clark highlighted several parenting strategies that distinguished poor children who were successful in school from those who were not. In Clark's study, Black parents who were very involved in their children's home activities; who worked with their children daily in studying, reading, and conversing around literacy; and who praised their children's talents and achievements were able to provide home environments that laid the basis for school success, even within poor homes.

Guadalupe Valdes argued that this model of successful family relations, which has been adopted by many family support programs, may conflict with the cultural values of Mexican-American families.[86] Valdes argues that Mexican childrearing focuses on developing respect and obedience in children (*respeto*). Consistent with *respeto*, Mexican mothers may not see it as their role to teach children skills; rather, they delegate this task to schools and teachers. The mother is responsible for the moral upbringing of her children. The U.S. view of childrearing— which has the family focused on the child, places the child's education as the highest priority, and seeks to develop independence and questioning of authority—conflicts (according to Valdes) with Hispanic parental practices, which seek to establish lines of authority within the family, stress familial bonds over individual interests, and emphasize respect for parents and elders. Indeed, Valdes argued that attempts to change parenting practices in Hispanic homes must be sensitive to their side effects: although having parents interact more with their children in ways that are linked to early school success may lead to more positive educational outcomes, there may also be real costs to families in de-emphasizing cultural values. Such parenting practices may force Mexican-American parents to choose between transmission of cultural values and academic success for their children.

The difficulty with cultural versus structural arguments is that they are hard to untangle. To what extent do the "values" that Valdes observed represent Mexican culture, as opposed to the impact of low parental education and family income? Luis Laosa and Ronald Henderson's work on parenting practices among Mexicans in the United States has challenged this "cultural interpretation."[87] Laosa and Henderson found that the teaching strategies used by mothers of Mexican descent varied by education levels. Mexican-American mothers who had not graduated from high school relied primarily on the directive and modeling techniques that Valdes identified as culturally Mexican (showing rather than verbally teaching). In comparison, Mexican-American mothers in this study who had graduated from high school were more likely to teach their children using techniques that Valdes identified as culturally American, such as use inquiry and praise. Thus, it is unclear to what extent the parenting practices observed by Valdes represent Mexican culture versus low education.

Cultural differences may make it more difficult for Hispanic families to adapt to changing American expectations—yet some of those same cultural differences, mainly a focus on family and respect for authority, may promote positive school performance. This is a second reason it is difficult to unpack cultural and structural debates. The Suarez-Orozcos' seminal studies of school attachment among Hispanic youths have challenged the view that poor educational performance among Mexican-Americans arises from cultural differences in familial values regarding education.[88] The Suarez-Orozcos compared the achievement orientation of four groups of students: Mexican adolescents who lived in Mexico, Mexican immigrants to the United States, Mexican-American second-generation youths, and White American youths. There was an obvious emphasis on academic achievement across groups, with Mexican immigrants showing the highest attachment to school and achievement orientation (followed by Mexican youths, Mexican-American second-generation students, and lastly White American youths).

The Suarez-Orozcos concluded that "although members of the immigrant generation typically demonstrate high expectations and an optimism that through schooling they can achieve status mobility, the second generation may adopt a less enthusiastic faith in the educational system."[89]

What accounts for the higher value placed on education by Mexican immigrants to the United States than by other groups? One explanation is that immigrants and native-born children have different reference groups. Immigrant students are more likely to compare their opportunities and status to that afforded in their home country; first- and second-generation youths are more likely to compare their opportunities and status to those of the dominant American culture. A second explanation is that immigrant and second-generation youths are treated differently and have different experiences in school. Many teachers perceive immigrant students as being motivated and valuing education, as compared to second-generation youth who are viewed as disrespectful and disengaged from schoolwork; these differences in perception may have important effects on the level of support and opportunities students receive.[90] Third, immigrant and second-generation students may experience different degrees of influence from traditional cultural norms regarding the behavior and decision making of children. In particular, Suarez-Orozco, in his research on Central American refugees, suggested that immigrant youth, who are more oriented toward family, may adopt compensatory achievement (a belief that investment in education is a responsibility to the community and to the family, as a means of paying families back for the hardships they endured).[91]

In summary, recent research on education and Hispanics has tended to stray from cultural perspectives toward structural perspectives. Yet as the pendulum swings away from cultural interpretations of family practices and home-school relations, it is important to recognize that policies and practices geared to Hispanic families and children need to build on and support cultural values and norms; attention to bridging cultural barriers is a central component of developing effective schools for Hispanic youth and their families.

Limited English Proficient Children and Bilingual Education: Special Issues and Concerns

Research findings regarding the higher academic orientation of immigrant youth stand in sharp contrast to school outcomes among limited English proficient (LEP) students. Despite being viewed by teachers as more highly motivated and well behaved, research finds that Hispanic immigrants (particularly LEP youth) have significantly poorer school performance and lower educational attainment than non-immigrant students.[92] All of the family and school characteristics identified as factors in the poorer educational opportunities and supports for Hispanic children are amplified for immigrant and LEP youths. One study found that LEP students in the United States, particularly Hispanics, tend to be poorer, have parents with lower education, have parents with limited English proficiency, and have families that are experiencing stresses such as unemployment.[93] LEP students are also more likely to be concentrated in high-poverty schools within large urban areas. More than 80 percent of LEP Hispanic first- and third-graders attended schools in which more than half of the student body was poor.[94]

Limited English proficient students face an additional barrier, because they require additional resources and supports from schools. Issues of bilingual education and of the effectiveness of alternative strategies for educating immigrant youths are heavily politicized and complex.[95] Pastora Cafferty, in chapter 3 of this book, offers an important analysis of approaches to bilingual education and the policy debate. Much of this debate focuses on the pace of English language acquisition and the effectiveness of alternative educational strategies in promoting language and skills acquisition among LEP students. Equally important, though, is whether LEP students have equal access to the kinds of training and supports that all students need to develop the skills critical for success in high school and beyond. A congressionally mandated study found that many LEP children are not receiving the help, early in their school careers, that is critical for school success. Limited English proficient students are less likely to attend preschool and, in particular, to participate in Head Start programs. Many do not receive the supplementary help in reading or math that is available through Chapter 1 funding. In both first and third grades, more than 40 percent of low-achieving LEP students receive no supplementary education assistance in reading or language arts, and more than two-thirds receive no supplementary help in math.[96] These issues of opportunity to learn are as important early in the elementary school years as later, when ensuring equal access to challenging, college-oriented curricula becomes critically important. Unfortunately, differences in early educational opportunities, as well as later differences in access to high-school-level courses, may reflect political ideology less than the resource limitations of the large urban school systems that serve immigrant youths.

Summary and Concluding Comments: Toward a Policy Agenda

Increasing educational achievement among Hispanics is a daunting challenge. When we look at trends in Hispanic education in the context of larger changes in education, the task seems overwhelming. Nevertheless, the research discussed in this chapter suggests some very clear strategies for improving educational attainment and achievement among Hispanic youths.

STRATEGY 1: SUPPORTING HISPANIC FAMILIES. If there is one clear theme in this chapter, it is that improving educational outcomes among Hispanic students requires support for Hispanic families. Regardless of what schools formally do, the nearly two-decade increase in the proportion of Hispanic children living in poverty and stagnant parental education undermine families' ability to provide the resources and supports that children need to succeed in school. This strategy begins with policies that support poor families and give families opportunities to invest in education and training. The earned income tax credit, child credit, and other family support policies are important poverty reduction initiatives, which have equally important educational impacts. The new educational incentives provided in the 1997 budget act (discussed later in this section) may also improve the capacity of Hispanic families to afford education for their children. However, these positive approaches are currently being offset by a withdrawal of the safety net in Hispanic communities.

Local communities and schools must also develop webs of support for Hispanic families. Supporting Hispanic families means calling on schools to develop and implement model school-home practices. If schools see it as their role to work with parents, overcome language difficulties, and assist parents in developing effective educational strategies for helping with homework, the schools' orientation will enhance Hispanic families' ability to support their children's education. A consistent finding of research on Hispanic education is that Hispanic families and adolescents are eager for such help.

STRATEGY 2: EXPANDING OPPORTUNITIES FOR PRESCHOOL PARTICIPATION. A second clear policy impetus is to address the widening gap in preschool enrollment between Hispanic families and other groups. The benefits of preschool education are widely documented, but Hispanic children (particularly children whose parents do not speak English) are the least likely to be enrolled in preschool programs, and this gap is widening over time. There is a pressing need for research on how much these gaps in preschool participation rates are due to lack of access to early childhood programs and how much to widening differences in the home environments and parental expectations of children. Such an inequity calls for targeted programs, at both federal and state levels, to expand Head Start resources and preschool slots in Hispanic communities, especially for immigrant youth.

STRATEGY 3: RAISING THE TOP AS WELL AS THE BOTTOM: RAISING ACHIEVEMENT AMONG HISPANIC YOUTH. In many ways, trends in Hispanic achievement are a glass half full and half empty. On the positive side, achievement test scores of Hispanic youth rose faster than those of non-Hispanic Whites during the 1970s and 1980s, reducing the ethnic gap in achievement. There has also been substantial progress in raising the proportion of Hispanic students who meet minimum standards for their grade. On the negative side, recent trends suggest some slowing and perhaps erosion of gains in Hispanic achievement, and much less progress has been made in increasing the proportion of Hispanic students with higher levels of the problem-solving and communication skills increasingly valued in today's economy.

The terms *accountability* and *standards* will most certainly characterize education policy initiatives of the 1990s and 2000s. Standard-raising approaches that hold teachers and schools accountable for student performance, regardless of the populations they serve, would appear to benefit Hispanic students. Policies such as those currently being implemented in Chicago include intervening and demanding higher performance from poorly performing schools, as well as setting and enforcing standards for student performance. Hispanics are the most recent minority group in America who bring to school cultural differences, language barriers, and low levels of parental education and income. Unfortunately, it is often too easy for teachers, many of whom do not feel prepared or effective in dealing with students who are different, to set lower and different standards and pursue less academically focused curricula for minority students, particularly bilingual-education and immigrant students. Given the importance of skills development for Hispanic children, and the historical tendency of teachers and schools to adopt compensatory coping techniques, external incentives may be necessary to ensure equal opportunity to learn. Such a strategy requires, however, that policy makers accompany standard-raising initiatives with the resources teachers, parents, and students will need as they work together to raise expectations and, ultimately, performance.

The current wave of standard-raising approaches tends to emphasize basic skills and to focus on poorly performing students and schools. This focus must be balanced with an equal emphasis on exposing Hispanic youth to enrichment experiences in writing, math, and science, to lay the basis for high-school- and college-level work. Without such balanced efforts, urban schools are truly selling Hispanic children and families short.

STRATEGY 4: INCREASING SOCIAL CAPITAL AND BUILDING EFFECTIVE HIGH SCHOOLS FOR HISPANIC YOUTH. The question of how to raise educational attainment among Hispanic youth is one of the most important challenges facing the U.S. education system and the Hispanic community. There is little evidence that payoffs for skills and higher educational attainment will wane in the next several decades. Yet, as we saw in this chapter, Hispanics as a group are distinguished by their high rate of school dropout. Raising educational attainment among Hispanic youths must begin with a focus on high schools. An emerging body of evidence shows that high schools as institutions are responding slowly to higher expectations and the fact that all students need higher levels of skills and greater educational attainment to be successful. National reports concur that the problems of high schools are widespread and not limited to urban schools, though this is where problems are most evident and where change has been lagging. The good news is that low-achieving students appear to benefit the most when high schools: (1) set high academic standards for students and have all students pursue more academically oriented coursework; (2) adopt reforms aimed at providing an infrastructure for school improvement, often called *restructuring approaches*; and (3) develop webs of support for students and teachers, providing more opportunities for teachers to interact and build instructional programs and for students to interact with teachers and work on critical skills.[97] Building twenty-first-century high schools will, however, require substantial human capital, programmatic, and infrastructure investment to reduce high school size; reinvigorate curricula; recruit and train high-quality teachers who are committed to success for all students; and develop programs and supports that will allow teachers to work with students and their families in building skills and making the link between high school and postsecondary institutions.

STRATEGY 5: INVESTING IN URBAN EDUCATION. Minority children will provide more than half of the net growth in the labor supply in the twenty-first century. These future workers are mostly being educated in major urban school systems, and the education they receive largely depends on the quality of those school districts.[98] Large urban school districts, those with enrollments of 10,000 students or more, serve half (46 percent) of the nation's students and more than two-thirds of the nation's Black and Hispanic students.[99] The growth in immigration and burgeoning populations of Hispanics in urban areas bring new resources to deteriorating inner cities. At the same time, these new students bring new burdens, as schools become overcrowded, new teachers are needed, and new services are needed to serve immigrant youth.

The large urban school systems in the United States have been handed a difficult task: mount the resources to address the educational needs of Hispanic and minority children *and* begin educational reform efforts that provide even greater levels of training and higher educational attainment for those children. The importance and magnitude of this task necessitate a new role for federal education. Standard-raising reforms do not deal with the key issues of educational finance and resource constraints on urban school systems. New federal and state support is needed to ameliorate those constraints, both in dealing with burgeoning population and in raising standards. For the first area, federal and state aid is needed to reduce school and class size; build and improve schools; hire, recruit, and train teachers; and add resources for bilingual education.

In the second area, these same school systems must be helped to invest in new programming and policy development. Approaches that seek to raise standards, like those being implemented in Chicago, are promising in that they promote higher standards for all children. But doing so, correctly and effectively, requires significant local resources for teacher development, new instructional materials, and extra supports for students. For example, the 1997–1998 cost of summer programs in Chicago, just for students who did not meet the standards, was estimated at $65 million. Preliminary evidence suggests that this summer school initiative was successful in providing low-achieving students with significant learning gains during the summer months.[100] Clearly, then, standard-raising approaches are not simply a matter of passing new requirements. Restructuring efforts and systemic reform initiatives require significant and ongoing monetary investments in summer schools, after-school programming, and additional preschool resources. It also requires investment in teacher training, in development of materials, in technology, and in expansion of these standards and resources to bilingual and LEP youths. Too often, though, disadvantaged urban school systems do not have the flexibility and capacity to mount such extra initiatives.

Reforming large urban school systems requires a commitment to change and the resources to do so. Ultimately, however, quality education for Hispanic children depends on the quality of their teachers. The federal government has an important role to play in investing in training for teachers, providing incentives for teachers to teach in urban areas, and in recruiting minorities to the teaching profession.

STRATEGY 6: BUILDING BRIDGES TO COLLEGE FOR HISPANIC YOUTH. Hispanics are not alone in facing barriers to college enrollment and completion. Neither Blacks nor Hispanics have improved the proportion of students who receive four-year college degrees, despite higher rates of college enrollment and aspirations. The Balanced Budget Act of 1997 contained a host of measures to increase the affordability of college, including tax deductions of up to $10,000 from taxable income and a tax credit of $1,500. There is much debate but little evidence on how these credits will shape overall demand for college enrollment, students' choice of two- or four-year institutions, and access to and attendance at institutions of higher education for poor and minority youths. Breaking down financial barriers to college is critical, but building bridges to college for Hispanic youth also requires that high schools and postsecondary institutions develop the supports that Hispanic families and adolescents need to translate these opportunities into college enrollment. Programs such as Upward Bound, the STEP Program at DePaul University, and AVID Learners are models that have demonstrated effectiveness. These programs work with students as early as their freshman year in high school to provide academic enrichment and ongoing support throughout students' high school careers, to develop an orientation to college and provide the roadmaps to get there.

Taken together, what these strategies suggest are that addressing the educational needs of Hispanic youth is not the sole responsibility of the Hispanic community or the local school systems that serve these children. Rather, improving the educational experiences and performance of Hispanic children must involve the participation and joint effort of the Hispanic community, local school systems, colleges and universities, foundation and nonprofit sectors, and federal and state governments. It also entails using a combination of broad-based efforts to support education and targeted efforts to address the special needs of Hispanic youth and the school systems that serve them.

Notes

1. Council of Economic Advisors, Executive Office of the President, *Economic Report of the President* (Washington, D.C.: Government Printing Office, 1996); Richard Freeman, "Toward an Apartheid Economy," *Harvard Business Review* (September-October 1996): 114–21; Sheldon Danziger and Peter Gottschalk, *America Unequal* (Cambridge, Mass.: Harvard University Press, 1995); Richard J. Murnane and Frank Levy, "Education and Training," in *Setting Domestic Priorities: What Can Government Do?*, ed. Henry J. Aaron and Charles Schultze (Washington, D.C.: Brookings Institution, 1992), 185–223; William Julius Wilson, *When Work Disappears: The World of the New Urban Poor* (New York: Alfred A. Knopf, 1997).
2. Leo R. Chavez and Rebecca Martinez, "Mexican Immigration in the 1980s and Beyond: Implications for Chicanas/Chicanos," in *Chicanas/Chicanos at the Crossroads: Social, Economic and Political Change*, ed. Leo Maciel and Isidro D. Ortiz (Tucson, Ariz.: University of Arizona Press, 1996), 25–51; Kristin Hansen and Carol S. Faber, *The Foreign Born Population: 1996* (Washington, D.C.: United States Bureau of the Census, 1996) (Current Population Reports Population Characteristics, Special Report Series P-20-494).
3. A *recent immigrant* is defined as a foreign-born person who arrived in the United States after 1980. Hansen and Faber, *The Foreign Born Population: 1996.*
4. Patricia Albjerg Graham, "Assimilation, Adjustment and Access: An Antiquarian View of American Education," in *Learning from the Past: What History Teaches Us About School Reform*, ed. Diane Ravitch and Maris Vinovskis (Baltimore, Md.: Johns Hopkins University Press, 1995), 3–24; David B. Tyak, *The One Best System: A History of American Urban Education* (Cambridge, Mass.: Harvard University Press, 1974); Maris Vinovskis, *Education Society and Economic Opportunity: A Historical Perspective on Persistent Issues* (New Haven, Conn.: Yale University Press, 1995).
5. Graham, "Assimilation, Adjustment and Access"; Tyak, *The One Best System.*
6. United States Department of Education, Office of Educational Research and Improvement, *120 Years of American Education: A Statistical Portrait* (Washington, D.C.: Author, 1993) (NCES 93-442).
7. United States Department of Education, *120 Years of American Education.*
8. Tyak, *The One Best System.*
9. Graham, "Assimilation, Adjustment and Access."
10. For a discussion of the growth of Catholic schools and the role that Catholic schools played in education and socialization for immigrants, see Anthony S. Bryk, Valerie E. Lee, and Peter B. Holland, *Catholic Schools and the Common Good* (Cambridge, Mass.: Harvard University Press, 1993).
11. Alejandro Portes and Ruben Rumbaut, *Immigrant America: A Portrait* (Berkeley, Cal.: University of California Press, 1996).
12. Earnings data presented in this section are from United States Department of Education, National Center for Educational Statistics, *Condition of Education: Supplemental and Standard Error Tables, 1996* (Washington, D.C.: Author, 1997) (NCES 97-998).

13. Frank D. Bean and Marta Tienda, *The Hispanic Population of the United States* (New York: Russell Sage Foundation, 1987); Portes and Rumbaut, *Immigrant America.*

14. United States Department of the Census, *The Hispanic Population in the United States: March 1993* (Washington, D.C.: Government Printing Office, 1994) (Current Population Report P-20, No. 475).

15. Ibid.

16. United States Department of Education, National Center for Education Statistics, *Condition of Education.*

17. Lutz Berkner, Stephanie Cucaro-Alamin, Alexander C. McCormich, and Larry G. Bobbit, *Descriptive Summary of 1989-90 Beginning Postsecondary Students Five Years Later* (Washington, D.C.: United States Department of Education, National Center for Education Statistics, 1996) (NCES 96-155); United States Department of Education, National Center for Education Statistics, *Minority Undergraduate Participation in Postsecondary Education* (Washington, D.C.: Author, 1995) (NCES 95-166); United States Department of Education, National Center for Education Statistics, *The Educational Progress of Hispanic Students* (Washington, D.C.: Author, 1995) (NCES 95-767).

18. United States Department of Education, National Center for Education Statistics, *Minority Undergraduate Participation in Postsecondary Education.*

19. Ibid., 16.

20. Ibid.; Berkner et al., *Descriptive Summary of 1989-90 Beginning Postsecondary Students.*

21. Commission on National Investment in Education, Council for Aid to Education, *Breaking the Social Contract: The Fiscal Crisis in Higher Education* (Washington, D.C.: Rand Corporation, 1997).

22. Council of Economic Advisors, *Economic Report of the President.*

23. Ibid.

24. Thomas Kane and Cecilia Elena Rouse, "Labor-Market Returns to Two- and Four-Year Colleges," *American Economic Review* 85, no. 3 (1995): 600–14.

25. Thomas Kane, "College Entry by Blacks Since 1970: The Role of College Costs, Family Background and the Returns to Education," *Journal of Political Economy* 102, no. 51 (1994): 878–911.

26. Data in this section on college attendance rates among seniors graduating in 1972 and 1989 are from United States Department of Education, National Center for Educational Statistics, *Condition of Education: Supplemental and Standard Error Tables 1996.*

27. Marilyn McMillen (project officer), *Dropout Rates in the United States* (Washington, D.C.: United States Department of Education, National Center for Education Statistics, 1997) (NCES 97-473).

28. McMillen, *Dropout Rates in the United States.*

29. Formal kindergarten participation rates are not available for periods prior to the 1970s. Historically, we do know the number of students each year who were enrolled in each grade. This data allows us to estimate kindergarten participation rates by dividing the number of children enrolled in kindergarten in one year by the number enrolled in first grade in the next year. For example, in 1910, 326,883 children were enrolled in kindergarten. In 1911, there were 3,889,542 first-graders in the United States. This gives us an estimate of kindergarten enrollment of .08 percent. In 1990, there were 3,486,358 children enrolled in kindergarten. In 1991, there were 3,499,091 first-graders in the United States, yielding an enrollment estimate of 99.6 percent. United States Department of Education, Office of Educational Research and Improvement, *120 Years of American Education.*

30. Katherine Chandler, Jerry West, and E. Hausken, *Approaching Kindergarten: A Look at Pre-schoolers in the United States* (Washington, D.C.: United States Department of Education, National Center for Education Statistics, 1995) (NCES 95-280); Laurie Shepard and Mary L. Smith, "Synthesis of Research on School Readiness and Kindergarten Retention," *Educational Leadership* 44 (1986): 78–86; Laurie Shepard and Mary L. Smith, "Escalating Academic Demands in Kindergarten: Counterproductive Policies," *Elementary School Journal* 44 (1988): 78–86.

31. Table 5.2 shows preschool participation rates estimated from the United States Department of Education's National Household Education Survey. Data from the Current Population Survey, a larger and more regular survey of families conducted by the United States Department of the Census, also finds a widening gap in preschool participation rates between Hispanics and Whites. In the early 1970s, less than 20 percent of White and slightly less than 15 percent of Hispanic 3- to 4-year-olds were enrolled in prekindergarten. By 1993, the Current Population Survey estimated that 38 percent of White and only 17 percent of Hispanic 3- to 4-year-olds were enrolled in a formal prekindergarten program. Importantly, although data from the National Household Education Survey suggests that Black children are not less likely to be enrolled in preschool, Current Population Survey data shows a widening gap over time, though not in any way as large as that between Hispanics and Whites. United States Department of Education, National Center for Education Statistics, *The Educational Progress of Hispanic Students*.

32. United States Department of Education, National Center for Education Statistics, *The Educational Progress of Hispanic Students*. (See also note 30.)

33. Janet Curre and Duncan Thomas, "Does Head Start Help Hispanic Children?," *Focus* 19, no. 1 (1997): 22–25; Doris S. Entwistle, Karl L. Alexander, and Linda Steffel, *Children, Schools, and Inequality* (Boulder, Colo.: Westview Press, 1997); Claude Goldenberg, Leslie Reese, and Ronald Gallimore, "Effects of Literacy Materials from School on Latino Children's Home Experiences and Early Reading Achievement," *American Journal of Education* (1992): 497–536; Arthur J. Reynolds, Emily Mann, Wendy Miedel, and Paul Smokowski, "The State of Early Childhood Intervention: Effectiveness, Myths and Realities, New Directions," *Focus* 19, no. 1 (1997): 5–11; Arthur J. Reynolds and Barbara Wolfe, "School Achievement, Early Intervention, and Special Education: New Evidence from the Chicago Longitudinal Study," *Focus* 19, no. 1 (1997): 18–21.

34. Chandler, West, and Hausken, *Approaching Kindergarten*; Goldenberg, Reese, and Gallimore, "Effects of Literacy Materials from School"; Guadalupe Valdes, *Con Respeto: Bridging the Distances Between Culturally Diverse Families and Schools: An Ethnographic Portrait* (New York: New York Teachers College Press, 1996).

35. Chandler, West, and Hausken, *Approaching Kindergarten*.

36. Judith R. Smith, Jeanne Brooks-Gunn, and Pamela Klebanov, "Consequences of Living in Poverty for Young Children's Cognitive and Verbal Ability and Early School Achievement," in *Consequences of Growing Up Poor*, ed. Greg J. Duncan and Jeanne Brooks-Gunn (New York: Russell Sage Foundation, 1997), 132–89.

37. Bean and Tienda, *The Hispanic Population of the United States*; Melissa Roderick, *The Path to Dropping Out: Evidence for Intervention* (Westport, Conn.: Auburn House, 1993); Russell Rumberger, "Dropping Out of High School: The Influence of Race, Sex and Family Background," *American Educational Research Journal* 20, no. 2 (1983):199–220; Shepard and Smith, "Synthesis of Research on School Readiness"; Mary Smith and Laurie Shepard, "What Doesn't Work:

Explaining Policies of Retention in the Early Grades," *Phi Delta Kappan* 69, no. 2 (1987): 129–34.

38. Susan Fuhrman, Richard F. Elmore, and Diane Massell, "School Reform in the United States: Putting It into Context," in *Reforming Education: The Emerging System Approach*, ed. Stephen L. Jacobson and Robert Berne (Thousand Oaks, Cal.: Corwin Press, 1993), 3–27; Diane Massell and Susan Fuhrman, *Ten Years of State Education Reform, 1983–1993: Overview with Four Case Studies* (Rutgers, N.J.: Consortium for Policy Research in Education, The State University of New Jersey, 1994).

39. Massell and Fuhrman, *Ten Years of State Education Reform*; Marshall Smith and Jennifer O'Day, "Systemic School Reform," in *Politics of Education Association Yearbook* (New York: Taylor and Francis, 1990), 233–67.

40. Fuhrman, Elmore, and Massell, "School Reform in the United States," 8.

41. Chicago Public Schools, *Guidelines for Promotion in the Chicago Public Schools* (Chicago: Author, 1997); The Chicago Panel, *Initiative Status Report: Summer Bridge* (Chicago: Author, 1998).

42. Chicago Panel, *Initiative Status Report*.

43. United States Department of Education, National Center for Education Statistics, *Report in Brief: NAEP 1994 Trends in Academic Progress* (Washington, D.C.: Author, 1996).

44. Data on trends in the NAEP in this section are from United States Department of Education, National Center for Education Statistics, *Report in Brief: NAEP 1994*.

45. Smith and O'Day, "Systemic School Reform."

46. United States Department of Education, National Center for Education Statistics, *NAEP 1994 Trends in Academic Progress* (Washington, D.C.: 1997) (NCES Report 97-095).

47. United States Department of Education, National Center for Education Statistics, *Condition of Education*.

48. Concha Delgado-Gaitan, "Research and Policy in Reconceptualizing Family-School Relationships," in *Renegotiating Cultural Diversity in American Schools*, ed. Patricia Phelan and Ann Locke Davidson (New York: Teachers College Press, 1993), 139–58; Jacquellynne Eccles and Rena Harold, "Family Involvement in Children's and Adolescents' Schooling," in *Family-School Links: How Do They Affect Educational Outcomes?*, ed. A. Booth and J. Dunn (Hillsdale, N.J.: Lawrence Erlbaum 1995); Anne Henderson and Nancy Berla, *A New Generation of Evidence: The Family Is Critical to Student Achievement* (Washington, D.C.: National Committee for Citizens in Education, 1994); Russell Rumberger, Rita Ghatak, Gary Poulus, Philip L. Ritter, and Sanford M. Dornbusch, "Family Influences on Dropout Behavior in One California High School," *Sociology of Education* 63 (October 1990): 283–99; Laurence Steinberg, Susie Lamborn, Stanford Dornbusch, and Nancy Darling, "Impact of Parenting Practices on Adolescent Achievement: Authoritative Parenting, School Involvement, and Encouragement to Succeed," *Child Development* 63 (1992): 1266–81.

49. Chandler, West, and Hausken, *Approaching Kindergarten*; Jeanne S. Chall, Vicki A. Jacobs, and Luke E. Baldwin, *The Reading Crisis: Why Poor Children Fall Behind* (Cambridge, Mass.: Harvard University Press, 1990); Goldenberg, Reese, and Gallimore, "Effects of Literacy Materials from School"; Luis M. Laosa and Ronald W. Henderson, "Cognitive Socialization and Competence: The Academic Development of Chicanos," in *Chicano School Failure and Success: Research and Policy Agendas for the 1990s*, ed. Richard R. Valencia (London: Falmer Press, 1991); Valdes, *Con Respeto*; Harold W. Stevenson, Chuansheng Chen, and David

Uttal, "Beliefs and Achievement: A Study of Black, White and Hispanic Children," *Child Development* 61 (1990): 508–23.

50. Goldenberg, Reese, and Gallimore, "Effects of Literacy Materials from School"; Stevenson, Chen, and Uttal, "Beliefs and Achievement."

51. United States Department of the Census, *Poverty in the University States: 1996* (Washington, D.C.: Government Printing Office, 1997) (Current Population Reports P-60-198).

52. Within the Hispanic population, families of Mexican origin tend to be larger. In 1993, according to the March Current Population Survey, the mean number of persons in a household of Mexican origin in the United States was 3.78, compared to 2.85 for Puerto Ricans, 2.65 for Cuban-origin households, and 3.25 for families of Central and South American origin. The mean number of persons in non-Hispanic White households was 2.52. United States Department of the Census, *The Hispanic Population in the United States: March 1993*.

53. United States Department of the Census, *The Hispanic Population in the United States: March 1993*.

54. Concha Delgado-Gaitan and Manuel Trueba, *Crossing Cultural Borders: Education for Immigrant Families in America* (London: Falmer Press, 1991).

55. Concha Delgado-Gaitan, "School Matters in the Mexican-American Home: Socializing Children to Education," *American Educational Research Journal* 29, no. 3 (1992): 495–516; Delgado-Gaitan and Trueba, *Crossing Cultural Borders*.

56. Stevenson, Chen, and Uttal, "Beliefs and Achievement."

57. Eccles and Harold, "Family Involvement in Children's and Adolescents' Schooling"; Rumberger, Ghatak, Poulus, Ritter, and Dornbusch, "Family Influences on Dropout Behavior in One California High School."

58. Melissa Roderick and Susan Stone, *Changing Standards, Changing Relationships: Building Family-School Relationships to Promote Student Achievement in Chicago High Schools* (Chicago, Ill.: Consortium on Chicago School Research, 1998).

59. Delgado-Gaitan and Trueba, *Crossing Cultural Borders*.

60. Valdes, *Con Respeto,* 166.

61. Roderick and Stone, *Changing Standards, Changing Relationships*.

62. David W. Grissmer, Sheila Nataraj Kirby, Mark Berends, and Stephanie Williamson, *Student Achievement and the Changing American Family* (Santa Monica, Cal.: Rand Corporation, 1994); Rumberger, "Dropping Out of High School"; Russell Rumberger, "Dropping Out of Middle School: A Multilevel Analysis of Students and Schools," *American Educational Research Journal* 32, no. 3 (1995): 583–626; Stevenson, Chen, and Uttal, "Beliefs and Achievement"; Gary D. Sanderfur, Sara McLanahan, and Roger A. Wojtkeiwicz, "Race and Ethnicity, Family Structure and High School Graduation" (Madison, Wis.: Institute for Research on Poverty, 1989) (Discussion Paper no. 893-89).

63. Grissmer, Kirby, Berends, and Williamson, *Student Achievement and the Changing American Family*; Rumberger, "Dropping Out of Middle School."

64. Grissmer, Kirby, Berends, and Williamson, *Student Achievement and the Changing American Family*; Sanderfur, McLanahan, and Wojtkeiwicz, "Race and Ethnicity, Family Structure and High School Graduation."

65. Grissmer, Kirby, Berends, and Williamson, *Student Achievement and the Changing American Family*.

66. Ibid., 106.

67. United States Department of the Census, *Poverty in the United States: 1996*.

68. Hector R. Cordero, "The Structure of Inequality and the Status of Puerto Rican Youth in the U.S.," in *Latinos and Education: A Critical Reader,* ed. Antonia

Darder, Rodolfo D. Torres, and Henry Gutierrez (New York: Routledge, 1997), 80–94.

69. Anthony S. Bryk and Mary Erina Driscoll, *The High Schools as Community: Contextual Influences and Consequences for Students and Teachers* (Madison, Wis.: National Center on Effective Secondary Schools, University of Wisconsin–Madison, 1988); Thomas Carter and Michael Chatfield, "Effective Bilingual Schools: Implications for Policy and Practice," *American Journal of Education* 95, no. 1 (1986): 200–31; 1992; Valerie E. Lee, Julie B. Smith, and Richard G. Croninger, "Another Look at High School Restructuring," in *Issues in Restructuring Schools* (Madison, Wis.: Center for School Restructuring, University of Wisconsin–Madison, 1995); Tamara Lucas, Rosemary Henze, and Ruben Donato, "Promoting the Success of Latino Language Minority Students: An Exploratory Study of Six High Schools," in Darder, Torres, and Gutierrez, *Latinos and Education*, 373–97; Fred M. Newmann, Gary G. Wehlage, and Susan D. Lamborn, "The Significance and Sources of Student Engagement," in *Student Engagement and Achievement in American Secondary Schools,* ed. Fred M. Newmann (New York: Teachers College Press 1992), 11–39; Penny Sebring, Anthony S. Bryk, Melissa Roderick, and Eric Camburn, *Charting Reform in Chicago: The Students Speak* (Chicago: Consortium on Chicago School Research, The University of Chicago, 1996).

70. Paul Jargowsky, in his analysis of the 1970, 1980, and 1990 censuses, found that the number of Hispanics living in high-poverty areas increased substantially between 1970 and 1990. However, this increase was accounted for by population growth and higher poverty rates for Hispanics in metropolitan areas, not a shift in the kinds of neighborhoods Hispanics were living in. The proportion of poor Blacks and Whites living in poor neighborhoods increased substantially between 1970 and 1990. Jargowsky does not find a similar increase in the proportion of Hispanics living in poor neighborhoods during this time. Paul Jargowsky, *Poverty and Place: Ghettos, Barrios, and the American City* (New York: Russell Sage Foundation, 1997). For a full discussion of trends in the segregation of Hispanic children in schools, see Gary Orfield, Mark Bachmeier, David R. James, and Tamela Eitle, *Deepening Segregation in American Public Schools* (Cambridge, Mass.: Harvard Project on School Desegregation, 1997).

71. Orfield, Bachmeier, James, and Eitle, *Deepening Segregation in American Public Schools.*

72. Ibid.

73. Ruban Espinosa and Alberto Ochoa, "Concentration of California Hispanic Students in Schools with Low Achievement: A Research Note," *American Journal of Education* 95, no. 1 (1986): 77–95; Laura Lippman, Shelley Burns, and Edith McArthur, *Urban Schools: The Challenge of Location and Poverty* (Washington, D.C.: United States Department of Education, Office of Educational Research and Improvement, 1996) (NCES 96-184).

74. M. Patricia Fernandez Kelley and Richard Schauffler, "Divided Fates: Immigrant Children and the New Assimilation," in *The New Second Generation,* ed. Alejandro Portes (New York: Russell Sage Foundation, 1996), 30–53; Maria Eugenia Matute-Bianchi, "Ethnic Identities and Patterns of School Success and Failure Among Mexican-Descent and Japanese-American Students in a California High School: An Ethnographic Analysis," *American Journal of Education* 95, no. 1 (1986): 233–55.

75. Donald J. Veldman and Julie P. Sanford, "The Influence of Class Ability Level on Student Achievement and Classroom Behavior," *American Educational Research Journal* 21, no. 3 (1984): 629–44; Andrew Fuligni, Jacquellynne S. Eccles, and

Bonnie Barber, "The Long Term Effects of Seventh-Grade Ability Grouping in Mathematics," *Journal of Early Adolescence* 15, no. 1 (1995): 58–89.

76. Victor Battistich, Daniel Solomon, Dong-il Kim, Marilyn Watson, and Eric Shaps, "Schools as Communities: Poverty Levels of Student Populations and Students' Attitudes, Motives and Performance, a Multilevel Analysis," *American Education Research Journal* 32, no. 3 (1995): 627–88; Anthony S. Bryk and Yeow Meng Thum, "The Effects of High School Organization on Dropping Out: An Exploratory Investigation," *American Educational Research Journal* 26, no. 3 (1989): 353–83; Valerie E. Lee and Anthony S. Bryk, "A Multilevel Model of the Social Distribution of High School Achievement," *Sociology of Education* 62 (1989): 172–92.

77. Battistich, Solomon, Kim, Watson, and Shaps, "Schools as Communities"; Valerie E. Lee and Julie B. Smith, "Effects of High School Restructuring and Size on Gains in Achievement and Engagement for Early Secondary School Students," *Sociology of Education* 68 (1995): 241–70.

78. Julia B. Smith, Bets Ann Smith, and Anthony S. Bryk, *Setting the Pace: Opportunities to Learn in Chicago's Elementary Schools* (Chicago: Consortium on Chicago School Research, 1998).

79. In 1995, for example, the average school size (student population) of a large central-city school was 686, compared to 500 for schools in large towns and 294 for rural school systems. The average class size of large central-city schools was 19.0, compared to 17.3 for large towns and 15.8 percent for rural areas. United States Department of Education, Office of Educational Research and Improvement, *SASS by State 1993–1994: School and Staffing Survey Selected Results* (Washington, D.C.: Author, 1996) (NCES 96-312).

80. Jargowsky, *Poverty and Place*.

81. Michael Rutter, Barbara Maughan, Peter Mortimore, and Janet Ouston, *Fifteen Thousand Hours: Secondary Schools and Their Effects on Children* (Cambridge, Mass.: Harvard University Press, 1979); Margaret C. Wang, Geneva D. Haertel, and Herbert J. Walberg, "Educational Resilience in Inner Cities," in *Educational Resilience in Inner-City America: Challenges and Prospects*, ed. Margaret C. Wang and Edmund W. Gordon (Hillsdale, N.J.: Lawrence Erlbaum Associates, 1994), 45–72.

82. Olga Reyes, Karen Gillock, and Kimberly Kobus, "A Longitudinal Study of School Adjustment in Urban, Minority Adolescents: Effects of a High School Transition Program," *American Journal of Community Psychology* 22 (1994): 341–69; Roderick, *The Path to Dropping Out*; Edward Seidman et al., "The Impact of School Transitions in Early Adolescence on the Self-system and Perceived Social Context of Poor Urban Youth," *Child Development* 65 (1994): 507–22; R. G. Simmons and D. Blyth, *Moving into Adolescence: The Impact of Pubertal Change and School Context* (Hawthorne, N.Y.: Aldine de Gruyter, 1987); R. G. Simmons, A. Black, and Y. Zhou, "African American versus White Children and the Transition into Junior High School," *American Journal of Education* 99, no. 4 (1991): 481–520.

83. Roderick and Stone, *Changing Standards, Changing Relationships*.

84. Ann Locke Davidson, *Making and Molding Identity in Schools* (Albany, N.Y.: State University of New York Press, 1996).

85. Reginald M. Clark, *Family Life and School Achievement: Why Poor Black Children Succeed or Fail* (Chicago: University of Chicago Press, 1983).

86. Valdes, *Con Respeto*.

87. Luis S. Laosa, "Maternal Teaching Strategies in Chicano Families of Varied

Educational and Socioeconomic Levels," *Child Development* 49 (1978): 1129–35; Laosa and Henderson, "Cognitive Socialization and Competence."
88. Marcelo M. Suarez-Orozco, *Central American Refugees in U.S. High Schools* (Stanford, Cal.: Stanford University Press, 1989); Marcelo M. Suarez-Orozco and Carola E. Suarez-Orozco, *Transformations: Migration, Family Life and Achievement Motivation Among Latino Adolescents* (Stanford, Cal.: Stanford University Press, 1995).
89. Suarez-Orozco and Suarez-Orozco, *Transformations*, 167.
90. Marc Moss and Michael Puma, *Prospects: The Congressionally Mandated Study of Educational Growth and Opportunity: First Year Report on Language Minority and Limited English Proficient Students* (Washington, D.C.: United States Department of Education, 1995); Marcelo M. Suarez-Orozco and Carola E. Suarez-Orozco, "Hispanic Cultural Psychology: Implications for Education Theory and Research," in Phelan and Davidson, *Renegotiating Cultural Diversity in American Schools*, 108–38.
91. Suarez-Orozco, *Central American Refugees in U.S. High Schools*.
92. Moss and Puma, *Prospects*; Laurence Steinberg, Patricia Blinde, and Kenyon S. Chan, "Dropping Out Among Language Minority Youth," *Review of Educational Research* 54 (1984): 113–32; McMillen, *Dropout Rates in the United States*.
93. Moss and Puma, *Prospects*.
94. Ibid.
95. In addition to Cafferty's chapter in this volume, see also Lorriane M. McDonnell and Paul T. Hill, *Newcomers in American Schools: Meeting the Educational Needs of Immigrant Youth* (Santa Monica, Cal.: Rand Corporation, 1993).
96. Moss and Puma, *Prospects*.
97. Characteristics associated with "restructured" high schools include such practices as keeping students in the same homeroom throughout high school, bringing parents into schools as volunteers, using interdisciplinary teaching, and developing smaller schools-within-schools. See Lee and Smith, "Effects of High School Restructuring and Size"; Lee and Bryk, "A Multilevel Model of the Social Distribution of High School Achievement."
98. McDonnell and Hill, *Newcomers in American Schools*; United States Department of Education, *Trends in School District Demographics 1986–1987 to 1990–1991*.
99. McDonnell and Hill, *Newcomers in American Schools*; United States Department of Education, *Trends in School District Demographics 1986–1987 to 1990–1991*.
100. Chicago Panel, *Initiative Status Report*.

Bibliography

Aaron, Henry J., and Charles Schultze, eds. *Setting Domestic Priorities: What Can Government Do?* Washington, D.C.: Brookings Institution, 1992.

Battistich, Victor, Daniel Solomon, Dong-il Kim, Marilyn Watson, and Eric Shaps. "Schools as Communities: Poverty Levels of Student Populations and Students' Attitudes, Motives and Performance, a Multilevel Analysis." *American Education Research Journal* 32, no. 3 (1995): 627–88.

Bean, Frank D., and Marta Tienda. *The Hispanic Population of the United States*. New York: Russell Sage Foundation, 1987.

Berkner, Lutz, Stephanie Cucaro-Alamin, Alexander C. McCormich, and Larry G. Bobbit. *Descriptive Summary of 1989-90 Beginning Postsecondary Students Five Years Later.* Washington, D.C.: United States Department of Education, National Center for Education Statistics, 1996 (NCES 96-155).

Booth, A., and J. Dunn, eds. *Family-School Links: How Do They Affect Educational Outcomes?* Hillsdale, N.J.: Lawrence Erlbaum, 1995.

Bryk, Anthony S., and Mary Erina Driscoll. *The High Schools as Community: Contextual Influences and Consequences for Students and Teachers.* Madison, Wis.: National Center on Effective Secondary Schools, University of Wisconsin–Madison, 1988.

Bryk, Anthony S., Valerie E. Lee, and Peter B. Holland. *Catholic Schools and the Common Good.* Cambridge, Mass.: Harvard University Press, 1993.

Bryk, Anthony S., and Yeow Meng Thum. "The Effects of High School Organization on Dropping Out: An Exploratory Investigation." *American Educational Research Journal* 26, no. 3 (1989): 353–83.

Carter, Thomas, and Michael Chatfield. "Effective Bilingual Schools: Implications for Policy and Practice." *American Journal of Education* 95, no. 1 (1986): 200–31.

Chall, Jeanne S., Vicki A. Jacobs, and Luke E. Baldwin. *The Reading Crisis: Why Poor Children Fall Behind.* Cambridge, Mass.: Harvard University Press, 1990.

Chandler, Katherine, Jerry West, and E. Hausken. *Approaching Kindergarten: A Look at Pre-schoolers in the United States.* Washington, D.C.: United States Department of Education, National Center for Education Statistics, 1995 (NCES 95-280).

Chavez, Leo R., and Rebecca Martinez. "Mexican Immigration in the 1980s and Beyond: Implications for Chicanas/Chicanos." In *Chicanas/Chicanos at the Crossroads: Social, Economic and Political Change*, edited by David Maciel and Isidro Ortiz, 25–51. Tucson, Ariz.: University of Arizona Press, 1996.

The Chicago Panel. *Initiative Status Report: Summer Bridge.* Chicago: Author, 1998.

Chicago Public Schools. *Guidelines for Promotion in the Chicago Public Schools.* Chicago: Author, 1997.

Clark, Reginald M. *Family Life and School Achievement: Why Poor Black Children Succeed or Fail.* Chicago: University of Chicago Press, 1983.

Commission on National Investment in Education, Council for Aid to Education. *Breaking the Social Contract: The Fiscal Crisis in Higher Education.* Washington, D.C.: Rand Corporation, 1997.

Council of Economic Advisors, Executive Office of the President. *Economic Report of the President.* Washington, D.C.: Government Printing Office, 1996.

Curre, Janet, and Duncan Thomas. "Does Head Start Help Hispanic Children?" *Focus* 19, no. 1 (1997): 22–25.

Danzinger, Sheldon, and Peter Gottshalk. *America Unequal.* Cambridge, Mass.: Harvard University Press, 1995.

Darder, Antonia, Rodolfo D. Torres, and Henry Gutierrez, eds. *Latinos and Education: A Critical Reader.* New York: Routledge, 1997.

Davidson, Ann Locke. *Making and Molding Identity in Schools.* Albany, N.Y.: State University of New York Press, 1996.

Delgado-Gaitan, Concha. "Research and Policy in Reconceptualizing Family-School Relationships." In *Renegotiating Cultural Diversity in American Schools*, edited by Patricia Phelan and Ann Locke Davidson, 139–58. New York: Teachers College Press, 1993.

———. "School Matters in the Mexican-American Home: Socializing Children to Education." *American Educational Research Journal* 29, no. 3 (1992): 495–516.

Delgado-Gaitan, Concha, and Manuel Trueba. *Crossing Cultural Borders: Education for Immigrant Families in America.* London: Falmer Press, 1991.

Duncan, Greg J., and Jeanne Brooks-Gunn, eds. *Consequences of Growing Up Poor.* New York: Russell Sage Foundation, 1997.

Eccles, Jacquellynne, and Rena Harold. "Family Involvement in Children's and Adolescents' Schooling." In *Family-School Links: How Do They Affect Educational Outcomes?*, edited by A. Booth and J. Dunn. Hillsdale, N.J.: Lawrence Erlbaum 1995.

Entwistle, Doris S., Karl L. Alexander, and Linda Steffel. *Children, Schools, and Inequality.* Boulder, Colo.: Westview Press, 1997.

Espinosa, Ruben, and Alberto Ochoa, "Concentration of California Hispanic Students in Schools with Low Achievement: A Research Note." *American Journal of Education* 95, no. 1 (1986): 77–95.

Freeman, Richard. "Toward an Apartheid Economy." *Harvard Business Review* (September-October 1996): 114–21.

Fuhrman, Susan H., Richard F. Elmore, and Diane Massell. "School Reform in the United States: Putting It into Context." In *Reforming Education: The Emerging System Approach*, edited by Stephen L. Jacobson and Robert Berne, 3–27. Thousand Oaks, Cal.: Corwin Press, 1993.

Fuligni, Andrew, Jacquellynne S. Eccles, and Bonnie Barber. "The Long Term Effects of Seventh-Grade Ability Grouping in Mathematics." *Journal of Early Adolescence* 15, no. 1 (1995): 58–89.

Goldenberg, Claude, Leslie Reese, and Ronald Gallimore. "Effects of Literacy Materials from School on Latino Children's Home Experiences and Early Reading Achievement." *American Journal of Education* (1992): 497–536.

Graham, Patricia Albjerg. "Assimilation, Adjustment and Access: An Antiquarian View of American Education." In *Learning from the Past: What History Teaches Us About School Reform*, edited by Diane Ravitch and

Maris Vinovskis, 3–24. Baltimore, Md.: Johns Hopkins University Press, 1995.

Grissmer, David W., Sheila Nataraj Kirby, Mark Berends, and Stephanie Williamson. *Student Achievement and the Changing American Family.* Santa Monica, Cal.: Rand Corporation, 1994.

Guzman, Hector R. Cordero. "The Structure of Inequality and the Status of Puerto Rican Youth in the U.S." In *Latinos and Education: A Critical Reader,* edited by Antonia Darder, Rodolfo D. Torres, and Henry Gutierrez, 80–94. New York: Routledge, 1997.

Hansen, Kristin, and Carol S. Faber. *The Foreign Born Population: 1996.* Washington, D.C.: United States Bureau of the Census, 1996 (Current Population Reports Population Characteristics, Special Report Series P20-494).

Henderson, Anne, and Nancy Berla. *A New Generation of Evidence: The Family Is Critical to Student Achievement.* Washington, D.C.: National Committee for Citizens in Education, 1994.

Jacobson, Stephen L., and Robert Berne, eds. *Reforming Education: The Emerging System Approach.* Thousand Oaks, Cal.: Corwin Press, 1993.

Jargowsky, Paul A. *Poverty and Place: Ghettos, Barrios, and the American City.* New York: Russell Sage Foundation, 1997.

Kane, Thomas. "College Entry by Blacks Since 1970: The Role of College Costs, Family Background and the Returns to Education." *Journal of Political Economy* 102, no. 51 (1994): 878–911.

Kane, Thomas, and Cecilia Elena Rouse. "Labor-Market Returns to Two- and Four-Year Colleges." *American Economic Review* 85, no. 3 (1995): 600–14.

Kelley, M. Patricia Fernandez, and Richard Schauffler. "Divided Fates: Immigrant Children and the New Assimilation." In *The New Second Generation,* edited by Alejandro Portes, 30–53. New York: Russell Sage Foundation, 1996.

Laosa, Luis M. "Maternal Teaching Strategies in Chicano Families of Varied Educational and Socioeconomic Levels." *Child Development* 49 (1978): 1129–35.

Laosa, Luis M., and Ronald W. Henderson. "Cognitive Socialization and Competence: The Academic Development of Chicanos." In *Chicano School Failure and Success: Research and Policy Agendas for the 1990s,* edited by Richard R. Valencia. London: Falmer Press, 1991.

Lee, Valerie E., and Anthony S. Bryk. "A Multilevel Model of the Social Distribution of High School Achievement." *Sociology of Education* 62 (1989): 172–92.

Lee, Valerie E., and Julie B. Smith. "Effects of High School Restructuring and Size on Gains in Achievement and Engagement for Early Secondary School Students." *Sociology of Education* 68 (1995): 241–70.

Lee, Valerie E., Julie B. Smith, and Richard G. Croninger. "Another Look at

High School Restructuring." In *Issues in Restructuring Schools*. Madison, Wis.: Center for School Restructuring, University of Wisconsin–Madison, 1995.

———. *Understanding How High School Organization Influences the Equitable Distribution of Learning in Mathematics and Science* (unpublished). Madison, Wis.: Center for School Restructuring, University of Wisconsin–Madison, 1996.

Lippman, Laura, Shelley Burns, and Edith McArthur. *Urban Schools: The Challenge of Location and Poverty*. Washington, D.C.: United States Department of Education, Office of Educational Research and Improvement, 1996 (NCES 96-184).

Lucas, Tamara, Rosemary Henze, and Ruben Donato. "Promoting the Success of Latino Language Minority Students: An Exploratory Study of Six High Schools." In *Latinos and Education: A Critical Reader,* edited by Antonia Darder, Rodolfo D. Torres, and Henry Gutierrez, 373–97. New York: Routledge, 1997.

Maciel, Leo, and Isidro Ortiz, eds. *Chicanas/Chicanos at the Crossroads: Social, Economic and Political Change*. Tucson, Ariz.: University of Arizona Press, 1996.

Massell, Diane, and Susan Fuhrman. *Ten Years of State Education Reform, 1983–1993: Overview with Four Case Studies*. Rutgers, N.J.: Consortium for Policy Research in Education, The State University of New Jersey, 1994.

Matute-Bianchi, Maria Eugenia. "Ethnic Identities and Patterns of School Success and Failure Among Mexican-Descent and Japanese-American Students in a California High School: An Ethnographic Analysis." *American Journal of Education* 95, no. 1 (1986): 233–55.

McDonnell, Lorriane M., and Paul T. Hill. *Newcomers in American Schools: Meeting the Educational Needs of Immigrant Youth*. Santa Monica, Cal.: Rand Corporation, 1993.

McLanahan, Sara S., and Larry Bumpass. "Comment: A Note on the Effect of Family Structure on School Enrollment." In *Minorities, Poverty, and Social Policy,* edited by Gary Sanderfur and Marta Tienda. New York: Plenum Press, 1988.

McMillen, Marilyn (project officer). *Dropout Rates in the United States*. Washington, D.C.: United States Department of Education, National Center for Education Statistics, 1997 (NCES 988-250).

Moss, Marc, and Michael Puma. *Prospects: The Congressionally Mandated Study of Educational Growth and Opportunity: First Year Report on Language Minority and Limited English Proficient Students*. Washington, D.C.: United States Department of Education, 1995.

Murnane, Richard J., and Frank Levy. "Education and Training." In *Setting Domestic Priorities: What Can Government Do?,* edited by Henry J. Aaron and Charles Schultze, 185–223. Washington, D.C.: Brookings Institution, 1992.

National Association of Secondary School Principals. *Breaking Ranks: Changing an American Institution.* Washington, D.C.: Author, 1996.

Newmann, Fred M., ed. *Student Engagement and Achievement in American Secondary Schools.* New York: Teachers College Press 1992.

Newmann, Fred M., Gary G. Wehlage, and Susan D. Lamborn. "The Significance and Sources of Student Engagement." In *Student Engagement and Achievement in American Secondary Schools,* edited by Fred M. Newmann, 11–39. New York: Teachers College Press 1992.

Orfield, Gary, Mark Bachmeier, David R. James, and Tamela Eitle. *Deepening Segregation in American Public Schools.* Cambridge, Mass.: Harvard Project on School Desegregation, 1997.

Ortiz, Vilma. "Reading Activities and Reading Proficiency Among Hispanic, Black and White Students." *American Journal of Education* (1986): 58–76.

Phelan, Patricia, and Ann Locke Davidson, eds. *Renegotiating Cultural Diversity in American Schools.* New York: Teachers College Press, 1993.

Portes, Alejandro, ed. *The New Second Generation.* New York: Russell Sage Foundation, 1996.

Portes, Alejandro, and Ruben Rumbaut. *Immigrant America: A Portrait.* Berkeley, Cal.: University of California Press, 1996.

Ravitch, Diane, and Maris Vinovskis, eds. *Learning from the Past: What History Teaches Us About School Reform.* Baltimore, Md.: Johns Hopkins University Press, 1995.

Reyes, Olga, Karen Gillock, and Kimberly Kobus. "A Longitudinal Study of School Adjustment in Urban, Minority Adolescents: Effects of a High School Transition Program." *American Journal of Community Psychology* 22 (1994): 341–69.

Reynolds, Arthur J., Emily Mann, Wendy Miedel, and Paul Smokowski. "The State of Early Childhood Intervention: Effectiveness, Myths and Realities, New Directions." *Focus* 19, no. 1 (1997): 5–11.

Reynolds, Arthur J., and Barbara Wolfe. "School Achievement, Early Intervention, and Special Education: New Evidence from the Chicago Longitudinal Study." *Focus* 19, no. 1 (1997): 18–21.

Roderick, Melissa. *The Path to Dropping Out: Evidence for Intervention.* Westport, Conn.: Auburn House, 1993.

Roderick, Melissa, and Eric Camburn. "Risk and Recovery from Course Failure in the Early Years of High School." Unpublished, 1997.

Roderick, Melissa, and Susan Stone. *Changing Standards, Changing Relationships: Building Family-School Relationships to Promote Student Achievement in Chicago High Schools.* Chicago: Consortium on Chicago School Research, 1998.

Ruenzel, David. "Avid Learners." *Education Week,* February 5, 1997. Internet posting.

Rumberger, Russell. "Dropping Out of High School: The Influence of Race,

Sex and Family Background." *American Educational Research Journal* 20, no. 2 (1983): 199–220.

———. "Dropping Out of Middle School: A Multilevel Analysis of Students and Schools." *American Educational Research Journal*. 32, no. 3 (1995): 583–626.

Rumberger, Russell, Rita Ghatak, Gary Poulus, Philip L. Ritter, and Sanford M. Dornbusch. "Family Influences on Dropout Behavior in One California High School." *Sociology of Education* 63 (October 1990): 283–99.

Rutter, Michael, Barbara Maughan, Peter Mortimore, and Janet Ouston. *Fifteen Thousand Hours: Secondary Schools and Their Effects on Children.* Cambridge, Mass.: Harvard University Press, 1979.

Sanderfur, Gary D., Sara McLanahan, and Roger A. Wojtkeiwicz. "Race and Ethnicity, Family Structure and High School Graduation." Madison, Wis.: Institute for Research on Poverty, 1989 (Discussion Paper no. 893-89).

Sanderfur, Gary D., and Marta Tienda, eds. *Minorities, Poverty, and Social Policy.* New York: Plenum Press, 1988.

Sebring, Penny, Anthony S. Bryk, and John Q. Easton. *Charting Reform in Chicago: Chicago Teachers Take Stock.* Chicago: Consortium on Chicago School Research, University of Chicago, 1996.

Sebring, Penny, Anthony S. Bryk, Melissa Roderick, and Eric Camburn. *Charting Reform in Chicago: The Students Speak.* Chicago: Consortium on Chicago School Research, The University of Chicago, 1996.

Seidman, Edward, A. LaRue, L. J. Aber, C. Mitchell, and J. Feinman, "The Impact of School Transitions in Early Adolescence on the Self-system and Perceived Social Context of Poor Urban Youth," *Child Development* 65 (1994): 507–22.

Shepard, Laurie A., and Mary L. Smith. "Escalating Academic Demands in Kindergarten: Counterproductive Policies." *Elementary School Journal* 44 (1988): 78–86.

———. "Synthesis of Research on School Readiness and Kindergarten Retention." *Educational Leadership* 44 (1986): 78–86.

Simmons, R. G., A. Black, and Y. Zhou. "African American versus White Children and the Transition into Junior High School." *American Journal of Education* 99, no. 4 (1991): 481–520.

Simmons, R. G., and D. Blyth. *Moving into Adolescence: The Impact of Pubertal Change and School Context.* Hawthorne, N.Y.: Aldine de Gruyter, 1987.

Smith, Judith R., Jeanne Brooks-Gunn, and Pamela Klebanov. "Consequences of Living in Poverty for Young Children's Cognitive and Verbal Ability and Early School Achievement." In *Consequences of Growing Up Poor*, edited by Greg J. Duncan and Jeanne Brooks-Gunn. New York: Russell Sage Foundation, 1997.

Smith, Julia B., Bets Ann Smith, and Anthony S. Bryk. *Setting the Pace: Opportunities to Learn in Chicago's Elementary Schools.* Chicago: Consortium on Chicago School Research, 1998.

Smith, Marshall, and Jennifer O'Day. "Systemic School Reform." In *Politics of Education Association Yearbook* 233–67. New York: Taylor and Francis, 1990.

Smith, Mary, and Laurie Shepard. "What Doesn't Work: Explaining Policies of Retention in the Early Grades." *Phi Delta Kappan* 69, no. 2 (1987): 129–34.

Steinberg, Laurence, Patricia Blinde, and Kenyon S. Chan. "Dropping Out Among Language Minority Youth." *Review of Educational Research* 54 (1984): 113–32.

Steinberg, Laurence, Susie Lamborn, Stanford Dornbusch, and Nancy Darling. "Impact of Parenting Practices on Adolescent Achievement: Authoritative Parenting, School Involvement, and Encouragement to Succeed." *Child Development* 63 (1992): 1266–81.

Stevenson, Harold W., Chuansheng Chen, and David Uttal. "Beliefs and Achievement: A Study of Black, White and Hispanic Children." *Child Development* 61 (1990): 508–23.

Suarez-Orozco, Marcelo M. *Central American Refugees in U.S. High Schools.* Stanford, Cal.: Stanford University Press, 1989.

Suarez-Orozco, Marcelo M., and Carola E. Suarez-Orozco. "Hispanic Cultural Psychology: Implications for Education Theory and Research." In *Renegotiating Cultural Diversity in American Schools,* edited by Patricia Phelan and Ann Locke Davidson, 108–38. New York: Teachers College Press, 1993.

———. *Transformations: Migration, Family Life and Achievement Motivation Among Latino Adolescents.* Stanford, Cal.: Stanford University Press, 1995.

Tyak, David B. *The One Best System: A History of American Urban Education.* Cambridge, Mass.: Harvard University Press, 1974.

United States Department of the Census. *The Hispanic Population in the United States: March 1993.* Washington, D.C.: Government Printing Office, 1994 (Current Population Report P-20, No. 475).

———. *Poverty in the University States: 1996.* Washington, D.C.: Government Printing Office, 1997 (Current Population Reports P-60-198).

United States Department of Education, National Center for Education Statistics. *Condition of Education: Supplemental and Standard Error Tables, 1996.* Washington, D.C.: Author, 1997 (NCES 97-998).

———. *The Educational Progress of Hispanic Students.* Washington, D.C.: Author, 1995 (NCES 95-767).

———. *Minority Undergraduate Participation in Postsecondary Education.* Washington, D.C.: Author, 1995 (NCES 95-166).

———. *NAEP 1994 Trends in Academic Progress.* Washington, D.C.: 1997 (NCES Report 97-095).

———. *Report in Brief: NAEP 1994 Trends in Academic Progress.* Washington, D.C.: Author, 1996.

———. *Trends in School District Demographics 1986–1987 to 1990–1991.* Washington, D.C.: Author, 1996 (NCES 96-399).

United States Department of Education, Office of Educational Research and Improvement. *Digest of Education Statistics, 1996.* Washington, D.C.: Author, 1996.

———. *The Educational Progress of Black Students: Findings from the Condition of Education 1994.* Washington, D.C.: Author, 1995. (NCES 95-765).

———. *120 Years of American Education: A Statistical Portrait.* Washington, D.C.: Author, 1993 (NCES 93-442).

———. *Projections of Education Statistics to the Year 2000.* Washington, D.C.: Author, 1997.

———. *SASS by State 1993-1994: School and Staffing Survey Selected Results.* Washington, D.C.: Author, 1996 (NCES 96-312).

Valdes, Guadalupe. *Con Respeto: Bridging the Distances Between Culturally Diverse Families and Schools: An Ethnographic Portrait.* New York: New York Teachers College Press, 1996.

Valencia, Richard R., ed. *Chicano School Failure and Success: Research and Policy Agendas for the 1990s.* London: Falmer Press, 1991.

Veldman, Donald J., and Julie P. Sanford. "The Influence of Class Ability Level on Student Achievement and Classroom Behavior." *American Educational Research Journal* 21, no. 3 (1984): 629–44.

Vinovskis, Maris. *Education Society and Economic Opportunity: A Historical Perspective on Persistent Issues.* New Haven, Conn.: Yale University Press, 1995.

Wang, Margaret C., Geneva D. Haertel, and Herbert J. Walberg. "Educational Resilience in Inner Cities." In *Educational Resilience in Inner-City America: Challenges and Prospects*, edited by Margaret C. Wang and Edmund W. Gordon, 45–72 (Hillsdale, N.J.: Lawrence Erlbaum Associates, 1994).

Wang, Margaret C., and Edmund W. Gordon, eds. *Educational Resilience in Inner-City America: Challenges and Prospects.* Hillsdale, N.J.: Lawrence Erlbaum Associates, 1994.

Wilson, William Julius. *When Work Disappears: The World of the New Urban Poor.* New York: Alfred A. Knopf, 1997.

6

Hispanics and the American Labor Market

Barry R. Chiswick and Michael E. Hurst

Introduction

This chapter presents a statistical portrait of Hispanics in the American labor market. The very rapid increase in the Hispanic population of the United States in recent decades has been due, in large part, to the large and increasing Hispanic immigration.[1] The different circumstances that immigrants experience in the United States compared to persons born in this country require that a study of Hispanics in the U.S. labor market consider differences by nativity. In addition, it is important to recognize that Hispanics are not necessarily a homogeneous group. Although Hispanics have a common linguistic origin or region of origin, the major groups of Hispanics are quite different in many important characteristics, including how they came to live in the United States, where they live, their fertility rates, and so on. This chapter evaluates differences in the characteristics of Hispanics that are relevant for the labor market.

The four groups of Hispanics identified in this chapter are Mexicans, Cubans, Puerto Ricans, and Other Hispanics. The "Other Hispanics" are primarily from Spanish-speaking Central and South America and other parts of the Caribbean area. Although persons born in Puerto Rico are citizens of the United States and thus are technically not foreign born, they are born into a linguistic and cultural environment that is closer to that of Hispanic immigrants than it is to that of Hispanics born on the mainland. Purely for the purpose of simplicity of exposition, persons born in Puerto Rico are referred to as foreign born throughout this study.

The most recent, reliable, large data set that permits an analysis of Hispanics in the American labor market is the 1990 Census of Population. Hispanics are identified in the 1990 census by the question on Hispanic ancestry, which asks whether the person is of Mexican, Cuban, Puerto Rican, other Spanish origin, or not of any Spanish origin. The data from the 5 percent sample of Hispanics in the United States (i.e., a 1-in-20 sample) are combined with data from a 0.5 percent sample (i.e., a 1-in-200 sample) of all non-Hispanics to provide the Hispanic/non-Hispanic comparison.[2] These provide very large samples for the statistical analysis.

Because of the focus on the labor market, this analysis is limited primarily to persons aged 25 to 64 years, and the data are differentiated by gender. The age restriction is introduced to exclude the aged, most of whom have retired from the labor market; and the young, who are still making investments in schooling and the early years of on-the-job training. An analysis of the youth labor market would require a separate investigation.

In spite of the dramatic change in gender roles in the United States in the post-World War II period, the genders have not attained full equality in activities. There is still a specialization of function in the household; that is, women are still more likely than men to withdraw from the labor force, either in whole or in part, to care for young children. Although many women return as the children grow older, others do not. For this reason, it is important that the analysis differentiate between men and women.

Thus, this chapter examines various characteristics of adults (aged 25 to 64) in the United States that influence or describe their labor market activities. These characteristics include schooling, English language proficiency, labor force participation, occupational attainment, and earnings, among other characteristics. Furthermore, the analyses permit an identification of differences between Hispanics and non-Hispanics, by nativity, gender, and type of Hispanic origin.

Educational Attainment

Educational attainment has been shown to be an important determinant of labor market status or success, whether measured by labor force participation, occupational attainment, earnings, or unemployment. The educational attainment adult Hispanics have obtained is much lower than that of non-Hispanics, both among men and women, and among the native born and foreign born (table 6.1).

Table 6.1
Educational Attainment of Hispanics and Non-Hispanics,
by Gender and Nativity, Aged 25–64 (1990)

Group	Mean Schooling (years)		Percent with			
			8 or fewer years		16 or more years	
	Male	Female	Male	Female	Male	Female
Hispanic	10.6	10.6	27.3	26.8	10.2	9.0
Native-born	12.1	11.9	11.1	11.8	12.1	10.4
Foreign-born[a]	9.5	9.6	38.7	38.3	8.8	7.9
Non-Hispanic	13.3	13.1	5.3	4.2	26.3	21.3
Native-born	13.3	13.1	4.9	3.6	25.4	20.9
Foreign-born	13.6	12.6	9.8	12.4	38.7	26.5
Mexican	10.1	10.9	33.3	32.0	7.2	6.3
Native-born	12.1	12.3	13.1	14.1	10.3	8.6
Foreign-born	8.0	8.5	54.1	55.5	4.0	3.4
Cuban	12.3	12.6	19.7	18.9	19.7	17.8
Native-born	14.0	14.0	3.7	2.8	29.2	28.1
Foreign-born	12.1	12.3	22.1	21.1	18.3	16.4
Puerto Rican	11.7	12.3	19.1	19.8	9.3	9.8
Native-born	12.8	13.2	5.6	4.5	12.2	13.1
Foreign-born[a]	11.0	11.7	26.4	27.5	7.7	8.2
Other Hispanic	11.8	11.7	19.4	21.6	15.4	12.2
Native-born	13.0	13.1	7.4	7.6	17.9	15.0
Foreign-born	11.3	11.1	24.1	26.9	14.4	11.1

[a] Includes persons born in Puerto Rico.

Source: 1990 Census of Population, Public Use Sample, 5 percent sample of the Hispanic population, and an 0.5 percent sample of the non-Hispanic population.

Among persons aged 25 to 64 years in 1990, Hispanics have an average level of schooling of 10.6 years for both men and women, in contrast to just about 13.2 years for non-Hispanics. The lower educational attainment is a characteristic of Hispanics born in the United States as well as foreign-born Hispanics. The educational deficiency of 1.2 years among the native born is, however, smaller than the deficiency among the foreign born (a gap of about 4.0 years for Hispanic men and 3.0 years for Hispanic women).

Hispanics are far from homogeneous in educational attainment even within nativity and gender categories. Immigrant men of Mexican origin have only 8.0 years of schooling. At the other extreme, men of Cuban origin born in the United States have 14 years of schooling, in part because most of them are young adults and completed schooling levels are higher among younger age cohorts. Overall, and within nativity groups, Cubans have the highest level of schooling, followed by Puerto Ricans and Other Hispanics with similar levels of schooling; those of Mexican origin clearly show the lowest educational attainment.

What is particularly striking is the difference in the proportions of those aged 25 to 64 years with very low levels and very high levels of schooling. Nearly 40 percent of foreign-born Hispanics have 8 or fewer years of schooling, in contrast to about 11 percent among foreign-born non-Hispanics. Even among the native born, about 11.5 percent of Hispanics have 8 or fewer years of schooling, in contrast to the 4.3 percent among non-Hispanics. Immigrants from Mexico show the lowest educational attainment, with 55 percent having 8 or fewer years of schooling. At the other extreme are persons of Cuban origin born in the United States, with only 3 percent having 8 or fewer years of schooling.

Those with 16 or more years of schooling are at the other end of the educational spectrum. About 10 percent of Hispanics have 16 or more years of schooling, with little difference by nativity. In contrast, nearly one-quarter of non-Hispanics and nearly 4 in 10 non-Hispanic foreign-born men have 16 or more years of schooling. Again, there is considerable heterogeneity among Hispanics. Only 4 percent of men and women born in Mexico have 16 or more years of schooling, though this is the case for nearly 30 percent of U.S.-born men and women of Cuban origin.

These data on educational attainment indicate a much lower level of schooling among Hispanics, especially among the foreign born. The educational gap is smaller among the native born, but it is still substantial. The gap in effective schooling may be greater than is suggested by the measure of years of schooling if, as is plausible, Hispanics received a lower quality of schooling than did the non-Hispanic population. Yet there is much heterogeneity among Hispanics, with Cubans, whether native or foreign born, having the highest level of schooling; and Mexicans, whether native or foreign born, having the lowest educational attainment.

English Language Proficiency

Another important determinant of labor market outcomes in the United States is the extent of proficiency in English. The 1990 census asked all persons aged five and over if they spoke a language other than or in addition to English at home. If they indicated another language, they were asked to identify that language and to report their speaking level in English as either "Very Well," "Well," "Not Well" (poor), or "Not at all" (only a few words). Table 6.2 reports the proportion of persons aged 25 to 64 who reported speaking only English or, if they speak another language at home, who speak English very well or have a lower level of proficiency.

Among native-born Hispanic men, English language proficiency is widespread, although not nearly as universal as it is among native-born non-Hispanic men (table 6.2). Among the native born, 84 percent of the Hispanics speak only English or, if they speak another language at home (nearly always Spanish), they report that they speak English very well. Among non-Hispanics, the comparable proportion is 99 percent speaking only English or speaking it very well, of whom all but 3 percent speak only English at home.

Not surprisingly, it is among immigrants that English language deficiencies are most dramatic. Only 5 percent of foreign-born Hispanic men speak only English at home, compared to 37 percent for native-born Hispanic men and 30 percent for foreign-born non-Hispanic men. About 65 percent of Hispanics do not consider themselves able to speak English very well, compared to 16 percent of native-born Hispanics and 35 percent of foreign-born non-Hispanics.

Table 6.2 shows that, on average, there is little difference between men and women in English language proficiency. Although native-born Hispanic women are about 2.5 percentage points less likely to speak only English at home than native-born Hispanic men, they are about 2.5 percentage points more likely to report that although they speak Spanish at home they speak English very well.

Table 6.2
English Language Proficiency of Hispanics and Non-Hispanics, by Gender and Nativity, Aged 25–64 (1990)
(percent)

Group	Males			Females		
	Speaks Only English	Speaks English Very Well[a]	Limited English[b]	Speaks Only English	Speaks English Very Well[a]	Limited English[b]
Hispanic	18.5	36.9	44.6	18.0	37.7	44.3
Native-born	37.4	46.7	15.9	34.9	49.3	15.8
Foreign-born[c]	5.2	30.1	64.7	5.1	28.8	66.1
Non-Hispanic	92.0	4.9	3.1	91.9	4.8	3.3
Native-born	96.5	2.7	0.8	96.6	2.6	0.8
Foreign-born	29.4	35.4	35.2	30.7	33.5	35.8
Mexican	19.2	36.2	44.6	19.8	38.5	41.7
Native-born	33.8	48.7	17.5	31.4	51.0	17.6
Foreign-born	4.1	23.3	72.6	4.6	21.8	73.6
Cuban	11.1	41.2	47.7	9.2	39.9	50.9
Native-born	44.1	48.7	7.2	41.8	51.9	6.3
Foreign-born	6.1	40.2	53.7	4.6	38.2	57.2
Puerto Rican	15.4	48.0	36.6	12.1	47.7	40.2
Native-born	31.8	55.0	13.2	25.4	60.6	14.0
Foreign-born[c]	6.6	44.2	49.2	5.4	41.4	53.2
Other Hispanic	20.0	31.8	48.2	19.2	30.4	50.4
Native-born	55.5	32.8	11.7	55.3	34.4	10.3
Foreign-born	6.1	31.4	62.5	5.6	28.9	65.5

[a] Speaks a language other than English at home and speaks English very well.
[b] Speaks a language other than English at home and speaks English well, not well, or not at all.
[c] Includes persons born in Puerto Rico.

Note: Row totals for each gender may not add to 100.0 due to rounding.
Source: 1990 Census of Population, Public Use Sample, 5 percent sample of the Hispanic population, and a 0.5 percent sample of the non-Hispanic population.

As with education, Hispanics are not a homogeneous group in terms of English language proficiency. Among native-born Hispanic men and women, Mexicans have the lowest percentage who speak only English or speak English very well: about 83 percent, compared to about 87 percent for Puerto Ricans and Other Hispanics, and about 93 percent for Cubans. This differential is even more dramatic among foreign-born Hispanics: only 4 percent of Mexican immigrants speak only English, compared to 6 to 7 percent for the other foreign-born Hispanic groups. Similarly, about half of those born in Puerto Rico and Cuba speak only English or speak English very well, compared to about a fourth of those born in Mexico.

The much lower proficiency in English among foreign-born Hispanics contributes to the gap in earnings with non-Hispanics and with native-born Hispanics, as is discussed in later in this chapter. The less-than-total English proficiency among native-born Hispanics contributes to their lower earnings as well.

Labor Force Participation

The *labor force* is defined as consisting of noninstitutionalized persons aged 16 and over who are employed or unemployed. The employed include those who work for pay (wages, salaries, and commissions) or for profit (the self-employed) and a numerically trivial group in the United States, unpaid workers in a family business. The unemployed include those who do not have a job but have engaged in a job search in the past four weeks and those with a job who are on a temporary job layoff. The labor force participation rate is the labor force as a percent of the relevant noninstitutionalized population.

Data from the 1990 census indicate that the labor force participation rate of adult (aged 25–64) Hispanics differs from that of the non-Hispanic population (table 6.3). Among men, the participation rate of Hispanics is 85 percent, not very different from the 86 percent among non-Hispanics. Among women, in contrast, the participation rate is 62 percent among Hispanics, compared to 70 percent among non-Hispanics.

By nativity, immigrant men have a higher participation rate than native-born Hispanic men, but the reverse is true among women. The higher labor force participation rate among Hispanic immigrant men appears to be due, in part, to the concentration in prime age groups (ages 25–45 years), but also in part because seeking employment in the

Table 6.3
Labor Force Participation Rates Among Hispanics and Non-Hispanics,
by Gender and Nativity, Aged 16–64 (1990)
(percent)

Group	Age 16–24		Age 25–64	
	Male	Female	Male	Female
Hispanic	68.8	54.8	84.6	62.2
Native-born	75.1	56.5	82.3	66.6
Foreign-born[a]	63.0	52.4	86.2	58.8
Non-Hispanic	65.4	62.9	86.2	69.9
Native-born	66.1	63.5	86.1	70.2
Foreign-born	52.5	51.6	87.6	66.1
Mexican	71.9	54.3	86.1	61.1
Native-born	64.8	56.2	83.2	66.2
Foreign-born	79.8	51.1	89.2	54.4
Cuban	66.7	66.6	85.2	69.3
Native-born	59.5	67.3	83.9	76.0
Foreign-born	75.9	65.6	85.4	68.4
Puerto Rican	59.7	50.3	75.7	54.3
Native-born	58.9	52.1	78.7	64.2
Foreign-born[a]	61.1	46.4	74.2	49.3
Other Hispanic	64.9	57.4	85.3	67.2
Native-born	60.0	59.9	80.6	69.1
Foreign-born	68.2	55.4	87.2	66.5

[a] Includes persons born in Puerto Rico.

Source: 1990 Census of Population, Public Use Sample, 5 percent sample of the Hispanic population, and a 0.5 percent sample of the non-Hispanic population.

United States is a primary motive for immigrating. Among the women, lower participation rates are in part due to higher fertility (i.e., more children tend to depress female labor supply), but may also reflect a tendency toward lower Hispanic female labor supply, other things being the same. This appears to be a characteristic of those of Mexican and Puerto Rican origins, in contrast to women of Cuban origin, who experience a labor force participation rate roughly comparable to that of non-Hispanic women.

Among younger persons (aged 16–24), Hispanic males are more likely to be in the labor force, 69 percent compared to 65 percent, with a very high participation rate (75 percent) for native-born Hispanic males. These higher labor force participation rates among young Hispanic males, compared to young non-Hispanics, are due to Hispanics' much lower rate of enrollment in high school and college.

The lowest participation rates are experienced by young Hispanic women, 55 percent (52 percent among the foreign born) compared to 63 percent for non-Hispanic women. This arises in spite of a low school enrollment rate. Rather, it is due to early age at first marriage, high youth fertility rates, and a lower propensity to work among mothers of Mexican and Puerto Rican origin than among other mothers, other things being the same.

Occupational Distribution

The occupational attainment of members of the labor force is determined, in part, by a series of demographic and skill characteristics. These include schooling level, past labor market experience, English language proficiency, nativity, duration of U.S. residency among the foreign born, gender, and other factors. The analysis of occupational attainment is reported only for men, in part because of the difficulty of interpreting occupational attainment for women with high rates of mobility in and out of the labor market. Furthermore, for simplicity of exposition, the myriad of occupations are collapsed into three broad groups: High Skilled (professional, technical, and managerial occupations); Middle Skilled (craft, clerical, and sales); and Low Skilled (service, operative, and laborer occupations). The frequency distributions of the occupations are reported in table 6.4.

The occupational distribution of Hispanic men differs sharply from that of non-Hispanic men, even within nativity categories. Among the non-Hispanic native born, somewhat more than one-third are in the high-skilled and middle-level occupations, and less than one-third are in the low-skilled jobs. Among native-born Hispanics, about one-quarter are in high-skilled occupations and nearly 4 in 10 are in the low-skilled category. Reflecting the group differences in schooling, the native born of Cuban origin have the highest occupational attainment (nearly 40 percent in high-skilled jobs) and the native born of Mexican origin have the lowest proportion in high-skilled jobs (23 percent). The Cubans have the smallest proportion in the lowest skilled occupations, in contrast to those of Mexican origin.

Table 6.4
Occupational Distribution Among Hispanic and Non-Hispanic Males,
by Nativity, Aged 25–64 (1990)
(percent)

| Group | Occupations[a] | | |
	High Skilled	Middle Skilled	Low Skilled
Hispanic	20.1	32.5	47.5
Native-born	24.9	35.9	39.2
Foreign-born[b]	16.7	30.0	53.3
Non-Hispanic	35.0	35.3	29.7
Native-born	34.6	35.5	29.9
Foreign-born	41.7	32.4	25.9
Mexican	16.3	32.0	51.7
Native-born	22.9	36.1	41.0
Foreign-born	9.7	27.7	62.6
Cuban	29.6	37.5	33.0
Native-born	37.9	36.2	25.9
Foreign-born	28.5	37.6	33.9
Puerto Rican	26.7	30.0	43.3
Native-born	28.1	34.7	37.2
Foreign-born[b]	26.0	27.5	46.5
Other Hispanic	23.9	33.6	42.5
Native-born	30.6	35.7	33.8
Foreign-born	21.2	32.8	46.0

[a] High Skilled includes professional, technical, and managerial occupations. Middle Skilled includes craft, clerical, and sales. Low Skilled includes service, operative, and laborer occupations.

[b] Includes persons born in Puerto Rico.

Note: Row totals may not add up to 100.0 due to rounding.

Source: 1990 Census of Population, Public Use Sample, 5 percent sample of the Hispanic population, and a 0.5 percent sample of the non-Hispanic population.

The differences among groups are even greater among the foreign born. More than 40 percent of foreign-born non-Hispanic men are in the highest occupational category, a proportion even greater than among the native born (35 percent). However, among the foreign-born Hispanic men, only 17 percent are in the high-skilled category. Whereas only one-quarter of non-Hispanic foreign-born men are in low-skilled jobs, this is the occupational category for more than half of the foreign-born Hispanic men.

Even among the foreign born, there are sharp differences in occupational attainment by type of Hispanic origin. Nearly one in three Cubans are in high-skilled jobs, compared to one in ten of Mexican origin. Whereas only one-third of Cuban immigrants are in low-skilled jobs, nearly two-thirds of Mexican immigrants are in these categories.

In summary, Hispanic men are in lower skilled occupations than non-Hispanic men, and the differences are larger among the foreign born than among the native born. There are particularly sharp differences in occupational attainment among Hispanic groups, with those of Cuban origin in more highly skilled occupations and those of Mexican origin more likely to be in the lowest skilled occupations.

Industrial Distribution

Another dimension of labor market activities is distribution by industry. Industry categories cut across skill levels. The agricultural sector includes unskilled fruit and vegetable pickers as well as highly educated veterinarians; the service sector includes carwash attendants and lawyers; manufacturing includes unskilled assembly-line workers and highly educated engineers. Nevertheless, industry categories indicate where people are working, and the relative proportions employed in industries change over the course of time. Agriculture (particularly farming) and manufacturing have been declining sectors in recent decades, with services the fastest growing industrial sector.

Overall, the distribution by industry of Hispanic men does not differ sharply from that of non-Hispanic men (table 6.5). Hispanics are, however, more likely to be in the agricultural sector (which includes farming and landscaping), 13 percent compared to 8 percent, and are more likely to be in construction and trade. Hispanics are less likely to be in the public administration, transportation, and service industries.

The differences in industrial distribution are greater by nativity within Hispanic and non-Hispanic groups than they are between Hispanics

Table 6.5
Industrial Distribution Among Hispanic and Non-Hispanic Males,
by Nativity, Aged 25–64 (1990)[a]
(percent)

Group	Agriculture	Construction	Manufacturing	Transportation	Trade	Service	Public Administration
Hispanic	12.7	13.2	20.9	7.9	18.3	22.0	5.2
Native-born	10.0	13.4	17.6	10.3	16.8	23.2	8.8
Foreign-born[b]	14.7	13.0	23.2	6.1	19.3	21.1	2.6
Non-Hispanic	8.2	11.8	21.6	9.6	16.2	25.8	6.9
Native-born	8.3	12.0	21.6	9.8	15.9	25.4	7.1
Foreign-born	6.9	8.5	20.5	7.1	20.5	32.5	4.0
Mexican	15.0	14.9	21.7	7.3	17.9	18.3	4.9
Native-born	10.3	14.2	18.5	10.2	16.9	21.4	8.5
Foreign-born	19.8	15.7	25.0	4.3	18.9	15.1	1.3
Cuban	7.4	10.8	16.3	9.6	21.7	29.9	4.4
Native-born	5.9	8.5	10.8	9.4	18.7	37.1	9.6
Foreign-born	7.6	11.1	17.1	9.6	22.1	28.9	3.7
Puerto Rican	13.1	6.9	21.1	9.3	15.3	26.1	8.1
Native-born	9.1	8.0	23.9	10.8	16.4	29.2	10.8
Foreign-born[b]	15.3	6.4	15.8	8.4	14.8	24.5	6.7

Other Hispanic	8.4	12.4	19.7	8.1	20.0	27.3	4.5
Native-born	9.4	13.6	15.2	10.4	16.5	26.1	8.9
Foreign-born	7.5	11.9	21.5	7.2	21.3	27.8	2.8

[a] Among the industries:

1) Agriculture includes agricultural services, landscaping, forestry, and fishing.
2) Construction includes mining.
3) Manufacturing includes durables and nondurables.
4) Transportation includes communication and utilities.
5) Trade includes retail and wholesale trade.
6) Services includes finance, insurance, and real estate (FIRE).
7) Public Administration includes civilian government employment and the military.

[b] Includes persons born in Puerto Rico.

Note: Row totals may not add to 100.0 due to rounding.

Source: 1990 Census of Population, Public Use Sample, 5 percent sample of the Hispanic population, and an 0.5 percent sample of the non-Hispanic population.

and non-Hispanics as a whole. Among Hispanic foreign-born men, nearly 15 percent are in agricultural industries, in contrast to only 7 percent of foreign-born non-Hispanic men or even 10 percent of native-born Hispanic men. The proportion of Hispanics in agriculture is greatest among men born in Mexico, of whom 1 in 5 (20 percent) is in the agricultural sector (including landscaping).

At the other extreme is the very low representation of foreign-born Hispanic men in public administration, which includes the government (federal, state, and local levels) and military sectors. Only 2.6 percent of foreign-born Hispanic men are in public administration, in contrast to 7 percent of non-Hispanic men. It is not Hispanic ethnicity per se that results in the low proportion in public administration. Among native-born Hispanics, who are U.S. citizens by birth and have a high degree of English language proficiency, 9 percent are in public administration, 2 percentage points greater than among native-born non-Hispanics. Moreover, among Hispanics born in Puerto Rico, and who therefore are U.S. citizens by birth, 7 percent are employed in public administration. Thus, the low representation of Hispanics in public administration appears to be due to the lower proportion who are U.S. citizens and the lower proportion fluent in English.

Overall, Hispanic men are somewhat underrepresented in the service industries, the fastest growing industrial sector, 22 percent compared to 26 percent. Yet this overall statistic masks sharp differences among Hispanics by origin. About 29 percent of Cuban immigrants and 37 percent of native-born men of Cuban origin are in the service industries. At the other extreme are men of Mexican origin, of whom 18 percent are in the service sector; only 15 percent of foreign-born Mexican-origin men are in services.

In summary, whereas Hispanic men have a greater tendency overall to be in certain industries (particularly agriculture) and a lower propensity to be in others (public administration and services) compared to non-Hispanic men, the differences are small. Larger differences appear among Hispanics by nativity and type of Hispanic origin. Foreign-born men of Mexican origin have a very high representation in agriculture and a very low proportion in public administration. Native-born Cubans and Puerto Ricans have a low proportion in agriculture and a high proportion in public administration. More important than ethnicity for explaining the industrial distribution of Hispanics are U.S. citizenship status and English language skills.

Earnings

Overall, Hispanic men have been shown to have lower levels of education and English language proficiency, to be more strongly represented in lower-skilled occupations, and to be more likely to work in the agricultural industry. These factors are associated with lower earnings. They would result in lower earnings on average for Hispanics compared to non-Hispanics, and lower earnings for immigrant Hispanics than for native-born Hispanics. Table 6.6 reports the earnings of adult (aged 25–64) men who worked in 1989. *Earnings* are defined as the sum of wage and salary income and net income from farm and nonfarm self-employment.

Hispanic men earned about $21,100 in 1989 on average, compared to $31,800 for non-Hispanic men, a gap of about 34 percent. The gap in earnings is somewhat smaller (25 percent) between native-born Hispanics and non-Hispanics. Native-born Hispanics earned about $4,700 more ($23,800) than foreign-born Hispanics, whereas native-born non-Hispanics actually earned about $400 less in 1989 than foreign-born non-Hispanics ($32,200). The low earnings of Hispanic immigrants thus tend to depress the average for Hispanics as a whole.

Length of time in the United States has been shown to be an important determinant of the earnings of foreign-born men. Over time, immigrants acquire greater proficiency in English, get more labor-market-specific and firm-specific education and training, work more weeks in the year, and move into higher-skilled occupations. Thus, foreign-born Hispanic men who had been in the United States for 5 or fewer years earned only about $13,200 in 1989, whereas those who had been in the United States between 15 and 20 years earned about $20,300. The latter earnings are substantially less than for non-Hispanics, but it is only about 15 percent less than among native-born Hispanics.

Among native-born Hispanics, earnings are not dramatically different by origin, with only about $2,000 separating Mexicans, Puerto Ricans, and Other Hispanics. Native-born men of Cuban origin, however, earned about 24 percent more ($29,500) than the average of other native-born Hispanics.

For foreign-born Hispanics, the differences in earnings are larger. Foreign-born Mexican men earned only about $16,000, and those who arrived since 1985 averaged only $11,000 in 1989. In contrast, Puerto Rican and Other Hispanic immigrants earned a little more than $21,000,

Table 6.6
Earnings Among Hispanic and Non-Hispanic Males,
by Nativity, Aged 25–64 (1990)[a]
(dollars)

| Group | All | Foreign-born | |
		Immigrated 1985-1990	Immigrated 1970-1974
Hispanic	21,089	—	—
Native-born	23,846	—	—
Foreign-born[b]	19,162	13,208	20,269
Non-Hispanic	31,825	—	—
Native-born	31,798	—	—
Foreign-born	32,215	23,844	34,541
Mexican	19,646	—	—
Native-born	23,267	—	—
Foreign-born	15,994	10,959	17,906
Cuban	27,666	—	—
Native-born	29,459	—	—
Foreign-born	27,396	16,436	23,561
Puerto Rican	22,541	—	—
Native-born	24,325	—	—
Foreign-born[b]	21,507	16,577	19,068
Other Hispanic	22,347	—	—
Native-born	25,443	—	—
Foreign-born	21,148	15,139	25,140

[a] Earnings include the wage, salary, and self-empolyment income of the respondent.

[b] Includes persons born in Puerto Rico.

Source: 1990 Census of Population, Public Use Sample, 5 percent sample of the Hispanic population, and a 0.5 percent sample of the non-Hispanic population.

whereas Cuban immigrants earned about $27,400, fully 71 percent more than Mexican immigrants.

The fastest earnings growth with duration in the United States seems to be with Other Hispanics, with earnings of $15,100 for recent immigrants, compared to $25,100 for those who had been in the United States for 15 to 20 years. The slowest growth appears to be for Puerto Ricans, with only about $2,500 separating the earnings of recent and longer-term immigrants.

The overall difference in earnings in 1989 between Hispanic men and non-Hispanic men was very large, about 34 percent lower earnings for Hispanic men. This is due, in part, to the very low earnings of Hispanic immigrants. Native-born Hispanic men earned about 25 percent less than non-Hispanics, whereas foreign-born Hispanic men earned about 40 percent less than foreign-born non-Hispanic men.

The differences in the skills that men bring to the labor market are important determinants of their earnings. Each additional year of schooling, for example, raises earnings by about 5 percent among Hispanic men, although it does so by about 10 percent for non-Hispanic men. Proficiency in English raises earnings among Hispanic men by about 17 percent compared to those who lack proficiency, in contrast to 10 percent among non-Hispanic men. Employment in agriculture depresses earnings for both groups, but more so among non-Hispanic men.

Much of the difference in earnings between Hispanic and non-Hispanic men within immigrant generations is explained by the differences in the skills that the two groups bring to the labor market. Among married men who have the same number of years of schooling, with the same total labor market experience, who were in the nonagricultural sector, who speak only English or who speak it very well, the weekly earnings of native-born Hispanic men were only 6 percent lower than that of native-born non-Hispanic men. The earnings of foreign-born Hispanic men were only about 15 percent lower than foreign-born non-Hispanic men with the same characteristics. Thus, most of the differences in earnings between Hispanic and non-Hispanic men are due to the differences in the skills they bring to the labor market.

Once again, there are substantial differences across the four major Hispanic groups. Among the native born, when other things are the same, Hispanic men's earnings are lower than those of non-Hispanic men by 7 percent for those of Mexican and Other Hispanic origins, and are on a par with non-Hispanic men for the Cubans and Puerto Ricans. Among the foreign born, the earnings gap with non-Hispanic men was consistently much larger, even when other variables are the same: about 19 percent lower earnings for those born in Puerto Rico, 16 percent lower earnings for Mexican immigrants, 11 percent lower earnings for those from Other Hispanic countries, and 9 percent lower earnings for Cuban immigrants.

Thus, there are very large differences in annual earnings between Hispanic and non-Hispanic men, and among Hispanic men by their nativity and origin. Most of these differences in earnings arise from the different levels of skill brought to the labor market, such as schooling, U.S. labor market experience, and English language proficiency. Among workers of the same level of skill in the nonagricultural sector, the earnings differences are much smaller, especially among the native born, though they still exist. Whether examined overall or when other variables are the same, the native-born Cubans have the highest earnings and the foreign-born Mexicans the lowest earnings among Hispanic men.

Conclusions

This chapter examines the skills of and labor market outcomes for Hispanics in the United States, in comparison to non-Hispanics. It uses data from the 1990 Census of Population. Levels of schooling, English language proficiency, labor force participation, occupation, industry, and earnings are all considered in turn.

The analysis shows lower levels of skill and lower levels of labor market outcomes among Hispanics. In terms of both skill levels and labor market outcomes, those of Cuban origin are the most successful and those of Mexican origin are the least successful. Within Hispanic groups, the disadvantages in skills and labor market outcomes compared to non-Hispanics are greater among the foreign born than among those born in the United States. The large differences in annual earnings between Hispanic and non-Hispanic men are primarily due to the lower levels of skill the former bring to the labor market. The lower participation in the public administration industry by Hispanics appears to be due to the smaller proportion who are United States citizens and the lower level of proficiency in English, because of the high proportion who are foreign born.

Thus, rather than viewing Hispanics in the labor market as a homogeneous group, the analysis finds substantial heterogeneity in their characteristics and economic circumstances.

Notes

1. For an earlier statistical portrait of Hispanics in the United States labor market, see Barry R. Chiswick, "The Labor Market Status of Hispanic Men," *Journal of American Ethnic History* (Fall 1987): 30–58. For an analysis of the growth of Hispanic immigration and the characteristics of Hispanic immigrants, see Barry R. Chiswick and Teresa A. Sullivan, "The New Immigrants," in *State of the Union: America in the 1990's* vol. 2, ed. Reynolds Farley, 211–70 (New York: Russell Sage Foundation, 1995).
2. These data refer to persons living in the United States—that is, the fifty states and the District of Columbia—in the first week of April 1990. Further information about these data can be obtained from the United States Bureau of Census, *Census of Population and Housing,1990, Public Use Microdata Sample, United States, Technical Documentation* (Washington, D.C.: Author, 1992).

Bibliography

Chiswick, Barry R. "The Labor Market Status of Hispanic Men." *Journal of American Ethnic History* (Fall 1987): 30–58.

Chiswick, Barry R., and Teresa A. Sullivan. "The New Immigrants." In *State of the Union: America in the 1990's* vol. 2, edited by Reynolds Farley. New York: Russell Sage Foundation, 1995.

Farley, Reynolds, ed. *State of the Union: America in the 1990's*. vol. 2. New York: Russell Sage Foundation, 1995.

United States Bureau of Census. *Census of Population and Housing, 1990, Public Use Microdata Sample, United States, Technical Documentation*. Washington, D.C.: Author, 1992.

7

Hispanics and Health Care

Zulema E. Suárez

Hispanics face significant barriers to health care use, including the highest chance of being uninsured despite their great participation in the labor force. These barriers are exacerbated by increasing health care costs as well as the increasing use of managed care. However, although access to medical care is of great importance to all individuals in our society, access to institutional medical care is not, by itself, sufficient to address the needs of the Hispanic population. Those who wish to understand Hispanic health care issues must appreciate not only the challenges facing this population in the context of national health care needs, but also the rich cultural and community resources that contribute to this population's wellness. To understand Hispanic health, one must appreciate the use of family, friends, and indigenous and religious healers in the Hispanic community.

This chapter is organized according to a model of health care use originally developed by Andersen[1] and later modified by Aday and Andersen.[2] According to this model, health care utilization is determined by three sets of variables: predisposing, enabling, and need. *Predisposing characteristics* precede the onset of an illness episode and "describe the biological or social 'given' characteristics which facilitate or inhibit individuals from using the medical care system."[3] These include such factors as age, sex, ethnicity, family structure, education, employment status, occupation, migration status, language, and cultural factors. *Enabling variables*, such as income, health insurance coverage, and other resources, as well as the characteristics of the health care system, can facilitate or inhibit entry to the health care system. This chapter also discusses the effects of welfare reform and immigration legislation on Hispanics' access to health care. Finally, *need* is the third component of the model and the most immediate predictor of health care services use. Mortality rates, risk of contracting HIV/AIDS, and women's health issues are discussed as indicators of need. This chapter concludes with a series of suggestions for research, public policy, and service delivery.

Predisposing Characteristics of the Hispanic Population

In this section, we examine the many factors that affect and describe Hispanic health in the United States and Hispanics' access to both medical and self-care.

Age

Age is an important variable in assessing health care needs. Younger populations are in the childbearing years and in need of greater prenatal and postnatal care.[4] Older groups, in contrast, struggle with the challenges of aging and the increasing likelihood of illness. Hispanics as a group tend to be younger than the general population, with a median age of 25 as compared to 35 for non-Hispanic Whites and 28 for non-Hispanic Blacks.[5] Disaggregation by subgroup, however, shows that although Mexicans, Puerto Ricans, and Central and South Americans all have median ages below 27, Cuban-Americans have a median age of 41.

Sex

Health care behavior differs across sexes. Females are more likely than males to seek help when ill.[6] Overall, the male-to-female ratio is about equal in the Hispanic population. Differences arise in some of the different subgroups, however. For example, there are more Mexican and Central and South American males (about 52 percent) than females (48 percent), but there are more Cuban and Puerto Rican (between 52 and 53 percent) females than there are males (about 47 percent for both).

Education

Researchers have directly linked low levels of education to increased health risks, lower levels of health insurance coverage, and the amount of health services used.[7] Specifically, less-educated people are less likely to use preventive services.[8] This is because persons with little education are less likely to have jobs that provide adequate wages and insurance coverage. The majority of all Hispanic subgroups aged 25 and older have no college education.[9] Of the three major groups plus South and Central Americans, Mexican-Americans are the least educated (less than half are high school graduates), followed by Puerto Ricans. Still, between 60 and 65 percent of Puerto Ricans, Cuban-Americans, and South and Central Americans are high school graduates. Hispanics' educational lag places them at a disadvantage in finding jobs and thus in their access to health care. In today's world, higher-paying jobs and jobs that provide benefits such as health insurance require greater education.[10]

Occupational Status

Hispanics are overrepresented in declining, lower-skilled, and semi-skilled jobs and underrepresented in fast-growing, service-sector occupations that demand more education.[11] Structural changes in the economy have resulted in a shift away from the manufacturing jobs that once provided Hispanics with high pay and good benefits. Most opportunities now are in service-sector jobs, such as retail trade, personnel and business, and health services, which require greater education and language skills, but are lower-paying industries. Given Hispanics' low educational levels, their access to these new jobs is restricted. Hence, Hispanics are becoming concentrated in low-wage, low-benefit work that often leaves them without health insurance and without money to buy it independently. According to a study by the National Council of La Raza (NCLR), 63 percent (208,153) of the 328,064 families sampled were uninsured even though they had at least one full-time, full-year worker.[12]

Poverty

For Hispanics who have low levels of education, escaping poverty is more difficult in a service-oriented, industrialized nation. In 1998, 27.1

percent of Hispanics were living in poverty, as opposed to 8.6 percent of non-Hispanic Whites. Poverty is associated with greater need of medical care for at least two reasons. First, low-income populations tend to have higher fertility rates and greater need of prenatal care.[13] At the same time, poor Hispanics are less likely to receive needed care if they are working and do not earn enough to buy health insurance, or if they are ineligible for services because of their immigration status (as will be discussed later). The working poor are especially vulnerable because, although the economy is booming, small businesses are creating most of the nation's new jobs and these are far less likely to provide health insurance than large companies. With the push for welfare reform, people leaving welfare are often forced to take jobs with no health benefits.[14] Moreover, poverty also relegates many U.S. Hispanics to living where drug abuse and other high-risk conditions are rampant.[15] Indeed, Mexican- and Puerto-Rican–origin Hispanics are among the poorest members of this society—almost 32 percent of the former and 39 percent of the latter are poor. Cuban-Americans (about 20 percent) and Central and South Americans (25.4 percent) are less likely to be poor.

Language

As a group, Hispanics have high retention of Spanish language, and many have limited English proficiency.[16] Poor English proficiency may prevent Hispanics from securing jobs that provide adequate salaries and health benefits. Limited language skills and a serious shortage of Spanish-speaking health care professionals in the United States have been linked to the restricted use of health care services by Hispanics.[17] Hispanics with limited or no English ability have a marked preference for Spanish-speaking physicians and often choose to travel longer distances for the sake of language facility.[18] This is understandable given the results of a recent study, which found that Hispanics experienced significant language barriers in emergency care, in part because of limited English proficiency.[19] Both language and culture seem to be important considerations in selecting a professional health care provider; the same study found that, in the state of California, Hispanic physicians cared for nearly three times as many Hispanic patients as did other physicians.

Migration Status

Researchers have found a relationship between migration status and use of formal medical services.[20] For one thing, immigration status determines eligibility for publicly funded health programs.

Stern and Giachello found an association between immigration status and the choice of prenatal care by Hispanic women living in a predominantly Mexican community in Chicago.[21] Immigration status was found to be associated with preferred ethnicity of the doctor. According to these findings, 21 out of 33 Mexican-born women expressed a clear preference for a Mexican or "Latino" doctor.[22] Further, participant observation by the researchers indicated that the illegal immigrant status of some women in the study area tended to influence their choice of health facilities. These women were reluctant to use public health settings, because of fear that they would be asked for documentation that would reveal their status, and that immigration authorities would be called by health personnel.[23] A more recent study of Mexican-immigrant and Mexican-American women, however, found no difference between the migrant and nonmigrant sample in the time they started prenatal care (at about 13 weeks).[24] This study, however, was conducted before the enactment of the Immigrant Responsibility Act of 1996, which restricts access to health care for all immigrants who were not living in the country prior to August, 1996. The effects of this law on Hispanics' access to health care is discussed later in this chapter.

Levels of Acculturation

Acculturation is "the process of change that occurs as a result of continuous contact between cultural groups" and the adoption by one group of the behavioral practices of the dominant society.[25] Acculturation has been associated in the literature with an increase in the morbidity and health-risk behaviors of Hispanics. Researchers have found an association between acculturation to U.S. society, high-risk behaviors, and specific psychiatric disorders.[26] According to a recent study, Mexican-immigrant women are more likely than Mexican-American women, who have been in the United States many years, to abstain from alcohol, drug, and cigarette use during pregnancy. The researchers found that a higher degree of integration in the United States was also associated with increased prenatal stress, which in turn was associated with fewer social supports and increased substance use.[27] It is hypothesized that as women of Mexican origin become integrated into U.S. culture, they are at risk of experiencing a decrease in culture-specific protective behaviors. These findings have prompted some to contend that adherence to traditional cultural values may have a protective effect.[28]

However, acculturation has also been found to be strongly associated with increased health knowledge and access to health information. For example, more acculturated Hispanics were found to have greater awareness about AIDS transmission.[29] Less acculturated Hispanics, in contrast, were less knowledgeable about HIV transmission and more likely to believe that mosquitoes, public toilets, eating utensils, and sneezes could transmit the virus. More acculturated Hispanics have greater access to English-language AIDS and other health information, as well as having more general education.

Ethnicity and Culture

Ethnicity is a significant factor affecting health-seeking behavior. Through socialization, ethnic groups teach group members characteristic ways of defining and responding to their problems.[30] When problems arise, individuals have group-prescribed ways of viewing them and of determining whether they are to be addressed, and if so by whom and how.[31] Not surprisingly, ethnicity has been linked to preferences as to the source of medical care.[32] *Culture*, defined as ethnic group membership, has also been found to influence "symptoms," that is, the complaints a patient presents to a physician and how these complaints are expressed.[33] Hence, sociocultural variables may lead to different interpretations of and responses to essentially the same experience.

Several historical and cultural currents affect health problem definition by Hispanics. The terms *popular medicine* or *folk medicine* refer to medical systems of indigenous rural and urban lower socioeconomic groups. This belief system is considered to be eclectic in nature because of its ability to assimilate practices from various popular and biomedical traditions, as it has done throughout the centuries.[34] According to Green, beliefs and knowledge about disease among Spanish-speaking persons living in the United States derive from medieval Spanish traditions brought to the "New World" by colonizers and influenced by indigenous Indian beliefs. Upon migration to the United States, these beliefs, in turn, have been incorporated with elements of Anglo popular traditions and scientific or biomedical knowledge. Elements of popular medicine are evident in and reinforced by mass media and advertising in the Spanish-language television and radio stations. Hence, Hispanics' etiological concepts and their use of diagnostic resources and curing approaches tend to reflect these multicultural influences. People adhering to this system make use of orthodox (mainstream medical) services as well as using the services of the local spiritist or *curandero* (folk healer).

Briefly, beliefs about causation of illness commonly cited by Hispanics adhering to popular medicine involve magical origins, natural causes, and strong emotional states.[35] Diseases of magical origin are believed to be caused by factors that are unverifiable and lie outside the realm of empirical knowledge. Diseases of natural causes, in contrast, are those in which external or environmental factors operate directly on the organism to cause illness. Finally, psychological disease may be attributed to the experiencing of strong emotional states, which are believed to lead to susceptibility to illness or to actual physiological dysfunction.

Santería, an Afro-Cuban religious practice that evolved from the syncretization of Spanish colonialists' Catholic beliefs and African world view and rituals, is burgeoning in the United States among Cubans and other communities, especially among persons of lower socioeconomic strata.[36] *Santeros* provide their followers with advice, spiritual cleansing, and other related services.[37] Another faith-healing system that may be practiced by Puerto Ricans and Cuban-Americans is *espiritismo*. In this tradition, a medium or spiritual counselor helps clients through the exorcism of spirits that produce illness or emotional distress.[38] Both *Santería* and *espiritismo* have been used as healing systems for health and mental health problems.[39] These folk healers do not view their roles as exclusive, however. The literature shows that *santeros* and *espiritistas* not only refer their clients to the orthodox health system, but also collaborate with mental health professionals in the treatment of emotional disorders.[40]

The practice of folk medicine may depend on the individual's level of acculturation and whether the person lives in an ethnic enclave or near the Mexican border. It is not unusual for immigrants living near the border to go back to Mexico to seek medicine, herbs, and consultations from folk healers. Also, the kind of traditions practiced may vary across Hispanic subgroups and their historical influences. Cubans,

Dominicans, and Puerto Ricans, for example, were exposed to and influenced by the African culture of the slaves brought to the islands by the Spaniards, whereas Mexicans and Central and South Americans were influenced by the great Native American civilizations that historically presided over their lands.

Finally, the extent to which Hispanics adhere to popular beliefs and use folk healers is not known. Studies documenting the use of folk medicine have been primarily ethnographic, based on small convenience samples and, at times, collected in foreign countries.[41] Spotlighting the use of indigenous healers, the findings of this research were generalized to different subgroups. This led to a perception of Hispanics as traditional and as skeptical of an alien medical system.[42] More representative samples have challenged the pervasiveness of the use of folk healers and popular medical practices. The family physician, not the folk healer, is the preferred treatment resource for health and mental health problems.[43]

Still, the constant influx of new immigrants from Latin America to the United States is likely to keep old, traditional practices alive. Moreover, a popular syndicated radio show, "*Salud en Cuerpo y Alma*" (which translates as "Health in Body and Soul"), featuring Dr. Manuel Rico Pérez, promotes the use of homeopathic and other natural remedies for problems such as male potency, female problems, blood enrichment, cancer prevention, cholesterol, and bad breath. This program is broadcast not only in the New York and Miami metropolitan areas, but also in Peru and the Dominican Republic.

The Extended Family

The Hispanic family, similar to families in cultures throughout the industrialized world, is the primary social support for individuals in times of crisis.[44] Yet the cultural tradition of, and a commitment to, the extended family has promoted certain myths about family relations among Hispanics. The family, in the context of the use of health and mental services, is viewed almost exclusively as a supportive, help-giving system that deters its members from seeking outside help. In the past, the generalization of this view has created romantic stereotypes that are counterproductive because they cloud the possibility of seeing the family as a potential source of mental distress; not all that goes on in Hispanic families is "supportive, harmonious and consensually based."[45] Moreover, it blames the underutilization of health services on Hispanics instead of on the inaccessible health care system.

Evidence for the existence of the extended family and its role in dealing with mental and physical disorders is inconclusive.[46] Although Hispanics are by tradition from close-knit families, and are more likely to live in family households than non-Hispanics,[47] the process of immigration can stimulate critical changes in behavior, including a redefinition of family life and kin obligations.[48] A study of several different immigrant groups in the United States found that nuclear families are the norm that emerges in the context of immigrant life in the United States.[49] Although immigrants may extensively use kin and quasi-kin relationships while establishing themselves during their early years of residence in the United States, after some time (possibly with the exception of aged parents) an attitude of permanent responsibility and mutual economic obligation may subside. Moreover, some studies of Mexican-Americans have shown that few of the respondents belonged to extended families. Only 11 percent of the respondents in Padilla's study reported belonging to extended families[50]; Grebler found that only 3 to 4 percent belonged to such a family unit.[51]

Evidence exists to support Rogler's contention that the value of the extended family in providing support for Hispanics has probably been overrated.[52] Studies examining the effects of the presence of an extended family on the utilization of mental health services have found no significant relationship between the two. A survey of the mental health service utilization patterns of 666 Mexican-American residents of three southern California urban towns found no relationship between the presence of an integrated extended family and contact with mental health clinics.[53] Similarly, Rodriguez's data on three ethnic groups—Puerto Ricans, Blacks, and Whites—did not show any relationship between underutilization and help by household members.[54] Some argue that the major difference between Hispanic and majority-culture group help-seeking may be Hispanics' more exclusive reliance upon the family for help, whereas non-Hispanic Whites will also seek help from friends and co-workers.[55]

In sum, Hispanics in this country are uncharacteristically young and poor. Their lower socioeconomic status and their youth predispose them to greater health risks and health needs. Although their immigration status and Spanish language hinder Hispanics' access to health care, they can also draw from a wealth of traditional healing practices.

Indeed, as they acculturate, they become more susceptible to riskier health behaviors. In the next section, we examine selected factors that either facilitate or hinder access to health care.

Enabling Characteristics

Enabling characteristics are the conditions that enable the individual or family "to act upon a value or satisfy a need regarding health service use."[56] Enabling conditions help the consumer to gain access to the health care system. A 1997 report on access to health care showed that families with a Hispanic head of household are more likely to report barriers to receiving care (15.1 percent) than families headed by Blacks (9.9 percent) or Whites or other ethnicities (11.4 percent).[57] Out of families experiencing problems in receiving care, Hispanic-headed families were more likely (69.1 percent) than families headed by persons in any other group (58.5 percent) to be unable to afford care. In addition to insurance coverage and having a usual source of care, the structuring or characteristics of the health care system can also enable or hinder access.

Although discussions of enabling factors traditionally begin with insurance coverage, a discussion of managed care (a growing model of both public and private health care financing) and its effects on Hispanics is in order. For example, in an effort to contain health care costs, for the past several years state Medicaid programs—the major safety net for low-income populations such as Hispanics—have been shifting from traditional fee-for-service to capitated managed care.

The structuring of the health care system can either facilitate or hinder access. A highly bureaucratized health care system may be experienced as insensitive and fragmented by users, and especially ethnic minorities.[58] Despite often-cited arguments in the literature that Hispanics are less likely to use health care services because of beliefs and attitudes, some researchers have found convincing evidence that characteristics of the health care system supersede cultural traits in explaining ethnic, racial, and class differences in use.[59]

Managed Care

Managed care is "basically characterized as the integration of financing, management, and the delivery of health services, with providers taking on financial risk."[60] One of the most popular forms of managed care is the health maintenance organization (HMO). Both privately and publicly insured patients are being steered to HMOs. Managed care can negatively affect Hispanics' access to health care, not only in terms of gaining entry to the system, but also in getting care once entry is gained.

Managed care shifts much of the burden of negotiating the health care system to the consumer, while at the same time placing more of the power in health care professionals' hands.[61] For example, in an HMO, patients must choose from a roster of primary doctors who act as "gatekeepers" and the central point for all medical care, as well as paying one monthly fee. Primary doctors decide on the need for treatment and whether a referral to a specialist is needed. Choosing a primary care physician is an important and rather daunting responsibility, as all health care decisions will have to go through this individual. Navigating the health care system is challenging for most people; for Hispanics who are not proficient in English and who are not experienced in dealing with complex bureaucracies, securing health services may be inordinately and increasingly difficult under managed care.

Managed care can significantly affect Hispanics' entry into the health care system. Because the fee does not change, regardless of how many times the physician is seen, healthier patients are more desirable than patients needing more or specialized care. To protect themselves from increased costs, managed care settings may establish enrollment practices that discourage minority participation (such as by not having sickle-cell specialists on panel to treat Blacks).[62] Hispanics' relative youth would, at first glance, make them appear to be desirable candidates for HMOs, as younger people tend to be healthier than older people. However, Hispanics "bear a disproportionate level of illness, disability, and mortality."[63] Because they are more likely to be poor, and poor people (as noted earlier) are more likely to have greater need for medical care, Hispanics may be denied membership in some HMOs. Of the three major Hispanic groups, Puerto Ricans may be the most vulnerable to exclusion from HMOs, because they have the worst health status of all the subgroups.

Hispanics may experience barriers even if they do manage to gain entry into the system. Critics of managed care fear that because doctors must pay for specialized treatment out of their fees, patients requiring specialized care may be denied treatment if it is too costly. If denied, it will be difficult for Hispanics who lack knowledge and language skills to act as advocates for themselves. It should be noted that both privately and publicly insured Hispanics are potentially affected. In an effort to restructure the traditional fee-for-service Medicaid program, states are increasingly steering Medicaid recipients and others who are poor into managed care through the use of waivers.[64]

The quality of care that Hispanics receive under managed care may also be affected by of the lack of Hispanic health care providers employed by HMOs. Despite many Hispanics' clear preference for Spanish-speaking physicians, they are less likely to find one in an HMO. According to the Office of Minority Health, minority providers have had difficulty being accepted into managed care organizations.[65] This practice discriminates not only against doctors, but also against patients, who may be discouraged from joining because of the absence of culturally appropriate health care services.

Finally, enrolling in an HMO most likely means giving up long-established relationships with outside health care providers. In sum, Hispanics who are poor and have low levels of education may be vulnerable to bureaucratic and procedural abuses of power by the managed care system.

Insurance Coverage

One of the most important factors facilitating access to medical care is health insurance. Insured persons are more likely to enter the health care system and to use more health services than persons who are not insured.[66] Conversely, persons who are uninsured are more likely to experience barriers to needed care, such as lacking a regular source of care. More specifically, a 1997 study reported that families with one or more members lacking insurance were 2.9 times more likely to experience difficulty or delay in securing care or to not receive needed care than families whose members were all insured.[67]

Hispanics are more likely to lack health insurance than any other ethnic/racial group in the United States.[68] Indeed, more than 33 percent of Hispanics were uninsured, as compared to 16 percent of other Americans.[69] This figure is consistent with findings from a 1976 health care utilization study.[70] Twenty years later, the Hispanic uninsurance rate remains unchanged.

Insurance coverage alone, however, does not guarantee access to adequate medical care. The type of insurance coverage determines health options and the quality of medical care. The insured may have insufficient or restricted coverage, whether private or public.[71] For example, persons who can afford a lower-cost private insurance policy may not seek care because they are not able to pay the higher deductible. Also, women who have Medicaid are more likely to encounter barriers to care and to not receive care during the first trimester of pregnancy. In a 1996 study, Trevino et al. found that uninsured or publicly insured individuals had greater need of health care.[72] Restrictions in Medicaid coverage particularly affect Puerto Ricans, who are far more likely than other Hispanic subgroups to have Medicaid as their insurance.[73]

Regular Source of Care

Having a regular source of care—a particular doctor's office, clinic, health center, or other place where Hispanics go if they are sick or need to consult about their health—is another strong predictor of use of medical services.[74] A regular source of care is important because persons without one may be less likely to receive treatment in a timely manner and to receive preventive health care services.[75] It also enhances the quality and continuity of care.[76] Persons without a usual source of care do not have an advocate who will help them with important health care decisions. Out of all the populations included in federal reports, Hispanics are least likely to have a regular source of care—about 30 percent (8.4 million) do not have one. Of all the Hispanic subgroups, Mexican-Americans are least likely to have a usual provider.

The type of regular source of care is also important in assessing access to medical care, as the content and accessibility of care may vary by facility. Persons who use a family doctor, private clinic, or prepaid group as a regular health provider are more likely to receive preventive services and to have continuity of care than those who obtain care from public facilities.[77] Among those having a source of care, Hispanics were more likely, along with Blacks, to have a hospital-based provider (including hospital clinics and outpatient departments) as their usual source of care.[78]

Hispanics having a hospital-based regular provider, however, often face intricate bureaucratic intake processes, long waiting periods for scheduled appointments, and excessive waiting time in the practitioner's office, as well as having to travel longer to receive care.[79] Hispanic users of outpatient departments have to wait longer than users of private physicians.[80] Nonetheless, Hispanics may be forced to use outpatient departments (OPDs) because of flexibility in arranging care, such as weekday evening and weekend coverage.

Other Determinants of Access

Effects of the Immigrant Responsibility Act and Welfare Reform on Hispanic Access to Health Care

In addition to the preceding factors, which are relevant to all health care consumers, Hispanics' health care is also affected by immigration policies. Although eligibility for publicly funded health care programs has always been determined by immigration status, recent legislation has made it even more difficult for immigrants to qualify for public benefits. In the past, refugees were eligible for all services, immigrants qualified for selected benefits, and undocumented immigrants were barred from participating in most safety-net programs. Today, however, all immigrants face increased restrictions when seeking care.

Fear of immigration authorities and deportation are real, contemporary issues. With the passage of the Illegal Immigration Reform and Immigrant Responsibility Act of 1996 (PRA), the definition of immigrants qualified to receive federal public benefits has become even more limited. Although the Balanced Budget Act (BBA), enacted on August 5, 1997, restored some benefits rescinded earlier, legal and undocumented immigrants are still significantly affected by these policy changes. For example, the PRA originally denied federal benefits to all unnaturalized legal immigrants; under the BBA, effective August 22, 1996, benefits were restored for legal immigrants who were receiving Supplemental Security Insurance (SSI) in August 1996, when President Clinton signed the welfare law.[81] The BBA also allows immigrants who were then living in this country to receive benefits should they become disabled. This change assures Medicaid eligibility for immigrants in states that provide Medicaid based on SSI benefits. However, immigrants who arrive in the future and become disabled will not be eligible for SSI benefits. The BBA restricts eligibility to qualified immigrants, unless the state enacts a law after August 22, 1996, specifically making nonqualified or undocumented immigrants eligible for state and local benefits. As a result of this law, Hispanics seeking services from any federally funded programs must show proof of citizenship under the Systematic Alien Verification for Eligibility program (SAVE).

The Personal Responsibility and Work Opportunity Act of 1996, while radically changing the structure of welfare programs and establishing major new restrictions on receipt of public benefits by legal immigrants, left the structure of Medicaid the same.[82] Parenthetically, while traditional fee-for-service programs still predominate, states are increasingly enrolling their Medicaid populations in managed care.[83] Consequently, recipients' loss of cash assistance under Aid to Families with Dependent Children (AFDC) and SSI does not automatically mean termination from Medicaid; beneficiaries may continue to receive assistance until found ineligible. Though this may seem favorable at first glance, it is not, because a state of residence may still choose to discontinue coverage under the state's Medicaid plan even if a recipient is eligible.

Under both laws, the federal government made provisions for reimbursement to state and local governments that provide emergency medical treatment, but only if reimbursement cannot be obtained from another federal program, from the immigrant, or from any other person.[84] This means that undocumented immigrants are eligible only for emergency medical services, such as labor and delivery or treatment of other conditions that, if left unattended, could immediately and seriously jeopardize the patient's health.[85] Hence, the law exempts Medicaid emergency medical care from the verification requirements, because emergency access to such care is considered a public health imperative.[86] Fortunately, nonprofit charitable organizations that provide both social and hospital services are entirely exempt from screening or verifying eligibility.

These laws further restrict Hispanics' access to health care, although some groups are affected more than others. It seems that Mexican-Americans and South and Central Americans would be most vulnerable under this legislation, because they are more likely to be legal immigrants or undocumented immigrants. This is alarming given that Mexican-Americans already have the lowest rates of health insurance of all the Hispanic subgroups.[87] For fear of deportation, undocumented immigrants may avoid medical care until the problem becomes a life-threatening emergency. Although medical emergencies are exempt from verification requirements, patients may not know this, nor would they know what technically constitutes a medical emergency. Moreover, legal immigrants may also abstain from seeking medical care in order to protect their sponsors, who would be held responsible for the medical bills. Despite the provision that nonprofit charitable organizations need not verify status and eligibility, Hispanics may lack the knowledge to determine which agency is "safe" or nonprofit. Less affected would be Puerto Ricans, who are citizens by birth and therefore eligible for services, although they too may be questioned. Cubans as a whole would be less affected because many have been in this country for decades and this subgroup has high naturalization rates. Cubans and other immigrants coming to the United States after August 22, 1996, would be denied services, including Supplemental Security Income, even if they are eligible. However, Cubans entering the country with refugee or asylee status would be deemed "qualified aliens" for cash assistance and other benefits. Because these laws are so recent, their full impact on the health and welfare of Hispanics will not be known until well into the next century.

Availability of Minority Physicians and Other Health Care Providers

It is vital to be able to communicate with a health practitioner in one's native language, to avoid misunderstandings that impede the provision of and access to care.[88] Studies show that Hispanics who are monolingual or have limited English proficiency encounter greater barriers to care.[89] Communication may be further impaired by cultural differences in communication styles and low educational attainment.[90]

There is a shortage of health care professionals who can relate to Hispanics both culturally and linguistically. Moreover, interpreters are often not used even when there are language barriers between patients and providers.[91] Though lacking current statistics, Trevino provided a sketch of Hispanic underrepresentation in the health professions. In 1988, Hispanics represented approximately 6 percent of all first-year medical and 7.6 percent of dental students. In 1991, Hispanics constituted only 3.1 percent of optometry students in the nation. Similarly, only 3.4 percent of first-year pharmacy students are Hispanic. Finally, in 1985 only 2.7 percent of nursing students were Hispanic. Trevino accounts for this underrepresentation by citing Hispanics' generally low educational levels, with more than 50 percent not going to or graduating from college.[92] At the same time, health careers are among the most competitive and educationally demanding. Often, the greater the educational requirements for a given profession, the lower the Hispanic representation.

A more recent study expands on the consequences of the shortage of Hispanic physicians.[93] This is of concern because, as noted earlier, Hispanics have a marked preference for Hispanic physicians.[94] Still, according to these researchers (who report more current statistics than those reported by Trevino), Hispanics make up 10.3 percent of the population but only about 5 percent of physicians. Hence, current attempts at dismantling affirmative action and programs that facilitate training of minority physicians—as was recently done in the California state university system—may threaten health care for both poor people and members of minority groups.[95] In other words, policies that reduce the number of minority physicians may indirectly reduce access to health care for poor people and minorities—and a federal survey reported that only 10 percent of non-Hispanic White medical students planned to practice in a critical manpower shortage area.[96]

In general, Hispanic and Black physicians are much more likely than other physicians to treat poor, Black, and Hispanic patients.[97] Based on a survey of 718 primary care physicians, researchers found that, on average, Black physicians cared for nearly 6 times as many Black patients and Hispanic physicians cared for nearly 3 times as many Hispanic patients as did other physicians.[98] These physicians were also more likely to care for patients covered by Medicaid (45 and 24 percent of their patients, respectively, compared with 18 percent of patients of non-Hispanic White physicians) than were other physicians. Hispanic doctors had a greater percentage of uninsured patients than did other doctors (9 percent compared with 3 to 6 percent for other physicians). Finally, Black and Hispanic doctors were more likely to have their practices in areas with large underserved groups. The facts that Hispanic doctors were more likely to care for Hispanic patients, had a greater percent of uninsured patients in their practices, and were more likely to locate their offices within their ethnic communities further underscore the prominence of Hispanic physicians in improving Hispanic patients' access to health care.

In sum, Hispanics are more likely to encounter barriers to receiving care than are Blacks and non-Hispanic Whites. They have the lowest rates of insurance coverage of any ethnic group in the United States. This is especially the case for Mexican-Americans, who are also less likely to have a regular source of care, another significant enabling variable. Changes in the health care environment brought about by managed care are likely to further hinder this group's ability to gain entry to the medical system. Even inside the system, however, Hispanics experience barriers to care because of a lack of Spanish-speaking physicians.

Need

Fertility Rates

Higher fertility rates predispose Hispanics to greater need for prenatal and postnatal care. According to a recent study by the National

Center for Health Statistics, 18 percent of the total number of births in the United States were to Hispanics, even though Hispanics make up only 10.3 percent of the nation's population.[99]

As with other indicators, fertility rates differ markedly among the different nationalities. These differences may be attributed to the high levels of immigration and fertility rates of Mexican-Americans, particularly recent immigrants. The overwhelming majority of Hispanic births (70 percent in 1995, up from 61 percent in 1989) were to this subgroup. Mexican-American women are estimated to average 3.32 births over their lifetimes, as compared to 1.7 births for Cuban-Americans and 2.2 births for Puerto Ricans, who have birth rates comparable to those of Black and non-Hispanic White women.[100] Unlike Cuban-Americans, who are older and have lower birth rates, Mexican-Americans continue to grow in number. This means that Mexican-Americans are especially in need of prenatal and postnatal care and of pediatric health care services.

Births to teen mothers (ages 15 to 19) are also higher among Hispanics.[101] Of all the Hispanic groups, Mexican-American teens also had higher birth rates (116.2 per 1,000 teens) as compared to 106.0 for Puerto Ricans and 87.9 for Central/South Americans. Cuban-Americans and non-Hispanic Whites had similar rates (40.2 and 40.4, respectively).

Mortality

Mortality rates are a basic measure of the standard of living of a population.[102] Not until 1988 did accurate estimates of Hispanic mortality rates become available, because prior to that date the national model death certificates did not include Hispanic identifiers.[103] Further, national data sets on health status also did not contain Hispanic identifiers until the 1980s. The most recent preliminary report on mortality patterns in the United States does not include general mortality data on Hispanics, because of "inconsistent reporting between death certificates and censuses and surveys."[104] Hence, available data continue to be insufficient to gather a realistic assessment of morbidity and mortality rates among this population.

The relative youth of Hispanics protects them from chronic diseases generally associated with aging. According to the limited data available, like non-Hispanic Whites and Blacks, Hispanics are more likely to be afflicted with or to die from diseases of the heart and malignant neoplasms.[105] Unlike the other two groups, for whom the third leading cause of death is cerebrovascular disease, Hispanics are more likely to die from accidents. These are followed by human immunodeficiency virus infection (HIV), homicide, and legal intervention. Interestingly, despite having lower access to health care, Mexican-Americans have death rates comparable to or lower than that of non-Hispanic Whites. The health status of Puerto Ricans, in contrast, is comparable to that of Blacks.[106]

HIV/AIDS

Perhaps the biggest health threat facing segments of the Hispanic community is HIV, either of two retroviruses that infect human T cells and cause AIDS (acquired immunodeficiency syndrome). AIDS is a condition in which progressive acquired deficiency in certain leukocytes results in a variety of infections, some forms of cancer, and degeneration of the nervous system. As a group, Hispanics are disproportionately affected by HIV/AIDS. Although they comprise between 10 and 12 percent of the population (including Puerto Rico), they account for 18 percent of total AIDS cases.[107] This figure shows an upward trend from 1995, when Hispanics accounted for only 15 percent of AIDS cases. Alarmingly, Hispanic children account for 24 percent of pediatric AIDS cases.[108]

HIV prevalence among Hispanics varies according to subgroup, however. Persons of Mexican descent have overall risk levels similar to those of Whites who are not Hispanic.[109] Of all the Hispanic subgroups, persons of Puerto Rican descent are the most likely to be afflicted with AIDS, due to their higher rates of intravenous drug abuse (IVDA). This subgroup's high rate of intravenous drug abuse may be explained by its concentration in New York City, Chicago, and cities in New Jersey. In these cities the rates of poverty and the availability of illicit drugs, both risk factors, are higher than in other parts of the country.[110] At the same time, according to a 1997 study, problem drug use and living in unstable housing conditions were associated with lower use of the most advanced combination drugs in the treatment of HIV/AIDS.[111] Therefore, although they are more likely to suffer from HIV/AIDS-related illnesses than non-Hispanic Whites, Puerto Ricans are less likely to receive the most effective treatment available.

Hispanic women of childbearing age show AIDS rates equal to those of men (18 percent).[112] Most HIV/AIDS cases among Hispanic women in the childbearing years have been related to intravenous drug (IV) use and by sexual contact with an IV drug user. Not surprisingly, given their higher rates of IV drug use, between 1988 and 1991 Puerto Rican women were found to be at much higher risk of contracting AIDS than Cuban- and Mexican-American women. Puerto Rican women with AIDS, both U.S.- and island-born, were more likely to contract the virus through their own drug use, or indirectly by sexual contact with an IV drug user, than other Hispanic women and non-Hispanic Whites.[113] Mexican-American women, in contrast, were more likely to contract AIDS from blood transfusions.[114] Cuban-American women, who had the lowest rate of AIDS cases during the same period of time, were most likely to contract the disease from sex with an HIV-positive man, and from IV drug use.

Infant Mortality

Infant mortality is the most widely used health indicator for a population.[115] In the United States, infant mortality rates among Hispanics were not evaluated at the national level until the Becerra study in 1991. The most current statistics available indicate that, as a whole, Hispanic infant deaths (IDs) are comparable to those of non-Hispanic Whites (6.5 per 1,000 live births).[116] Separating the Hispanics into subgroups reveals differences between groups, as is to be expected. Although Mexican-Americans' rate of IDs is identical to that of non-Hispanic Whites, Cubans and Central/South Americans have lower rates (4.4 and 5.7, respectively), and Puerto Ricans have a significantly higher rate (8.7 deaths per 1,000 live births). Similar relationships appear when one looks at low birth weight (LBW). In this case, however, Mexican-Americans have slightly lower rates of LBW (5.8) than non-Hispanic Whites (6.1), who have rates similar to Cubans (6.3) and Central/South Americans (6.0). Again, Puerto Ricans' LBW rate was higher than that of the other groups (9.1). That Hispanic infant birth weight distribution and infant deaths are comparable to those of the non-Hispanic White population, given Hispanics' greater levels of poverty, is considered a paradox, leading some to question whether reproductive outcomes serve as an aggregate indicator of socioeconomic well-being.[117]

It may also seem paradoxical that Puerto Ricans, who as citizens have access to publicly funded health and social service programs, have higher rates of IDs and LBW than Mexican-Americans, who are more likely to be uninsured. Although both subgroups are poor, and poverty is associated with greater health risks, Puerto Ricans are more likely to live in female-headed households and to exhibit high-risk behaviors (such as substance abuse) than Mexican-Americans.[118] Studies show that greater integration in the United States is associated with increased prenatal stress, which in turn is associated with fewer social supports and more substance use.[119]

In sum, although the relative youth of Hispanics protects them from most chronic diseases generally associated with aging, like Blacks and non-Hispanic Whites they are likely to be afflicted by heart disease and cancers. Hispanics are also more likely to die from preventable events such as accidents, homicide, and legal intervention. However, the biggest threat facing segments of the Hispanic community is HIV/AIDS. Puerto Ricans are more likely to be infected than other Hispanic subgroups, because of their higher rates of intravenous drug use. Finally, Hispanics as a group have high fertility rates that predispose them to increased need of prenatal care.

Access to Health Care

Access to health care refers to those dimensions describing the potential and actual entry of a given group to the health care system.[120] Some key measures of access are whether a person in need of care is able to enter the medical care system (realized access), the volume of physician visits and hospital days relative to their need, and the quality of care.[121]

Use of Medical Care

It is difficult to assess Hispanics' actual use of medical care, for a number of reasons. First, government agencies traditionally classified Hispanics as White, precluding access to Hispanic morbidity and utilization data.[122] Second, federal and state agencies have used inconsistent criteria to define Hispanic ethnic identity over the years. This has made it difficult to compare study findings and to assess trends.[123] Third, some studies have been limited to specific Hispanic subgroups living in a particular geographical area. Fourth, with few exceptions, such as the Hispanic Health and Nutrition Examination Survey (HHANES) and the 1987 National Medical Expenditures Survey (NMES), national and state databases have inadequate racial/ethnic identifiers to conduct meaningful analyses of Hispanic subpopulations.[124] Because the collection of national data requires oversampling, and is labor- and cost-intensive, it takes a long time before the data are available to researchers.

Nevertheless, some studies have shown that Hispanics generally have lower utilization of health services.[125] Others studies have found that Hispanics have higher use than the general population. For example, using a national data set, Trevino and Moss found, using aggregate data, that "white, black, and Hispanic populations had an approximately equal number of physician visits per person per year."[126] Analysis by subgroup, however, revealed that Mexican-Americans had, on average, about half as many visits to physicians as did the mainland Puerto Ricans and Cubans in the sample. These differences persisted even after the data were age-adjusted. In another national study, researchers found that Hispanics did not differ significantly from Whites in use of health services.[127] Yet another study, of barriers to care among hypertensives across three different ethnic groups, found that although Hispanics on the whole had fewer physician visits (2.1) than Whites (3.4) and Blacks (2.3), self-reported hypertensives across groups had higher numbers of physician visits (3.8, 4.5, and 4.1, respectively).[128]

Although the 1996 study found that Hispanics had fewer physician visits than non-Hispanic Whites and Blacks, their access problems have, in the past, also been in the areas of satisfaction with services and reported difficulty in obtaining care.[129] Indeed, Hispanics also experience more delays when receiving health care, are more likely to travel longer to the source of care, and must wait longer to see the physician once they get there.[130]

Use of Medical Care by Hispanic Women

Routine medical examinations are important for screening and health maintenance. According to HHANES data, 44.6 percent of Mexican-American, 40.5 percent of Cuban-American, and 38.4 percent of Puerto Rican women had not had a physical exam in more than 2 years.[131] Hispanic women are also less likely to have preventive exams such as Pap smears. Despite higher rates of cervical cancer, Hispanic women have lower rates of late Pap smears and higher rates of late-stage diagnoses.[132] The HHANES shows that 75.3 percent of Mexican-American, 68.2 percent of Cuban-American, and 79.6 of Puerto Rican women in the sample had not had a Pap smear in more than 2 years.[133] These rates fall below the federal Year 2000 objectives, which call for at least 85 percent of women to have received a Pap smear within the past 3 years, and have improved very little since 1985.[134] The likelihood of not receiving a Pap smear is even greater for Hispanic women who speak only or mostly Spanish.[135]

Access to prenatal care is especially important for a population in its childbearing years. With the exception of Cubans (89.2 percent), however, who are more likely to have early prenatal care than non-Hispanic Whites (87.1 percent), Hispanics have lower rates of early prenatal care. Of the three remaining subgroups, Mexican-Americans, who have the highest fertility rates, have the lowest rate of prenatal care (69.1 percent). This compares to approximately 74 percent for Puerto Ricans and Central and South Americans.[136]

In sum, it is difficult to form an accurate picture of Hispanics' use of medical care, because of methodological problems. Some studies suggest, however, that although Hispanics may not lack access when entering the health care system, they are more likely to experience barriers when receiving care, due to language difficulties, longer travel times, and longer delays at the practitioner's office.

Recommendations

The preceding sections provided an overview of Hispanic health issues using Andersen and Aday's 1975 model of health care use. This framework is also used to organize a series of recommendations for policy and research that emerge from the review.

Predisposing Variables

By now it is well established that there are significant differences among Hispanic subgroups. This diversity has implications for program and policy development. For example, although Hispanics are one of the youngest groups in the country as a whole, Cubans are older than the general population: while the former are in the midst of childbearing, Cubans are dealing with issues of aging. Moreover, even younger Cubans have lower fertility rates than the general population. Hence, health care dollars must be targeted according to the specific developmental health needs of the different Hispanic subgroups.

Investments in the education of Hispanics can have a significant effect on the health of this population. Higher education results in better occupations and in better-paying jobs with good health insurance benefits. English as a second language (ESL) and other language training would not only enhance Hispanics' ability to get jobs in the service sector, but would also facilitate their access to health care, as they would not have to rely on Spanish-speaking doctors. In sum, increasing Hispanics' levels of education would ultimately raise them from poverty and from living under high-risk conditions in inner-city neighborhoods. That Cubans are doing better financially and otherwise than Mexican-Americans and Puerto Ricans could be attributed in part to their being more educated.

Migration status and recent immigration legislation significantly affect the health-seeking behavior of Hispanics, both documented and undocumented. By dramatically limiting immigrants' eligibility for health services, the federal government may be contributing to the deterioration of the health of the nation's soon-to-be largest ethnic minority group. With the passage of the Immigrant Responsibility Act, the government created an atmosphere of fear and mistrust. Hence, even Hispanics qualified for services may be hesitant to seek them, out of concern that their papers may not be in order. Ironically, although the government passed this legislation to contain costs, neglecting the health of such a sizeable population can result in unprecedented financial, social, and economic costs for society as a whole.

The relationship between acculturation and increased health-risk behaviors should be better understood. Hispanics eventually and inevitably acculturate, so it is important to understand why this is likely to lead to increased morbidity. With an understanding about why this occurs, health practitioners can design health education programs that encourage the retention of healthy cultural behaviors. This, of course, would require a commitment to preventive services from both government and nonprofit sources.

Hispanics have a rich history of healing that can be drawn upon and supported to enhance their health. Up until recently, Hispanic folkways were seen as backward in contrast to modern medicine. It is becoming increasingly evident, however, that non-Western cultures have viable healing systems that can benefit Western societies. The Office of Alternative and Complementary Medicine Center has assumed the responsibility of documenting the effectiveness of these "alternative" or complementary healing systems. These efforts are finally lending credence to practices that some Hispanics have traditionally adhered to. This will, it is hoped, eventually cause physicians to incorporate some of these practices in the treatment of patients who believe in them. Thus, the health care system would feel more accommodating to Hispanics.

Finally, more research is needed on the relationship of socioeconomic status to health care issues. Although in the past ethnicity has been blamed for Hispanics' underrepresentation in the health care system, poverty and low wages seem to be greater determinants of use than is culture. To better understand which health behaviors are due to culture and which are due to social and financial barriers, efforts should be made to study upper- and middle-class Hispanics, in contrast to low-income populations. Controlling for class would enable us to better understand the relationships among culture, socioeconomic status, and health care use.

Enabling Variables

If Hispanics are to remain healthy and vital, they need to have access to health insurance. Declining rates of coverage in a growing population will result in increased levels of disability and poverty. Efforts to improve the educational and occupational status of Hispanics, as mentioned earlier, would result in improved benefits. This is critical, given that many of the uninsured are working but cannot afford coverage.[137] Because educating a population takes time, policymakers should seriously consider extending instead of restricting health care benefits. Although denying Hispanics insurance today may save some money, the economic, social, and moral costs this action will have in the future will be magnified.

As Keith and LaVeist pointed out, extending coverage to the uninsured may not have the desired effects if adequate health care providers are not available.[138] Given the importance of having a regular source of care (especially one that is Spanish-speaking), policies such as those abolishing affirmative action programs, which reduce the number of minority physicians, also may reduce access to health care for Hispanics.[139] Efforts must be made to ensure that Hispanics will have providers with whom they feel comfortable. Multiple strategies have been identified to achieve this goal.[140] Increasing the pool of Hispanic health professionals requires a financial commitment from federal, state, and nonprofit sources, but it is essential.

Because managed care restricts freedom of choice in health care practitioners, Hispanics should be provided with coverage that allows them to seek services from practitioners who understand their language and culture. Growing a cadre of Hispanic providers will take time; in the meantime, potential discrimination by HMOs must be averted. This can be done through the collection of data to monitor utilization patterns by race, ethnicity, national origin, and primary language.[141] Federal and local governments should assess an HMO's representation of minority providers before awarding it the care of Medicaid patients.

Need Variables

Hispanics' health status is not, as might be expected, that of a youthful population. Instead, they are afflicted with preventable illnesses. Some argue that the overall state of Hispanic health reflects the great economic disparity when compared with the health status of the rest of the U.S. population.[142] Still, until the ideal of economic parity can be achieved, the health of this population can be significantly improved through health promotion and disease prevention (HPDP) programs.

Strategies for HPDP have been outlined elsewhere by a cadre of Hispanic health professionals and researchers and are summarized here.[143] First, it is essential to advocate for federal legislation that will appropriate funding for the development and evaluation of HPDP programs for Hispanics. Second, such programs should integrate paraprofessionals, lay leaders from the community, indigenous healers, and other community health workers in the development and implementation of HPDP programming for Hispanics. Third, media resources and community networks at local, state, and federal levels should be used to educate Hispanic communities regarding HPDP issues. Finally, mass media marketing plans targeting Spanish-speaking and bilingual Hispanics could be used to inform the public how to gain access to and properly utilize health services.

Barring a universal health insurance program and socioeconomic equity, implementation of these strategies would improve Hispanics' use of health care services. Because Hispanics are such a diverse population, health care policies should allow for cultural and regional differences in clinical and administrative measurements; what is appropriate for one subgroup may not be appropriate for another.[144] The inclusion of a cultural index of access to health care as part of quality measurements and requirements, and providing financial resources to systems that need infrastructure development to meet this requirement, would address some of the issues regarding satisfaction with care.

In conclusion, the effort needed to ensure a healthy Hispanic population may seem daunting. However, the goals are achievable if society is willing to support and build on the rich resources that Hispanics already have—youth, vitality, strong support networks, and rich healing traditions. A commitment of resources and creative ways of providing health care to this population is essential. Not only are Hispanics not going to go away, their numbers are growing exponentially. Investing in the health of Hispanics is an investment in the health of the nation.

Notes

1. R. M. Andersen, *A Behavioral Model of Families' Use of Services*, Center for Health Administration Studies Research Series no. 25 (Chicago: University of Chicago Press, 1968).

2. L. A. Aday and R. M. Andersen, "A Framework for the Study of Access to Medical Care," *Health Services Research* 9, no. 3 (1974): 208–20.

3. A. L. Giachello, "Hispanics and Health Care," in *Hispanics in the United States: A New Social Agenda*, ed. Pastora San Juan Cafferty and William McCready (New Brunswick, N.J.: Transactions Books, 1985), 159–94.

4. Zulema E. Suárez and K. Siefert, "Latinas and Sexually Transmitted Diseases: Implications of Recent Research for Prevention," *Social Work in Health Care* 28, no. 1 (1998): 1–20.

5. United States Bureau of the Census, *March 1994 Population Reports: Age of Population by Ethnicity*, Internet posting, www.census.gov/Age/sex94.txt.

6. Giachello, "Hispanics and Health Care."

7. R. K. Peters, D. G. Thomas, T. M. Mack, and B. D. Henderson, "Risk Factors for Invasive Cervical Cancer Among Latinas and Non-Latinas in Los Angeles County," *Journal of the National Cancer Institute* 77, no. 5 (1986): 1063–77; P. Kilborn, "Nation's Uninsured Seek Healthcare Any Way They Can," *New York Times*, August 5, 1997, Internet posting.

8. R. M. Andersen, A. L. Giachello, and L. A. Aday, "Access of Hispanics to Health Care and Cuts in Services: A State of the Art Overview," *Public Health Reports* 101, no. 3 (1986): 238–52.

9. United States Bureau of the Census, *March 1994 Population Reports: Age of Population by Ethnicity*.

10. S. M. Pérez and D. Martinez, *State of Hispanic America 1993: Toward a Latino Anti-Poverty Agenda* (Washington, D.C.: Policy Analysis Center Office of Research, Advocacy, and Legislation, National Council of La Raza, 1993).

11. Ibid.

12. Ibid.

13. E. Ginzberg, "Access to Health Care for Hispanics," *Journal of the American Medical Association* 265, no. 2 (January 1991): 238–41.

14. R. Pear, *New York Times* archive article, National Desk, September 26, 1998.

15. L. Bonilla, L. Porter, and S. Mendez, "*Tenemos que Protegernos*: AIDS in Puerto Rican Communities," *Latinos Studies Journal* 1, no. 1 (1994): 83–104.

16. D. S. Massey, R. E. Zambrana, and A. Bell, "Contemporary Issues in Latino Families: Future Directions for Research, Policy and Practice," in *Understanding Latino Families: Scholarship, Policy and Practice*, ed. Ruth E. Zambrana (Thousand Oaks, Cal.: Sage Publications, 1995).

17. A. M. Padilla, M. L. Carlos, and S. E. Keefe, "Mental Health Services Utilization by Mexican Americans," in *Psychotherapy with the Spanish-Speaking: Issues in Research and Service Delivery*, ed. M. R. Miranda, 9–20 (Los Angeles: Univer-

sity of California, 1976) (Spanish Speaking Mental Health Research Center, Monograph no. 3); L. M. Cohen, *Culture, Disease, and Stress Among Latino Immigrants,* Special Study Research Institute on Immigration and Ethnic Studies (Washington, D.C.: Smithsonian Institution, 1979); L. H. Rogler et al., *A Conceptual Framework for Mental Health Research on Hispanic Populations* (Bronx, N.Y.: Fordham University, 1983) (Hispanic Research Center Monograph no. 10); M. Komaromy et al., "The Role of Black and Hispanic Physicians in Providing Health Care for Underserved Populations," *New England Journal of Medicine* 334 (May 16, 1996): 1305–10; C. A. Stroup-Benham and L. Perkowski, "A Comparison of Financial, Access, and Sociocultural Barriers to Care Among Hypertensives Across Three Ethnic Groups," in *Achieving Equitable Access: Studies of Health Care Issues Affecting Hispanics and African Americans,* ed. Marsha D. Lillie-Blanton, Wilhemina A. Leigh, and Ana I. Alfaro-Correa (Washington, D.C.: Joint Center for Political and Economic Studies, 1996), 119–42; Ruth E. Zambrana, "The Relationship of Health Perceptions, Physical and Mental Health, and Language Use to Usual Source of Care," in Lillie-Blanton, Leigh, and Alfaro-Correa, *Achieving Equitable Access,* 75–98.

18. R. Ailinger, "A Study of Illness Referral in a Spanish-Speaking Community," *Nursing Research* 26, no. 1 (1977): 53–56; Cohen, *Culture, Disease, and Stress Among Latino Immigrants*; G. Stern and A. L. Giachello, "Applied Research: The Mother-Infant Project," paper presented at the American Anthropology Research Conference annual meeting (New York, N.Y., 1977); Stroup-Benham and Perkowski, "A Comparison of Financial, Access, and Sociocultural Barriers to Care"; Zambrana, "The Relationship of Health Perceptions, Physical and Mental Health, and Language Use."

19. David W. Baker et al., "Use and Effectiveness of Interpreters in an Emergency Department," *Journal of the American Medical Association* 275, no. 10 (March 13, 1996): 783–88.

20. S. Z. Nagi and E. Haavio-Mannila, "Migration, Health Status and Utilization of Health Services," *Sociology of Health and Illness* 2, no. 2 (1980): 175–93; Stern and Giachello, "Applied Research: The Mother-Infant Project."

21. Stern and Giachello, "Applied Research: The Mother-Infant Project."

22. Also see M. Gaviria, G. Stern, and S. L. Schensul, "Sociocultural Factors and Perinatal Health in a Mexican-American Community," *Journal of the National Medical Association* 74, no. 10 (1982): 40–46.

23. Also see ibid.

24. Ruth E. Zambrana, C. M. Scrimshaw, N. Collins, and C. Dunkel-Schetter, "Prenatal Health Behaviors and Psychosocial Risk Factors in Pregnant Women of Mexican Origin: The Role of Acculturation," *American Journal of Public Health* 87, no. 6 (June 1997): 1022–26.

25. J. M. Solis, G. Marks, M. Garcia, and D. Shelton, "Acculturation and the Risk of AIDS Among Hispanics in the United States," *American Journal of Public Health* 80 (Supplement) (1990): 11–19, at 11.

26. Alejandro Portes and Ruben G. Rumbaut, *Immigrant America: A Portrait* (Los Angeles, Cal.: University of California Press, 1990); A. Nyamathi et al., "AIDS-Related Knowledge, Perceptions, and Behaviors among Impoverished Minority Women," *American Journal of Public Health* 83, no. 1 (1993): 65–71.

27. Zambrana, Scrimshaw, Collins, and Dunkel-Schetter, "Prenatal Health Behaviors and Psychosocial Risk Factors."

28. Nyamathi et al., "AIDS-Related Knowledge, Perceptions, and Behaviors."

29. B. Marin and G. Marin, "Knowledge about HIV Transmission in Hispanics in

San Francisco: Acculturation Effects" (International Conference on AIDS, June 4–9, 1989, No. 5:801; abstract no. D. 658).

30. J. W. Green, *Cultural Awareness in the Human Services: A Multi-ethnic Approach* (Boston: Allyn & Bacon, 1995).

31. G. H. Weber and L. M. Cohen, eds., *Beliefs and Self-Help* (New York: Human Sciences Press, 1982).

32. E. Berkanovic and L. G. Reeder, "Ethnic, Economic, and Social Psychological Factors in the Source of Medical Care," *Social Problems* 21, no. 2 (1973): 246–59; Stern and Giachello, "Applied Research: The Mother-Infant Project."

33. I. K. Zola, "Culture and Symptoms: An Analysis of Patients' Presenting Complaints," *American Sociological Review* 31 (1966): 615–30.

34. Green, *Cultural Awareness in the Human Services.*

35. Ibid.

36. M. C. Sandoval, "Santería as a Mental Health Care System: An Historical Overview," *Social Science and Medicine* 13B (1979): 137–51, at 137.

37. R. Jimenez-Vazquez, "Hispanics: Cubans," in *Encyclopedia of Social Work,* 19th ed. (Washington, D.C.: NASW Press, 1995), 1223–31.

38. G. Bernal, "Cuban Families," in *Ethnicity and Family Therapy,* ed. M. McGoldrick, J. K. Pearce, and J. Giordano (New York: Guilford Press, 1984), 186–207; Jimenez-Vazquez, "Hispanics: Cubans."

39. S. Field, "Folk Healing for the Wounded Spirit: Storefront Psychotherapy Through Séance," *Innovations* 3, no. 1 (1976): 3–11; V. Garrison, "Doctor, Espiritista or Psychiatry?: Health-Seeking Behavior in a Puerto Rican Neighborhood of New York City," *Medical Anthropology* 1, no. 2 (1977): 65–91; Sandoval, "Santería as a Mental Health Care System."

40. Field, "Folk Healing for the Wounded Spirit"; Garrison, "Doctor, Espiritista or Psychiatry?"; Sandoval, "Santería as a Mental Health Care System."

41. Ailinger, "A Study of Illness Referral in a Spanish-Speaking Community"; Cohen, *Culture, Disease, and Stress Among Latino Immigrants*; C. S. Scott, "Health and Healing Practices Among Five Ethnic Groups in Miami, Florida," *Public Health Reports* 89 (1974): 524–32; C. H. Teller, "Access to Medical Care of Migrants in a Honduran City," *Journal of Health and Social Behavior* 14 (1973): 214–26.

42. Zulema E. Suárez, "Use of Self-Care by Hispanics in Chicago: Culture, Access or Need?," *Journal of Health and Social Policy* 4, no. 2 (1992): 32–44.

43. F. X. Acosta, "Barriers Between Mental Health Services and Mexican Americans: An Examination of a Paradox," *American Journal of Community Psychology* 7, no. 5 (1979): 503–19; L. A. Aday, R. M. Andersen, and G. V. Fleming, *Access to Medical Care in the United States: Equitable to Whom?* (Beverly Hills, Cal.: Sage Publications, 1980); Suárez, "Use of Self-Care by Hispanics in Chicago."

44. M. Delgado and D. Humm-Delgado, "Natural Support Systems: Source of Strength in Hispanic Communities," *Social Work* 27, no. 1 (1982): 83–89; J. Veroff, R. A. Kulka, and E. Douvan, *Mental Health in America* (New York: Basic Books, 1981).

45. Rogler et al., *A Conceptual Framework for Mental Health Research on Hispanic Populations,* 21.

46. A. Baron, *The Utilization of Mental Health Services by Mexican Americans: A Critical Analysis* (Palo Alto, Cal.: R & E Associates, 1979); Rogler et al., *A Conceptual Framework for Mental Health Research on Hispanic Populations.*

47. United States Bureau of the Census, *March 1994 Population Reports: Age of Population by Ethnicity.*

48. G. Grant, "Impact of Immigration on the Family and Children," in *Newcomers to the United States,* ed. M. Frank (New York: Haworth Press), 26–37, at 27.

49. Rogler et al., *A Conceptual Framework for Mental Health Research on Hispanic Populations.*
50. Padilla, Carlos, and Keefe, "Mental Health Services Utilization by Mexican Americans."
51. Cited in Baron, *The Utilization of Mental Health Services by Mexican Americans,* at 78.
52. Rogler et al., *A Conceptual Framework for Mental Health Research on Hispanic Populations.*
53. S. E. Keefe, "Why Mexican Americans Underutilize Mental Health Clinics: Fact and Fallacy," in *Family and Mental Health in the Mexican American Community,* ed. J. M. Casas and S. E. Keefe (Spanish Speaking Mental Health Center Monograph no. 7) (Los Angeles: University of California, 1979), 91–106.
54. O. Rodriguez, "Barriers to Clinical Services Among Chronically Mentally Ill Hispanics," *Fordham University Hispanic Research Bulletin* 6, nos. 3/4 (1983): 1–10.
55. Rogler et al., *A Conceptual Framework for Mental Health Research on Hispanic Populations*; Keefe, "Why Mexican Americans Underutilize Mental Health Clinics"; Aday, R. M. Andersen, and G. V. Fleming, *Access to Medical Care in the United States.*
56. Andersen, *A Behavioral Model of Families' Use of Services,* 16.
57. R. M. Weinick, S. H. Zuvekas, and S. Drilea, *Research Findings #3: Access to Health Care—Sources and Barriers, 1996* (Washington, D.C.: Agency of Health Care Policy and Research, 1997).
58. R. Valdez, "Improving Access to Health Care in Hispanic/Latino Communities," in *One Voice, One Vision—Recommendations to the Surgeon General to Improve Hispanic/Latino Health* 15–17 (Washington, D.C.: United States Department of Health and Human Services, 1993).
59. V. Keith and T. LaVeist, "Social, Economic, and Health Determinants of the Use of Health Care Services by Whites, African Americans, and Mexican Americans," in Lillie-Blanton, Leigh, and Alfaro-Correa, *Achieving Equitable Access.*
60. United States Department of Health and Human Services, Public Health Service, "The State of Minority Health: OMH State Representatives Meeting Addresses Managed Care," *Closing the Gap: A Newsletter of the Office of Minority Health* (March/April 1996): 1–4, at 2.
61. Ibid., 2.
62. Ibid., 3.
63. Zambrana, "The Relationship of Health Perceptions, Physical and Mental Health, and Language Use."
64. United States Department of Health and Human Services, Public Health Service, "The State of Minority Health."
65. Ibid.
66. Center for Health Economic Research, *Access to Health Care: Key Indicators for Policy* (Princeton, N.J.: Robert Wood Johnson Foundation, 1993).
67. Weinick, Zuvekas, and Drilea, *Research Findings #3: Access to Health Care— Sources and Barriers.*
68. R. P. Trevino, F. M. Trevino, and R. Medina, "Health Care Access Among Mexican Americans with Different Health Insurance Coverage," *Journal of Health Care for the Poor and Underserved* 7, no. 2 (1996): 112–21.
69. R. Pear, *New York Times* archive article, National Desk, September 26, 1998.
70. R. M. Andersen, S. Z. Lewis, A. L. Giachello, L. A. Aday, and G. Chiu, "Access

to Medical Care Among the Hispanic Population of the Southwestern United States," *Journal of Health and Social Behavior* 22, no. 3 (1981): 78–89.

71. J. M. Piper, W. A. Ray, and M. R. Griffin, "Effects of Medicaid Eligibility Expansion on Prenatal Care and Pregnancy Outcome in Tennessee," *Journal of the American Medical Association* 264, no. 17 (1990): 2219–23; Center for Health Economic Research, *Access to Health Care*.

72. Trevino, Trevino, and Medina, "Health Care Access Among Mexican Americans."

73. F. M. Trevino, E. Moyer, R. B. Valdez, and C. A. Stroup-Benham, "Utilization of Health Services by Mexican Americans, Mainland Puerto Ricans, and Cuban Americans," *Journal of the American Medical Association* 265 (1991): 233–37.

74. Trevino, Moyer, Valdez, and Stroup-Benham, "Utilization of Health Services by Mexican Americans, Mainland Puerto Ricans, and Cuban Americans"; Zulema E. Suárez, "Latino Health Care Utilization: Mexican-Americans and Puerto Ricans in Chicago," *Latino Studies Journal* 3, no. 2 (1992): 87–98; Trevino, Trevino, and Medina, "Health Care Access Among Mexican Americans."

75. L. S. Caplan and S. G. Haynes, "Breast Cancer Screening for Older Women," *Public Health Review* 24, no. 2 (1996): 193–204.

76. Aday, Andersen, and Fleming, *Access to Medical Care in the United States*.

77. Solis, Marks, Garcia, and Shelton, "Acculturation and the Risk of AIDS Among Hispanics in the United States"; L. J. Cornelius and Zulema E. Suárez, "What Accounts for the Dependency of African Americans and Hispanics on Hospital-Based Outpatient Care?," in Lillie-Blanton, Leigh, and Alfaro-Correa, *Achieving Equitable Access*.

78. Cornelius and Suárez, "What Accounts for the Dependency of African Americans and Hispanics on Hospital-Based Outpatient Care?"; Weinick, Zuvekas, and Drilea, *Research Findings #3: Access to Health Care—Sources and Barriers*.

79. M. Aguirre-Molina, "Health Promotion and Disease Prevention," in *One Voice, One Vision*, 23–25; Stroup-Benham and Perkowski, "A Comparison of Financial, Access, and Sociocultural Barriers to Care."

80. Cornelius and Suárez, "What Accounts for the Dependency of African Americans and Hispanics on Hospital-Based Outpatient Care?"

81. R. Pear, "Legal Immigrants to Benefit under New Budget Accord," *New York Times* archives article, National Desk, July 30, 1997.

82. C. Schlosberg and T. Nemore, *Welfare Reform Implementation: Issue paper 1* (National Law Project, 1996), Internet posting: www.healthlaw.org/analyses.html

83. Kaiser Family Foundation, *The Medicaid Fact Sheet* (November 1997), Internet posting.

84. National Health Law Program, *Health Related Provisions in the Illegal Immigration Reform and Immigrant Responsibility Act of 1996* (Los Angeles, Cal.: National Health Law Program, October 1996), at 3.

85. Schlosberg and Nemore, *Welfare Reform Implementation*.

86. Ibid.

87. Trevino, Trevino, and Medina, "Health Care Access Among Mexican Americans."

88. Stroup-Benham and Perkowski, "A Comparison of Financial, Access, and Sociocultural Barriers to Care."

89. Zambrana, "The Relationship of Health Perceptions, Physical and Mental Health, and Language Use"; Stroup-Benham and Perkowski, "A Comparison of Financial, Access, and Sociocultural Barriers to Care."

90. Baker et al., "Use and Effectiveness of Interpreters in an Emergency Department."

91. Ibid.

92. F. Trevino, "Increasing the Representation of Hispanics/Latinos in the Health

Professions," in *One Voice, One Vision*, 19–21.

93. Komaromy et al., "The Role of Black and Hispanic Physicians in Providing Health Care."

94. Zambrana, "The Relationship of Health Perceptions, Physical and Mental Health, and Language Use."

95. Komaromy et al., "The Role of Black and Hispanic Physicians in Providing Health Care."

96. Trevino, "Increasing the Representation of Hispanics/Latinos in the Health Professions."

97. Komaromy et al., "The Role of Black and Hispanic Physicians in Providing Health Care."

98. Ibid.

99. S. A. Holmes, "Hispanic Births in U.S. Reach Record High," *New York Times on the Web,* archives article, National Desk, February 13, 1998, at 1–2.

100. Ibid.

101. Ibid.

102. W. A. Leigh, *The Health Status of Women of Color* (Washington, D. C.: Joint Center for Political and Economic Studies, 1994).

103. Council on Scientific Affairs, "Hispanic Health in the United States," *Journal of the American Medical Association* 265, no. 2 (1991): 248–52.

104. Centers for Disease Control, "Mortality Patterns—Preliminary Data, United States, 1996," *MMWR: Morbidity and Mortality Weekly* 46, no. 40 (October 10, 1997): 941–44.

105. P. D. Sorlie, E. Backlund, N. J. Johnson, and E. Rogot, "Mortality by Hispanic Status in the United States," *Journal of the American Medical Association* 270 (1993): 2464–68.

106. Leigh, *The Health Status of Women of Color.*

107. Kaiser Family Foundation, *The Medicaid Fact Sheet.*

108. Centers for Disease Control and Prevention, "HIV/AIDS Surveillance Report," *MMWR: Mortality and Morbidity Weekly Report* 39, no. 6 (1994): 1–39.

109. R. M. Selik, K. G. Castro, M. Pappaioanou, and J. W. Buehler, "Birthplace and Risk of AIDS Among Hispanics in the United States," *American Journal of Public Health* 79, no. 7 (1989): 836–39.

110. P. DeCarlo, Marín VanOss, C. Gómez, and R. Díaz, *What Are Latinos' HIV Prevention Needs?* (San Francisco, Cal.: University of San Francisco Center for AIDS Prevention Studies, HIV Prevention Fact Sheet, 1996).

111. L. Richardson, "White Patients Have More Access to New AIDS Drugs, a Survey Shows," *New York Times* archives article, Metropolitan Desk, July 27, 1997, at 1–3.

112. Centers for Disease Control, "AIDS in Women—United States," *MMWR: Morbidity and Mortality Weekly* 39, no. 47 (1990): 845–46.

113. Ibid.

114. T. Diaz, J. W. Buehler, K. G. Castro, and J. W. Ward, "AIDS Trends Among Hispanics in the United States," *American Journal of Public Health* 83, no. 4 (1993): 504–10.

115. J. E. Becerra, C. J. R. Hogue, H. Atrash, and N. Pérez, "Infant Mortality Among Hispanics: A Portrait of Heterogeneity," *Journal of the American Medical Association* 265, no. 2 (1991): 217–21.

116. Holmes, "Hispanic Births in U.S. Reach Record High."

117. Becerra, Hogue, Atrash, and Pérez, "Infant Mortality Among Hispanics."

118. Selik, Castro, Pappaioanou, and Buehler, "Birthplace and Risk of AIDS Among Hispanics"; Peters, Thomas, Mack, and Henderson, "Risk Factors for Invasive

Cervical Cancer Among Latinas and Non-Latinas"; Solis, Marks, Garcia, and Shelton, "Acculturation and the Risk of AIDS Among Hispanics in the United States."

119. Zambrana, Scrimshaw, Collins, and Dunkel-Schetter, "Prenatal Health Behaviors and Psychosocial Risk Factors."

120. Aday, Andersen, and Fleming, *Access to Medical Care in the United States.*

121. Andersen, Lewis, Giachello, Aday, and Chiu, "Access to Medical Care Among the Hispanic Population of the Southwestern United States."

122. Keith and LaVeist, "Social, Economic, and Health Determinants of the Use of Health Care Services."

123. Ibid.

124. Zambrana, "The Relationship of Health Perceptions, Physical and Mental Health, and Language Use"; Cornelius and Suárez, "What Accounts for the Dependency of African Americans and Hispanics on Hospital-Based Outpatient Care?"

125. Giachello, "Hispanics and Health Care."

126. F. M. Trevino and A. J. Moss, "Health Insurance Coverage and Physician Visits Among Hispanic and Non-Hispanic People," in *Health United States, 1983* (Washington, D.C.: Government Printing Office, 1983) (National Center of Health Statistics, U.S. Public Health Service, no. 84-1576).

127. Andersen, Lewis, Giachello, Aday, and Chiu, "Access to Medical Care Among the Hispanic Population of the Southwestern United States."

128. Stroup-Benham and Perkowski, "A Comparison of Financial, Access, and Sociocultural Barriers to Care."

129. L. A. Aday, R. M. Andersen, and G. V. Fleming, *Access to Medical Care in the United States: Who Has It, Who Doesn't?* (Chicago: Pluribus Press, 1984); Andersen, Lewis, Giachello, Aday, and Chiu, "Access to Medical Care Among the Hispanic Population of the Southwestern United States"; Teller, "Access to Medical Care of Migrants in a Honduran City"; S. Welch, J. Comer, and M. Steinman, "Some Social Attitudinal Correlates of Health Care Among Mexican Americans," *Journal of Health and Social Behavior* 14 (1973): 205–13.

130. Stroup-Benham and Perkowski, "A Comparison of Financial, Access, and Sociocultural Barriers to Care"; Cornelius and Suárez, "What Accounts for the Dependency of African Americans and Hispanics on Hospital-Based Outpatient Care?"

131. Solis, Marks, Garcia, and Shelton, "Acculturation and the Risk of AIDS Among Hispanics in the United States."

132. L. C. Harlan, A. B. Bernstein, and L. G. Kessler, "Cervical Cancer Screening: Who Is Screened and Why?," *American Journal of Public Health* 81, no. 7 (July 1991): 890–95; Center for Health Economic Research, *Access to Health Care.*

133. Solis, Marks, Garcia, and Shelton, "Acculturation and the Risk of AIDS Among Hispanics in the United States."

134. Center for Health Economic Research, *Access to Health Care.*

135. Harlan, Bernstein, and Kessler, "Cervical Cancer Screening."

136. March of Dimes Infant Health Statistics, "Perinatal Statistics by Maternal Ethnicity, US, 1995," Internet posting: http://modimes.org/stats.htm.

137. Pérez and Martinez, *State of Hispanic America 1993.*

138. Keith and LaVeist, "Social, Economic, and Health Determinants of the Use of Health Care Services."

139. Komaromy et al., "The Role of Black and Hispanic Physicians in Providing Health Care."

140. *One Voice, One Vision—Recommendations to the Surgeon General to Improve Hispanic/Latino Health* 15–17 (Washington, D.C.: United States Department of Health and Human Services, 1993).

141. United States Department of Health and Human Services, Public Health Service, "The State of Minority Health."

142. *One Voice, One Vision.*
143. Ibid.; Suárez and Siefert, "Latinas and Sexually Transmitted Diseases."
144. *One Voice, One Vision.*

Bibliography

Acosta, F. X. "Barriers Between Mental Health Services and Mexican Americans: An Examination of a Paradox." *American Journal of Community Psychology* 7, no. 5 (1979): 503–19.

Aday, L. A., and R. M. Andersen. "A Framework for the Study of Access to Medical Care." *Health Services Research* 9, no. 3 (1974): 208–20.

Aday, L. A., R. M. Andersen, and G. V. Fleming. *Access to Medical Care in the United States: Equitable to Whom?* Beverly Hills, Cal.: Sage Publications, 1980.

———. *Access to Medical Care in the United States: Who Has It, Who Doesn't?* Chicago: Pluribus Press, 1984.

Aguirre-Molina, M. "Health Promotion and Disease Prevention." In *One Voice, One Vision—Recommendations to the Surgeon General to Improve Hispanic/Latino Health*, 23–25. Washington, D.C.: United States Department of Health and Human Services, 1993.

Ailinger, R. "A Study of Illness Referral in a Spanish-Speaking Community." *Nursing Research* 26, no. 1 (1977): 53–56.

Andersen, R. M. *A Behavioral Model of Families' Use of Services.* Center for Health Administration Studies Research Series no. 25. Chicago: University of Chicago Press, 1968.

Andersen, R. M., A. L. Giachello, and L. A. Aday. "Access of Hispanics to Health Care and Cuts in Services: A State of the Art Overview." *Public Health Reports* 101, no. 3 (1986): 238–52.

Andersen, R. M., S. Z. Lewis, A. L. Giachello, L. A. Aday, and G. Chiu. "Access to Medical Care Among the Hispanic Population of the Southwestern United States." *Journal of Health and Social Behavior* 22, no. 3 (1981): 78–89.

Baker, David W., et al. "Use and Effectiveness of Interpreters in an Emergency Department." *Journal of the American Medical Association* 275, no. 10 (March 13, 1996): 783–88.

Baron, A. *The Utilization of Mental Health Services by Mexican Americans: A Critical Analysis.* Palo Alto, Cal.: R & E Associates, 1979.

Becerra, J. E., C. J. R. Hogue, H. Atrash, and N. Pérez. "Infant Mortality Among Hispanics: A Portrait of Heterogeneity." *Journal of the American Medical Association* 265, no. 2 (1991): 217–21.

Berkanovic, E., and L. G. Reeder. "Ethnic, Economic, and Social Psychological Factors in the Source of Medical Care." *Social Problems* 21, no. 2 (1973): 246–59.

Bernal, G. "Cuban Families." In *Ethnicity and Family Therapy*, edited by M. McGoldrick, J. K. Pearce, and J. Giordano, 186–207. New York: Guilford Press, 1984.

Bonilla, L., L. Porter, and S. Mendez. *"Tenemos que Protegernos*: AIDS in Puerto Rican Communities." *Latinos Studies Journal* 1, no. 1 (1994): 83–104.

Cafferty, Pastora San Juan, and William McCready, eds. *Hispanics in the United States: A New Social Agenda*. New Brunswick, N.J.: Transactions Books, 1985.

Caplan, L. S., and S. G. Haynes. "Breast Cancer Screening for Older Women." *Public Health Review* 24, no. 2 (1996): 193–204.

Casas, J. M., and S. E. Keefe, eds. *Family and Mental Health in the Mexican American Community*. Los Angeles: University of California, 1979 (Spanish Speaking Mental Health Center Monograph no. 7).

Castillo, R. J. *Culture and Mental Illness: A Client-Centered Approach*. Pacific Grove, Cal.: Brooks/Cole, 1997.

Center for Health Economic Research. *Access to Health Care: Key Indicators for Policy*. Princeton, N.J.: Robert Wood Johnson Foundation, 1993.

Centers for Disease Control. "AIDS in Women—United States." *MMWR: Morbidity and Mortality Weekly* 39, no. 47 (1990): 845–46.

———. "Mortality Patterns—Preliminary Data, United States, 1996." *MMWR: Morbidity and Mortality Weekly* 46, no. 40 (October 10, 1997): 941–44.

Centers for Disease Control and Prevention. "HIV/AIDS Surveillance Report." *MMWR: Mortality and Morbidity Weekly Report* 39, no. 6 (1994): 1–39.

Cohen, L. M. *Culture, Disease, and Stress Among Latino Immigrants*. Washington, D.C.: Smithsonian Institution, 1979 (Special Study Research Institute on Immigration and Ethnic Studies).

Cornelius, L. J., and Zulema E. Suárez. "What Accounts for the Dependency of African Americans and Hispanics on Hospital-Based Outpatient Care?" In *Achieving Equitable Access: Studies of Health Care Issues Affecting Hispanics and African Americans*, edited by Marsha D. Lillie-Blanton, Wilhemina A. Leigh, and Ana I. Alfaro-Correa. Washington, D.C.: Joint Center for Political and Economic Studies, 1996.

Council on Scientific Affairs. "Hispanic Health in the United States." *Journal of the American Medical Association* 265, no. 2 (1991): 248–52.

DeCarlo, P., Marín VanOss, C. Gómez, and R. Díaz. *What Are Latinos' HIV Prevention Needs?* San Francisco, Cal.: University of San Francisco Center for AIDS Prevention Studies, HIV Prevention Fact Sheet, 1996.

Delgado, M., and D. Humm-Delgado. "Natural Support Systems: Source of Strength in Hispanic Communities." *Social Work* 27, no. 1 (1982): 83–89.

Diaz, T., J. W. Buehler, K. G. Castro, and J. W. Ward. "AIDS Trends Among Hispanics in the United States." *American Journal of Public Health* 83, no. 4 (1993): 504–10.

Edgerton, R. B., and M. Karno. "Mexican Bilingualism and the Perceptions of Mental Illness." *Archives of General Psychiatry* 24, no. 6 (1971): 286–90.

Field, S. "Folk Healing for the Wounded Spirit: Storefront Psychotherapy Through Séance." *Innovations* 3, no. 1 (1976): 3–11.

Frank, M., ed. *Newcomers to the United States.* New York: Haworth Press, 1983.

Freidson, E. "Client Control and Medical Practice." *American Journal of Sociology* 65 (1960): 374–82.

Garrison, V. "Doctor, Espiritista or Psychiatry?: Health-Seeking Behavior in a Puerto Rican Neighborhood of New York City." *Medical Anthropology* 1, no. 2 (1977): 65–91.

Gaviria, M., G. Stern, and S. L. Schensul. "Sociocultural Factors and Perinatal Health in a Mexican-American Community." *Journal of the National Medical Association* 74, no. 10 (1982): 40–46.

Giachello, A. L. "Hispanics and Health Care." In *Hispanics in the United States: A New Social Agenda*, edited by Pastora San Juan Cafferty and William McCready, 159–94. New Brunswick, N.J.: Transactions Books, 1985.

Giachello, A. L., and R. M. Andersen. *Self-Care Behavior Among the Hispanic Population in the U.S.: Analysis of National Data.* Unpublished paper presented at the Spring Institute, Department of Sociology, University of Chicago, 1981.

Gil, R. M. "Puerto Rican Mothers' Cultural Attitudes Toward Children's Problems and Toward the Use of Mental Health Services." In *Special Education and the Hispanic Child. Proceedings from the Second Annual Colloquium on Hispanic Issues*, edited by H. Martinez, 49–60. N.p.: 1980 (Eric/Cue Urban Diversity Series, no. 74).

Ginzberg, E. "Access to Health Care for Hispanics." *Journal of the American Medical Association* 265, no. 2 (January 1991): 238–41.

Gottlieb, B. H. "Lay Influences on the Utilization and Provision of Health Practices: A Review." *Canadian Psychological Review* 17, no. 2 (1976): 126–36.

Grant, G. "Impact of Immigration on the Family and Children." In *Newcomers to the United States*, edited by M. Frank, 26–37. New York: Haworth Press, 1983.

Green, J. W. *Cultural Awareness in the Human Services: A Multi-ethnic Approach.* Boston: Allyn & Bacon, 1995.

Harlan, L. C., A. B. Bernstein, and L. G. Kessler. "Cervical Cancer Screening: Who Is Screened and Why?" *American Journal of Public Health* 81, no. 7 (July 1991): 890–95.

Health United States, 1983. Washington, D.C.: Government Printing Office, 1983 (National Center of Health Statistics, U.S. Public Health Service, no. 84-1576).

Holmes, S. A. "Hispanic Births in U.S. Reach Record High." *New York Times on the Web* archives article. National Desk, February 13, 1998, at 1–2.

Jimenez-Vazquez, R. "Hispanics: Cubans." In *Encyclopedia of Social Work*, 19th ed., 1223–31. Washington, D.C.: NASW Press, 1995.

Kaiser Family Foundation. *The Medicaid Fact Sheet.* November 1997. Internet posting: http://www.kff.org/archive/health_policy/kcfm/glance/glance.html

Keefe, S. E. "Why Mexican Americans Underutilize Mental Health Clinics: Fact and Fallacy." In *Family and Mental Health in the Mexican American Community*, edited by J. M. Casas and S. E. Keefe, 91–106. Los Angeles: University of California, 1979 (Spanish Speaking Mental Health Center Monograph no. 7).

Keith, V., and T. LaVeist. "Social, Economic, and Health Determinants of the Use of Health Care Services by Whites, African Americans, and Mexican Americans." In *Achieving Equitable Access: Studies of Health Care Issues Affecting Hispanics and African Americans*, edited by Marsha D. Lillie-Blanton, Wilhemina A. Leigh, and Ana I. Alfaro-Correa. Washington, D.C.: Joint Center for Political and Economic Studies, 1996.

Kilborn, P. "Nation's Uninsured Seek Healthcare Any Way They Can." *New York Times*, August 5, 1997, Internet posting.

Komaromy, M., et al. "The Role of Black and Hispanic Physicians in Providing Health Care for Underserved Populations." *New England Journal of Medicine* 334 (May 16, 1996): 1305–10.

Leigh, W. A. *The Health Status of Women of Color.* Washington, D. C.: Joint Center for Political and Economic Studies, 1994.

Lillie-Blanton, Marsha D., Wilhemina A. Leigh, and Ana I. Alfaro-Correa, eds. *Achieving Equitable Access: Studies of Health Care Issues Affecting Hispanics and African Americans.* Washington, D.C.: Joint Center for Political and Economic Studies, 1996.

March of Dimes Infant Health Statistics. "Perinatal Statistics by Maternal Ethnicity, US, 1995." Internet posting: http://modimes.org/stats.htm

Marin, B., and G. Marin. "Knowledge about HIV Transmission in Hispanics in San Francisco: Acculturation Effects." International Conference on AIDS, June 4–9, 1989 (No. 5:801; abstract no. D. 658).

Massey, D. S., R. E. Zambrana, and A. Bell. "Contemporary Issues in Latino Families: Future Directions for Research, Policy and Practice." In *Understanding Latino Families: Scholarship, Policy and Practice*, edited by Ruth E. Zambrana. Thousand Oaks, Cal.: Sage Publications, 1995.

McGoldrick, M., J. K. Pearce, and J. Giordano, eds. *Ethnicity and Family Therapy.* New York: Guilford Press, 1984.

McKinlay, J. B. "Some Approaches and Problems in the Study of the Use of Services: An Overview." *Journal of Health and Social Behavior* 13 (1972): 115–51.

Miranda, M. R., ed. *Psychotherapy with the Spanish-Speaking: Issues in Re-*

search and Service Delivery. Los Angeles: University of California, 1976 (Spanish Speaking Mental Health Research Center, Monograph no. 3).

Nagi, S. Z., and E. Haavio-Mannila. "Migration, Health Status and Utilization of Health Services." *Sociology of Health and Illness* 2, no. 2 (1980): 175–93.

National Health Law Program. *Health Related Provisions in the Illegal Immigration Reform and Immigrant Responsibility Act of 1996.* Los Angeles, Cal.: National Health Law Program, October 1996. Internet posting: http://www.healthlaw.org/mmigrant.html

Nyamathi, A., et al. "AIDS-Related Knowledge, Perceptions, and Behaviors among Impoverished Minority Women." *American Journal of Public Health* 83, no. 1 (1993): 65–71.

One Voice, One Vision—Recommendations to the Surgeon General to Improve Hispanic/Latino Health. Washington, D.C.: United States Department of Health and Human Services, 1993.

Padilla, A. M., M. L. Carlos, and S. E. Keefe. "Mental Health Services Utilization by Mexican Americans." In *Psychotherapy with the Spanish-Speaking: Issues in Research and Service Delivery*, edited by M. R. Miranda, 9–20. Los Angeles: University of California, 1976 (Spanish Speaking Mental Health Research Center, Monograph no. 3).

Pear, R. "Legal Immigrants to Benefit under New Budget Accord." *New York Times* archives article. National Desk, July 30, 1997.

———. *New York Times* archives article. National Desk, September 26, 1998.

Pérez, S. M., and D. Martinez. *State of Hispanic America 1993: Toward a Latino Anti-Poverty Agenda.* Washington, D.C.: Policy Analysis Center Office of Research, Advocacy, and Legislation, National Council of La Raza, 1993.

Peters, R. K., D. G. Thomas, T. M. Mack, and B. D. Henderson. "Risk Factors for Invasive Cervical Cancer Among Latinas and Non-Latinas in Los Angeles County." *Journal of the National Cancer Institute* 77, no. 5 (1986): 1063–77.

Piper, J. M., W. A. Ray, and M. R. Griffin. "Effects of Medicaid Eligibility Expansion on Prenatal Care and Pregnancy Outcome in Tennessee." *Journal of the American Medical Association* 264, no. 17 (1990): 2219–23.

Portes, Alejandro, and Ruben G. Rumbaut. *Immigrant America: A Portrait.* Los Angeles, Cal.: University of California Press, 1990.

Richardson, L. "White Patients Have More Access to New AIDS Drugs, Survey Shows." *New York Times* archives article. Metropolitan Desk, July 27, 1997, at 1–3.

Rodriguez, O. "Barriers to Clinical Services Among Chronically Mentally Ill Hispanics." *Fordham University Hispanic Research Bulletin* 6, nos. 3/4 (1983): 1–10.

Rogler, L. H., and A. Hollingshead. *Trapped: Families and Schizophrenia.* New York: John Wiley, 1965.

Rogler, L. H., et al. *A Conceptual Framework for Mental Health Research on Hispanic Populations.* Bronx, N.Y.: Fordham University, 1983 (Hispanic Research Center Monograph no. 10).

Sandoval, M. C. "Santería as a Mental Health Care System: An Historical Overview." *Social Science and Medicine* 13B (1979): 137–51.

Schlosberg, C., and T. Nemore. *Welfare Reform Implementation: Issue paper I.* National Law Project, 1996. Internet posting: www.healthlaw.org/analyses.html

Scott, C. S. "Health and Healing Practices Among Five Ethnic Groups in Miami, Florida." *Public Health Reports* 89 (1974): 524–32.

Selik, R. M., K. G. Castro, M. Pappaioanou, and J. W. Buehler. "Birthplace and Risk of AIDS Among Hispanics in the United States." *American Journal of Public Health* 79, no. 7 (1989): 836–39.

Solis, J. M., G. Marks, M. Garcia, and D. Shelton. "Acculturation and the Risk of AIDS Among Hispanics in the United States." *American Journal of Public Health* 80 (Supplement) (1990): 11–19.

Sorlie, P. D., E. Backlund, N. J. Johnson, and E. Rogot. "Mortality by Hispanic Status in the United States." *Journal of the American Medical Association* 270 (1993): 2464–68.

Stern, G., and A. L. Giachello. "Applied Research: The Mother-Infant Project." Paper presented at the American Anthropology Research Conference annual meeting. New York, N.Y., 1977.

Stroup-Benham, C. A., and L. Perkowski. "A Comparison of Financial, Access, and Sociocultural Barriers to Care Among Hypertensives Across Three Ethnic Groups." In *Achieving Equitable Access: Studies of Health Care Issues Affecting Hispanics and African Americans,* edited by Marsha D. Lillie-Blanton, Wilhemina A. Leigh, and Ana I. Alfaro-Correa. Washington, D.C.: Joint Center for Political and Economic Studies, 1996.

Suárez, Zulema E. "Latino Health Care Utilization: Mexican-Americans and Puerto Ricans in Chicago." *Latino Studies Journal* 3, no. 2 (1992): 87–98.

———. "Use of Self-Care by Hispanics in Chicago: Culture, Access or Need?" *Journal of Health and Social Policy* 4, no. 2 (1992): 32–44.

Suárez, Zulema E., and K. Siefert. "Latinas and Sexually Transmitted Diseases: Implications of Recent Research for Prevention." *Social Work in Health Care* 28, no. 1 (1998): 1–20.

Teller, C. H. "Access to Medical Care of Migrants in a Honduran City." *Journal of Health and Social Behavior* 14 (1973): 214–26.

Trevino, F. "Increasing the Representation of Hispanics/Latinos in the Health Professions." In *One Voice, One Vision—Recommendations to the Surgeon General to Improve Hispanic/Latino Health,* 19–21. Washington, D.C.: United States Department of Health and Human Services, 1993.

Trevino, F. M., and A. J. Moss. "Health Insurance Coverage and Physician Visits Among Hispanic and Non-Hispanic People." In *Health United States, 1983*. Washington, D.C.: Government Printing Office, 1983 (National Center of Health Statistics, U.S. Public Health Service, no. 84-1576).

Trevino, F. M., E. Moyer, R. B. Valdez, and C. A. Stroup-Benham. "Utilization of Health Services by Mexican Americans, Mainland Puerto Ricans, and Cuban Americans." *Journal of the American Medical Association* 265 (1991): 233–37.

Trevino, R. P., F. M. Trevino, and R. Medina. "Health Care Access Among Mexican Americans with Different Health Insurance Coverage." *Journal of Health Care for the Poor and Underserved* 7, no. 2 (1996): 112–21.

United States Bureau of the Census. *March 1994 Population Reports: Age of Population by Ethnicity*. Internet posting: http://www.census.gov/Age/sex94.txt.

———. "Table 2. Selected Economic Characteristics of All Persons and Hispanic Persons, by Type of Origin: March 1994." http://www.census.gov/population/socdemo/hispanic/table2.txt

United States Department of Health and Human Services, Public Health Service. "The State of Minority Health: OMH State Representatives Meeting Addresses Managed Care." *Closing the Gap: A Newsletter of the Office of Minority Health* (March/April 1996): 1–4.

Valdez, R. "Improving Access to Health Care in Hispanic/Latino Communities." In *One Voice, One Vision—Recommendations to the Surgeon General to Improve Hispanic/Latino Health* 15–17. Washington, D.C.: United States Department of Health and Human Services, 1993.

Veroff, J., R. A. Kulka, and E. Douvan. *Mental Health in America*. New York: Basic Books, 1981.

Warren, D. *Helping Networks*. Notre Dame, Ind.: University of Notre Dame Press, 1981.

Weber, G. H., and L. M. Cohen, eds. *Beliefs and Self-Help*. New York: Human Sciences Press, 1982.

Weinick, R. M., S. H. Zuvekas, and S. Drilea. *Research Findings #3: Access to Health Care—Sources and Barriers, 1996*. Washington, D.C.: Agency of Health Care Policy and Research, 1997.

Welch, S., J. Comer, and M. Steinman. "Some Social Attitudinal Correlates of Health Care Among Mexican Americans." *Journal of Health and Social Behavior* 14 (1973): 205–13.

Zambrana, Ruth E. "The Relationship of Health Perceptions, Physical and Mental Health, and Language Use to Usual Source of Care." In *Achieving Equitable Access: Studies of Health Care Issues Affecting Hispanics and African Americans*, edited by Marsha D. Lillie-Blanton, Wilhemina A. Leigh, and Ana I. Alfaro-Correa (Washington, D.C.: Joint Center for Political and Economic Studies, 1996), 75–98.

Zambrana, Ruth E., ed. *Understanding Latino Families: Scholarship, Policy and Practice.* Thousand Oaks, Cal.: Sage Publications, 1995.

Zambrana, Ruth E., C. M. Scrimshaw, N. Collins, and C. Dunkel-Schetter. "Prenatal Health Behaviors and Psychosocial Risk Factors in Pregnant Women of Mexican Origin: The Role of Acculturation." *American Journal of Public Health* 87, no. 6 (June 1997): 1022–26.

Zola, I. K. "Culture and Symptoms: An Analysis of Patients' Presenting Complaints." *American Sociological Review* 31 (1966): 615–30.

8

Hispanics and the Social Welfare System

Katie McDonough and Alvin Korte

Over the past thirty years, the function and structure of social welfare have undergone sustained criticism that led to episodic reforms. The federal government has turned over more responsibility to states to create social welfare policy and to shape the delivery of services. Whereas government once assumed primary responsibility for funding and providing social welfare services and programs, that is no longer the case. The delivery of social welfare programs is increasingly contracted out to nonprofit and for-profit private agencies. Despite these changes, Hispanics and other populations remain poorly served by the social welfare system.

All too often, social welfare programs are designed to react to problems rather than to solve or prevent them. Many social welfare providers approach clients in a rigid, bureaucratic manner that creates alienation and disempowerment. The social welfare system often operates on a pathology model of human behavior at the individual and family levels, which emphasizes the need to control deviancy. Social welfare programs and services are not geared toward solving problems on the community level. The existing structure of social welfare does not provide the basic investments in communities needed to foster social institutions that would support the health, safety, and welfare of community members.

The social welfare system must undergo reconceptualization and restructuring if Hispanic and other poor populations are to be well served in the United States. For this to happen, attitudes about social welfare, as well as social welfare practices that frame the construction and provision of services, must be examined and transformed. To transform social welfare services, collaborative arrangements between government and communities are necessary. Such arrangements include reinvestment in communities and recognition of the strength and capacity of communities to develop local solutions to problems and needs. Community-based services offer the promise that social welfare can be more attentive to the needs of Hispanics.

Vulnerable Populations

Hispanics experience social problems because of poverty, marginalization, and discrimination. A large proportion of Hispanics are Mexican-Americans (62.6 percent), followed by Puerto Ricans (14.9 percent), Cubans (13.8 percent), Central and South Americans (7.6 percent), and a residuum of "other Hispanic." This is a young population with corresponding population growth: the Hispanic population grew 53 percent between 1980 and 1990, 5 times as fast as the total population and 8 times as fast as the non-Hispanic population. At the current rate of growth, Hispanics will be the largest ethnic group in the United States by the year 2020.[1] Much of the growth of the Hispanic population results from natural increases such as high fertility, but about half of the growth in population comes from immigration.[2]

Although the actual number of poor non-Hispanic Whites is greater than the numbers of poor Hispanics and Blacks, the likelihood of living below the poverty level is greater for Blacks and Hispanics. At the start of the 1990s, 1 in 3 Blacks (32.7 percent), more than 1 in 4 Hispanics (28.7 percent), and about 1 in 10 non-Hispanic Whites (11.3 percent) were poor.[3] Much of the poverty among Hispanics can be found among those who are working. "In 1991, 27.5 percent of all Hispanic families below poverty had at least one year-round, full-time worker. This compares to 21.8% of White and 11.9% of Black families in poverty."[4] Of Hispanic families below the poverty line in 1990, almost half (48.3 percent) were Hispanic female-headed households. Mainland Puerto Rican female-headed households had the highest poverty rate (64.4 percent), compared to less than one-third (31.7 percent) of non-Hispanic female-headed families.[5] The problem of poverty, which is so obvious for the working poor and female-headed households, also differentially affects infants and children, youth who fall outside the educational systems available to them, and the many elderly poor who never worked in jobs that built up Social Security.

Poverty statistics illustrate the failure of the social welfare system. Whereas 15.1 percent of the people in the United States were poor in 1993 (below the poverty threshold of $14,763 for a family of four), 30.6 percent of Hispanics in the United States were below that threshold.[6] For the general population, child poverty is the highest in thirty years, at more than one in five. Appalling as that proportion is, more than 40 percent of Hispanic children are living below the poverty level.[7]

Hispanic Infants and Children

The proportion of Hispanic children is increasing rapidly, relative to children of other racial and ethnic groups, and they now outnumber Black and non-Hispanic White children. The 40 percent of Hispanic children (as well as 40 percent of Black children) who live below the poverty line are disparately affected by social and developmental problems. The well-being of children who live below the poverty line compares unfavorably to those living above it on many indicators: general health (poorer), health care (no usual source), housing (multiple problems), nutrition (more hunger), early childhood education (less enrollment), and likelihood of having a parent working full-time all year.[8]

The quality of life for Hispanic children is seriously degraded by these factors. The number of Hispanic children entering the child welfare system is increasing. Methods of data collection identifying Hispanics in child welfare vary within and between states, so these children may be "underrepresented, overrepresented, or not counted at all."[9] For example, in Massachusetts, the Hispanic population is 4.7 percent and child abuse victims are reported as being 17 percent Hispanic; in Florida, "Hispanic" is not used as a category in the data, so none are reported. Thus, the data reveal no clear picture of how many Hispanic children are involved in the child welfare system.

In 1996, the National Latino Child Welfare Advocacy Group conducted a unique study that included child welfare service providers and participants from the community.[10] The researchers concluded that the welfare needs of Hispanic[11] children can be expressed in three main areas: (1) the need to improve the quality of data to track Hispanic children in the system; (2) the need to move Hispanic participation away from the margins of the child welfare system toward central participatory roles; and (3) the need to think more holistically about these children or to consider their welfare outside and beyond their condition in the child welfare system. This means policy attention that supports community environments assuring safety, care, and security for these vulnerable children. Ortega further outlined recommendations for the welfare of the children, including increased collaboration between services for children and linking of children's systems in the form of schools, child welfare services, the courts, and religious facilities.[12] These approaches are inherent in the community-based social policies and services recommended to more fully address the needs of this population.

Youth and the Educational System

The Hispanic population is a young population. The median age in 1990 was 34.6 years for non-Hispanic Whites, 27.7 for Blacks, and 26.3 for the Hispanic population overall. The median age for Mexican-Americans is 24.3 years, followed by 26.7 for Puerto Ricans, 27.9 for Central and South Americans, and 39.3 for Cubans.[13]

However, these young Hispanics are at great risk educationally. *Dropouts from school* refers to persons not enrolled in school who have no high school diploma. Regardless of the definition used for dropouts, Hispanics continue to have the highest school dropout rates of any major group. About 43 percent of Hispanics aged 19 years old or over are not enrolled in high school and have no high school diploma. Hispanic females tend to drop out earlier than Hispanic males. By ages 16 to 17, 21.4 percent of Hispanic females have dropped out of school, compared to 18.1 percent of Hispanic males; at ages 18 to 19, 27.3 percent of Hispanic females have dropped out, compared to 35.2 percent for Hispanic males. Gender differences of this magnitude are not found for Blacks or non-Hispanic Whites. One of the factors that impel students to leave school is family socioeconomic status. Using the National Education Longitudinal Study of 1988 (NELS) and data from the National Council of La Raza (NCLR), De La Rosa and Maw pointed out that among some of the factors leading to dropping out are single-parent families, low parental education and income, limited English proficiency, and having a sibling who dropped out of school.[14] These factors are not to be taken as purely causative, as there may be intervening variables of a personal nature as well.

Factors within the schools' control are attendance policies, discipline, promotion, resource allocation, hiring practices, availability of special instruction to meet special needs, in-service training for counselors and teachers, and mechanisms for involving parents.[15] Early marriage and/or pregnancy were often listed by Hispanic females as contributing reasons for leaving school. One-third reported leaving because of marriage or plans to marry, and one-fourth listed pregnancy. Twenty-six percent of the male dropouts left because they chose to work after getting job offers, but another 17 percent indicated that they had been expelled or suspended. The largest group, 34 percent of males and 32 percent of females, left school because of poor grades. Other studies have supported the contention that low attainment led students to conclude that school was "not for them." Again, the authors added a cautionary note not to infer cause-and-effect relationships, as other factors—within the student, the family, or the school—may cause poor grades.[16]

The Elderly

The population of elderly is growing in the United States. The Hispanic elderly are also a rapidly growing population, which experiences serious economic, physical, and emotional vulnerability.[17] Cubillos and Prieto cited the 1986 Census Bureau publication, "Projections of the Hispanic Population: 1983 to 2080," which shows that increases in the number of Hispanic elderly will account for one-quarter of the total Hispanic growth over the next twenty years. Since 1970, the Hispanic population has grown by 61 percent, well above the growth rate of the total elderly population.[18] Another estimate projected that "between 1990 and 2030, the Hispanic elderly population is expected to grow by 395 percent."[19]

Hispanics are the least educated elderly subgroup. The median number of school years completed for Hispanics 65 years of age and older in 1987 was 7.4, compared to 8.4 for Black elderly and 12.1 for non-Hispanic White elderly. In 1985, more than one-third (34.6 percent) of Hispanic elderly had less than 5 years of schooling, as compared to 1 in 4 (23.3 percent) of Black elderly and 1 in 20 (5.0 percent) for non-Hispanic White elderly. The Mexican-American elderly were the most likely to have completed less than 5 years of education (47.2 percent) and the least likely to be high school graduates (11.2 percent). Cubans were nearly three times as likely to be high school graduates. As expected, schooling varies by age, with the oldest persons (aged 75 and over) having less schooling than those aged 65 to 74.[20]

It is commonly assumed that low income in old age is less of a problem for elderly Mexican-Americans, as their immediate kin will take care of them. However, modernization and urbanization continue to erode a value system that mandates caring for the elderly.[21] Several authors have proposed that older Mexican-Americans are likely to feel abandoned by their families.[22] Many younger, U.S.-born Mexican-Americans have moved into the middle class, and the elderly may have problems dealing with these upwardly mobile children. The result of this adjustment is often that they cannot expect much help from adult children. Finally, language difficulties and economic hardships, as well as the need to balance independence with close family relationships, are great burdens to Mexican-American elderly.[23]

The poorest of the Hispanic elderly are the Puerto Ricans. Poor economic conditions in Puerto Rico, coupled with the lure of better jobs and better wages, have led many to migrate from the island to New York and other northeastern states. "Older Puerto Ricans face low income, poor health and urban ghettoization—a marked contrast to the rural village background of most of them, and not likely what they had in mind when they originally migrated to the United States."[24] Most older Cubans emigrated to the greater Miami-Dade County of southern Florida. Weeks[25] stated that "many Cuban elders have adapted remarkably well. Though some elders have suffered considerably with the disappearance of the extended family, many have adjusted well to peer group support systems .... Adaptation to America has required the development of new styles of living that are faster, more impersonal and individualistic."[26]

Lack of a good education is the one factor that seems to link Hispanic youth and elderly in time. Hispanic youth continue to experience high dropout rates. One consequence of this is that they will spend many years in low-income employment, often without good benefits. This will lead to a future like that of the present Hispanic poor elderly.

The 1990s and Social Services

The basic reason for a government social welfare system is to support the well-being of the people. Poverty is the force driving all the welfare needs exhibited by the vulnerable, marginalized, and oppressed populations within the social system. These conditions result in serious deprivations and require social welfare strategies to alleviate the suffering.

Social welfare policy in the United States has rarely met the challenge of delivering effective services to diverse peoples. Many system alterations have been made over several decades, in attempts to respond to plural needs. These included the "maximum feasible participation" of the War on Poverty years, as demonstrated in community action programs and Head Start. Attention has been given to recruiting, educating, placing, and advancing persons of diverse backgrounds and ethnicities as the professionals in the delivery system. Theories and policies have been implemented to affirm the right and need to have services delivered in the recipient's own language, by persons who are recognizably one with the clients' identity and culture. Many other approaches have attempted to adjust the technology of service delivery systems. These alterations in the culture, structure, and staffing of social service agencies were derived from important motivations and were necessary for the improvement of services. However, the delivery system has not achieved consistent success in improving the daily lives of the children, families, and individuals in the Hispanic community. They continue to experience high levels of need, and thus suffer disproportionately because of the failure of the service system.

Structures for service delivery in the United States are experiencing enormous upheaval. The era of conservativism during the late 1970s through 1990s led to reduced domestic spending for social programs. The rhetoric of values such as the work ethic, "getting ahead," and individual responsibility for one's own circumstances took a moralistic turn. Huge budget deficits, interpreted as scarcity of resources, added to the prevailing conservative ideologies and worsened the condition of the poorest in the nation through reduction of means-tested programs. It was impossible for the reduction in federal funding to be balanced by local and state funding, much less by private charity. The delicately woven and yet incomplete system of social services for the lowest income people lost funding to tax cuts, military spending, and interest on the hugely expanding national debt. This move away from the commitment to programs of social support is accelerating in the late 1990s, driven by the ideology and energy of the New Right. These change proponents are thriving while the nation's diverse peoples are becoming more oppressed by intensifying social problems.

The problems of increasing poverty, family violence, inadequate medical insurance, child welfare concerns, immigrant service needs, community health needs, and more are so intense and immediate that existing social service delivery systems seem inadequate to address them. Beyond the delivery system's problems, the foci of major federal efforts are questionable. Sometimes in the past government policy effectively countered the effects of racism and prejudice, and created programs that transformed the social order. In the late 1990s, though, the federal government appears to be creating a "police war against low-income Americans of color, not to mention teenagers, immigrants, and other designated misfits."[27] For example, incarceration levels can be a measure of repression, and the United States leads the world in this measure. Hispanics, as well as other persons of color, are disproportionately represented in U.S. jails. At year end in 1998, 688 Hispanics per 100,000 were inmates in federal and state prisons, compared to 193 White inmates per 100,000 non-Hispanic Whites.[28]

The federal government itself has taken on the role of control agent and surveillance leader in this repressive era, using the slogan "law and order" to justify the priority. The government is protecting the predominant ideology of the market system, acting to privatize services and passing tax law that accepts and increases income and wealth inequality. So, at the close of the century, the social service systems constructed by that government are struggling to survive. They have few resources and little energy left for the task of developing remedies for the problems experienced by the diverse peoples who make up the Hispanic population. This system, which has been relatively unresponsive to the needs of Hispanics, has facilitated and advanced the "otherness" of this group through increasing stigmatization of social services participants, and has been ineffective in reversing increasing poverty.

The social welfare system is embedded in a society that considers individuals responsible for their life condition and gives limited attention to the societal conditions that produce poverty, preventing families and communities from transforming their social situations. This system has consistently focused on individual interventions, a strategy that supports the status quo of structural inequities and oppression built into society and its operations. The causes of problems are seen by the system as the social welfare client's own malfunctioning.[29]

Additionally, the current residual policy approach places responsibility upon the poor for their condition—even while it creates programs that respond based only upon need. Residual concepts are built upon the "premise that an individual's needs should be met through the market system and through the family. This is the normative system in society." Further, when need is established, as it must be in the residual system, it proves "the breakdown of the other normative systems that should be working."[30]

In a more functional model, social welfare policy would provide support for the tangible survival and instrumental needs of the populations whose participation in the market system has been most limited by societal factors, including Hispanics and their families. It would also be organized to support their socioemotional needs, intervene in crises, and deliver long-term support. There would be validation of the membership and capability of the Hispanic community to build upon its own strengths. There would be participation by those community members, creation or expansion of neighborhood-based services, and increasing control by the community itself.

Government has the responsibility to provide resources and social supports to people through social welfare policy. To do so, it must innovate and, tapping the roots of social work, employ social and community assets to construct that policy. Social welfare and social programs must provide services and, at the same time, attack the larger economic and social structures that foster inequality, poverty, and dependence. Comprehensive, collaborative, multilevel policy and action programs can reduce poverty, unemployment, and homelessness. These initiatives could ease the unbearable stresses that increase child neglect and abuse, addictions, violence, and all the other maladaptive behaviors that tear at the heart of Hispanic and other peoples who have become mere objects in the system.

Adherence to Outdated and Inappropriate Economic Theory

In the United States, social welfare policy is intricately connected to the widespread belief that capitalism and democracy are not only mutually enhancing, but are required if either is to be accomplished. This unbending notion produces the dichotomous values demonstrated by conservative and liberal ideologies. Conservative economic theory purports that hard work produces success in the free market; thus, character separates those who deserve success from those who do not. Liberal approaches counter with an understanding that capitalism needs to be regulated to decrease the inequalities that result from the system itself. Both approaches continue to define capital and its contribution to the welfare of the society in limited and outmoded market-based terms.

This earlier definition of *capital* is anchored in viewpoint of an industrialized society. Policy leaders have been socialized to the nineteenth and twentieth centuries' industrialization history and its narrow financial and physical definition of *capital*. This prevents focus on and appreciation of the social capital ready to be tapped within communities.

Contemporary economic realities are far removed from those earlier notions. No longer an economy centered on labor and production, the present and future economy is knowledge- and communications-based and global in domain; it demands a revised understanding of capital to include humans. Production in the new economy requires that technical capital be part of the economic equation, in the form of individuals who have personal competence, ability to access information, and basic technological capacities. Skills and knowledge for such economic activities as computer programming, development of new scientific theories, entertainment, specialized services, and medical or biotechnical research are each domains of technical capital. If this type of capital is missing from society, the economy cannot prosper.[31]

Other expansions of the definition of *capital* recognize social and cultural participation and environmental or natural systems as part of its base. "The creation of wealth in fact rests fundamentally on the increase of social and natural capital."[32] Fundamental economic stability depends on this. Social capital includes all the human participants in the social structure: individuals, family members, households, volunteers, and community members. All societal members are potential contributors to a society that has goals for its people (such as social welfare policy that supports the instrumental and active needs of people). "Recognition of this broader concept of social capital extends economic decisions into a public or social sphere, and underlines the importance of relationships," social networks, and investment in these for the economic performance of a society. Social capital is policy-relevant and must not be defined as "economically inactive" or separate from economic theory.[33] Neither can it be seen as empty investment, nor deficit-producing; in fact, it is critical to basic economic stability.

Social capital is nested within its ecological system and cannot be separated from it. The environment itself is critical to the well-being of all the peoples who live within it. Industrial-age economics has focused more upon the pillage and exploitation of environmental resources than upon a perception of natural human systems as capital to be sustained and nurtured.

These definitions of the economy, based upon a changing world and particularly embracing the social and cultural capital view, will work to actively move Hispanics away from the margins of the economic system, into a central role in the continued well-being of the society. When the social institutions and natural networks valued by Hispanic peoples become a valued part of "productive" society—seen as capital to be invested in, rather than a deficit-producing welfare expenditure—some movement can occur in recreating social welfare policy.

Mechanistic Worldview and Top-Down Decision Making

The worldview issue in crises of social welfare is what is called the modern mechanistic worldview. This view is based on overreliance on ideologies emphasizing measurement, quantification, objectivity, and prediction about how the world works, while completely ignoring or devaluing the lives of human beings who are experiencing poverty, oppression, and discrimination. Social welfare systems had until recently ignored and devalued the assets of the diverse Hispanic community, particularly natural social networks and family relationships. Even the identification of the Hispanic group as a valid social category was a construction proclaimed by the United States government on May 4, 1978. The "validity" of the category stems from the law that names it rather than the lived experiences of the heterogenetic people who have been grouped into the category.[34]

Generic labeling and a western worldview of this markedly diverse group of individuals tend to create generalizations that impede real understanding of social welfare issues that need the energy of public policy for correction. The overbroad label is a mechanistic tool of a hierarchy that tends to gloss over the wide variances in the histories and perspectives of the peoples themselves. These differences have huge social, economic, cultural, and political ramifications that are often obscured by politically convenient terminology.

Hispanic is such a "scientifically problematic label," because it "glosses over salient national, ethnic and racial variations of a highly heterogeneous population with significantly different histories and perspectives."[35] Some Hispanics have been in the United States for hundreds of years, predating English-speaking settlers. Others in the population are very recent immigrants. The vast majority of immigrants are documented permanent residents, though some are undocumented. There are documented and undocumented refugees from socialist governments such as Cuba; others are political refugees from Mexico, Guatemala, El Salvador, Peru, and Chile. Additionally, the label includes Puerto Ricans, who as American citizens participate in the nation's highly mobile search for opportunity by moving to urban areas on the mainland. "Hispanic" ethnicity is further variegated by descendants of pre-Columbian Indian peoples, descendants of Africans brought as slaves to the New Spain, and all manner of hybrid Hispano-Indies *mestizos.*[36]

Since construction of the category *Hispanic*, government institutions have unilaterally identified, controlled, and provided systems-identified needed services to members of the "new" group.[37] This top-down direction affords limited attention to the real lives of the people placed in that category. The service delivery process has been constructed using problem definitions that are based on variation from the norms exemplified by those in leadership roles in the service institutions. Examples of this are found even in relatively progressive agencies, such as the Department of Health and Human Services (HHS), which appointed the Departmental Working Group on Hispanic Issues (DWGHI) in 1995 to examine the HHS's programs and services to Hispanic-Americans. The leaders of the working group were nominated by service divisions, using the criteria "senior representatives with experience serving Hispanic populations and/or in multi-cultural affairs, who had a *familiarity with organizational structures, programs, policies and resources for improving the services to Hispanic customers.*"[38] These criteria tend to ensure that the systems of service already in place will be viewed as the one best way to construct service delivery.

Characteristics of the typical system include planning models which presume that knowledge resides with those who are in lead positions; methods of assessment which presume that diagnostic approaches capture the nature and reality of problems; and case handling which presumes that those problems are located primarily and specifically within the individuals in which they are documented. These system characteristics are reinforced and protected by limiting access to leadership positions by people who come out of the Hispanic cultures and by depending on "generalized" research results that set forth stereotypical views of the lived experiences of the peoples themselves. This gap between policy makers and the diverse needs and characteristics of the peoples at the bottom of the decision-making structure devalues the significant and diverse basic elements that make up the real lives of the people identified. It ignores the social context of the human lives to which social welfare policy is directed. The values, rituals, traditions, and beliefs that define the identity of Hispanic peoples are minimized, and thus the persons who make up the group are also dismissed in the interest of creating efficient, effective policy. The typical system ignores the fact that life as lived in the neighborhood or community contains basic elements upon which social services could be modeled.

Another example of mechanistic structures is the widespread use of the *Diagnostic and Statistical Manual* (DSM) classification of human problems. By classifying another's reality as typified, the social worker gains surety of understanding and control. According to Sands, the various editions of the *Diagnostic and Statistical Manual* (currently DSM-IV) have dubious reliability, validity, and objectivity. Nevertheless, the DSM has been used to label those whose "constructs of reality" do not match trained professionals' views, and whose behaviors are a threat to mental health workers and the social order. Specifically, Sands argued that this tool of public policy can be used to segregate and oppress the poor, the fragile, and the disempowered, among whom are women, elderly, and minorities of color. Citing Esterson, she stated that "[e]ffective psychological study requires involvement—personal, reciprocal relatedness leading to an understanding of the nature of another person's experience."[39]

Social welfare professionals become agents and objects of the mechanistic approach as they identify with the funding sources that support them. Thus, child protection services, neonatal social work, medical social work, forensic social work, and other agency positions give identity and respectability to the practitioner. This narrowing of focus prevents the practitioner from considering the wider and more pervasive problems of poverty, economic insecurity, racism, and discrimination. Community- and neighborhood-based programs, which identify more closely with the people experiencing need, must hustle for funding from multiple sources and struggle to maintain their identity as community agencies. This requires people who are adept at handling proposals, garnering funds, and coordinating them for services that will not be reduced to a narrow-problem focus, but are understood to be part of systems at multiple levels. The mechanistic approach, which identifies problems from an elitist, expert space, names them, and pronounces the intervention to be used, is totally antithetical to methods that draw from the community itself understanding of and participation in meeting its own needs. Reinvention of the relationship between centralized funding approaches and self-identified community needs is called for.

Postmechanistic approaches in some scientific circles recognize dynamic systems in which behaviors and interactions re-create formerly devalued organizations. These groups are less rigid, nonhierarchical, and utilize the experience of members of the society to develop dynamic structures through which the well-being of people can be supported.

Language of Deficit

Social service workers have also tended to frame Hispanic populations in the language of deficit. Descriptions of the Hispanic community of need, by the words that are used, project specific views that may prevent addressing the actual needs of Hispanic persons. For example, consider this description of need:

> Hispanics suffer a 50 percent high school dropout rate, the highest of all groups; 64 percent of Hispanic heads of households do NOT have a high school diploma—the highest rate of all groups; 31 percent of Hispanic children with working parents lack medical insurance coverage as compared to 12 percent for non-minority children; 40 percent of Hispanic children live in poverty which is the highest for all minority groups; 11 percent or one in nine Hispanic families lives in poverty (based on 1989 census data); and in 1994, 23 percent of Hispanic elderly (sixty-five or older) lived in poverty.[40]

These demographics are, to a great degree, the results of macro-level problems of social stratification, economic inequality, and decrement of community. They are maintained through the structures of society, including social welfare programs, that miss important components of the interactional relationships that produce stable, functional systems.

The numbers may be crucial to understand the need for and the importance of more effective social welfare services. The language itself tends to "frame" the persons who are Hispanic in particular and peculiar ways. One overriding social welfare approach in the United States has been to blame the victim; thus, the very fact that Hispanics experience the disproportionate social ills demonstrated by these social indicators casts the whole population as suspect, to be subjected to investigation by social service delivery systems. As people are investigated, they become even more stigmatized and subjugated, and hence are made the objects of closer observation. This intensifies the exclusion of the group, increases the power and authority of those who investigate, and reinforces the institutional controls and paternalistic methods used by the social welfare systems.[41] Additionally, Margolin stated, "By focusing on the characteristics of clients [Hispanics in this case], on *their* pathology, *their* delinquency, *their* failures, attention was diverted from the conditions external to them that constrained and limited their choices." The negative language used by social welfare workers regarding Hispanic clients "legitimize[s] the existing social order by deflecting attention from the unequal distribution of social resources and opportunities responsible for turning some people into clients and others into judges."[42]

The language of deficit can place negative moral and behavioral attributes upon a large, diverse group of people. Strengths existing within the groups can be lost, ignored, or devalued in the problem-saturated recounting of the conditions existing in the group. Deficit views issues through a single lens, which contributes to faulty analysis and thus to the continued dysfunction of the social welfare systems. If there is ever to be preventive and appropriate social policy making, then alternative, more appropriate methods of analysis are needed. Herbert J. Gans proposed that an assertive "debunking" program to end the undeservingness of the poor could be achieved through applying differing methods of analysis, including "popular ethnography," analysis of the difference between "divergent" and "harmful" behaviors, exposure of the limited utility of blaming, and critical application of antiracism experiences to an attack on "classism."[43] Popular ethnography would show the lived experiences of the poor, and their survival efforts, along with the daily activities of the agencies that work with them. Stereotypes can be debunked with reality. This approach in the popular media could foster the inclusion (membership) of those who experience the social issues, and replace the value of financial efficiency with enhancement of the well-being of members of the society. Gans's proposals for altering the analytic approaches could be highly useful in facilitating greater knowledge of issues affecting Hispanics today and developing ways to address these issues.

Conceptually, issues surrounding social welfare services for Hispanics have centered upon accessibility, language issues, availability of Hispanic professionals, relevance to the particular Hispanic population, and cultural differences between Hispanics and non-Hispanics.[44] These certainly are important considerations for improving existing social welfare services. However, there has been little conversation about the social service structure itself and the dire need to alter this structure, which claims to support the well-being of all persons in the society and particularly those who have historically been defined as outside the "mainstream." The language of policy and thus of social welfare services shapes the way the identified people are viewed and becomes the basis for action.[45]

The Creation of "Other"

Majority group members (usually non-hispanic White, middle- or upper-class, and heterosexual) live within their own experience of entitlement and privilege. This forms their identity and constructs that experience as normative.[46] This construction fosters the tendency to view all persons of other races, classes, and sexual orientation as "other." There is a credible struggle for inclusiveness taking form in the emergence of multiculturalism in academia and the popular press. Yet members of society continue to be socialized to see difference and to make judgments about the relative worth of groups in terms of their differences.[47] Those judgments can be the basis for continuing racism, silencing of other voices, and social oppression through social welfare practices conducted by those who have not yet extinguished their learned behaviors.

Michael Soldatenko traced the "continuous process of 'othering'" as it is particularly connected to imperialist expansion:

> The colonial territories are transformed into worlds of possibilities where the norm is antithetical to the European and therefore inadequate. Moreover, this colonial space becomes part of the very imperialist nations themselves. Thus the othering of the alien is not only done externally to those communities but occurs to "those" people as immigrants (short- and long-term), forced emigrés, and conquered peoples living in these core societies.[48]

This construction has prevailed over the centuries and is constitutive to the culture of the Western mind. This type of thought denies the likelihood of knowledge of and by the other and invalidates their very being.[49] In this way, for more than 500 years, Hispanic persons in the United States have been made into an inverted image of the Euro-Americans, the opposite image representing social attributes that are considered negative. Created in negative and barbaric images, with the social problems of the times attributed to them, there is erasure of the persons within the groups and complicity by the group itself in accepting the reflected identity as real.

Social work education requires curriculum content that prepares graduates to recognize the salience of race, ethnicity, and culture for social welfare practice. This focus presumes that cultural "sensitivity" or "competence" will alter the relationships of the social workers to persons who are racially or ethnically different from themselves. It does not address the carefully constructed, fundamental social divisions that create the separations in society, and that are such vicious contradictions of equality. The social workers' relationships to the Hispanic community do not change by the workers' being sensitive and competent, but by their knowing and acting wholeheartedly upon the reality that difference is not deviance.

An alternative socialization of all members of society relative to their social space and the relationships within it could be based in some elements of Hans Falck's Membership Perspective.[50] Falck's theory of membership is anchored in the view that living things are always linked to other living things. Life and survival are contingent upon this permanent linkage. "It is lawful, it crosses all boundaries of race, ethnicity, time, place, social class, gender and age." One cannot resign from the linkage. It is irreversible. It is beyond choice. One group or person cannot eliminate the linkage of another. The linkage is called *membership*. From this, Falck developed the "Principle of Constant Connectedness" and suggested that social workers can adapt from this principle a second stance called the "Principle of Conditional Accessibility." With membership established beyond doubt, social workers must examine and act upon the conditional accessibility constructed by biological, social, psychological, and symbolic factors. These have "unlawfully" (without scientific or factual basis) divided individuals, groups, systems, races, ethnicities, and genders into parts that are separated from membership.[51] Social welfare systems can turn their efforts toward eliminating such conditionality for Hispanics and affirm Hispanics' full membership. There can be no expectation or requirement that they lose their language, culture, mores, and ways of being Hispanic to gain access to the policy resources available to full members.

An example of a social factor that constructs conditional accessibility is the assimilation model of racial and ethnic relations. This continues to be the dominant model taught in sociology, and it informs the social science research agenda dealing with racial and minority peoples.[52] The model assumes that acceptance—or membership, to use Falck's term—increases as minority group members become more like the members of the majority group. Assimilation thus creates access to constant connectedness *conditioned* on how closely the minority person comes to the prescribed idealized social order. The model gives theoretical support to political views promoting English-only and other such policy agendas, along with promoting the view of difference as deviance. Of course, there has been some discrediting of assimilation theory in the past forty years, because it is not actually a theory but more of a prescription for success within the dominant society.[53] Nonetheless, the approach socializes many people into a way of perceiving membership. Until we adopt the fundamental stance that humans are constantly connected, so that there can be no construction of "other," we will continue to wonder how to achieve a just social system. The differential effects of a flawed social welfare system upon Hispanics give evidence of the "unlawful" separation from membership constructed through privilege. Once a separation from full unconditional membership is constructed, the people who hold membership move in the direction of ignoring those who have been separated, seeing them as expendable, disposable, and dispossessed—or not seeing them at all!

Reactions to Changing Demographics

Other chapters of this book discuss at length the specifics of the changing ethnic composition and demographics of the United States. These profound shifts fuel political and economic tensions that affect the social welfare system. Historically, new immigrants have settled in enclaves within inner cities, where the most socially disadvantaged remained, and competed with additional new arrivals for community resources. The more skilled immigrants have been shifting their settlement patterns toward the suburbs, where their skills and education allow movement into middle-class enterprises located there. Manning gave evidence that there has been a profound shift in immigrant settlement patterns, with more immigrants flowing to the suburbs than to the central cities, and thereby changing the sociocultural "complexion" of the metropolitan suburban landscape.[54] This shift (mostly in major metropolitan areas such as Washington, D.C., Chicago, Los Angeles, and New York) represents a loss of political control in the suburbs by the dominant non-Hispanic White majority. This raises political tensions and threatens the existing power structures. The resultant movement toward fundamental social change, at a time when there are glimpses of impending collapse within industrial capitalism, produces some of the hysteria demonstrated within major social systems and by those who have power therein.

The rapidly shifting demographics of the nation drive an urgent discussion of multiculturalism. While there is no denying that social categories exist (whether artificially constructed or occurring within the unique experiences of each group), there is urgency in deciding the place of these categories within social welfare policy. Tensions exist between the values and strength of a culturally plural society acting to construct policy, on the one hand; and the unity of a national identity in which there is marginalization of cultures other than the dominant one, on the other. In this second approach, social welfare policy is constructed within the ideological values of the dominant group. This typical approach stands accused of supporting multilayered patterns of social inequality (stratification by class) that are politically constructed and maintained, which overemphasize harmony between groups while overlooking the political and economic forces that divide them. The overemphasis on harmony is also driven by a reemergence of the idea of restoring a national unity—which has never been an actuality. The danger in that discussion is that once again we will fall prey to a preoccupation with national cohesiveness and collectivity, seeking harmonious and unified national activities by elitists who may even hold hostile views of the strength and moral authority of the local community.[55] The demographic changes, which are quickly making the Hispanic minority into a majority, incite a frantic national discussion bent upon restoring to dominance the idea that middle-class lifestyles and values should be expected and attained by the less privileged, even without the resources to achieve them. This idea has already borne fruit in the welfare "reforms" of 1996, under which welfare mothers are forced to enter the labor market and are stigmatized for single parenthood.

The demographic changes and resultant tensions have contributed to some of the farthest-reaching changes in social welfare policy in more than fifty years. The increase in numbers of Hispanic immigrants and undocumented persons was a background stimulus to the changes in social welfare that reduced or eliminated their public welfare benefits. As of the enactment date of H.R. 3734, the Personal Responsibility and Work Opportunity Reconciliation Act of 1996, legal immigrants entering the United States are not eligible for Supplemental Security Income (SSI), food stamps, Medicaid, unemployment benefits, or other federal programs until they have been residents in the United States for five years or until they obtain citizenship. There are a few exceptions, such as a legal immigrant who is a political refugee, or one who has worked for forty quarters paying into Social Security, or a legal immigrant who is an honorably discharged veteran of the U.S. armed services. The act also amended SSI so that most legal immigrants who are older and disabled and had qualified for SSI benefits would lose them at the annual recertification of eligibility. States were also given the power to ban Medicaid coverage after the five-year residency requirement. In 1997, the states were also given the option to *terminate* Medicaid coverage, food stamps, and many other services to legal immigrants, under the Title XX Social Service Block Grants. Although some of those options were repealed, they indicate major alterations in government's basic investment in the social well-being of members of society, driven by the tensions in the dominant society about the changing demographics.

Panethnicity

One development that can have great effect on the ways social welfare services are constructed and implemented with Hispanic populations is panethnicity. *Panethnicity* is defined as "the development of bridging organizations and solidarities among subgroups of ethnic collectivities that are often seen as homogeneous."[56] While continuing to recognize the heterogeneous nature of the Hispanic-labeled group, it is also possible to recognize the political power to be gained by establishing collaboration and coalition between and among the groups. This is not a simple process. It is affected by many factors, which can be grouped into cultural and structural categories. Lopez and Espiritu identified these as language and religion, race, class, generation, and geography.[57] For Hispanics, language and religion are potentially powerful cultural bases for bridging the dividing structural factors. There is great variation, however, in the structural factors that could divide Hispanics. Class differences are reflected in the contrast between Cuban middle-class political refugees, Puerto Ricans, and Mexican and Central American immigrants. Group members who have been in the United States for a longer time have a greater likelihood of sharing concerns with each other than with those who are newly arrived. New arrivals may be seen as competitors, and newcomers may feel excluded. The fact that Hispanic subgroups have occupied geographically dispersed spaces within the United States has worked against their unification efforts. "A Puerto Rican in New York City and the Hispano in rural New Mexico may share a language, a religion, and a heritage of exploitation but they still have little common ground on which to cooperate."[58]

Therefore, in general, the structural factors that work against Hispanic panethnicity are exceedingly salient. There have been small successes in bridging these differences, but separation is still apparent. The demographic transitions now taking place provide new opportunities to overcome the disunity, and to organize around a common understanding of economic deprivation, political exclusion, and similar class positions, without giving up the particularism that is highly valued within the subgroups. Ethnic culture could be bound together through common language. Even though Hispanics in the United States rapidly become English-language dominant, retention of the unifying language factor among all the subgroups of Hispanics has enormous political ramifications. The possibility of the language contribution to panethnic organizing is constantly diminished through policy offensives that advocate "English only" and reduction of bilingual education, both of which were popular political foci in the late 1990s. Religion could be an organizing arena for building social power and regaining government funding for partnerships between local communities and the national policy system. Even though the traditional membership in the Catholic Church is diminishing, reflecting worldwide trends toward Protestant and other denominations, claims to Christianity continue as a unifying element.

Another counter-influence to divisive structural factors could be for Hispanics to assertively embrace a view of one community, based upon the understanding that community does not necessarily rely upon place or differences but can be based upon choice. A *chosen community* is one that focuses "on people who are distributed throughout social and ethnic groupings and who do not themselves constitute a traditional community of place."[59] The political decision that created the Hispanic grouping in this society could be a foundation for diverse groups to form a chosen community. This determined choice—to be members in such a community—would construct a Hispanic people who could resist the dominant attributions maintained in the social welfare policy systems and subvert the identities constructed about them. They could disallow an identity as atomistic components of systems, or as "like minded subjects of an authoritarian community of place."[60] Then, to gain the power to achieve effective social welfare policy, Hispanics might focus on the cross-cutting issues that influence their chosen community. The dividing factors can be supplanted with a commitment to develop a cohesive community of choice which is tied together by a common concern for the well-being of the whole group and appreciation for the resources residing in its members. There is implicit understanding of these issues in organizations such as La Raza, a currently existing organization that could be a foundation for panethnic organizing.

Other examples of chosen communities that have activated social policy on behalf of large numbers of diverse members are the American Association of Retired Persons (AARP) and the American Legion. AARP has demonstrated resounding success in supporting the social policy agenda of middle-class elderly persons, across phenomenal dividing factors. This organization is influential in protecting its own agenda in the policy arena.

The American Legion is often viewed as a local voluntary civic organization. However, organizing around a single salient binding experience—serving in the military—it became a nationwide community of officers and soldiers who served in North America's wars. It has more than 10,000 posts across the United States and enrolls up to 25 percent of veterans from those wars.[61] The best example of the American Legion's uniting of interests of a diverse membership is its initiation of and support for the GI Bill of 1944. This major expansion of the welfare state, equaled only by the Social Security Act of 1935, demonstrates the power of a panethnic organization to overcome huge obstacles to produce policy that addresses a common need. The GI Bill is social welfare policy that invested in social capital by providing universal benefits to veterans and their families; it made them stakeholders in their own future and organized them into a widely diverse group committed to the well-being of much of society.

The differences among the multiple ethnic groups represented under the term *Hispanic* can also be bridged by using the advanced methods of rapid communication afforded through easily available information and electronic technology. If more than 1 million veterans of all socioeconomic and racial backgrounds could be organized in 1944 to pass a social policy agenda, there is great hope that a like community can be formed by Hispanic persons committed to the well-being of the panethnic community they organize.

This type of commitment already exists for Hispanics at the family level. Cuellar specified that there are "unifying cultural themes or patterns that underlie the beliefs and values that most Hispanic Americans share, and that, besides Spanish language use, [these themes] distinguish them from the dominant Anglo American cultural tradition."[62] Some of the most important of these, which could be built upon to create community-based social welfare policy and services, are *familismo, personalismo, espiritismo,* and *presentismo.* These values (discussed further later in this chapter) or others might be good basic starting points to consider for building a panethnic approach to welfare with the diverse community of choice.

Revitalizing of Communities and the Community-Based Model

The rapid and continuing increase in the Hispanic population, along with the intensification of social welfare problems, provides a context in which to return to the historic mission of social welfare. This mission, briefly stated, is to ensure the freedom and well-being of all in the society, particularly those who are most disadvantaged. The current policy approaches to fulfilling this mission have been based on limited definitions of social capital; mechanistic, hierarchical, and bureaucratic structures; disempowering language; and the segregation of Hispanics into one of several problem-saturated minority groups.

National social welfare policy could comprehensively reverse the effects of these approaches. The growing dissatisfaction with social welfare programs has led to community-based, client-centered, and neighborhood-style approaches for rebuilding community services. These approaches are not new; they had precursors in the settlement movement and the War on Poverty, to name only two. The community initiative addresses specific problems in neighborhoods and communities by reinvigorating traditional agencies in collaboration and coordination to create more responsive services. This approach requires a different way of viewing "the client," as well as forging different relationships with the people in neighborhoods and communities. The structural changes needed in social policy are already appearing in some social science literature. The approach with the most potential for just and effective activities is based on partnerships with communities and neighborhoods. Social welfare policy can take the lead in reversing the beginning point for intervention, placing this point at the community level and using the resources, social networks, assets, and social capital of community members.

The overall policies for social welfare in the United States have largely ignored one of the most basic elements of Hispanic peoples' communities: the natural support system.[63] These natural network systems tend to be overlooked or suppressed as a source of needed social welfare service. Although a large body of research gives evidence of the buffering effects of social support on stresses, social welfare policies and systems have given only limited acknowledgment to the potential outcomes of collaboration with them. There has been even less effort to shift the central focus to building social welfare services that use natural networks as the foundation of the services. Hispanic communities historically do not seek the help of deductively constructed social service systems, but very frequently access the social networks naturally available. It therefore follows logically that collaboration with those networks could result in more accessibility, closer fit between providers and recipients, and more appropriate services. Gottlieb organized the strong appeal of such an approach in three areas.[64] First, governments and social service planners should be impressed by the widely applicable empirical demonstrations of the way social supports offset the "negative effects of stress that are produced by environmental adversity."[65] Second, use of the natural support network, with professionals collaboratively involved in the delivery of resources to support the interventions and for research purposes, would cost less than the labor-intensive technologies currently employed. The third area of appeal is what Gottlieb called "their ecological validity." Historically underserved or unserved communities most usually turn to informal natural systems and voluntary groups in their host culture. The influence of "cultural blueprints" on the structures of social networks—"their norms about helping, their patterns of help seeking, and the very meanings that support takes on"[66]—produces social support that is more accessible, culturally valid, and acceptable than traditional social services.

For Hispanics, the well-documented presence of natural support/help systems existing within each community can become a foundation upon which to develop social welfare organizations and services. This can be accomplished in collaboration with federal, state, and local policies and professionals. This community context for social welfare services has been called "the pendulum of the 1990s,"[67] and is a central movement that could make a vast difference in the kinds of support Hispanics receive from social welfare policy. Delgado and his colleague found, though, that in sixteen Office of Substance Abuse Planning (OSAP) Hispanic grant applications, none had included use of existing social networks in their service planning, nor had the natural support system been conceptualized as a valuable resource.[68] Delgado provided some fruitful ideas for the incorporation of natural support systems in the curbing of alcohol, drug, and tobacco use.[69]

Politically, social support through natural networks would be supported by conservatives because they value self-help. Liberals might see the use of natural support systems as an empowering approach, giving more control over personal lives to individuals. However, as Gottlieb asserted, there could be "more pernicious" political uses of the approach.[70] If the informal systems take on more responsibility for service delivery, any failures could deflect blame away from policy makers onto the indigenous system.

Realistically, community-based services cannot be claimed as a panacea for the disproportionate and troubling welfare needs of Hispanics. "Securing a modest share of social power for the residents of disadvantaged communities is eminently worthwhile, but it has serious limitations when the levers of meaningful political and economic power hover far above the grasp of the players."[71] The democratic political process and informal interactions must become the central focus if the market ideology that has dominated policies meant to address inequality is to be overcome. "Take back the rhetoric" might be one rallying cry. The market-ideology-driven language of personal responsibility over collective and shared responsibility, community members as "consumers" of the "products" of social services, and the "numbers who have gone off welfare" versus the well-being of competent, resourceful, family- and community-oriented Hispanics is a possible organizing point. "Rather than adopting the 'official' language and modifying policies to conform to the rhetoric of the market or appealing to market efficiency, advocates need to attack the ideological basis of public policy and expose market rationales as legitimizing the current unequal distribution of wealth and power."[72] Beyond the critical need for strengthening the political and social power of the Hispanic community, the movement toward community-based services can best be built upon the knowledge and success of the approach utilized during the past decade.

P. Ewalt, the editor of *Social Work*, succinctly addressed the matter of poor people, the restructuring of social services, and the need for comprehensive community approaches to solve entrenched problems. The core of the problem is the continued concentration of poor people in central cities and is characterized by lack of basic resources such as transportation, employment, health care, public safety, and good education for children. It is clear, she wrote, that because of the compounding and interrelatedness of problems, "redevelopment of impoverished communities requires a multifaceted approach that addresses the physical and economic conditions of neighborhoods and as well as the social and cultural aspects."[73] She further pointed out that sectional funding may not be as promising as funding for comprehensive community initiatives. Traditional social services such as child welfare agencies and juvenile probation offices cannot attack the problem alone.

A pooling of resources, development of interagency collaborative and coordination agreements, and redirected effort are needed. The new approach to social services, besides being less stigmatizing, is

less reactive, more proactive and preventative, building on the strengths and resources of families and communities rather than focusing on individual and neighborhood deficits. In forming partnerships with family members, their social networks, schools, churches, and formal and informal organizations of many kinds, workers share responsibility rather than shouldering the burden of social problems alone.[74]

There are many illustrations, including the aforementioned volume of *Social Work* dedicated to illustrating how communities are attempting to renegotiate, revitalize, and redevelop needed community linkages and agreements to combat the problems of ATOD (alcohol, tobacco, and drug use), juvenile delinquency, neighborhood violence, school dropouts, and services to elderly people.

Community policing shares some concerns with this new/old social service thinking. For example, one article argued that well-functioning, well-organized communities have the capacity to assess and propose solutions to community problems, including crime. Thus, community policing as compared to the formal model of policing involves community organizing in socially disorganized areas.[75] Some of these linkages may involve only a few community agencies agreeing to share client information, pool resources, and redirect efforts. Other efforts may involve complex structures needed to redirect the available resources in a more focused endeavor.

There are qualitative differences in how clients are treated in these organizations. For one thing, a partnership with the people to be served requires a sense of equality among the partners. Persons seen as partners become stakeholders in the agency and its purposes. This was seen in one organization in which one of the authors did a program evaluation. The program involved underachieving Spanish-speaking students in an education program. These youth came from migrant families that followed the crops and had settled in the area because of the year-round availability of agricultural and farm work. A program evaluation determined that these underachieving youth had one thing in common: a father serving time in jail or prison. It was also determined that the mother needed skills to better manage family affairs. Outreach was conducted by a Spanish-speaking person who understood the needs of newly arrived migrants and others at the edges of society. Classes in citizenship, English as a second language, budgeting, community services, family problem solving, clothing and food provision, and other services were made available according to family needs. Mothers were listed in the program records as "volunteers." Indeed, they came to the point of participating with their children in a community graffiti cleanup. They had developed ownership in and a partnership with the agency. During the life of the program to date, not one of the thirty-three families involved has had a child referred to the juvenile probation office. One father returned from prison during the program evaluation and had employment waiting for him. Unfortunately, he lost this job after having to wait for hours for a designated and mandatory appointment with an adult probation officer, who rudely neglected to see this man during the scheduled time. The probation officer's lack of participation in the coalition, despite the agreement between the agencies, could derail efforts to normalize these Mexican-American immigrant families. Rather than allowing the family to fail and therefore become eligible for services by a policy default (what is now euphemistically being called "clientized"[76]), the managers of this community center elected to provide the family with the citizenship and community participation skills they needed to survive. It is important to note that program funding did not filter through many channels, but was made site-ready. This meant that there was local access and control of the dollars by the local community and a reduction in the role of state and federal bureaucracies. The services were driven by their goals and missions, not by mandated compliance with rules and regulations.

Another success is the work of the Hispanic Health Council (HHC), a community-based health research, service, and advocacy organization in Hartford, Connecticut. The major identified work of the council is AIDS prevention education with Puerto Ricans. Although this organization is basically constructed on a public health model, and reports mostly with an institutional viewpoint, the institutional purpose includes a strong focus on critically understanding the structural "determinant roles of social inequality, racism, homophobia, and sexism in shaping the [AIDS] epidemic."[77] The analysis of the organization's experiences over a fifteen-year period is helpful in pinpointing supports for and obstacles to effective community-based social services. Some of the challenges encountered by HHC, which would apply to any community-based service enterprise, were: institutionalizing the service, resisting co-optation, and resisting depoliticalization. Any organization that is serious about reinventing services to ensure community self-determination and social *conscientization*, so that change can be constructed, will confront these issues.

People need to be seen as valued *vecinos*, persons or families who share the life of the neighborhood and with whom one shares in the solution of neighborhood problems. In the agency described earlier, a community link person was found to be key in bringing people into the agency.[78] Link persons interpret what the agency/service organization offers. This is vital in working with Hispanics, as this person "authenticates" the agency to the people in need and paves the way for participation. In the cited case, a bilingual-bicultural worker who herself had been a migrant worker was exceptionally well placed to facilitate connections into the network of agency and community services.

The last part of Ewalt's equation has to do with cultural and social values that must be incorporated in services to Hispanics. Cuellar articulated a set of values that have appeared in the literature in a number of places.[79] Cuellar defined *familismo* as the value that family locality comes first. It is within the family system that family members are taught cooperation versus competition, mutual assistance as opposed to individual problem solving, sharing as differentiated from withholding resources.[80] It is interesting to note the number of social services agencies that use the word *familia* as an ethnic symbol in either the organization's name (Familias Unidas, La Familia, Somos Familia) or in subcomponents of a program. This appeal to ethnic loyalty is characteristic of organizations serving Hispanics[81] and may be a way to identify the nature and intent of services.

Personalismo means more than personal inner qualities that make for good interpersonal relationships.[82] As Lauria pointed out,[83] it is the quality of interpersonal interactions that foster *respeto*, respect between two interactants. *Personalismo* may be important in persons' getting to know the agency link person well enough before revealing more serious aspects of their lives.[84] In fact, all manner of symbolic *valores* (values) evolve in these interactions, such as *confianza* (trust) and allowing persons to maintain *dignidad* (dignity). There is a lot of variability in how these symbolic interactions are expressed among Hispanics. For example, *plática* (chat or talk) is seen as a means of understanding one's interlocutor in northern New Mexico, a means of maintaining another person's *vergüenza* (one's family and social personage).

Espiritismo, spirituality expressed in folk medicine and religion-based healing, comprises varied approaches—as varied as the groups of Hispanics themselves. However, as Cuellar explained, the approach generally reflects "a value orientation based on the perceived working relationships of humans to their natural and supernatural environments, one that is neither completely subjugated to, nor in complete domination of, their physical and spiritual worlds."[85] This approach in social and community services recognizes the whole person. It can particularly counterbalance the diagnostic pathological approach, by recognizing that humans are physical and spiritual beings, with both aspects in need of healing.

The value of *presentismo* emphasizes the here and now. This cultural approach, when seen as a valued orientation, can place appropriate emphasis on the current situation. When social welfare services effectively address today's concern, they become dependable in the eyes in the participant. When an urgent need expressed by a family within a community is addressed well, the reaction prepares that family to join in the collaboration to address other larger needs. As thus defined, these cultural traditions cut across the multiple Hispanic groups, and can be viewed as social capital or an asset base upon which communities of choice can be built and through which social welfare needs can be addressed.

Several other issues and concerns also have to be taken up. Dhooper, writing about services to Asians, made some points that are also relevant in Hispanic communities.[86] Citing the work of Hirayam and Cetingok,[87] Dhooper pointed out that people in need should be provided with:

1. Knowledge about where and how to secure resources, such as money, jobs, housing, health care, and education;

2. Knowledge about civil, political, and legal systems as well as American methods of problem solving;

3. Attitudes and behavior or interpersonal skills that are effective when dealing with social systems and organizations; and

4. Social support both within and outside the ethnic community.[88]

Finally, Dhooper and others advocated for large-scale efforts at attacking powerlessness by mobilizing efforts at several levels—individual, interpersonal, organizational, institutional, and societal. The agency should be community-oriented and "willing and capable of undertaking class advocacy and helping the community to organize itself, build alliances and form coalitions with other groups with similar problems."[89] Halpern[90] put the matter even more pointedly, noting that initiatives in poor neighborhoods will not improve the life chances of their residents if the focus is only on the neighborhood itself.

Chaskin, Joseph, and Chipenda-Dansokho raised the issue of what operational structure best promotes comprehensive programming that exploits the interconnections among the components. In addition, they asked what supportive staff, technical assistance, funding, and evaluation will best support a community development group in fully developing and implementing a comprehensive development strategy. They answered their own questions by positing that:

1. "[T]he charge to be comprehensive has facilitated the engagement of actors with varying interests in the strategic planning process, [so] there is a need for greater clarity of what comprehensive development means in operational terms."

2. "[S]trategic plans provide a map of potential activities, [but] competing motivating factors (such as arising opportunities and existing network of associations) have and probably will continue to provide a stronger and clearer impetus for program development and implementation."

3. "[A] recognition of the depth and persistence of problems affecting low-income neighborhoods and the structural and resource limitations of comprehensive community building initiatives suggest a need for more responsive, long-term funder-grantee relationships."[91]

Community-centered or neighborhood-based services can move the members of Hispanic communities into the center of attention, away from the margins of society. This approach can amplify the voices of those members, so that their wisdom can be utilized in the recognition and definition of their need and the construction and delivery of social services. They can build social capital to become competent in working with dollars and community resources to resolve problems. Finally, the vulnerable and unequal position to which many Hispanic peoples have been yoked might be a central theme in reconstructing social welfare policies affecting them.

Notes

1. See chapter 1 in this book.
2. National Council of La Raza, *State of Hispanic America 1991: An Overview* (Washington, D.C.: Author, February 1992).
3. Sonia Pérez and Deirdre Martínez, *State of Hispanic America: Toward a Latino Anti-Poverty Agenda* (Washington, D.C.: National Council of La Raza, July 1993), at 4.
4. Ibid., 2.
5. Ibid.
6. United States Bureau of the Census, *Statistical Abstract of the United States*, 115th ed. (Washington, D.C.: Author, 1995), 479–83.
7. Katherine Van Wormer, *Social Welfare: A World View* (Chicago: Nelson Hall, 1997), 310.
8. ChildStats.gov, "America's Children: Key National Indicators of Well-Being," Internet posting (version current at 10 December 1998).

9. Child Welfare League of America, "National Council of Latino Executives: Advocating for Latinos in Child Welfare," Internet posting (version current at 8 December 1998).

10. Robert M. Ortega, Cindy Guillean, and Lourdes Gutierrez Najera, "Latinos and Child Welfare/*Latinos y el Bienestar Del Niño—Voces de la Communidad* Executive Summary," *Prevention Report* (National Resource Center for Family Centered Practice) (Fall 1996): 21–23.

11. The term *Latino* used by these researchers has been changed to *Hispanic* in this chapter for consistency.

12. Ortega, Guillean, and Najera, "Latinos and Child Welfare," 23.

13. Diane Naranjo, "Health Promotion Fact Sheet: Hispanic Women's Health Status" (Washington, D.C.: National Council of La Raza, 1992).

14. Denise De La Rosa and Carlyle Maw, *Hispanic Education: A Statistical Portrait 1990*, Special Conference Edition (Washington, D.C.: National Council of La Raza, June 1990). 33. This report contains both information from the NCLR report and additional data prepared for NCRL.

15. De La Rosa and Maw, *Hispanic Education*.

16. Ibid.

17. Hermina L. Cubillos and Margarita M. Prieto, *The Hispanic Elderly: A Demographic Profile* (Washington, D.C.: National Council of La Raza, October 1987).

18. Ibid., 3.

19. United States Senate Special Committee on Aging, American Association of Retired Persons, Federal Council on Aging, and United States Administration on Aging, *Aging America: Trends and Projections*, 1991 ed. (Washington, D.C.: Authors, 1991) (DHHS Pub. No. FcoA 91-28001).

20. Cubillos and Prieto, *The Hispanic Elderly*.

21. David Maldonado, Jr., "The Chicano Aged," *Social Work* 20, no. 3 (1975): 213–16.

22. Ibid.; J. Moore, "Mexican Americans (Part II)," *The Gerontologist* 11, no. 1 (1971): 30–35.

23. John R. Weeks, *Aging Concepts and Social Issues* (Belmont, Cal.: Wadsworth, 1984).

24. Ibid., 186.

25. Ibid., citing J. Szapocznik et al., "Life Enhancement Counseling: A Psychological Model of Service for Cuban Elders," in *Minority Mental Health*, ed. E. Jones and S. Kardin (New York: Holt, Rinehart & Winston, 1980), 41.

26. Weeks, *Aging Concepts and Social Issues*, 186.

27. Barbara Ehrenreich, "When Government Gets Mean: Confessions of a Recovering Statist," *The Nation* 265, no. 16 (1997): 11.

28. United States Department of Justice, Bureau of Prison Statistics, Internet posting (accessed February 23, 1999).

29. C. Zastrow, *Introduction to Social Work and Social Welfare*, 5th ed. (Pacific Grove, Cal.: Brooks/Cole, 1993).

30. R. Dolgoff, D. Feldstein, and L. Scolnic, *Understanding Social Welfare* (New York: Longman, 1993), 109–10.

31. Michio Kaku, *Visions: How Science Will Revolutionize the 21st Century* (New York: Anchor Books, 1997), 123.

32. Rod Dobell, "The 'Dance of the Deficit' and the Real World of Wealth: Re-thinking Economic Management for Social Purpose" (1994), 4. Internet posting (version current at 12 June 1998).

33. Ibid.

34. Santiago Rodriguez, "Hispanics in the United States: An Insight into Group Char-

acteristics" (July 1995). Internet posting (version current at 21 October 1996).
35. Jose B. Cuellar, "Hispanic American Aging; Geriatric Education Curriculum Development for Selected Health Professionals" (Washington, D.C.: United States Department of Health and Human Services, Health Resources and Services Administration, 1990) (Minority Aging Essential Curriculum Content for Selected Health and Allied Health Professionals), 369.
36. Ibid.
37. Graciela M. Castex, "Providing Services to Hispanic/Latino Populations: Profiles in Diversity," *Social Work* 39, no. 3 (May 1994): 289; C. H. Enloe, "The Growth of the State and Ethnic Mobilization: The American Experience," *Ethnic and Racial Studies* 4 (1981): 123–36; D. E. Hayes-Bautista and J. Chapa. "Latino Terminology: Conceptual Bases for Standardized Terminology," *American Journal of Public Health* 77 (1987): 61–68; C. Nelson and Marta Tienda, "The Structuring of Hispanic Ethnicity: Historical and Contemporary Perspectives," *Ethnic and Racial Studies* 8 (1985): 49–74.
38. Departmental Working Group on Hispanic Issues, "Hispanic Agenda for Action: Improving Services to Hispanic Americans, July, 1996," Internet posting (version current at 21 October 1996). Italics added.
39. Roberta Sands, "The DSM-III and Psychiatric Nosology: A Critique from the Labeling in Perspective," *California Sociologist* (Winter 1983): 79.
40. United States Department of Health and Human Services, "Hispanic Demographics," Internet posting (version current at 21 October 1997).
41. L. Margolin, *"Framing the Poor": Under the Cover of Kindness* (Charlottesville, Va.: University Press of Virginia, 1997), 98.
42. Ibid., 105.
43. Herbert J. Gans, *The War Against the Poor: The Underclass and Antipoverty Policy* (New York: Basic Books 1995), 119–28.
44. Carmen Rivera-Martinez, "Hispanics and the Social Service System," in *Hispanics in the United States: A New Social Agenda*, ed. Pastora San Juan Cafferty and William C. McCready (New Brunswick, N.J.: Transaction Publishers, 1985), 187–201.
45. Stanley L. Witkin, "Philosophy and Advocacy," *Philosophical Issues in Social Work* 3, nos. 3 & 4 (1992): 3.
46. See especially Ian Haney López, *White by Law: The Legal Construction of Race* (New York: New York University Press, 1996).
47. R. G. McRoy and E. M. Freeman, "Racial-Identity Issues Among Mixed-Race Children," *Social Work in Education* 8 (1986): 164–74.
48. Michael Soldatenko, "The Quincentenary of an Erasure: From Caliban to Hispanic," *Mexican Studies/Estudios Mexicanos* 13, no. 2 (Summer 1997): 386–87.
49. Ibid., 387.
50. Hans S. Falck, *Social Work: The Membership Perspective* (New York: Springer, 1988).
51. Hans S. Falck, "Investigations of Membership Theory in Social Work: Their Current State," *Philosophical Issues in Social Work* 3, nos. 3 & 4 (1992): 5–6.
52. J. Niemonen, "Some Observations on the Problem of Paradigms in Recent Racial and Ethnic Relations Texts," *Teaching Sociology* 21 (1993): 271–86.
53. H. H. Bash, *Sociology, Race, and Ethnicity: A Critique of American Ideological Intrusions upon Sociological Theory* (New York: Gordon and Breach, 1979).
54. Robert D. Manning, "Multiculturalism in the United States: Clashing Concepts, Changing Demographics, and Competing Cultures," *International Journal of Group Tensions* 25, no. 2 (1995): 144.
55. William A. Schambra, "Local Groups Are the Key to America's Civic Renewal,"

Brookings Review 15 (Fall 1997): 20–22.
56. David Lopez and Yen Espiritu, "Panethnicity in the United States: A Theoretical Framework," *Ethnic and Rural Studies* 13, no. 2 (April 1990): 198.
57. Ibid., 202–04.
58. Ibid., 207.
59. Marilyn Friedman, "Feminism and Modern Friendship: Dislocating the Community," *Ethics* 99, no. 2 (1989): 290.
60. Ibid.
61. Theda Skocpol, "Delivering for Young Families: The Resonance of the GI Bill," *American Prospect* 28 (September-October 1996): 66–77.
62. Cuellar, "Hispanic American Aging," 385.
63. Melvin Delgado, "Hispanic Natural Support Systems and Alcohol and Other Drug Services: Challenges and Rewards for Practice," *Alcoholism Treatment Quarterly* 21, no. 1 (1995): 17–31.
64. Benjamin H. Gottlieb, ed., *Marshaling Social Support: Formats, Processes, and Effects* (Newbury Park, Cal.: Sage Publications, 1988), 12–15.
65. S. Cohen and T. A. Wills, "Stress, Social Support, and the Buffering Hypothesis," *Psychological Bulletin* 98 (1985): 310–57, cited in Gottlieb, *Marshaling Social Support*, 12.
66. H. W. Neighbors and J. S. Jackson, "The Use of Informal and Formal Help: Four Patterns of Illness Behavior in the Black Community," *American Journal of Community Psychology* 12 (1984): 629–44 (cited in Gottlieb, *Marshaling Social Support*); Ramon Valle and William Vega, *Hispanic Natural Support Systems: Mental Health Promotion Perspectives* (Sacramento, Cal.: State of California Department of Mental Health, 1980); A. Vaux, "Variations in Social Support Associated with Gender, Ethnicity, and Age," *Journal of Social Issues* 41 (1985): 89–110 (cited in Gottlieb, *Marshaling Social Support*); W. Vega and M. R. Miranda, *Stress and Hispanic Mental Health* (Washington, D.C.: Government Printing Office, 1985) (DHHS Publication No. ADM 85-1410).
67. Claudia J. Coulton, "Riding the Pendulum of the 1990s: Building a Community Context for Social Work Research," *Social Work* 40, no. 4 (1995): 437.
68. Delgado, "Hispanic Natural Support Systems."
69. Ibid.
70. Gottlieb, *Marshaling Social Support*.
71. J. Zalenski and M. Mannes, "Romanticizing Localism in Contemporary Systems Reform," *Prevention Report* no. 1 (1998): 8.
72. Peter S. Fisher, "The Economic Context of Community-Centered Practice: Markets, Communities, and Social Policy," in *Reinventing Human Services: Community- and Family-Centered Practice*, ed. Paul Adams and Kristine Nelson (New York: Aldine de Gruyter, 1995), 41.
73. P. Ewalt, "Editorial: The Revitalization of Impoverished Communities," *Social Work*, 42, no. 5 (September 1997): 413.
74. Paul Adams and Kristine Nelson, "Introduction," in Adams and Nelson, *Reinventing Human Services*, 1.
75. M. Wiatrowski and C. Campoverde, "Community Policing and Community Organization: Assessment and Consensus Development Strategies," *Journal of Community Practice* 3, no. 1 (1996): 1–17.
76. Gerald Smale, "Integrating Community and Individual Practice," in Adams and Nelson, *Reinventing Human Services*, 59–80.
77. Merrill Singer, "The Evolution of AIDS Work in a Puerto Rican Community Organization," *Human Organization* 55, no. 1 (1996): 67–75, at 70.
78. Ramon Valle and Lydia Mendoza, *The Elder Latino* (San Diego, Cal.: Campanile

Press (San Diego State University), 1978).
79. Cuellar, "Hispanic American Aging."
80. Ibid.
81. David M. Tirado, "Mexican American Community Political Organizations," *Aztlan Chicano Journal of the Social Sciences* 1, no. 1 (1970): 53–78.
82. Cuellar, "Hispanic American Aging."
83. Anthony Lauria, "Respeto, Relajo and Interpersonal Relations in Puerto Rico," *Anthropological Quarterly* 37 (1964): 54–55.
84. I. Aguilar, "Initial Contacts with Mexican-American Families," *Social Work* 17, no. 2 (1972): 144–52.
85. Cuellar, "Hispanic American Aging," 391.
86. Surjit Singh Dhooper, "Toward an Effective Response to the Needs of Asian-Americans," *Journal of Multicultural Social Work* 1, no. 2 (1991): 65–81.
87. H. Hirayam and M. Cetingok, "Empowerment: A Social Work Approach for Asian Immigrants," *Social Casework* 69, no. 1 (1988): 41–47.
88. Dhooper, "Toward an Effective Response to the Needs of Asian-Americans," 74.
89. Ibid., 75.
90. R. Halpern, "Neighborhood-Based Initiative to Address Poverty: Lessons from Experience," *Journal of Sociology and Social Welfare* 20 (1993): 111–25, cited in Elizabeth Mulroy and Sharon Shay, "Nonprofit Organizations and Innovations: A Model of Neighborhood-Based Collaboration to Prevent Child Maltreatment," *Social Work* 42, no. 5 (1997): 515–26.
91. Robert J. Chaskin, Mark L. Joseph, and Selma Chipenda-Dansokho, "Implementing Comprehensive Community Development: Possibilities and Limitations," *Social Work* 42, no. 5 (1997): 442.

Bibliography

Adams, Paul, and Kristine Nelson. "Introduction." In *Reinventing Human Services: Community- and Family-Centered Practice*, edited by Paul Adams and Kristine Nelson. New York: Aldine de Gruyter, 1995.

Adams, Paul, and Kristine Nelson, eds. *Reinventing Human Services: Community- and Family-Centered Practice*, edited by Paul Adams and Kristine Nelson. New York: Aldine de Gruyter, 1995.

Aguilar, I. "Initial Contacts with Mexican-American Families." *Social Work* 17, no. 2 (1972): 144–52.

Bash, H. H. *Sociology, Race, and Ethnicity: A Critique of American Ideological Intrusions upon Sociological Theory*. New York: Gordon and Breach, 1979.

Burnett, Denise, and Ada C. Mui. "In-Home and Community-Based Service Utilization by Three Groups of Elderly Hispanics: A National Perspective." *Social Work Research* 19 (December 1995): 197–206.

Cafferty, Pastora San Juan, and William C. McCready, eds. *Hispanics in the United States: A New Social Agenda*. New Brunswick, N.J.: Transaction Publishers, 1985.

Castex, Graciela M. "Providing Services to Hispanic/Latino Populations: Profiles in Diversity." *Social Work* 39, no. 3 (May 1994): 288–95.

Chaskin, Robert J., Mark L. Joseph, and Selma Chipenda-Dansokho. "Implementing Comprehensive Community Development: Possibilities and Limitations." *Social Work* 42, no. 5 (1997): 435–44.

ChildStats.gov. "America's Children: Key National Indicators of Well-Being." Internet posting: http://www.childstats.gov/ac1998/highlite.htm (version current at 10 December 1998).

Child Welfare League of America. "National Council of Latino Executives: Advocating for Latinos in Child Welfare." Internet posting: cwla.org/cwla/latexecs/councillatinoexecs.html (version current at 8 December 1998).

Cohen, S., and T. A. Wills. "Stress, Social Support, and the Buffering Hypothesis." *Psychological Bulletin* 98 (1985): 310–57.

Coulton, Claudia J. "Riding the Pendulum of the 1990s: Building a Community Context for Social Work Research." *Social Work* 40, no. 4 (1995): 437.

Cubillos, Hermina L., and Margarita M. Prieto. *The Hispanic Elderly: A Demographic Profile*. Washington, D.C.: National Council of La Raza, October 1987.

Cuellar, Jose B. "Hispanic American Aging; Geriatric Education Curriculum Development for Selected Health Professionals." Washington, D.C.: United States Department of Health and Human Services, Health Resources and Services Administration, 1990. (Minority Aging Essential Curriculum Content for Selected Health and Allied Health Professionals).

De La Rosa, Denise, and Carlyle Maw. *Hispanic Education: A Statistical Portrait 1990*. Special Conference Edition. Washington, D.C.: National Council of La Raza, June 1990.

Delgado, Melvin. "Hispanic Natural Support Systems and Alcohol and Other Drug Services: Challenges and Rewards for Practice." *Alcoholism Treatment Quarterly* 21, no. 1 (1995): 17–31.

Departmental Working Group on Hispanic Issues. "Hispanic Agenda for Action: Improving Services to Hispanic Americans, July, 1996." Internet posting: hhs.gov/about/heo/wghi.html (version current at 21 October 1997).

Dhooper, Surjit Singh. "Toward an Effective Response to the Needs of Asian-Americans." *Journal of Multicultural Social Work* 1, no. 2 (1991): 65–81.

Dobell, Rod. "The 'Dance of the Deficit' and the Real World of Wealth: Rethinking Economic Management for Social Purpose." 1994. Internet posting: http://mai.flora.org/library/deficit1.html (version current at 12 June 1998).

Dolgoff, R., D. Feldstein, and L. Scolnic. *Understanding Social Welfare*. New York: Longman, 1993.

Enloe, C. H. "The Growth of the State and Ethnic Mobilization: The American Experience." *Ethnic and Racial Studies* 4 (1981): 123–36.

Ehrenreich, Barbara. "When Government Gets Mean: Confessions of a Recovering Statist." *The Nation* 265, no. 16 (1997): 11.

Ewalt, P. "Editorial: The Revitalization of Impoverished Communities." *Social Work* 42, no. 5 (September 1997): 413–14.

Falck, Hans S. "Investigations of Membership Theory in Social Work: Their Current State." *Philosophical Issues in Social Work* 3, nos. 3 & 4 (1992): 5–6.

———. *Social Work: The Membership Perspective.* New York: Springer, 1988.

Fisher, Peter S. "The Economic Context of Community-Centered Practice: Markets, Communities, and Social Policy." In *Reinventing Human Services: Community- and Family-Centered Practice*, edited by Paul Adams and Kristine Nelson, 41. New York: Aldine de Gruyter, 1995.

Friedman, Marilyn. "Feminism and Modern Friendship: Dislocating the Community." *Ethics* 99, no. 2 (1989): 290–95.

Gans, Herbert J. *The War Against the Poor: The Underclass and Antipoverty Policy.* New York: Basic Books 1995.

Gottlieb, Benjamin H., ed. *Marshaling Social Support: Formats, Processes, and Effects.* Newbury Park, Cal.: Sage Publications, 1988).

Halpern, R. "Neighborhood-Based Initiative to Address Poverty: Lessons from Experience." *Journal of Sociology and Social Welfare* 20 (1993): 111–25.

Haney López, Ian. *White by Law: The Legal Construction of Race.* New York: New York University Press, 1996.

Hayes-Bautista, D. E., and J. Chapa. "Latino Terminology: Conceptual Bases for Standardized Terminology." *American Journal of Public Health* 77 (1987): 61–68.

Hirayam, H., and M. Cetingok. "Empowerment: A Social Work Approach for Asian Immigrants." *Social Casework* 69, no. 1 (1988): 41–47.

Jones, E., and S. Kardin, eds. *Minority Mental Health.* New York: Holt, Rinehart & Winston, 1980.

Kaku, Michio. *Visions: How Science Will Revolutionize the 21st Century.* New York: Anchor Books, 1997.

Kaufman, R. "Planning Educational Systems: A Results Based Approach." In *Planning and Conducting Needs Assessments: A Practical Guide*, edited by Belle Ruth Witkin and James W. Altshuld, 9. Thousand Oaks, Cal.: Sage Publications, 1995.

Lauria, Anthony. "Respeto, Relajo and Interpersonal Relations in Puerto Rico." *Anthropological Quarterly* 37 (1964): 54–55.

Lopez, David, and Yen Espiritu. "Panethnicity in the United States: A Theoretical Framework." *Ethnic and Rural Studies* 13, no. 2 (April 1990): 188–224.

Maldonado, David Jr. "The Chicano Aged." *Social Work* 20, no. 3 (1975): 213–16.

Manning, Robert D. "Multiculturalism in the United States: Clashing Concepts, Changing Demographics, and Competing Cultures." *International Journal of Group Tensions* 25, no. 2 (1995): 117–68.

Margolin, L. *"Framing the Poor": Under the Cover of Kindness.* Charlottesville, Va.: University Press of Virginia, 1997.

McRoy, R. G., and E. M. Freeman. "Racial-Identity Issues Among Mixed-Race Children." *Social Work in Education* 8 (1986): 164–74.

Moore, J. "Mexican Americans (Part II)." *The Gerontologist* 11, no. 1 (1971): 30–35.

Mulroy, Elizabeth, and Sharon Shay. "Nonprofit Organizations and Innovations: A Model of Neighborhood-Based Collaboration to Prevent Child Maltreatment." *Social Work* 42, no. 5 (1997): 515–26.

Naranjo, Diane. "Health Promotion Fact Sheet: Hispanic Women's Health Status." Washington, D.C.: National Council of La Raza, 1992.

National Council of La Raza. *State of Hispanic America 1991: An Overview.* Washington, D.C.: Author, February 1992.

Neighbors, H. W., and J. S. Jackson. "The Use of Informal and Formal Help: Four Patterns of Illness Behavior in the Black Community." *American Journal of Community Psychology* 12 (1984): 629–44.

Nelson, C., and Marta Tienda. "The Structuring of Hispanic Ethnicity: Historical and Contemporary Perspectives." *Ethnic and Racial Studies* 8 (1985): 49–74.

Niemonen, J. "Some Observations on the Problem of Paradigms in Recent Racial and Ethnic Relations Texts." *Teaching Sociology* 21 (1993): 271–86.

Ortega, Robert M., Cindy Guillean, and Lourdes Gutierrez Najera. "Latinos and Child Welfare/*Latinos y el Bienestar Del Niño—Voces de la Communidad* Executive Summary." *Prevention Report* (National Resource Center for Family Centered Practice) (Fall 1996): 21–23.

Pérez, Sonia, and Deirdre Martínez. *State of Hispanic America: Toward a Latino Anti-Poverty Agenda.* Washington, D.C.: National Council of La Raza, July 1993.

Rivera-Martinez, Carmen. "Hispanics and the Social Service System." In *Hispanics in the United States: A New Social Agenda,* edited by Pastora San Juan Cafferty and William C. McCready, 187–201. New Brunswick, N.J.: Transaction Publishers, 1985.

Rodriguez, Santiago. "Hispanics in the United States: An Insight into Group Characteristics." July 1995. Internet posting: hhs.gov/about/heo/hgen.html (version current at 21 October 1997).

Sands, Roberta. "The DSM-III and Psychiatric Nosology: A Critique from the Labeling in Perspective." *California Sociologist* 6, no. 1 (Winter 1983): 77–87.

Schambra, William A. "Local Groups Are the Key to America's Civic Renewal." *Brookings Review* 15 (Fall 1997): 20–22.

Singer, Merrill. "The Evolution of AIDS Work in a Puerto Rican Community Organization." *Human Organization* 55, no. 1 (1996): 67–75.

Skocpol, Theda. "Delivering for Young Families: The Resonance of the GI Bill." *American Prospect* 28 (September-October 1996): 66–77.

Smale, Gerald. "Integrating Community and Individual Practice." In *Reinventing Human Services: Community- and Family-Centered Practice*, edited by Paul Adams and Kristine Nelson, 59–80. New York: Aldine de Gruyter, 1995.

Soldatenko, Michael. "The Quincentenary of an Erasure: From Caliban to Hispanic." *Mexican Studies/Estudios Mexicanos* 13, no. 2 (Summer 1997): 384–87.

Szapocznik, J., et al. "Life Enhancement Counseling: A Psychological Model of Service for Cuban Elders." In *Minority Mental Health*, edited by E. Jones and S. Kardin (New York: Holt, Rinehart & Winston, 1980).

Tirado, David M. "Mexican American Community Political Organizations." *Aztlan Chicano Journal of the Social Sciences* 1, no. 1 (1970): 53–78.

United States Bureau of the Census. "No. 53. Social and Economic Characteristics of the Hispanic Population: 1995." In *Statistical Abstract of the United States.* 116th ed. Washington, D.C.: Author, 1996.

United States Bureau of the Census. *Statistical Abstract of the United States.* 115th ed. Washington, D.C.: Author, 1995.

United States Bureau of the Census. *Statistical Abstract of the United States.* 116th ed. Washington, D.C.: Author, 1996.

United States Department of Education, National Center for Education Research. *A Profile of the American Eighth Grader: National Education Longitudinal Study: Base Year Student Survey, 1988.* Washington, D.C.: Author, April 1990 (NELS:88).

United States Department of Education, National Center for Education Statistics. *High School and Beyond, Sophomore Cohort, Second Follow up Study (1982).* Washington, D.C.: Author, 1986.

United States Department of Health and Human Services. "Hispanic Demographics." Internet posting: www.hhs.gov/about/heo/hisp.html (version current at 21 October 1997).

United States Department of Justice, Bureau of Prison Statistics. Internet posting: http://www.ojp.usdoj.gov/bjs/prisons.htm (version current at 23 February, 1999).

United States Senate Special Committee on Aging, American Association of Retired Persons, Federal Council on Aging, and United States Administration on Aging. *Aging America: Trends and Projections.* 1991 ed. Washington, D.C.: Authors, 1991. (DHHS Pub. No. FcoA 91-28001).

Valle, Ramon, and Lydia Mendoza. *The Elder Latino.* San Diego, Cal.: Campanile Press (San Diego State University), 1978.

Valle, Ramon, and William Vega. *Hispanic Natural Support Systems: Mental Health Promotion Perspectives.* Sacramento, Cal.: State of California Department of Mental Health, 1980.

Van Wormer, Katherine. *Social Welfare: A World View*. Chicago: Nelson Hall, 1997.

Vaux, A. "Variations in Social Support Associated with Gender, Ethnicity, and Age." *Journal of Social Issues* 41 (1985): 89–110.

Vega, W., and M. R. Miranda. *Stress and Hispanic Mental Health*. Washington, D.C.: Government Printing Office, 1985. (DHHS Publication No. ADM 85-1410).

Weeks, John R. *Aging Concepts and Social Issues*. Belmont, Cal.: Wadsworth, 1984.

Wiatrowski, M., and C. Campoverde. "Community Policing and Community Organization: Assessment and Consensus Development Strategies." *Journal of Community Practice* 3, no. 1 (1996): 1–17.

Williams, N., Kelly F. Himmel, Andree F. Sjoberg, and Diana J. Torrez. "The Assimilation Model, Family Life, and Race and Ethnicity in the United States: The Case of Minority Welfare Mothers." *Journal of Family Issues* 16, no. 3 (May 1995): 387.

Witkin, Belle Ruth, and James W. Altshuld, eds. *Planning and Conducting Needs Assessments: A Practical Guide*. Thousand Oaks, Cal.: Sage Publications, 1995.

Witkin, Stanley L. "Philosophy and Advocacy." *Philosophical Issues in Social Work* 3, nos. 3 & 4 (1992): 1–3.

Zalenski, J., and M. Mannes. "Romanticizing Localism in Contemporary Systems Reform." *Prevention Report* no. 1 (1998): 5–9.

Zastrow, C. *Introduction to Social Work and Social Welfare*. 5th ed. Pacific Grove, Cal.: Brooks/Cole, 1993.

9

Hispanics and the Criminal Justice System

Cruz Reynoso*

The most important role of government is to secure the physical safety of those governed. Many institutions participate in that process: the police; the legislature; the bar, specifically prosecutors and defense attorneys; the courts, including judges and juries; and the prisons. In a democracy, those institutions must serve and protect all communities with equal vigor and equal fairness. This chapter explores whether Hispanic communities are being well and fairly served by those institutions. The last ten years have provided the beginnings of studies and documentation that will help, in part, to answer the question. Still, too often the facts and figures are provided in an amalgam of "minority" statistics, leaving the scholar to interpret the specific relation of that information to Hispanic communities. In the decade to come, researchers would be wise to increase focus on Hispanic communities as worthy of independent study. Indeed, legislators should mandate the collection of data on Hispanics.

What emerges from the current research is the following. The long-standing suspicion and distrust of the institutions that form the criminal justice system persist in the Hispanic community. New immigrants are particularly wary of authority. Language differences may be a major reason for this distrust. As detailed in this chapter, language issues play a major role not only in how Hispanics perceive the criminal justice system, but also in how they are treated by it. Overall, many facets of

---

*   Invaluable assistance in research and drafting was provided by Cynthia A. Valenzuela, Esq.

the criminal justice system discussed herein are replete with language issues, such as the use of excessive force by police officers, the right to a court interpreter, and the right of monolingual Hispanic defendants to have a jury composed of bilingual speakers.

Nevertheless, progress has been made. In the last decade, Hispanics have seen their numbers increase in the institutions that serve the criminal justice system. That increased presence in influential positions has had the effect of heightening awareness of the importance of better serving Hispanic communities. In this chapter, the reality of Hispanics in the criminal justice system and the promise of increased participation in positions of power are explored.

Police-Community Relations and Civil Liberties

The police are the front-line representatives of the criminal justice system. It is the local police departments that most often interact with Hispanics. The tenor of that interaction is of special importance to the relationship between Hispanic communities and the criminal justice system. In the aftermath of the Los Angeles riots of 1992 and the beating of two undocumented persons in Riverside County, California, in 1996, the importance of this relationship has become increasingly evident. These events graphically depict a growing sense of hostility between Hispanic communities and law enforcement officials.

This section begins with a look at the Hispanic community's current perception of police officers. It then deals with three related topics: the use of excessive force by police, language barriers as they relate to excessive force, and the number of Hispanic law enforcement officials. Finally, the relationship between local law enforcement agencies and the Immigration and Naturalization Service (INS) is examined.

Perceptions of Police in Hispanic Communities

Perceptions regarding the police seem to be largely influenced by the ethnicity and race of the observer. National surveys report that non-Hispanic Whites and minorities entertain different perspectives regarding police. For example, with respect to fair treatment by local police, Hispanics and Blacks were less likely to rate the police as "excellent" or "pretty good" than were their non-Hispanic White counterparts.[1] With respect to police brutality, Hispanics and other minority groups were more likely to believe that there was police brutality in their communities.[2]

According to a poll taken in Orange County, California, 37 percent of the Hispanic population report that they have "a lot of confidence" in police, compared to 52 percent of non-Hispanic White and 27 percent of the Asian population.[3] Twenty-seven percent of the county's residents, including all ethnic groups, felt that law enforcement officials were unfairly tough on Hispanics.[4] Hispanics perceived themselves as the group most mistreated by police, with 46 percent responding that officers are unfairly tougher on Hispanics. Fifteen percent of Hispanics reported being victims of police abuse, as opposed to 5 percent of non-Hispanic Whites and Asians (Blacks were not included in the Orange County poll).[5]

An Amnesty International report concluded that police brutality in the United States is widespread and that Latinos and Blacks are disproportionately victims of the abuse.[6] Two independent reports concurred in that conclusion (the Kolts Commission report and the Christopher Commission report, which are discussed later in this chapter).[7]

The negative views of so many Hispanics can be better understood by examining the issue of excessive force by the police, and the importance of language in police-community encounters as they relate to excessive force.

Excessive Force

In May 1991, a civil disturbance erupted in the Mount Pleasant area of Washington, D.C. The neighborhood is largely Hispanic. The disturbance was sparked by the shooting of a Salvadoran male by a rookie police officer who was attempting to arrest the man on charges of public drunkenness. However, the underlying cause of the uprising was a history of poor police-community relations. Hispanic residents of Mount Pleasant reported, and the U.S. Commission on Civil Rights found, a pattern of police misconduct, including "harassment, racial and demeaning language, excessive use of force, and the abuse of discretionary arrest power."[8]

Concerns were also voiced regarding the lack of sufficient bilingual personnel in the metropolitan police department and the inadequacy of police training and monitoring of police misconduct. A statistical analysis of citizen complaints to the Civilian Complaint Review Board (CCRB) revealed that, during the 1985–1991 period, the Third District, which covers the Mount Pleasant and Adams Morgan areas, had the highest overall CCRB complaint rate, the highest resident complaint rate, and the highest number of officers against whom multiple complaints had been lodged.[9]

The commission's report included several recommendations. Among them, the commission suggested cultivating the newly formed "early warning system" to identify violence-prone officers. It noted the lack of comprehensive training in the use of force, human relations, and multicultural sensitivity, both for new recruits and experienced officers. The commission also endorsed the implementation of an ambitious written recruitment plan for Hispanics and other minorities, which made bilingualism a factor in hiring and offered incentives for the use and enhancement of bilingual skills. Finally, the commission recommended adequate funding for the operation of the Civilian Complaint Review Board, to support expeditious and effective resolution of citizen complaints.[10]

Only one year later, in 1992, a civil disturbance erupted in Los Angeles following the Rodney King verdict. As in Mount Pleasant, one of the underlying causes of the uprising was poor police-community relations. Frustration and resentment at historical and present-day police misconduct was not limited to the Black community. Of those arrested during the riots, 51 percent were Hispanic.[11] Further, Hispanics represented 43 percent of the persons convicted of riot-related felonies.[12]

The Christopher Commission was established in Los Angeles after the infamous Rodney King beating, but before the verdict and the accompanying civil unrest. The Christopher Commission was directed to "examine all aspects of the law enforcement structure in Los Angeles that might cause or contribute to the problem of excessive force."[13] One of the main concerns identified by the commission was the attitudes of Los Angeles police officers toward ethnic and racial minorities.[14] The report documented discrimination against minority civilians and officers. The Christopher Commission further reported that Black and Hispanic men were detained, harassed, humiliated, and excessively beaten by Los Angeles Police Department (LAPD) officers.[15]

The Kolts Commission specifically reviewed the Los Angeles County Sheriff's Department. This commission was established in December of 1991, following widespread community outrage over the LAPD police abuse revealed by the Christopher Commission report and a series of questionable shootings by Los Angeles deputy sheriffs involving minority victims in the summer after the King beating.[16] The Kolts Commission investigated practices and policies in relation to allegations of excessive force, community sensitivity, and citizen complaint procedures.[17] Like the Christopher report, the Kolts report documented systematic racial and ethnic bias within the department.

About the same time, the Nevada State Advisory Committee (SAC) to the U.S. Commission on Civil Rights published a report on police-community relations in Reno. The report found that the Hispanic community of Washoe County was growing, and that most of the newcomers spoke primarily Spanish. Realizing that officers must provide police service to non-English speakers, the Nevada SAC recommended additional recruitment and hiring of bilingual officers, and salary incentives for sworn officers and unsworn staff who speak Spanish. In 1991, only 21 out of 723 sworn personnel in the Reno Police Department, and the surrounding community, were Hispanic.[18] The report did not indicate whether there has been an increase in the number of Hispanic sworn personnel since 1991.

The federal government has also responded to the seeming upsurge in police brutality. In 1994, Congress passed the Violent Crime Control and Law Enforcement Act. This Act includes a provision targeting departments and police tactics that lead to abusive conduct:

> It shall be unlawful for any governmental authority, or any agent thereof, or any person acting on behalf of a governmental authority, to engage in a pattern or practice of conduct by law enforcement officers that deprives persons of rights, privileges, or immunities secured or protected by the Constitution or laws of the United States.[19]

The Act requires the Attorney General to collect and publish data about the use of excessive force by law enforcement officers and authorizes her to bring civil actions to obtain equitable and declaratory relief for violations of the Act. This law should contribute significantly to remedying problems of police misconduct by the identification, assessment, and prosecution of police abuse cases.

The Act does not specify what data must be collected and reported; there is wide latitude in the type of information that could be gathered. Presently, two national data collection efforts have been initiated in response to the Act's mandate.[20] The Bureau of Justice Statistics (BJS), which administers the ongoing National Crime Victimization Survey, intended to develop a police-public contact supplement to the survey. The supplement was scheduled to be pretested in late spring of 1996, to help the BJS determine the types of questions that would yield reliable information regarding police use of force. The International Association of Chiefs of Police was awarded a grant by the BJS and the

National Institute of Justice (NIJ) to begin compiling a national database containing information from police departments on their incidence of force.[21] These two initial efforts have not yet resulted in written reports.

Incidents of police abuse directed at Hispanics, and patterns of disrespect, insensitivity, and hostility toward Hispanics, can be ameliorated, in part, by increasing Hispanic representation on police forces. Such representation also provides credibility to the police department.

Mandel found that the lack of representation of minority groups on police forces was a factor contributing to distrust of law enforcement by communities of color.[22] When the police are representative of the community, the "us versus them" mentality begins to erode and an increasingly cooperative relationship between police and community develops. The potential for tension and violence thus decreases.

Bilingual officers ensure that non-English-speaking communities are served, especially in life-threatening situations. Misunderstandings due to language barriers, which can so easily escalate, could be prevented. Indeed, Mandel found that the major advantages of having a fair representation of Hispanic police officers were "(1) their knowledge of Spanish, (2) their understanding of Hispanic culture, and (3) their ability to limit excessive force through education, example, and peer pressure."[23]

Mandel also found, however, that some respondents identified Hispanic officers as being harder on fellow Hispanics than "Anglo" police. Mandel surmised that some Hispanic police officers may be more violent because of they feel pressure to perform according to a majority Anglo environment.[24] Another theory is that Hispanics lose their individual identities and adopt the attitudes of the "Anglo" officers, whom they emulate when dealing with other Hispanics.[25] Mandel reported that Hispanic leaders nonetheless believe that an increase in Hispanic officers and better representation of Hispanics in administrative and policy positions will minimize the use of excessive force against Hispanics and will lead to improved police-community relations.[26]

Hispanic Representation on Police Forces

The number of Hispanic police officers is important inasmuch as their representation (or lack thereof) on police forces affects the community's perception of the legitimacy of law enforcement. Hispanic representation on police forces has been increasing slowly but steadily. As a whole, the ranks of law enforcement, including local police and sheriff's deputies, are beginning to reflect the percentage of Hispanics in their various communities.

The United States Department of Justice provided a comprehensive collection of statistical estimates on the number of Hispanic male and female sworn personnel in local police departments.[27] The report reflects the percent of full-time sworn employees who are Hispanic by size of population served. For "all sizes," there are 5.5 percent Hispanic male and 0.7 percent Hispanic female full-time sworn personnel. In departments serving a population of 1 million or more, Hispanic males constitute 10 percent and Hispanic females constitute 2 percent of full-time sworn employees. Among those serving a population of 50,000 to 99,999, the respective percentage of Hispanic full-time sworn employees is 4.7 percent and 0.5 percent. In small geographic areas where the population is less than 2,500, the percentages were 1.8 percent and 0.1 percent respectively.

The following figures reflect a steady increase in the number of Hispanic police. Overall, the percentage of Hispanic full-time sworn personnel increased from 4 percent in 1987, to 5 percent in 1990, and to approximately 6 percent in 1993.[28] With the Hispanic population increasing nationally by more than 1 million per year, a 1 percent increase in Hispanic sworn police officers every few years suggests that efforts to recruit and retain Hispanic officers could stand improvement. Presently available information does not delineate the status of Hispanic sworn personnel; for example, the reports do not specify the number of Hispanics who are in patrol divisions or supervisory roles. Such positions often enjoy greater authority, corresponding salary benefits, and increased visibility.

Not surprisingly, there appears to be a correlation between the percentage of Hispanics in the general population of any given city and the percentage of Hispanic police officers in that city. Miami and Los Angeles, for example, both have large Hispanic populations, and the percentage of Hispanic police officers in those two cities is correspondingly large. The respective population and police representation are as follows:

- Miami: 62.5 percent Hispanic population[29] and 47.2 percent Hispanic police officers.[30]

- Los Angeles: 36 percent Hispanic population[31] and 29.91 percent Hispanic police officers.[32]

In 1982, Mandel predicted that by the end of the decade, five selected cities would significantly increase the number of Hispanic police and perhaps reach parity with the general population.[33] Although all five cities have increased Hispanic representation within their local departments, only one city—Albuquerque, New Mexico—has reached parity. Other local police departments that achieved parity between the number of Hispanic officers and the total Hispanic population in 1992 include: Minneapolis, Minnesota; Buffalo, New York; Toledo, Ohio; Omaha, Nebraska; El Paso, Texas; and Milwaukee, Wisconsin.[34]

In most jurisdictions, the sheriff's department also serves significant portions of the Hispanic community. The number of full-time sworn personnel in sheriff's departments for "all sizes" is 5.0 percent male and 0.8 percent female. In local sheriff's departments serving a population of 1 million or more, Hispanic males constitute 11.5 percent and Hispanic females constitute 1.8 percent of full-time sworn employees. Among those serving a population of 50,000 to 99,999, the percentages are 2.1 percent and 0.4 percent, respectively. Where the population is less than 10,000, the respective percentages are 3.4 percent and 0.7 percent.[35] As with police officers, information regarding recruitment, retention, rank, and salary incentives for Hispanics is lacking with regard to sheriff's deputies.

The Relationship Between Police and the Immigration and Naturalization Service

Another point of tension between the Hispanic community and local police is the interaction of local law enforcement officials with the Immigration and Naturalization Service (INS). The relationship between INS agents and local police is an ambiguous one, varying from jurisdiction to jurisdiction.

State and local law enforcement officials are prohibited from enforcing immigration laws. Some local law enforcement agencies have established internal policies barring officers from conducting investigations solely as a pretext for determining immigration status. The Los Angeles Police Department has such a policy. It provides that the INS is to be notified only when "an undocumented alien is [arrested and] booked for multiple misdemeanor offenses, a high grade misdemeanor, a felony offense, or has been previously arrested for a similar offense."[36]

According to the American Civil Liberties Union (ACLU), immigrants' rights groups, and civil rights groups, the policy is not followed in practice.[37] Indeed, during the civil disturbance of April 29–May 5,

1992, 196 persons were relinquished to the INS by sheriff's deputies. By May 20, the total was 1,090. The LAPD turned over 372 persons to the INS during the uprising and 452 total by May 20. It is not clear whether these people were booked for multiple or high misdemeanors, or had prior criminal records justifying their release to INS officials. However, such a scenario is unlikely.

Whether stated policies are followed in practice is a valid concern. The proper role of local law enforcement in border situations was at issue in the aftermath of the clubbing of two undocumented immigrants by Riverside County sheriff's deputies. The high-speed chase that preceded the beating began at a border checkpoint pursuant to a Border Patrol request for assistance from the local deputies.[38]

Policies that limit police cooperation with the INS may be ignored in practice, especially when immigration becomes a heated issue in politics. The backdrop in the "Riverside beating" was a strong anti-immigrant climate; in particular, an anti-Hispanic immigrant sentiment. During the 1996 local and national campaigns, many candidates seeking public office endorsed anti-immigrant proposals. The campaign tactics, particularly directed at Hispanics, stereotyped immigrants as an invasion of brown-faced hordes. When high public officials so dehumanize and demonize Hispanics, discrimination by law enforcement is impliedly justified.

In New York, proposed legislation would have enabled local police to cooperate with the INS by reporting suspected undocumented persons. As proposed, the legislation would have prohibited localities from preventing or limiting such cooperation.[39] At the time of this writing, the legislation had not passed.

In a report entitled *Federal Immigration Law Enforcement in the Southwest: Civil Rights Impacts on Border Communities*,[40] incidents of misconduct by Border Patrol agents were found. These incidents included reports of "shootings, beatings, and sexual assault; racial and ethnic insults; rude and abusive language; threats and coercion; illegal or inappropriate searches and arrest; and confiscation of documents."[41] Equally disturbing, the report found that there was a negative impact on citizens of Hispanic ancestry in border communities that experienced the increased presence of federal immigration forces. Many allegations of civil rights violations were made. Hispanics, irrespective of citizenship or immigration status, continue to suffer at the hands of law enforcement because of xenophobic prejudices.[42]

Hispanic Officials in the Criminal Justice System

In the Orange County, California, poll, Hispanics were the most likely to report the perception that the criminal justice system is biased (39 percent of Hispanics versus 28 percent of Asians and 24 percent of non-Hispanic Whites). What effect do the involvement and participation of Hispanics at various stages of the criminal justice system have on the reality and the perception of justice? This question cannot yet be answered. More information is needed on the numbers of Hispanics working within the criminal legal system. Further, more research is needed into how the proportion of Hispanic criminal justice officials affects Hispanics in the criminal justice system.

Hispanic Lawyers and Judges

Information regarding Hispanic lawyers and judges is sparse. Statistics showing raw numbers of members of the bar have begun to appear only within the last ten years. These numbers, however, fail to delineate the areas of law in which Hispanics are practicing, and what influence Hispanic lawyers and judges are having on the administration of justice.

The limited information that is available reveals that there are currently 1,310 local, state, and federal Hispanic judges in the nation.[43] Puerto Rico (358), Texas (352), California (188), and New Mexico (95) have the highest numbers of Hispanic judges. Of President Clinton's appointees to the United States Courts of Appeal, between 1993 and 1996, 10.3 percent were Hispanic.[44] This percentage increased significantly from 5.4 percent during the Bush administration and 0 percent in the second term of the Reagan administration.[45] For district court judgeships, the percentage of Hispanic appointments by President Clinton was 6.5 percent.[46] The percentages were 4 percent and 4.3 percent in the Bush and Reagan administrations respectively.[47]

In California, the state with the largest number of Hispanics, the Hispanic population is 25.8 percent of the total population. According to a report issued by the California Judicial Council Advisory Committee on Racial and Ethnic Bias in the Courts (Bias Report), Hispanics constitute 4.3 percent of superior court judges and 6.5 percent of municipal court judges.[48] As of September 1996, there were 4 Hispanic judges out of 82 positions at the courts of appeal. No Hispanics were represented on the California Supreme Court.[49] Hispanic attorneys, the pool from which judges are selected, constituted just 3 percent of active bar members.[50]

Very little data about Hispanic attorneys are available. Research revealed limited information regarding attorneys' backgrounds, self-perceptions, selected fields of practice, and professional success. The information that is available does not address attorneys involved in the criminal justice system—namely, prosecutors and public defenders—but rather focuses on Hispanic attorneys in private law firms.

Cheek found that many large law firms continue to maintain preconceived notions about the competence of Hispanic attorneys.[51] Hispanic attorneys reported feeling that they are "not respected as qualified, equally capable and even more skillful litigators by the traditional legal community."[52] Further, the respondent attorneys reported feeling an obligation to give back to the community and to accept added responsibilities that are thrust upon Spanish-speaking attorneys. Cheek surmised that such obligations could hamper the career advancement of Hispanic attorneys.[53]

The National Association for Law Placement (NALP) reported that in 1996, 2.93 percent of partners in the nation's major law firms were minority. The NALP report did not dissect the "minority" category. The report noted that the figure indicates an underrepresentation of minorities among partnership ranks, but stated that the numbers continue to increase slightly.[54] The American Bar Association (ABA) reported a steady increase in Hispanic law student enrollment over the past ten years.[55] If the trend continues, an increase in Hispanic lawyers and judges is inevitable. However, the recent curtailment of affirmative action laws, and the consequent proscription of consideration of race and ethnicity as factors in law school admissions, poses a threat to continued progress.

Courtroom Interpreters

A 1997 study indicated that approximately 13 percent of the United States population are speakers of non-English languages.[56] Mendez found that more than half of those whose primary language is other than English speak Spanish.[57] Spanish is the most frequently used language in court-interpreted proceedings. In southwestern state and federal courts, in 1982, approximately 96 percent of court interpreter appearances were for Spanish. In the northeastern federal courts in 1987, 81.3 percent of court interpreter appearances were for Spanish. In the United States federal district courts for fiscal year 1986, Spanish-language interpreters were used 43,166 times. (By contrast, Haitian Creole interpreters came in second as being used 381 times.) The need for Spanish-speaking interpreters appears to be no less in state courts. In one midwestern state court, for example, 92 percent of court interpreter appearances were for Spanish.[58]

The federal government has shown sensitivity to the hindrances that language barriers pose to access to justice. The Federal Court Interpreters Act of 1978 assured the availability of certified court interpreters in federal court.[59] That Act states that a certified court interpreter shall be utilized "if the presiding judicial officer determines ... [that a party, defendant, or witness] (A) speaks only or primarily a language other than the English language."[60]

Nine states have enacted statutes guaranteeing the right to a court-appointed interpreter, including Arizona, California, Colorado, Illinois, Massachusetts, Minnesota, New Mexico, New York, and Texas. California and New Mexico have demonstrated the highest commitment to ensuring that language is not a barrier in the courtroom, by making the provision of an interpreter a constitutional right.[61] The remainder of the twenty-four states that provide for court interpreters do so by way of administrative or judicial regulation.[62]

However, even at the federal level and in states that provide for court interpreters, the scope of the right is unclear. For example,

interpreters play three different but essential roles in criminal proceedings: (1) They make the questioning of a non-English-speaking witness possible ("witness interpreter"); (2) they facilitate the non-English-speaking defendant's understanding of the colloquy between the attorneys, the witness, and the judge ("proceeding interpreter"); and (3) they enable the non-English-speaking defendant and his English-speaking attorney to communicate ("defense interpreter").[63]

At least one scholar has argued that the separate functions of each interpreter role represent the different needs of limited-English-speaking litigants and witnesses.[64] Mendez observed that courts generally do not consider the separate functions of the interpreter or the different needs of the non-English-speaker when assessing the need for an interpreter. Furthermore, courts often fail to appreciate the difference in linguistic skills between understanding the proceedings and testifying directly (or indirectly through cross-examination).[65]

The scope of the right is also limited to certain cases. The federal law provides for an interpreter only in federal criminal actions and civil actions initiated by the United States in the federal district courts. Similarly, in California, a party to a civil proceeding does not have a constitutionally based right to an interpreter or a right to have an interpreter appointed at court expense.[66]

The trial judge has broad discretion in making the determination of whether an interpreter should be provided. Unfortunately, the California legislature has failed to provide guidance to judges in their determination of whether a limited-English witness or litigant should be assisted by a certified or qualified courtroom interpreter.[67]

The importance of judicial discretion in the absence of legislative guidance is exemplified in *Gonzalez v. United States*.[68] Gonzalez sought to overturn his convictions or modify his sentence, claiming that the federal district court judge had failed, under the Court Interpreters Act, to appoint an interpreter at the hearing where he entered a guilty plea. Gonzalez asserted that his limited English-speaking ability interfered with his ability to understand the nature of the charges against him and the potential consequences of a guilty plea.[69] The Ninth Circuit affirmed the decision of the district court judge in holding "that Gonzalez's comprehension was not sufficiently inhibited as to require an interpreter." The decision was based upon the fact that Gonzalez had been a resident of Oregon for ten years, was buying a home, and worked in the auto sales business.[70] In addition, Gonzalez admitted that he could not read well but that he could understand English "[a] little bit."[71]

Of the three appellate judges, one dissented. He noted that Gonzalez was capable of responding to the judge's questions only when they required simple yes or no answers; Gonzalez's answers were nonresponsive when the questions required more than a one-word answer.[72] He argued further that even though Gonzalez may have been able to understand English at a "very basic level," his language difficulties obviously inhibited his understanding of the complex criminal trial proceedings, and therefore a court interpreter should have been appointed.

There is also concern regarding the accuracy of interpreters. At the federal level and in some states, interpreters are required to successfully complete a rigorous certification examination. California has provided the most extensive framework to achieve high-quality court interpreting services for non-English speakers. Its statutory scheme requires interpreters for court proceedings to be "certified."[73] A statewide program provides coordination of interpreter services, including recruitment, testing, certification, renewal of certification, and continuing education.[74] However, Perea suggested that if a certified court interpreter is not available, or if the state allows "qualified" interpreters rather than mandating certified interpreters, the translation can be negatively affected.[75]

Berk-Seligson documented the various ways in which interpreters affect courtroom proceedings. According to Professor Berk-Seligson's findings, court interpreters play an active role in the courtroom.[76] They often interrupt the flow of the question-and-answer dialogue to ask for clarification; they challenge and correct attorneys as witnesses are questioned; and they correct "non-sensical" answers to distance themselves from such responses. Interpreters can affect the witness's testimony through linguistic mechanisms that shape the presentation of the witness's testimony, perhaps even altering meaning.[77]

Hispanics as Jurors

In part for these reasons, Perea asserted that bilingual Hispanics should serve on juries. Bilingual jurors, Perea suggested, could complement the efforts of the interpreter and ensure a proper interpretation. However, the United States Supreme Court apparently has a quite different view. In 1954, the Supreme Court considered discrimination against Hispanics as jurors in *Hernandez v. Texas*.[78] It held that persons with Mexican or Latin American surnames had been unconstitutionally discriminated against and denied the opportunity to serve as jury commissioners, grand jurors, and petit jurors throughout the previous twenty-five years.

In contrast, the current Court, in *Hernandez v. New York*,[79] allowed the peremptory exclusion of prospective jurors who were Hispanic and bilingual from a jury considering Spanish-language testimony. The prosecutor allegedly excused the two jurors because they were reluctant to swear that they would defer to the interpreter's version of the Spanish-language testimony. The Court held that although the striking of all venire members who speak a given language may be a pretext for racial discrimination, under the particular circumstances of this case, and because of the individual responses of these two jurors, no such pretext existed.

The *Hernandez* case sets a dangerous precedent. As a direct impact of the decision, monolingual and Spanish-dominant Hispanic litigants may be denied their right to a trial by a jury of their peers. In general, those who share similar cultural or ethnic traits with the defendant are more likely to identify with the defendant's situation. Although there is no constitutional right to have members of the defendant's race or ethnicity on the jury, courts are obligated to ensure that no groups are systematically excluded from the jury pool. Perea surmised that, outside of the courtroom, the decision will perpetuate and encourage the myth that Hispanics are unqualified and alien.[80] Perea hypothesized that bilingual Hispanics will likely be denied the opportunity to serve on a jury; that juries will be deprived of the experience and knowledge of bilingual Hispanics; and that the perception, within the Hispanic community, of the illegitimacy of jury verdicts will persist.[81]

Hispanics as Victims of Crime

Hispanics were victims of violent crime more often than non-Hispanics.[82] Similarly, Hispanic households experienced a significantly higher rate of property crime than non-Hispanics (426 incidents per 1,000 households versus 298, respectively). A Bureau of Justice Statistics report included those general findings on the relative frequency of Hispanic victimization. The study was based on a representative sample of persons aged 12 and over living in approximately 100,000 households across the nation. One hypothesis to explain the higher rate of Hispanic victimization is that Hispanics embody the characteristics associated with high crime rates, including youth, poverty, and residence in urban areas.[83]

Both male and female Hispanics in urban areas were victims of crime at a higher rate than Hispanics in suburban or rural areas. The comparative figures for males were 76.1 incidents per 1,000 households, versus 66.3 and 58.7, respectively. For females the figures were 62.0 incidents per 1,000 households, versus 51.2 and 57.3, respectively.[84]

Hispanics are victimized by strangers at a higher rate than other groups (65 percent of Hispanics, compared to 58 percent of non-Hispanic Whites and 54 percent of Blacks).[85] Conversely, Hispanics are least likely to be victimized by persons known to them (12 percent per 50,000 Hispanic households versus 22 percent per 50,000 Black households).[86]

In the past ten years, Hispanics contacted police regarding their victimization as often as non-Hispanic Whites or Blacks.[87] This is a change from 1980, when Hispanics reported crimes at lower rates than Blacks and non-Hispanic Whites, even though Hispanics experienced higher victimization rates.[88] Interestingly, however, Hispanic victims of robbery, personal theft, and household crimes who chose not to report the crime refrained because they felt the police would be unresponsive. That Hispanic victims would refrain from contacting police should not be surprising considering the factors discussed earlier: underrepresentation of Hispanics, particularly bilingual Hispanics, on police forces; the lack of good community-police relations; and the cooperation of local police with the INS.

Hate Crimes

A *hate crime* is defined by the federal Hate Crime Statistics Act (HCSA) as a crime motivated by "prejudice based on race, religion, sexual orientation, or ethnicity."[89] The HCSA, passed in 1990, directs the Attorney General to collect data from state and local law enforcement agencies on the number of hate crimes committed each year. The central repository of hate crime statistics is the Federal Bureau of Investigation's (FBI) Uniform Crime Report.

The FBI reported that 698 people were victims of anti-Hispanic crimes in 1995.[90] In 1996, 728 persons fell victim to anti-Hispanic violence.[91]

It is unclear whether the hate crime rate is rising or falling. The uncertainty is due in part to the fact that submission of hate crime data is voluntary. "As of October 1996, five states still did not collect hate crime data."[92] What is clear is that there has been a sharp rise in such crimes in the Southwest, particularly in California.

In 1994, 59 percent of the voters in California passed Proposition 187, which denies undocumented immigrants access to public services, including education and nonemergency health care. Bigotry and hate speech directed at Hispanics swelled during the emotionally charged debate surrounding the proposition. Perhaps the atmosphere created by the campaign provided a hate crime climate.

The Coalition for Humane Immigrants' Rights of Los Angeles (CHIRLA) issued a report in 1995 summarizing and documenting civil rights violations against Hispanics in the wake of Proposition 187. The report found that hate crimes and hate speech against Hispanics had increased, as had discrimination against Hispanics by businesses, police officers, and neighbors. The report concluded that nativism, scapegoating, anti-immigrant rhetoric, and inflammatory political campaigning had incited the violence.

The Los Angeles County Commission on Human Relations tracks hate crime in Los Angeles on an annual basis. According to its 1994 report, hate crimes against Hispanics increased by more than 23 percent, from 68 to 84 incidents in 1 year. Interestingly, Hispanic perpetration of racial hate crimes also increased from 2 to 9 for females, and from 89 to 96 for males.[93] Again, in 1995, hate crimes against Hispanics rose 11.9 percent, from 84 to 94 incidents. The number of Hispanic perpetrators of racial hate crimes remained constant for females and decreased by 6.3 percent for males.[94] In 1996, racial hate crimes against Hispanics decreased from 94 to 84 incidents (10.6 percent). Hispanic perpetration of racial hate crimes increased by 44.4 percent (from 9 to 13) and 35.6 percent (from 90 to 122) for females and males, respectively.[95]

To deal with the root causes of hate crimes, structural approaches must be taken to ensure security, equality, and access to opportunity for all Americans. Beyond tightening of penalties for hate crime offenders, a culture of prevention must be created. Education casting an appreciation of cultures in a broad sense should be promoted by the schools, the media, the business community, religious leaders, political leaders, and other organizations. Creation of a positive atmosphere of mutual respect and cooperation would improve the underlying racial tensions that too often result in violence.

Hispanics in Prison

Other than the death penalty, imprisonment is the ultimate punishment society imposes on convicted criminals. That punishment is not an isolated step in criminal procedure. A prison sentence can result from disparate treatment at each stage of the justice system: from selective deployment of law enforcement personnel; to police misconduct, such as stops and arrests based on racial profiles; to prosecutorial discretion as to whom to charge and with what crime; to lack of diversity in jury pools; to improper use of peremptory challenges to remove Hispanics from juries; to the disproportionate effect of mandatory minimum sentences.[96] The net effect is a disproportionately high representation of Hispanics in the prison population.

According to the Federal Bureau of Prisons, in 1994, 25.9 percent of the prison population was Hispanic. A Bureau of Justice Statistics report indicated that Hispanics constitute the fastest growing minority group being imprisoned.[97] Between 1985 and 1995, the percentage of Hispanics in state and federal prison increased by 219 percent, from 10.9 percent to 15.5 percent; an average of 12.3 percent each year. By the end of the 1995 calendar year, the Hispanic population in state or federal prisons was at least 174,000.[98]

The Sentencing Project found that Blacks and Hispanics constituted 90 percent of offenders sentenced to state prison for drug possession. The study cited difficulties in obtaining accurate information about

Hispanics within the criminal justice system. However, the study reviewed imprisonment statistics indicating that the Hispanic inmate population in both the state and federal prison systems has doubled since 1980.[99]

A 1997 report noted that Whites are arrested more often than Blacks or Hispanics.[100] Similarly, Jackson found that Whites commit more violent offenses than do Blacks or Hispanics.[101] Yet Blacks and Hispanics are sentenced to prison more often than non-Hispanic Whites, who often receive only probation. Further, Jackson found that Black and Hispanic inmates are disproportionately represented when their imprisonment rates are compared to their proportions in the general population.[102] Jackson contended that these disparities are, in part, a result of federal drug sentencing policies. He noted that although Whites have been found to use drugs at a higher rate than Blacks or Hispanics, mandatory minimum sentencing laws for drug offenders have had the greatest impact on Blacks and Hispanics.[103]

Researchers have debated the cause of these disparate imprisonment rates among the various ethnic groups. Jackson noted that the general belief is that race is a significant factor. Some researchers[104] have asserted "that racial disparity in the prison population is due to the seriousness of the crimes committed and the offender's prior criminal history, thereby eliminating race as a causal factor and suggesting that a relationship exists between crime and incarceration rates."[105] Jackson's study, however, rejected the hypothesis that "differential incarceration rates stem directly from differential rates of delinquency involvement."[106]

In comparing the three racial groups, Jackson found that Blacks and Hispanics shared the burden of economic stress and familial responsibility more than non-Hispanic Whites. Hispanic inmates also had lower levels of educational attainment.[107] Individuals with these characteristics, the report confirmed, are disproportionately represented in the prison population. Jackson found that, even in light of these contributing factors, racial discrimination is undeniably "a major factor" in the differential incarceration rates among non-Hispanic Whites, Blacks, and Hispanics.

Sentencing

The federal Sentencing Reform Act of 1984 was enacted to reduce sentencing disparities by limiting judges' discretion and making sentencing more uniform.[108] The Act charged the U.S. Sentencing

Commission with the task of developing guidelines (the Guidelines) that allowed consideration of only certain characteristics during sentence determination. Because the Guidelines restricted the discretion of judges, many federal judges resisted the law until it was declared constitutional in 1989. McDonald and Carlson found that prior to full implementation of the Guidelines, between 1986 and 1988, federal courts distributed similar sentences to Whites, Blacks, and Hispanics.[109] After implementation of the Guidelines, beginning in late 1987 and 1988, disparities in sentencing based on race became more pronounced. Thus, between 1989 and 1990, 85 percent of Hispanic offenders were sentenced to prison, compared to 78 percent of Black and 72 percent of White offenders.[110] As a result of the Act, sentencing disparities have actually increased, to the detriment of Hispanics and other people of color.

Several explanations have been offered as to why the Sentencing Reform Act has failed to bring about more equitable sentencing and eliminate sentencing disparities between non-Hispanic Whites and people of color. One explanation, offered by Professor Albert Alschuler, focuses on the movement to a harm-based scheme that tends to ignore situational and offender characteristics. According to Alschuler, the Guidelines' mechanistic uniformity and excessive aggregation (which can be defined as the grouping of unlike cases) ignore crucial distinctions among offenders, and frequently group offenders on the basis of meaningless criteria. For example, drug couriers or human "mules" are usually charged under the same statute as drug dealers—possession with intent to distribute—even though their personal circumstances often vary greatly. As Alschuler noted, couriers tend to be naïve poor persons (and often minorities) who generally do not know the amount, value, or type of drug they are carrying.[111] This led Professor Alschuler to conclude that although the Guidelines may have come closer to treating all offenders who commit the same crime alike, it has not been successful in treating persons with similar culpability alike.[112]

Another explanation offered for the failure of the Sentencing Reform Act to bring about more equitable sentencing concerns prosecutorial discretion. With the discretion of judges severely limited, the length of sentence is usually a function of the crime charged. Federal prosecutors have formidable power in determining how to frame charges or whether to bring charges at all against a particular defendant.[113] An example of the potential impact this can have on sentencing can be seen clearly upon examination of the use of mandatory minimum sentences. The Comprehensive Crime Control Act of 1984, which included the Sentencing Reform Act, included new mandatory minimum sentences for drug and firearm offenses.[114] "Mandatory minimums are statutory provisions binding courts to impose specific criminal penalties for certain criminal conduct."[115] Prosecutors, however, can avoid mandatory minimums in a variety of ways. For example, in drug cases prosecutors can avoid the mandatory sentences by omitting the quantity of drugs found or by indicating a smaller quantity than could actually be produced and proven in court.[116] Prosecutors can even decline to bring charges and allow state courts, which usually impose lesser sentences, to handle the case.

The result of these practices has been that non-Hispanic Whites more often than minorities elude mandatory minimums, even when the record suggests that they could have been prosecuted under the stiffer penalties.[117] Illene H. Nagel, who was part of a task force of U.S. Attorneys appointed by the Justice Department in 1995 to study whether there are racial patterns in prosecutions, suggested that social class, race, and gender may influence a prosecutor's decision to pursue a case or to be lenient.[118] Overall, mandatory minimums have resulted in severe sentences for young minority males.[119]

A further source of the disparity in sentencing is the Anti-Drug Abuse Act of 1986, which stiffened the federal sentencing laws and prescribed harsh penalties for those trafficking crack as opposed to cocaine powder.[120] This is significant because although non-Hispanic Whites who regularly use cocaine (75 percent in 1991; 52 percent crack) outnumber Blacks (15 percent in 1991; 38 percent crack) and Hispanics (10 percent in 1991; 10 percent crack),[121] Blacks constitute the vast majority (83 percent) of federal crack prosecutions.[122] According to McDonald and Carlson, drug trafficking (importing, manufacturing, cultivating, or distributing) has become the crime most commonly prosecuted in federal courts.[123] It is also one of the crimes receiving the severest punishment.

Of those convicted in federal courts for drug trafficking, Blacks and Hispanics were disproportionately represented. Between January 20, 1989, and June 30, 1990, 40 percent of all non-Hispanic White offenders were convicted of federal drug offenses, as were 49 percent of all Black offenders and 59 percent of all Hispanic offenders. Blacks and Hispanics were given more severe sentences. Length of sentence was about equal for non-Hispanic Whites and Hispanics, and higher for Blacks. Of those convicted for drug offenses, 25 percent were trafficking marijuana. Hispanics were convicted of marijuana trafficking at a higher rate (39.3 percent) than Blacks (2.8 percent) or non-Hispanic Whites (18.6 percent); 95 percent of all Hispanic marijuana traffickers were incarcerated.[124]

McDonald and Carlson suggested that legitimate considerations— such as the offense of conviction, the offender's role in the crime, criminal history, dependence on crime for a livelihood, and physical impairment—can explain the sentencing disparities.[125] For drug offenses, legitimate considerations also include the type of drug and whether weapons were used in commission of the crime. However, McDonald and Carlson further noted that some of the characteristics are associated with race or ethnicity and strongly influence sentences under federal guidelines. The most notable finding in this report is that modification of laws or guidelines relating to crack/cocaine trafficking (for example, making the sentence identical for the same weight of cocaine regardless of the form [crack or powder]) would essentially eliminate the racial and ethnic differences in federal sentencing.[126]

Three-Strikes Laws

The war on drugs has affected people of color not only through mandatory sentencing laws, but also through "three-strikes" laws. Although the purpose of such laws is to reduce the risks posed by repetitive, dangerous offenders, one report found that 85 percent of all offenders sentenced under these laws are sentenced for nonviolent offenses, including drug offenses.[127] Under California's three-strikes law, sentencing for second and third offenses has affected twice as many marijuana possessors (192) as murderers (4), rapists (25), or kidnappers (24).

Washington state became the first state to enact a three-strikes law, in 1993. Since then, at least twenty-two other states have enacted such laws, and the federal government has followed suit. Three-strikes laws have been used infrequently in jurisdictions other than California.[128]

The application of the three-strikes laws has raised many concerns. The racial disparity among those sent to prison under such laws is particularly distressing. Blacks are sentenced under the law thirteen times as often as Whites. Although Blacks constitute only 7 percent of the state's population, they account for 43 percent of the three-strike inmates.[129] Statistics specifically relating to Hispanics were not found. However, related data suggest a similar disparity.

As discussed earlier, Hispanics were convicted for marijuana trafficking at a higher rate than Blacks or Whites, and 95 percent of all

Hispanic marijuana traffickers were incarcerated. If marijuana users are being hardest hit by such laws, and Hispanics are convicted at higher rates for marijuana possession and trafficking, it seems logical to assume that three-strikes laws are likely to result in a disproportionate number of Hispanics being sentenced to prison.

Death Penalty

Capital punishment data are collected and published annually by the Bureau of Justice Statistics as part of the National Prisoner Statistics Program. The most recent report reviewed the status of the death penalty in 1996. The report indicated that out of 3,219 state and federal prisoners under sentence of death, there were 259 Hispanics (4 female and 255 male). This is an increase from 239 in 1995. In 1996, twenty-eight Hispanics received a death sentence, six were removed from death row, and two were executed. More than 75 percent of Hispanic death-row inmates were incarcerated in the states of Texas, California, Arizona, and Florida.[130]

Since a revised death penalty statute went into effect in 1988, the federal government has sought the death penalty ninety-two times.[131] Eleven out of these ninety-two cases involved a Hispanic defendant.

Of the defendants executed since 1977, 7 percent were Hispanic, compared to 51 percent White and 41 percent Black.[132] During the 20-year period from 1977 to 1996, 5 percent of Hispanics were removed from death row by other means, as compared to 52 percent of Whites and 41 percent of Blacks. Hispanics constituted 8.8 percent of death-row inmates[133] and 3 percent of the victims in death penalty cases.[134]

Reports that the death penalty is disproportionately applied to Hispanics and Blacks may stem from the fact that persons of different ethnicities are lumped together under an overinclusive category such as "minorities."[135] For more meaningful analysis to occur, future researchers must look beyond the White/minority dichotomy and address the paucity of information on Hispanics and the death penalty.

Hispanic Juveniles and Crime

The existing empirical data on Hispanic juvenile delinquents are very sparse. What is available is scattered information that can be pieced together to yield a "bare bones" analysis of what causal factors affect Hispanic juvenile delinquency rates in correlation with current statistical data.

It was not until 1980 that the Uniform Crime Reports (UCR) began asking reporting law enforcement agencies to report the ethnic designations of Hispanic and non-Hispanic. This request has not effectively permeated statistical intake, and even today the majority of statistical data in the UCR does not include figures on Hispanics as a separate ethnic group. Most reports from the Office of Juvenile Justice and Delinquency Prevention (OJJDP) use the racial classifications of "White" or "non-White," or "Black" and "White," with Hispanics being included in the White category.[136] The most current data available on juvenile arrest rates, contained in an OJJDP report entitled "Juvenile Arrests 1995," stated that "juvenile arrests disproportionately involved minorities," yet once again classified Hispanics as White.[137] Recent fact sheets published by the OJJDP concerning drug offense cases in juvenile court, delinquency cases waived to criminal court, and detention and delinquency cases all fail to mention the Hispanic juvenile. These areas are especially important for determining the social impact of the processing, holding, and rehabilitation of Hispanic youth.

Fortunately, concrete statistics on the number of Hispanic juveniles in correctional facilities (both state and federal, private and public) are available. The most recent data for private facilities nationwide show that Hispanic juveniles account for 4,116 inmates of these 39 facilities (approximately 10 percent).[138] Out of 69 public facilities holding 14,653 total juveniles, 725 inmates are Hispanic.[139] Compiling the two surveys, as of 1996 approximately 6 percent of the juvenile population in public and private correctional facilities is Hispanic. Perhaps the significance of these figures is more properly illustrated by an OJJDP report,[140] which found that the Hispanic juvenile population in private facilities over a 5-year period increased at a rate of 31 percent, reflecting an overall 1.7 percent population increase. This growth rate (31 percent) is extremely high and is quite alarming when put in perspective: it was double the percentage change for Blacks, and well above the 2 percent change for White juvenile delinquents in private facilities.

In the federal criminal justice system, out of the total 124 juvenile delinquents confined in 1994, Hispanics were the group with the second highest representation, 15.3 percent. In addition, 4 percent of the juvenile delinquents were of Mexican citizenship. Surprisingly, the majority of juvenile delinquents in the federal criminal justice system were Native Americans, representing an overwhelming 60.5 percent.[141]

In light of this statistical data, it is clear that Hispanic juveniles are being incarcerated at an increasing rate. What is not so clear is why

Hispanic juveniles are coming into conflict with the law more frequently than in the past. Perhaps socioeconomic status, discrimination, language barriers, immigration, culture conflict, and socialization processes are all factors that can help explain this dilemma. Unfortunately, however, sociological studies have not taken up these questions with specific reference to either Hispanic juvenile delinquents or to adult Hispanic offenders.

It is widely known that by early in the next century, Hispanics will be the nation's largest minority group. The juvenile justice system must be equipped to respond to the needs of this ethnic group. "[A]n increased awareness of the values and norms," along with a heightened sensitivity to social factors contributing to Hispanic delinquency, is needed.[142] Only by seeking to understand the root causal factors contributing to Hispanic delinquency can the criminal justice system, and society as a whole, hope to cure the increasing prevalence of Hispanic youth incarceration.

Most of the sociological literature pertaining to the delinquent Hispanic juvenile revolves around the two key elements of family and education. Various studies have consistently suggested that one of the most important predictors of juvenile crime is the significance of family relations.[143] Indeed, an ethnographic study by Orlando Rodriguez and David Weisburd found that "family involvement was significantly related to delinquency."[144] The significance of familial relationships can also be viewed against the background of high levels of Hispanic immigration to the United States; some hypothesize "that recent immigrants have fewer stabilizing social structures, such as strong family ties ... that would tend to make them law abiding."[145]

It also seems that the Hispanic family has a large correlation with the academic success of youth. A study by Bedard et al. found that the major cause of Hispanic youth's dropping out of school was lack of parental involvement. This belief "remained relatively constant across place of birth, gender, and origin" of the Hispanics polled.[146] In addition, "a strong majority of [Hispanics felt] that dropping out of high school is a very serious problem,"[147] indicating that the Hispanic community views education as valuable and is concerned with their young completing their education. The results of this study correlate with a study done by Jackson, which found that a majority of Hispanic offenders had a much lower level of education when compared to Blacks and Whites.[148] The OJJDP, in a publication entitled "Improving Literacy Skills of Juvenile Detainees," stated that the "average reading ability of youth confined in correctional institutions is at the fourth-grade level."[149]

The lower level of education and high dropout rate among Hispanics may be related to the dangers associated with school attendance. A government study found that Hispanic students were more likely than non-Hispanics to indicate fear of attack at school; 30 percent of Hispanic students, contrasted with 27 percent of Blacks and 24 percent of Whites, reported fear in school.[150] Another study done by the National Center for Education Statistics found that Hispanic students were more worried about crime than Blacks and Whites.[151]

Lack of parental involvement was also the largest identifiable factor contributing to gang involvement.[152] In 1991, gang members by ethnicity were 42.7 percent Hispanic. Between 1990 and 1991, the number of Black gang members increased by 13 percent, while the number of Hispanic gang members increased by 18 percent.[153]

A prevalent practice among law enforcement in the war on gangs is the use of "gang profiling." This practice typically involves stopping persons who fit a gang profile, taking their pictures, and documenting them as members of a gang. The problem is that "stereotyping and institutional racism make it hard for cops to separate the hard core gang members from other people who hang out in certain areas and dress a certain way."[154] Taking pictures of Hispanics simply because of their ethnicity, without permission or evidence of gang membership, is harassment. Such harassment punishes young Hispanics for noncriminal behavior like gathering in certain areas and associating with certain friends.[155]

Another tactic used by police that can result in harassment is the use of civil injunctions against alleged gang members. Injunctions are easier to obtain than criminal convictions. Injunctions require a lower burden of proof and do not trigger any right to a lawyer or trial by jury.

Georges-Abeyie found that the "misuse of racial and cultural delineators" as classifiers, exemplified in the confused application of race and ethnicity (particularly in statistical compilation for crime), "is bound to result in cognitive confusions and negative practical consequences."[156] This confused state creates a "social distancing," which is defined as a cultural and spatial isolation of ethnic minorities, which can, in turn, lead to the formation of ethnically based subcultures and even contra-cultures. The main effect is "generalization of negative cultural and social attributions" and the subsequent criminalization of such attributions. The result: overcriminalization, prosecution, and sentencing discrepancies.[157]

Public Policy Issues

The criminal justice system is said to be "one of the most important hierarchy-enhancing social institutions within the social system."[158] As such, the hierarchy-enhancing institution is concerned with preserving the status quo, namely the entrenchment of the hegemonic group. "The net output of this institution will be an unequal distribution of negative social value to members of subordinate groups," such as Hispanics.[159]

Attention should be focused on the changing perception of Hispanic communities. Do the suspicion and distrust of the criminal justice system abate as the number of Hispanics in law enforcement, the legal profession, and the judiciary increases? Studies should measure the *actual* social impact such increased representation yields. If the criminal justice system protects the status quo and punishes subordinate groups such as Hispanics, will change come only as the status of Hispanics changes educationally, professionally, politically, economically, and socially? Are there differences among the various Hispanic groups? If so, are those differences instructive respecting Hispanic involvement in the criminal justice system?

The current paucity of data on Hispanics prevents deeper analysis. Criminologists, sociologists, educators, policy makers, and other professionals who study the criminal justice system cannot effectively make policy recommendations without facts. Therefore, legislators should mandate the collection of data that includes Hispanics. Researchers should also resist categorizations based on the White/Black or White/ minority dichotomy. When possible, the diversity within the Hispanic community should be reported. The varying experiences of distinct Hispanic groups may help explain the relationship of Hispanics to the criminal justice system. Only a multifaceted approach, which gathers data on Hispanics as well as other groups, will provide the specific data necessary to support a more in-depth evaluation of Hispanics in relation to the criminal justice system.

With this in mind, the following is a list of policy recommendations, each corresponding to a particular concern raised in one of the various sections of this chapter.

1. To combat police discrimination and police abuse directed at Hispanics so as to improve police-community relations:

   * Municipalities, counties, and states should increase Hispanic representation on police forces and in administrative and policy positions relating to law enforcement decision making.

- There must be an increased effort on the part of government authorities to identify, assess, and prosecute cases involving police abuse and misconduct. Rigorous enforcement of the federal Violent Crime Control and Law Enforcement Act passed in 1994 should help.

- State and local law enforcement officials should avoid enforcing immigration laws.

2. To change both the perception and the reality that the criminal justice system is biased against Hispanics:

   - Studies should be conducted to determine what effect Hispanic involvement and participation at the various stages in the criminal justice system has on the reality and perception of justice.

   - There should be a clearly delineated right for non-English-speaking defendants to have a courtroom interpreter.

   - Bilingual Hispanics should be allowed to serve on juries in cases involving monolingual or Spanish-dominant Hispanic defendants.

3. To reduce the number of hate crimes committed against Hispanics, a culture of prevention must be created, beyond just the stiffening of penalties for hate crime offenders. Schools, the media, and community leaders should work together to create a positive atmosphere that promotes mutual respect and cooperation among different cultures.

4. To ensure more equitable treatment of Hispanic perpetrators of crime:

   - Sentencing laws that severely limit judicial discretion and flexibility, like the Sentencing Reform Act of 1984 and mandatory minimum sentences, should be modified or repealed.

   - Three-strikes laws should be limited to violent offenses only.

5. To reduce the number of Hispanic juveniles involved in crime, much more empirical data and information must be collected on Hispanic juvenile delinquents. This information should include sociological studies that attempt to explain the increasing incarceration rate of Hispanic juveniles. Overall, only after a wealth of information has been collected on Hispanic juvenile delinquents can more than just a cursory analysis be made of the possible causal factors that lead to incarceration of these youths.

Notes

1. Jesse Smith and Robert Johns, eds., *Statistical Record of Black America* (3d ed. 1995).
2. Ibid.
3. Alicia Di Rado, "The *Times* Poll: Fear of Crime Is the Unifying Factor in Orange County," *Los Angeles Times*, October 25, 1993, Metro, Part A, at 1.
4. Ibid.
5. Ibid.

6. Roberto Rodriguez, "Scholars Document Pattern of Police Brutality Against Latinos," *Black Issues in Higher Education* 8 (April 1993): 26–27.
7. Ibid.
8. United States Commission on Civil Rights, "Racial and Ethnic Tensions in American Communities: Poverty, Inequality, and Discrimination," vol. 1 of *The Mount Pleasant Report* (Washington, D.C.: Author, January 1993).
9. Ibid.
10. Ibid.
11. Robert Garcia, "Latinos and Criminal Justice," *Chicano-Latino Law Review* 14 (Winter 1994): 6.
12. Ibid.
13. Independent Commission on the Los Angeles Police Department, *Report of the Independent Commission on the Los Angeles Police Department* (Los Angeles, Cal.: Author, 1991) (Christopher Commission Report).
14. Ibid.
15. Ibid.
16. Paul Hoffman, "The Feds, Lies, and Videotape: The Need for Effective Federal Role in Controlling Police Abuse in Urban America," *Southern California Law Review* 66 (May 1993): 1453.
17. *Los Angeles County Sheriff's Department: A Report by Special Counsel James G. Kolts & Staff* (Los Angeles, Cal.: Los Angeles County Sheriff's Department, July 1992) (Kolts Commission Report).
18. Nevada Advisory Committee to the United States Commission on Civil Rights, *Police-Community Relations in Reno, Nevada* (Washington, D.C.: United States Commission on Civil Rights, May 1992).
19. 42 U.S.C. § 14141(a).
20. United States Department of Justice, Bureau of Justice Statistics, "National Data Collection on Police Use of Force" (by Tom McEwen) (Washington, D.C.: Author, 1996).
21. Ibid.
22. Jerry Mandel, Jay Alire, and Emily E. McKay, eds., "Hispanic Police," Chapter 5 of *Final Report: Police Use of Deadly Force in Hispanic Communities* (Washington, D.C.: National Council of La Raza, 1982).
23. Ibid.
24. Ibid.
25. Ibid.
26. Ibid.
27. United States Department of Justice, Bureau of Justice Statistics, "Local Police Departments" (by Brian A. Reaves) (Washington, D.C.: Author, 1993).
28. Ibid.
29. United States Department of Commerce, Economics, and Statistics Administration, Bureau of the Census, *1990 Florida Census of Population and Housing* (Washington, D.C.: Author, 1993).
30. United States Department of Justice, Bureau of Justice Statistics, *Sourcebook of Criminal Justice Statistics* (ed. Kathleen Maguire and Ann L. Pastore) (Washington, D.C.: Author, 1994) [hereinafter "*Sourcebook* 1994"].
31. United States Department of Commerce, Economics, and Statistics Administration, Bureau of the Census, *1990 California Census of Population and Housing* (Washington, D.C.: Author, 1992).
32. Los Angeles Police Department, "Sworn Personnel by Rank, Gender, & Ethnicity" (Report PR 91 and HLRPT 17, July 7, 1997).
33. Mandel, *Final Report.*

34. *Sourcebook* 1994.
35. United States Department of Justice, Bureau of Justice Statistics, *Sourcebook of Criminal Justice Statistics* (ed. Kathleen Maguire and Ann L. Pastore) (Washington, D.C.: Author, 1996) [hereinafter "*Sourcebook* 1996"].
36. Los Angeles Police Department, memo from Chief of Police, 1979.
37. American Civil Liberties Union of Southern California, *The Call for Change Goes Unanswered: Los Angeles Police Department Citizen Complaint Procedure* (Los Angeles, Cal.: Author, 1992).
38. Kenneth Noble, "Before They Beat Mexicans, Police Gave Orders in English," *New York Times*, April 10, 1996, at A12; "Taped Aliens' Beating Sparks Protests," *Facts on File World News Digest*, April 11, 1996, at D3, p. 245.
39. N.Y. Assembly Bill 3499, S. 2210 (1997).
40. United States Commission on Civil Rights, *Federal Immigration Law Enforcement in the Southwest: Civil Rights Impacts on Border Communities* (Los Angeles, Cal.: Author, 1997).
41. Ibid.
42. Ibid.
43. ABA Judicial Division, Task Force on Minorities in the Judiciary, *The Directory of Minority Judges of the United States*, 2d ed. (Chicago: ABA/Martindale-Hubbell, 1997).
44. *Sourcebook* 1996.
45. Ibid.
46. Ibid.
47. Ibid.
48. California Judicial Council Advisory Committee on Racial and Ethnic Bias in the Courts, *Final Report* (Oakland, Cal.: Abbey Press, January 1997) [hereinafter "Bias Report 1997"].
49. Ibid.
50. Ibid.
51. R. Garfield Cheek, "Ethnicity and Inclusion into the Legal Profession: The Latin American Experience," *Career Planning and Adult Development Journal* 9 (1996): 71–79.
52. Ibid.
53. Ibid.
54. National Association for Law Placement, "Women and Minority Partners Make Small Gains at Major Law Firms" (Press release, December 11, 1996).
55. American Bar Association, *Approved Law Schools: Statistical Information on American Bar Association Approved Law Schools, 1998 Edition*, ed. Rick L. Morgan and Kurt Snyder (New York: Macmillan, 1998).
56. Miguel Mendez, "Lawyers, Linguists, Story-Tellers, and Limited English-Speaking Witnesses," *New Mexico Law Review* 27 (Winter 1997): 77.
57. Ibid.
58. Ibid.
59. Ibid.
60. 28 U.S.C. § 1827.
61. Susan Berk-Seligson, *The Bilingual Court* (Chicago: University of Chicago Press, 1990).
62. Ibid.
63. People v. Mata Aguilar, 35 Cal. 3d 785, 790 (1984).
64. Mendez, "Lawyers, Linguists, Story-Tellers, and Limited English-Speaking Witnesses."
65. Ibid.

66. Jara v. Municipal Court, 21 Cal. 3d 181 (1978).
67. Mendez, "Lawyers, Linguists, Story-Tellers, and Limited English-Speaking Witnesses."
68. Gonzalez v. United States, 33 F.3d 1047 (9th Cir. 1994).
69. Mendez, "Lawyers, Linguists, Story-Tellers, and Limited English-Speaking Witnesses."
70. *Gonzalez*, 33 F.3d at 1051.
71. Ibid. at 1050.
72. Ibid. at 1053.
73. Cal. Gov't Code § 68561.
74. Bias Report 1997.
75. Juan Perea, "*Hernandez v. New York*: Courts, Prosecutors, and the Fear of Spanish," *Hofstra Law Review* 21 (Fall 1992): 1–61.
76. Berk-Seligson, *The Bilingual Court.*
77. Ibid.
78. Hernandez v. Texas, 347 U.S. 475 (1954).
79. Hernandez v. New York, 111 S. Ct. 1859 (1991).
80. Perea, "*Hernandez v. New York*: Courts, Prosecutors, and the Fear of Spanish."
81. Ibid.
82. United States Department of Justice, Office of Justice Programs, "Criminal Victimization in the United States" (Washington, D.C.: Author, 1994).
83. United States Department of Justice, Bureau of Justice Statistics, "Hispanic Victims" (by Lisa D. Bastian) (Washington, D.C.: Author, 1990).
84. United States Department of Justice, Office of Justice Programs, "Criminal Victimization in the United States."
85. United States Department of Justice, Bureau of Justice Statistics, "Hispanic Victims."
86. Ibid.
87. Ibid.
88. United States Department of Justice, Bureau of Justice Statistics, "Hispanic Victims: Advance Report" (National Crime Survey Report) (Washington, D.C.: Author, 1980).
89. United States Department of Justice, Bureau of Justice Statistics, "A Policymaker's Guide to Hate Crimes" (by Owen Holden et al.) (Washington, D.C.: Author, 1997).
90. United States Department of Justice, Federal Bureau of Investigation, "Hate Crime" (Uniform Crime Reports) (Washington, D.C.: Author, 1995).
91. United States Department of Justice, Federal Bureau of Investigation, "Hate Crime Statistics" (Uniform Crime Reports) (Washington, D.C.: Author, 1996).
92. United States Department of Justice, Bureau of Justice Statistics, "A Policymaker's Guide to Hate Crimes."
93. Los Angeles County Commission on Human Relations, *Hate Crime in Los Angeles County in 1994* (Author, 1994).
94. Los Angeles County Commission on Human Relations, *Hate Crime in Los Angeles County in 1995* (Author, 1995).
95. Los Angeles County Commission on Human Relations, *Hate Crime in Los Angeles County in 1996* (Author, 1996).
96. Nkechi Taifa, "Beyond Institutionalized Racism: 'The Genocidal Impact of Executive, Legislative & Judicial Decision-making in the Crack Cocaine Fiasco,'" *National Bar Association Magazine* 10, no. 5 (September/October 1996): 13–17.
97. United States Department of Justice, Bureau of Justice Statistics, "Prisoners in

1996" (by Christopher J. Murnola and Allen J. Beck) (Washington, D.C.: Author, 1996).

98. Ibid.
99. R. Ostrow, "Sentencing Study Sees Race Disparity," *Los Angeles Times*, October 5, 1995, at A1.
100. Kevin L Jackson, "Differences in the Background and Criminal Justice Characteristics of Young Black, White, and Hispanic Male Federal Prison Inmates." *Journal of Black Studies* 27 (March 1997): 494–509.
101. Ibid.
102. Ibid.
103. Ibid.
104. Alfred Blumstein, "On the Racial Disproportionality of United States Prison Populations," *Journal of Criminal Law & Criminology* 73 (1982): 1259; Patrick A. Langan, "Racism on Trial: New Evidence to Explain the Racial Composition of Prisons in the U.S.," *Journal of Criminal Law & Criminology* 76 (1985): 666; Stephen P. Klein, Susan Turner, and Joan Petersilia, *Racial Equity in Sentencing* (Santa Monica, Cal.: Rand, 1988).
105. Jackson, "Differences in the Background and Criminal Justice Characteristics of Male Federal Prison Inmates."
106. Ibid.
107. Ibid.
108. Douglas C. McDonald and Kenneth E. Carlson, "Sentencing in the Federal Courts: Does Race Matter?" (December 1993 (NCJ-145328)), at 18.
109. Ibid.
110. Ibid.
111. Albert Alschuler, "The Failure of the Sentencing Guidelines: A Plea for Less Aggregation," *University of Chicago Law Review* 58 (1991): 901.
112. Ibid.
113. Philip Oliss, "Mandatory Minimum Sentencing: Discretion, the Safety Valve, and the Sentencing Guidelines," *University of Cincinnati Law Review* 63 (Summer 1995): 1851.
114. Ibid.
115. Ibid.
116. Ibid.
117. Mary Pat Flaherty, and Joan Biskupic, "Judges Protest Racial Disparity by Ignoring Sentencing Guidelines," *Dallas Morning News*, October 11, 1996, at 41A.
118. Ibid.
119. Ibid.
120. McDonald and Carlson, "Sentencing in the Federal Courts: Does Race Matter?"
121. Taifa, "Beyond Institutionalized Racism."
122. United States Department of Justice, Bureau of Justice Statistics, "Prisoners in 1996."
123. McDonald and Carlson, "Sentencing in the Federal Courts: Does Race Matter?"
124. Ibid.
125. Ibid.
126. Ibid.
127. Campaign for an Effective Crime Policy, "The Impact of 'Three Strikes and You're Out' Laws: What Have We Learned?" (Washington, D.C.: Author, September 1996).

128. Ibid.
129. Ibid.
130. United States Department of Justice, Bureau of Justice Statistics, "Bulletin" (by Tracy L. Snell) (Washington, D.C.: Author, 1997).
131. Robert Suro, "Verdict Destined to Be a Benchmark in Age-Old Debate," *Buffalo [N.Y.] News*, June 14, 1997, at A4.
132. United States Department of Justice, Bureau of Justice Statistics, "Bulletin."
133. Ibid.
134. "Facing Death: The Numbers Behind the Ultimate Penalty," *Los Angeles Times*, January 21, 1996, Metro, Part B, at 2.
135. R. Hernandez, "Death Row Not Hispanic," *Portland Oregonian*, June 27, 1997, section B, at 8.
136. United States Department of Justice, Office of Justice Programs—Office of Juvenile Justice and Delinquency Prevention, "Juvenile Court Statistics" (by Carl E. Pope and William Feyerherm) (Washington, D.C.: Author, 1988).
137. United States Department of Justice, Office of Justice Programs—Office of Juvenile Justice and Delinquency Prevention, "Juvenile Arrests 1995" (by Howard N. Snyder) (Washington, D.C.: Author, 1995), at 3.
138. United States Department of Justice, Office of Justice Programs—Office of Juvenile Justice and Delinquency Prevention, "1995 Juvenile Facility Census" (Washington, D.C.: Author, 1995).
139. Ibid.
140. United States Department of Justice, Office of Justice Programs—Office of Juvenile Justice and Delinquency Prevention, "Juveniles in Private Facilities, 1991–1995" (by Joseph Moore) (Washington, D.C.: Author, 1995).
141. United States Department of Justice, Office of Justice Programs, "Juvenile Delinquents in the Federal Criminal Justice System" (by John Scalia) (Washington, D.C.: Author, 1997).
142. Laura Bedard, Sarah Eschholz, and Marc Gertz, "Perceptions of Crime and Education Within the Hispanic Community and the Impact on Corrections," *Journal of Correctional Education* 45, no. 2 (1994): 72–80.
143. Jean-Marie Lyon, Scott Henngeler, and James A. Hall, "The Family Relation, Peer Relations, and Criminal Activities of Caucasian and Hispanic-American Gang Members," *Journal of Abnormal Child Psychology* 20, no. 5 (1992): 439–49.
144. Orlando Rodriguez and David Weisburd, "The Integrated Social Control Model and Ethnicity: The Case of Puerto Rican American Delinquency," *Criminal Justice and Behavior* 18, no. 4 (1991): 464–79.
145. Garcia, "Latinos and Criminal Justice," at 8.
146. Bedard, Eschholz, and Gertz, "Perceptions of Crime and Education Within the Hispanic Community."
147. Ibid.
148. Jackson, "Differences in the Background and Criminal Justice Characteristics of Male Federal Prison Inmates."
149. United States Department of Justice, Office of Justice Programs—Office of Juvenile Justice and Delinquency Prevention, "Improving Literacy Skills of Juvenile Detainees" (by Jane Hodges, Nancy Giuliotti, and F. M. Porpotage II) (Washington, D.C.: Author, 1994).
150. United States Department of Justice, Office of Justice Programs—Office of Juvenile Justice and Delinquency Prevention, "Juvenile Offenders and Victims: 1996" (by Howard N. Snyder, Melissa Sickmund, and Eileen Poe-Yamagata) (Washington, D.C.: Author, 1995).

151. Ibid.
152. Bedard, Eschholz, and Gertz, "Perceptions of Crime and Education Within the Hispanic Community."
153. United States Department of Justice, Office of Justice Programs, "Gang Crime and Law Enforcement Recordkeeping" (National Institute of Justice) (by G. David Curry, Richard A. Ball, and Robert J. Fox) (Washington, D.C.: Author, 1994).
154. Ron Nixon, "Crime & Punishment: How the Criminal Justice System Fails Hispanics," *Hispanic* 9 (September 1996): 26–32.
155. Ibid.
156. Daniel E. Georges-Abeyie, "Defining Race, Ethnicity, and Social Distance: Their Impact on Crime, Criminal Victimization, and the Criminal Justice Processing of Minorities," *Journal of Contemporary Criminal Justice* 8, no. 2 (1992): 100–113.
157. Ibid.
158. Jim Sidanius, James H. Liu, John S. Shaw, and Felicia Pratto, "Social Dominance Orientation, Hierarchy Attenuators and Hierarchy Enhancers: Social Dominance Theory and the Criminal Justice System," *Journal of Applied Social Psychology* 24 (1994): 338–66.
159. Ibid.

Bibliography

ABA Judicial Division, Task Force on Minorities in the Judiciary. *The Directory of Minority Judges of the United States* (2d ed.). Chicago: ABA/Martindale-Hubbell, 1997.

Abrams, Norman, et al. *Federal Criminal Law and Its Enforcement*, 2d ed. St. Paul, Minn.: West, 1993.

Alschuler, Albert. "The Failure of the Sentencing Guidelines: A Plea for Less Aggregation." *University of Chicago Law Review* 58 (1991): 901.

American Bar Association. *Approved Law Schools: Statistical Information on American Bar Association Approved Law Schools, 1998 Edition*, edited by Rick L. Morgan and Kurt Snyder. New York: Macmillan, 1998.

———. *Achieving Justice in a Diverse America: Summit on Racial & Ethnic Bias in the Justice System* (interim report). Chicago: Author, 1994.

American Civil Liberties Union of Southern California. *The Call for Change Goes Unanswered: Los Angeles Police Department Citizen Complaint Procedure*. Los Angeles, Cal.: Author, 1992.

Bedard, Laura, Sarah Eschholz, and Marc Gertz. "Perceptions of Crime and Education Within the Hispanic Community and the Impact on Corrections." *Journal of Correctional Education* 45, no. 2 (1994): 72–80.

Berk-Seligson, Susan. *The Bilingual Court.* Chicago: University of Chicago Press, 1990.

Blumstein, Alfred. "On the Racial Disproportionality of United States Prison Populations." *Journal of Criminal Law & Criminology* 73 (1982): 1259.

California Judicial Council Advisory Committee. *Racial and Ethnic Compo-

sition of the California Trial Courts 1991–1992. Oakland, Cal.: Abbey Press, 1992.

California Judicial Council Advisory Committee on Racial and Ethnic Bias in the Courts. *Final Report.* Oakland, Cal.: Abbey Press, January 1997.

Campaign for an Effective Crime Policy. "The Impact of 'Three Strikes and You're Out' Laws: What Have We Learned?" Washington, D.C.: Author, September 1996.

Cheek, R. Garfield. "Ethnicity and Inclusion into the Legal Profession: The Latin American Experience." *Career Planning and Adult Development Journal* 9 (1996): 71–79.

Coalition for Humane Immigrant Rights of Los Angeles (CHIRLA). "Hate Unleashed: Los Angeles in the Aftermath of 1987." Los Angeles, Cal.: CHIRLA, 1995.

Days, Drew. "Race and the Federal Criminal Justice System: A Look at the Issue of Selective Prosecution." *Maine Law Review* 48 (1996): 179.

Di Rado, Alicia. "The *Times* Poll: Fear of Crime Is the Unifying Factor in Orange County." *Los Angeles Times,* October 25, 1993, Metro, Part A, at 1.

"Drug Prosecutions Are Biased, Some Minorities Say; Problem Is 'Among Inner-City Street Gangs, Not Suburban Bowling Leagues,' Retorts Official." *St. Louis Post-Dispatch,* May 18, 1996, at 4B.

"Facing Death: The Numbers Behind the Ultimate Penalty." *Los Angeles Times,* January 21, 1996, Metro, Part B, at 2.

Federal Bureau of Prisons Fact Card. June 1994.

Flaherty, Mary Pat, and Joan Biskupic. "Judges Protest Racial Disparity by Ignoring Sentencing Guidelines." *Dallas Morning News,* October 11, 1996, at 41A.

Florida State Advisory Committee to the United States Commission on Civil Rights. "Police-Community Relations in Miami." Washington, D.C.: United States Commission on Civil Rights, 1989.

The Fund for Free Expression, A Committee of Human Rights Watch. "English Only—The Attack on Minority Language Speakers in the United States." *Fund for Free Expression* 4, no. 1 (1992): 2–9.

Garcia, Robert. "Latinos and Criminal Justice." *Chicano-Latino Law Review* 14 (Winter 1994): 6.

Georges-Abeyie, Daniel E. "Defining Race, Ethnicity, and Social Distance: Their Impact on Crime, Criminal Victimization, and the Criminal Justice Processing of Minorities." *Journal of Contemporary Criminal Justice* 8, no. 2 (1992): 100–113.

Harlan, Vernon T. *Youth Street Gangs: Breaking the Gangs Cycle in Urban America.* San Francisco, Cal.: Austin & Winfield, 1997.

Harris, David. "'Driving While Black' and All Other Traffic Offenses: The Supreme Court and Pretextual Traffic Stops." *Journal of Criminal Law and Criminology* 87, no. 2 (1997): 544–82.

Hernandez, R. "Death Row Not Hispanic." *Portland Oregonian*, June 27, 1997, section B, at 8.

Hispanic Americans: A Statistical Sourcebook, edited by Louise L. Hornor. California: Information Publications, 1997.

Hoffman, Paul. "The Feds, Lies, and Videotape: The Need for Effective Federal Role in Controlling Police Abuse in Urban America." *Southern California Law Review* 66 (May 1993): 1453.

Independent Commission on the Los Angeles Police Department. *Report of the Independent Commission on the Los Angeles Police Department.* Los Angeles, Cal.: Author, 1991 (Christopher Commission Report).

Jackson, Kevin L. "Differences in the Background and Criminal Justice Characteristics of Young Black, White, and Hispanic Male Federal Prison Inmates." *Journal of Black Studies* 27 (March 1997): 494–509.

Klein, Stephen P., Susan Turner, and Joan Petersilia. *Racial Equity in Sentencing*. Santa Monica, Cal.: Rand, 1988.

Langan, Patrick A. "Racism on Trial: New Evidence to Explain the Racial Composition of Prisons in the U.S." *Journal of Criminal Law & Criminology* 76 (1985): 666.

Leadership Conference on Civil Rights. "Cause for Concern: Hate Crimes in America." January 1997.

Leonard, Kimberly, Carl Pope, and William Feyerherm, eds. *Minorities in Juvenile Justice*. Thousand Oaks, Cal.: Sage Publications, 1995.

Lopez, Antoinette Sedillo. *Latinos in the United States.* New York & London: Garland, 1995.

Los Angeles County Commission on Human Relations. *Hate Crime in Los Angeles County in 1996*. Author, 1996.

———. *Hate Crime in Los Angeles County in 1995*. Author, 1995.

———. *Hate Crime in Los Angeles County in 1994*. Author, 1994.

Los Angeles County Sheriff's Department: A Report by Special Counsel James G. Kolts & Staff. Los Angeles, Cal.: Los Angeles County Sheriff's Department, July 1992 (Kolts Commission Report).

Los Angeles Police Department. Memo from Chief of Police. 1979.

———. "Sworn Personnel by Rank, Gender, & Ethnicity." Report PR 91 and HLRPT 17, July 7, 1997.

Los Angeles Police Department Manual § 4/604.41. 1997, based on 1995 edition.

Lyon, Jean-Marie, Scott Henngeler, and James A. Hall. "The Family Relation, Peer Relations, and Criminal Activities of Caucasian and Hispanic-American Gang Members." *Journal of Abnormal Child Psychology* 20, no. 5 (1992): 439–49.

Mandel, Jerry, Jay Alire, and Emily E. McKay, eds. "Hispanic Police." Chapter 5 of *Final Report: Police Use of Deadly Force in Hispanic Communities*. Washington, D.C.: National Council of La Raza, 1982.

McDonald, Douglas C., and Kenneth E. Carlson. "Sentencing in the Federal Courts: Does Race Matter?" December 1993 (NCJ-145328).

Mendez, Miguel. "Lawyers, Linguists, Story-Tellers, and Limited English-Speaking Witnesses." *New Mexico Law Review* 27 (Winter 1997): 77.

Mendoza, Salvador. "When Maria Speaks Spanish: *Hernandez*, the Ninth Circuit, and the Fallacy of Race Neutrality," *Chicano-Latino Law Review* 18 (Fall 1996): 196.

Mirande, Alfredo. "Now That I Speak English, *No Me Dejan Hablar*: The Implications of *Hernandez v. New York*." 18 *Chicano-Latino Law Review* 18 (Fall 1996): 115.

National Association for Law Placement. "Women and Minority Partners Make Small Gains at Major Law Firms." Press release, December 11, 1996.

National Conference on Sentencing Advocacy. *Race, Sentencing, and Criminal Justice*. New York: Practising Law Institute, 1991 (Litigation and Administrative Practice Course Handbook Series, Criminal Law and Urban Problems).

National Council of La Raza. *The Death Penalty and Hispanics*. Washington, D.C.: Author, 1986.

Nevada Advisory Committee to the United States Commission on Civil Rights. *Police-Community Relations in Reno, Nevada*. Washington, D.C.: United States Commission on Civil Rights, May 1992.

Nixon, Ron. "Crime & Punishment: How the Criminal Justice System Fails Hispanics." *Hispanic* 9 (September 1996): 26–32.

Noble, Kenneth. "Before They Beat Mexicans, Police Gave Orders in English." *New York Times*, April 10, 1996, at A12.

Oliss, Philip. "Mandatory Minimum Sentencing: Discretion, the Safety Valve, and the Sentencing Guidelines." *University of Cincinnati Law Review* 63 (Summer 1995): 1851.

Ostrow, R. "Sentencing Study Sees Race Disparity." *Los Angeles Times*, October 5, 1995, at A1.

Perea, Juan. "*Hernandez v. New York*: Courts, Prosecutors, and the Fear of Spanish." *Hofstra Law Review* 21 (Fall 1992): 1–61.

Rivera, Carla. "Faith in LAPD Returns on Eve of Volatile Trials." *Los Angeles Times*, February 6, 1993, Metro, Part A, at 1.

Rodriguez, Orlando, and David Weisburd. "The Integrated Social Control Model and Ethnicity: The Case of Puerto Rican American Delinquency." *Criminal Justice and Behavior* 18, no. 4 (1991): 464–79.

Rodriguez, Roberto. "Scholars Document Pattern of Police Brutality Against Latinos." *Black Issues in Higher Education* (April 1993): 26–27.

Seager, Susan. "A Matter of Race." *Daily Journal* 106 (1993): 1.

Shoemaker, Donald J. *Theories of Delinquency*. New York: Oxford University Press, 1990.

Sidanius, Jim, James H. Liu, John S. Shaw, and Felicia Pratto. "Social Dominance Orientation, Hierarchy Attenuators and Hierarchy Enhancers: Social Dominance Theory and the Criminal Justice System." *Journal of Applied Social Psychology* 24 (1994): 338–66.

Smith, Jacqueline. "Latino Gang Male Youth and Risk Factors: Time Preference, Time Perception, and Locus of Control." Ph.D. diss., University of California at Los Angeles, 1995.

Smith, Jesse, and Robert Johns, eds. *Statistical Record of Black America*. 3d ed., 1995.

Spencer, Gary. "Sentence Disparities Cited by Democratic Legislators." *New York Law Journal* 215, no. 93 (1996): 1 (col. 3).

Starrett, Richard. "The Crime Reporting Behavior of Hispanic Older Persons: A Causal Model." *Journal of Criminal Justice* 16 (1988): 413–23.

Suro, Robert. "Verdict Destined to Be a Benchmark in Age-Old Debate." *Buffalo [N.Y.] News*, June 14, 1997, at A4.

Taifa, Nkechi. "Beyond Institutionalized Racism: 'The Genocidal Impact of Executive, Legislative & Judicial Decision-making in the Crack Cocaine Fiasco.'" *National Bar Association Magazine* 10, no. 5 (September/October 1996): 13–17.

"Taped Aliens' Beating Sparks Protests." *Facts on File World News Digest*, April 11, 1996, at D3, p. 245.

Tinker, John, John Quiring, and Yvonne Pimentel. "Ethnic Bias in California Courts: A Case Study of Chicano and Anglo Felony Defendants." *Sociological Inquiry* 55 (1985): 83–96.

United States Commission on Civil Rights. *Federal Immigration Law Enforcement in the Southwest: Civil Rights Impacts on Border Communities*. Los Angeles, Cal.: Author, 1997.

———. "Racial and Ethnic Tensions in American Communities: Poverty, Inequality, and Discrimination." Vol. 1, *The Mount Pleasant Report*. Washington, D.C.: Author, January 1993.

United States Department of Commerce, Economics, and Statistics Administration, Bureau of the Census. *1990 California Census of Population and Housing*. Washington, D.C.: Author, 1992.

———. *1990 Florida Census of Population and Housing*. Washington, D.C.: Author, 1993.

United States Department of Justice, Bureau of Justice Statistics. "Bulletin" (by Tracy L. Snell). Washington, D.C.: Author, 1997.

———. "Census of State and Federal Correctional Facilities, 1995" (by James J. Stephan). Washington, D.C.: Author, 1995.

———. "Correctional Populations in the United States, 1994" (by Brown et al.). Washington, D.C.: Author, 1996.

———. "Hispanic Victims" (by Lisa D. Bastian). Washington, D.C.: Author, 1990.

————. "Hispanic Victims: Advance Report" (National Crime Survey Report). Washington, D.C.: Author, 1980.

————. "Local Police Departments" (by Brian A. Reaves). Washington, D.C.: Author, 1993.

————. "National Data Collection on Police Use of Force" (by Tom McEwen). Washington, D.C.: Author, 1996.

————. "A Policymaker's Guide to Hate Crimes" (by Owen Holden et al.). Washington, D.C.: Author, 1997.

————. "Prisoners in 1996" (by Christopher J. Murnola and Allen J. Beck). Washington, D.C.: Author, 1996.

————. "Prisons and Prisoners in the United States" (by Lawrence A. Greenfield). Washington, D.C.: Author, 1992.

————. "Race of Prisoners Admitted to State and Federal Institutions, 1926–86" (by Patrick A. Langan). Washington, D.C.: Author, 1991.

————. *Sourcebook of Criminal Justice Statistics* (ed. Kathleen Maguire and Ann L. Pastore). Washington, D.C.: Author, 1994.

————. *Sourcebook of Criminal Justice Statistics* (ed. Kathleen Maguire and Ann L. Pastore). Washington, D.C.: Author, 1996.

————. "Special Report: Lifetime Likelihood of Going to State or Federal Prison" (by Thomas P. Bonczar and Allen J. Beck). Washington, D.C.: Author, 1997.

United States Department of Justice, Bureau of Justice Statistics, Federal Justice Statistics Program. "Noncitizens in the Federal Criminal Justice System, 1984–94" (by John Scalia). Washington, D.C.: Author, 1996.

United States Department of Justice, Federal Bureau of Investigation. "Hate Crime" (Uniform Crime Reports). Washington, D.C.: Author, 1995.

————. "Hate Crime Statistics" (Uniform Crime Reports). Washington, D.C.: Author, 1996.

United States Department of Justice, Office of Justice Programs. "Criminal Victimization in the United States." Washington, D.C.: Author, 1994.

————. "Gang Crime and Law Enforcement Recordkeeping" (National Institute of Justice) (by G. David Curry, Richard A. Ball, and Robert J. Fox). Washington, D.C.: Author, 1994.

————. "Juvenile Delinquents in the Federal Criminal Justice System" (by John Scalia). Washington, D.C.: Author, 1997.

United States Department of Justice, Office of Justice Programs—Bureau of Justice Statistics. "School Crime: A National Crime Victimization Survey Report" (by Lisa D. Bastian and Bruce M. Taylor). Washington, D.C.: Author, 1991.

United States Department of Justice, Office of Justice Programs—Office of Juvenile Justice and Delinquency Prevention. "A Comprehensive Response to America's Youth Gang Problem" (by James H. Burch II and Betty M. Chemers). Washington, D.C.: Author, 1997.

———. "Delinquency Cases Waived to Criminal Court, 1985–1994" (by Jeffrey A. Butts). Washington, D.C.: Author, 1997.

———. "Detention and Delinquency Cases, 1985–1994" (by Eileen Poe-Yamagata). Washington, D.C.: Author, 1997.

———. "Drug Offense Cases in Juvenile Court, 1985–1994" (by Jeffrey A. Butts). Washington, D.C.: Author, 1997.

———. "Epidemiology of Serious Violence" (by Barbara Tatem Kelley et al.). Washington, D.C.: Author, 1997.

———. "Improving Literacy Skills of Juvenile Detainees" (by Jane Hodges, Nancy Giuliotti, and F. M. Porpotage II). Washington, D.C.: Author, 1994.

———. "Juvenile Arrests 1995" (by Howard N. Snyder). Washington, D.C.: Author, 1995.

———. "Juvenile Court Statistics" (by Carl E. Pope and William Feyerherm). Washington, D.C.: Author, 1988.

———. "Juveniles in Private Facilities, 1991–1995" (by Joseph Moore). Washington, D.C.: Author, 1997.

———. "Juvenile Offenders and Victims: 1996" (by Howard N. Snyder, Melissa Sickmund, and Eileen Poe-Yamanata). Washington, D.C.: Author, 1995.

———. "Minorities and the Juvenile Justice System" (by Carl E. Pope and William Feyerherm). Washington, D.C.: Author, 1995.

———. "1995 Juvenile Facility Census." Washington, D.C.: Author, 1995.

Welch, Susan, John Gruhl, and Cassia Spohn. "Dismissal, Conviction, and Incarceration of Hispanic Defendants: A Comparison with Anglos and Blacks." *Social Science Quarterly* 65 (1985): 257–64.

10

Hispanics and the Political Process

Christine Marie Sierra*

The beginning of a new millennium provides an important benchmark by which to assess Hispanic involvement in the U.S. political system. Over the final decades of the twentieth century, important developments unfolded in the nature and scope of Hispanic participation in American politics. Much attention focused on the burgeoning numbers of Hispanics in the U.S. population and their potential impact on American political institutions and the public policy-making process. Although pronouncements of expanded political power for Hispanics tended to overstate the case, by the century's end, Hispanics legitimately claimed attention and recognition from political observers, the mass media, policy makers, and scholars as a significant sector of the American body politic.

This chapter offers a synthesis of the scholarly literature on Hispanic political participation. Recognizing the vast scope and complexity of Hispanic politics, only selected dimensions of Hispanic political involvement are examined for their major patterns and implications for the future. Through a composite portrait of Hispanic political participation, the chapter suggests issues to be considered in the crafting of a Hispanic agenda for the twenty-first century.

It is important to note that scholarship in Hispanic politics has greatly expanded since the mid-1980s, when the previous edition of *Hispanics*

---

*   The author completed this chapter while in residence as a Visiting Scholar with the Mexican American Studies & Research Center (MASRC) at the University of Arizona. She would like to acknowledge the MASRC for its support of her research.

in the United States was published. The literature reflects a much more expansive list of topics as well as methodological and interdisciplinary approaches. Noteworthy are two groundbreaking national studies of the Hispanic population, the 1988 National Latino Immigrant Survey and the 1990 Latino National Political Survey (LNPS), that provide comprehensive data on Hispanic political values, attitudes, and behaviors. A number of scholarly books and articles have since been published analyzing data from these surveys.[1] Although there continue to be significant gaps in the literature—for example, studies of women and politics that focus specifically on Hispanic women[2]—a rich and substantial body of research provides a fuller understanding of Hispanic politics than was the case in the 1980s.

Demographic Considerations

"The steady beat [of] demographics" underlies Hispanic politics in multiple ways.[3] Research identifies the growth, distribution, concentration, and diversification of the Hispanic population as important considerations in the fashioning of contemporary Hispanic politics. Touted as a source of political strength, the burgeoning numbers of Hispanics, especially in the final decades of the twentieth century, have indeed been impressive. In 1970, the U.S. Census counted 9.1 million Hispanics in the nation. By 1996, Hispanics approximated 28.4 million—an increase of more than 200 percent.[4] Given that numbers constitute an important resource in American politics, especially with regard to voting, elections, political apportionment, and representation, the tremendous growth of the Hispanic population, in both absolute and relative terms, implies enhanced political clout for Hispanics in the U.S. system.

To be sure, population growth has created new possibilities for the exercise of Hispanic political power. At the same time, research shows that numbers do not necessarily or easily translate into political influence and power. For example, additional demographic characteristics of the Hispanic population, such as its youthfulness, relatively low socioeconomic standing, and sizeable percentage of noncitizens, tend to limit Hispanic political influence. Hence, while the tremendous demographic growth has enhanced the overall political profile of Hispanics in the U.S. political system, scholarship tends to temper and qualify the claims made about the political payoffs to be realized from the increase in Hispanic numbers.

Concurrent with continued growth has been a broader distribution of the Hispanic population throughout the country. The 1990 census revealed a Hispanic population that fanned out beyond the more traditional areas of Hispanic concentration—the Southwest, the Midwest, and major urban areas in the Northeast and Florida. By 1990, Hispanics were present in every state of the Union, including such areas as the Deep South and Plains states. Moreover, the Hispanic population became increasingly suburbanized, with 48 percent of the population residing in suburbs rather than in central cities or rural areas.[5] The expanded presence of Hispanics across the country has provided more exposure and recognition for the group in national politics. Scholars contend that these patterns of population dispersion have elevated the Hispanic population from a "regional minority" to a national one.[6]

It is important to note that as Hispanics have increased their presence in American society, political forces have also risen in opposition to Hispanic interests, perhaps as a result of Hispanics' increased visibility. Political campaigns to enact "English-only" laws, to end bilingual education and affirmative action programs, and to target immigrants (both legal and undocumented) in punitive and restrictive ways are particularly illustrative of the backlash politics that Hispanics have had to counter at the close of the twentieth century. Hence, political challenges as well as opportunities are associated with the ongoing process of Hispanic "nationalization."

Notwithstanding population dispersion, Hispanics remain geographically concentrated in particular regions of the country and in selected states and urban areas. Their patterns of geographic concentration carry important political implications. With regard to national politics, Hispanic numbers are strategically poised to influence presidential elections. In 1990, Hispanics claimed a significant presence (8+ percent) in nine states: California, with 7.7 million Hispanics (25.8 percent of its state population); Texas, 4.3 million Hispanics (25.5 percent of residents); New York, 2.2 million (12.3 percent); Florida, 1.6 million (12.2 percent); Illinois, 900,000 (7.9 percent); New Jersey, 740,000 (9.6 percent); Arizona, 688,000 (18.8 percent); New Mexico, 579,000 (38 percent); and Colorado, 424,000 (12.9 percent).[7] Five of these states are among the most populous in the country and thus account for a significant number of electoral college votes: California (54), New York (33), Texas (32), Illinois (22), and Florida (25). Together, these 5 states claim 166 electoral votes, almost two-thirds of the number necessary to elect a president (270). Adding the states of New Jersey (15), Arizona (8),

Colorado (8), and New Mexico (5), the electoral vote count reaches 202, 75 percent of the number needed to win the presidency.

Although a number of conditions must prevail for Hispanics to play a decisive role in the outcome of a presidential contest,[8] their geographic concentration in key states assures some measure of attention and potential influence, especially in close elections. Likewise, at the state and local levels, a significant Hispanic presence figures into electoral contests and outcomes, reapportionment and redistricting plans, governing coalitions, and the crafting of public policy agendas.

Alongside these demographic factors, the composition of the Hispanic population raises important questions regarding Hispanic political participation. As a case in point, researchers have pointed out how the tremendous growth of the Hispanic population since the 1970s has also resulted in more diversification of this population. Although persons of Mexican origin continue to account for the largest percentage of the Hispanic population, other national-origin groups, especially those from Central and South America and the Caribbean, have also increased their numbers. Census figures for March 1996 reveal the following breakdown: Mexican origin, 63 percent of the Hispanic population; Puerto Rican, 11 percent; Cuban, 4 percent; Central and South American, 14 percent; and "Other Hispanic," 7 percent.[9]

Such diversity has prompted questions that strike at the very core of Hispanic politics. For example, to what extent do these groups share a common politics? Do they in fact represent a political community or multiple communities of diverse political interests? Do they behave in politically similar ways? Do the differences across groups call into question the construction of Hispanic politics as a real, actual, and viable political force? Relatedly, because immigrants or the foreign-born have increased their proportion of the total U.S. Hispanic population, distinctions on the basis of citizenship and legal status within the Hispanic population have become increasingly salient for their political implications.

In the end, a theme to emerge from studies of Hispanic political participation is the dialectic of similarity and difference.[10] That is, an understanding of the demographic and political similarities and differences across and within multiple sectors and subgroups of the Hispanic population remains a major concern for students of Hispanic politics. Investigations of Hispanic political culture, attitudes, and behavior will continue to grapple with these questions as the Hispanic population grows, transforms, and reinvents itself in the next millennium. With these broad demographic considerations in mind, a closer examination of major dimensions to Hispanic political participation follows.

Hispanic Political Culture

A major aspect of political participation is the concept of *political culture*, which broadly refers to the political beliefs, values, attitudes, and general political orientations of a population. Prior to 1990, research on Hispanic political culture focused on specific national-origin groups (mostly Mexican-American), largely at the local level.[11] Studies of Hispanic political culture with national or statewide samples of Hispanics were relatively few in number and tended to suffer from methodological shortcomings.[12] With the completion of the Latino National Political Survey (LNPS) in 1990, research in this area greatly expanded. The LNPS was the first national survey to examine in depth the political attitudes, values, and behaviors of the three largest Hispanic groups—those of Mexican, Puerto Rican, and Cuban origin—in the United States. The LNPS continues to serve as a primary source of data for analyses of Hispanic political culture.[13]

Hispanic political culture is a broad topic addressed only selectively here. Leading texts on Hispanic politics analyze Hispanic political culture by focusing on the following aspects: (1) group identity, (2) political values and orientations, (3) political ideology, (4) public policy perspectives, and (5) partisan affiliation. Group identity and its political implications constitute one of the most compelling areas of investigation for scholars of Hispanic politics. A variety of theoretical and methodological approaches inform discussion and debate on this question. Prominent among them are examinations of ethnic self-identification and the "political construction" of ethnic labels.

Group Identity

Authors of the Latino National Political Survey signaled as a major finding of their study distinctive patterns of ethnic self-identification. Most of the LNPS respondents self-identified through national-origin labels rather than panethnic designations, such as Latino or Hispanic. That is, when asked how they preferred to identify themselves ethnically, clear majorities of Mexican-Americans, both native- and foreign-born, chose Mexican origin-based terms (i.e., Mexican-American, Mexican, Mexicano(a), Chicano(a)). Similarly, Puerto Ricans preferred a Puerto Rican designation over a panethnic one, and Cubans followed suit, preferring terms associated with Cuban origin over panethnic designations. The authors noted that the native-born in all groups were much more likely to use panethnic labels, although they constituted a minority in all groups as well.[14]

Additional differences among national-origin groups on other dimensions of political culture and political participation provided the LNPS authors with a compelling argument: notions of a singular Hispanic identity, and hence an overarching Hispanic politics, were overdrawn and misleading. Rather, national-origin distinctions were too important to ignore and, in many ways, defined the parameters for how the Hispanic population thought about politics and acted politically. The LNPS findings and their implications extended and amplified the ongoing debate among social scientists regarding the origins, nature, cohesiveness, and authenticity of Hispanic ethnic identity.[15]

Subsequent analysis of LNPS data, however, suggests a more complex picture of ethnic self-identification. Jones-Correa and Leal reexamined LNPS data and found substantial use of panethnic designations among LNPS respondents as a secondary form of identification. Whereas only 14 percent of the survey's respondents gave a panethnic label as their primary identifier, "most respondents chose to give more than one answer to the question asking for their identification. That is, they gave some indication not only of their primary choice for ethnic identification but also of their other preferences as well." In all, almost 42 percent of the respondents chose a panethnic label among the number of other labels with which they identified.[16]

By broadening their analysis, then, beyond respondents' preferred or primary ethnic identifications—the sole focus of the original LNPS researchers—Jones-Correa and Leal found stronger evidence of panethnic identity taking hold across all three national-origin groups. Hence, their findings challenged, or broadened, the original contentions regarding ethnic identification made by LNPS researchers.

Although the political implications of panethnic identification were ambiguous, the authors did find clear indications that panethnic identification is an "American creation." That is, Hispanic panethnicity increased with factors associated with life in the United States: distance from the immigration experience, youth, and education. In the end, the authors concluded that it would be fruitful to consider panethnicity "as part of a constellation of individuals' multiple identifications and that individuals may manage these identities in very different ways."[17]

As growth and diversification of the Hispanic population continue in the next millennium, transformations of Hispanic ethnic identity are sure to occur. At best, research underscores the multifaceted, fluid, and situational character of ethnic identity. It is unclear how, in the long term, ethnic identity will be expressed within and across Hispanic groups. But it is a good bet that the tension between similarity and difference, distinctiveness and commonality, will continue to provide the subtext to this provocative question.

Political Orientations and Political Values

Political orientations and political values generally refer to individuals' psychological and attitudinal predispositions toward political participation and the political system. That is, how individuals relate to the political system—for example, their interest in politics and trust in government—as well as their political values inform the extent to which they are likely to be active participants in the political process. Research has produced mixed results regarding Hispanics. On the one hand, scholars have characterized specific national-origin groups as exhibiting "weak participant political cultures," as in the case of Puerto Ricans, Cubans, and Dominicans in New York City. Similar findings have applied to Mexican-Americans in Texas, who have shown lower levels of interest in politics when compared to non-hispanic Whites and Blacks in their respective locales.[18]

On the other hand, in their analysis of a nationally representative sample of Mexican-ancestry households in the United States, Garcia and Arce found Mexican-Americans to exhibit strong civic orientations to politics. On the basis of additional research, John Garcia summarized, "[a]ttitudinally, Mexican Americans express support for participatory norms and behavior, while feeling less efficacious and confident in their understanding of the political process. Levels of trust for this group tend to fall in the mid-range." He noted that available evidence suggests similar findings for other Hispanic subgroups.[19]

Research on Hispanic political values provides further support for the proposition that Hispanics appear to be engaged with the U.S. political system, at least in an attitudinal or psychological sense. De la Garza et al. argued that Mexican-Americans, Puerto Ricans, and Cuban-Americans show strong psychological attachment to the United States and support for "core American political values." In like manner,

DeSipio maintained that public policy positions held by Hispanics, native-born as well as immigrants, fall "within the mainstream" of American politics. As these scholars contend, such findings counter the popular perception that the Hispanic population, and in particular Hispanic immigrants, constitute a fractionalizing force in American society.[20]

Given these findings, a major paradox emerges in Hispanic politics: Hispanics actively participate in politics at relatively lower levels than other groups. Clearly, participatory attitudes and orientations do not necessarily or directly translate into modes of political activity. Scholarship does offer some answers to the puzzle of disconnection between attitudes and behavior, between participatory orientations and political action. Demographic characteristics (such as income, age, education, citizenship) are significant factors in determining whether individuals participate in politics. Additional explanations include contextual, structural, historical, and political factors to account for lower levels of Hispanic involvement in the U.S. political system.

For example, several scholars point out that Puerto Ricans and Dominicans show much more interest *and* higher levels of involvement in electoral politics in their respective homelands than they exhibit as citizens in U.S. cities. Accordingly, Hero drew attention to the contextual aspects of politics as a partial explanation for levels of citizenry involvement. Similarly, Hardy-Fanta critiqued the American system of political parties and elections for their failure to engage and mobilize Hispanics (and Americans in general) in the political process. At the same time, F. C. Garcia pointed to difficulty in overcoming "a legacy of discouragement and exclusion" as a likely factor in Hispanics' lower levels of participation. Indeed, it is rather astounding to see the extent to which positive and participatory attitudes toward the political system are held by a population that has confronted discrimination and inequality, in both its historical and contemporary manifestations. An additional set of arguments emphasizes the availability of material and political resources, opportunities for participation, and the role of agents of political mobilization (leaders, activists, organization) for translating attitudinal predispositions into political behavior.[21]

Political Ideology and Public Policy Perspectives

Political scientists characterize the ideological or philosophical orientations of Americans as falling along a left-right continuum, ranging from "liberal" to "conservative," with the largest percentage of Americans self-identifying as "moderates." Hispanics show a range of ideological orientations with variations across national-origin groups. Mexican-Americans self-identify in roughly equal proportions as moderate and conservative, with a lesser but substantial percentage indicating liberal orientations. Puerto Ricans and Cubans, in contrast, are more likely to self-describe as conservative than as liberal or moderate.[22] The meanings of these ideological orientations are questionable, however, when considered in light of Hispanic positions on public policies.

McClain and Stewart observed that, "[r]egardless of their self-identified ideological label, large majorities of all three groups support what could be characterized as core elements of a liberal domestic agenda." For example, they favor increased government spending on a broad range of policy issues, including public education, health care, the environment, crime control and drug prevention, and child care. In the same vein, DeSipio maintained that a "relatively liberal attitude toward the role and scope of government" predominates among the three groups, despite some evidence of conservative attitudes on several specific issues, such as abortion and capital punishment.[23]

The dialectic of similarity and difference extends to additional considerations of Hispanic public policy positions. With regard to issue saliency, LNPS data indicate that majorities among all three groups identify social issues, such as crime and drug control, as the most important problems at both the national and local levels. Moreover, economic issues, such as employment, rank second in importance for all three groups.[24] At the same time, particular issues carry more saliency for particular groups. Debates over the status of Puerto Rico are more intense among Puerto Ricans, and U.S. policy toward Cuba generates more attention and mobilization from Cuban-Americans than from the other groups.

Hispanic distinctiveness from other racial and ethnic groups provides another dimension to consider. For example, substantial majorities of the three main Hispanic subgroups show support for bilingual education; slight majorities across all three groups oppose making English the official language of the United States.[25] These positions are in stark contrast to those held by other groups, especially non-Hispanic Whites.

It appears, then, that there is a basis for a common agenda for mobilization across various Hispanic groups, even though differences with regard to issue saliency and policy positions will surface on particular issues. Of course, it is important to keep in mind that further analysis of Hispanic public policy positions may well reveal additional differences, both within and across Hispanic groups (for example, along social class, generational, and gender lines), that will carry important implications for the building of a Hispanic public policy agenda.[26]

Partisan Affiliation

Affiliation or identification with a political party provides a ready cue for understanding and predicting an individual's or group's political behavior. For Hispanics, partisan affiliation shows clear differences among the major Hispanic groups. Overall, Mexican-Americans and Puerto Ricans identify with the Democratic Party. Indeed, it is ironic that, given their tendency to self-identify as conservative, Puerto Ricans overall identify more strongly with the Democratic Party than do Mexican-Americans. Cuban-Americans, in contrast, overwhelmingly identify with the Republican Party, and a near majority considers itself strongly Republican.[27] Voting patterns for all three groups support these general patterns of partisan identification.

Questions arise, however, regarding the strength and durability of these group affiliations over time. Cuban-Americans serve as an interesting case in point. Cuban affiliation with the Republican Party appears closely tied to foreign policy concerns. To the extent that domestic issues overtake foreign policy concerns, Cuban affiliations may shift away from the Republican Party. As previously pointed out, Cubans show substantial support for liberal positions on a host of domestic policies. Such a shift is not unlikely as a younger generation of Cuban-Americans becomes increasingly involved in politics and places domestic issues at the forefront of its political agenda.[28]

Furthermore, Hispanics could conceivably begin to reflect the increasing tendency among American voters to identify as "independents" rather than as partisans, especially if the major political parties ignore Hispanic concerns. To be sure, some Hispanic groups have broken away from the major two parties in the past. Mexican-Americans, most notably in the Southwest, formed *El Partido de la Raza Unida* in the late 1960s. However, such efforts achieved only minimal success in electoral terms. Given the difficulties encountered by third parties in the American party system, it is more likely that any Hispanic disaffection with the two major parties will be expressed through a weakening of partisan ties or through noninvolvement altogether.

Hispanic Political Behavior

Participation in the electoral process is a key indicator of Hispanic involvement in politics. Although a broad range of activities—both electoral and nonelectoral—constitutes political participation, voting is the most common activity engaged in by Americans. Hence, Hispanic rates of voter registration and turnout provide a good basis for comparing Hispanic involvement vis-à-vis other groups and to assess the group's incorporation into the American political system. As previously mentioned, the increasing and rapid growth of the Hispanic population in the closing decades of the twentieth century has generated claims of enhanced political power for Hispanics. Though the potential for enhanced power certainly exists, the reality of Hispanic political power— at least as expressed through the voting booth—reflects constraints and limits as well as possibilities.

Voter Registration and Turnout

Data on Hispanic voting behavior have consistently shown lower rates of participation for Hispanics in comparison to other racial and ethnic groups. For more than three decades, studies have shown that Hispanics fall behind other groups, most notably non-Hispanic Whites and Blacks, in their rates of voter registration and turnout. At the close of the twentieth century, that long-standing pattern persists. In terms of actual numbers, however, more Hispanics have become voters and a significant sector comprises a potential electorate. Nevertheless, demographic characteristics of the Hispanic population, as well as the noncitizenship status of a significant proportion of Hispanic adults, continue to place serious limits on Hispanic voting strength.

Census data for the 1992 general election provide a stark portrait of voting gaps across groups when voting-age populations are compared: 70 percent of Whites, 64 percent of Blacks, and 35 percent of Hispanics registered to vote in 1992. Although the White-Black differential is problematic, the lag in Hispanic registration rates is dramatic. Registration rates for 1996 showed only minor changes: Whites (68 percent), Blacks (64 percent), and Hispanics (36 percent).[29]

Importantly, studies that compare voting-age populations of U.S. citizens only (hence adjusting for noncitizenship status) show much smaller gaps between Hispanics and other groups. A report on the 1996 election showed the Hispanic voter registration rate to be 64 percent (taking into account citizenship), comparable to the rate of Blacks (64 percent) and only slightly lower than that of Whites (68 percent).[30] LNPS data for Hispanic citizens in 1989–1990 also showed smaller gaps as well as important differences across national-origin groups. The Cuban-American rate of registration (78 percent) is at parity with that of Whites (78 percent), whereas Mexican-Americans (65 percent) and Puerto Ricans (64 percent) lag behind.[31]

Voting in the 1992 and 1996 presidential elections showed similar voting gaps for racial and ethnic groups. Among the age-eligible population, 64 percent of Whites voted in 1992, as compared to 54 percent of Blacks and 29 percent of Hispanics. In 1996, voter turnout results did not alter the relative ranking of groups, but showed a decline for each: Whites (56 percent), Blacks (51 percent), and Hispanics (27 percent). As a percentage of registered voters, Hispanic voting rates improved, although they still lagged behind those of others: White turnout (83 percent), Black turnout (80 percent), and Hispanic turnout (75 percent).[32]

The importance of demographics in accounting for lower rates of Hispanic voting cannot be overemphasized. Research pinpoints the effects of age, education, and income on Hispanic participation. In general, the propensity to participate in voting and other political activities increases with age, education, and income. On each of these characteristics, Hispanics are at a disadvantage. In comparison to other groups, especially non-Hispanic Whites, Hispanics are relatively younger and have lower levels of formal education and income. The impact of noncitizenship further compounds the problem of Hispanic nonvoting.

Accordingly, studies show that when Hispanic citizens are compared to non-Hispanics of similar sociodemographic status, differences in participation diminish or disappear altogether. Comparisons across Hispanic subgroups make the point as well. Cuban-Americans show higher rates of registration and turnout when compared to Mexican-Americans and Puerto Ricans. Their higher levels of involvement can be explained in large part by demographics: Cuban-Americans are a relatively older population and enjoy higher levels of educational attainment and income than the other groups. Moreover, they naturalize at a higher rate than does the Mexican-origin population.

Hispanic Voting: Possibilities and Limits

Elections in the 1990s reveal both the potential and limits of Hispanic voting.[33] On the one hand, an unprecedented number of Hispanics registered and voted in the 1996 presidential election. According to the U.S. Bureau of the Census, a record number of Hispanic voters—4.9 million—cast ballots in 1996. This figure represented a 16 percent increase over the 4.2 million Hispanics who voted in 1992. Similarly, the number of Hispanics registered to vote hit a new high of 6.6 million, a 28 percent increase over the number registered in 1992. Importantly, underlying these increases was the unprecedented number of Hispanic immigrants who naturalized from 1992 to 1996, thus expanding the pool of eligible voters. In the end, Hispanics increased their presence among all voters, accounting for 5 percent of the total electorate in 1996 as opposed to the 4 percent they represented in 1988 and 1992. The 1996 election thus sustained and expanded a trend apparent over the 1980s and 1990s: continued growth in the number of Hispanics who made their way to the polls. Although impressive for their numbers, these gains are also somewhat misleading, in that they belie important and persistent limitations in Hispanic voting strength.

Growth in the Hispanic electorate is evident in raw numbers, but not as a percentage of the eligible electorate that turns out to vote. Although the numbers of Hispanic voters increased in every presidential election from 1984 to 1996, Hispanic turnout remained essentially the same. Turnout among Hispanic citizens was 48 percent in 1984, 46 percent in 1988, 48.3 percent in 1992, and 47.6 percent in 1996. Ironically, although the total number of Hispanic voters hit a record high in 1996, Hispanic voter turnout actually *declined* from its 1992 level. As one political observer noted, Hispanics were able to increase their percentage of the voting electorate from 1992 to 1996 because they increased their proportion of the population over those years and "Hispanic turnout [in 1996] went down less than [that for] the rest of the population in an abysmally low turnout year."[34]

Paralleling the growth in Hispanic voters was an increase in the number of Hispanic nonvoters. In 1992, Hispanic nonvoters, comprised of Hispanic citizens who did not vote as well as noncitizens who were ineligible to vote, numbered 10,450,000; in 1996 their number soared to 13,500,000, representing an increase of 29 percent.[35] Given that the rate of growth for Hispanic voters during that same period was 16 percent (as mentioned earlier), it is clear that the increase in voters was far surpassed by the increase of Hispanic nonvoters.

In sum, at the end of the twentieth century, a rapidly expanding Hispanic population continued to add numbers to its voting electorate. But the general structure of the Hispanic electorate did not appear to be changing, as low levels of Hispanic participation in elections persisted. At least in terms of the voting process, Hispanic political incorporation appeared paradoxically to both advance and remain unchanged.

Looking at the big picture, scholars have identified political mobilization efforts as key to the further advancement of Hispanics in the political process. Uhlaner contended that empirical research has removed much of the mystery surrounding low participation rates; hence, "activists can concentrate on either changing or compensating for [those] concrete factors [that affect participation], such as noncitizenship, language, education, income, youth, and so forth."[36] DeSipio argued for broad-based, community-wide mobilization to naturalize Hispanic immigrants as a long-term strategy to enhance the political power of the Hispanic population as a whole.[37] De la Garza and DeSipio contended that "[i]f the Latino vote is to count, campaigns, candidates, elites and organizations must find strategies to mobilize *new* voters" through targeted outreach to Hispanic communities.[38] A pressing challenge for Hispanic empowerment, then, is the conversion of Hispanic citizens into voters and immigrants into citizens and voters—both daunting but compelling tasks.

Political Representation

Although its political potential has not yet been realized, Hispanic participation in U.S. politics has produced important results, perhaps most clearly seen in terms of political representation. Since the 1970s, significant gains have been made in the number of Hispanics elected to public office. A combination of legal and institutional changes in the electoral process, as well as political mobilization on the part of Hispanics, has been key to bringing about substantial increases in representation. Civil rights legislation in the 1960s and 1970s removed many of the obstacles (e.g., the poll tax and literacy tests) that had prevented Hispanics, particularly Mexican-Americans in the Southwest, from voting. Although some of its provisions are currently under challenge, the Voting Rights Act (VRA), first extended to language minority populations in 1975, continues to offer legal protections against minority vote dilution. In addition, Hispanic advocacy organizations have used multiple strategies, including litigation and voter mobilization campaigns, to increase Hispanic representation in the political system.

By the end of the twentieth century, an unprecedented number of Hispanic elected officials (HEOs) had made their way to public office.

The National Association of Latino Elected and Appointed Officials (NALEO) estimated the total number of HEOs in 1994 as 5,459, of which 1,694 were women. Although they occupied positions at every level of government, most were found in city government and on local school boards. They held office in thirty-five states and the District of Columbia. At the same time, reflecting the geographic concentration of the Hispanic population, the five states of the Southwest, plus New York, New Jersey, Florida, and Illinois, held the greatest number of HEOs. Indeed, Texas, New Mexico, and California accounted for almost 70 percent of the total.

From 1984 to 1994, the number of Hispanic elected officials in the nation increased by 48 percent, close to the Hispanic population's rate of growth over the decade (53 percent). Although the increase for HEOs was impressive, women officeholders made even more dramatic gains. The number of Hispanic women in public office increased by 194 percent over the same period. Although they continued to be underrepresented in public office, Hispanic women accounted for 31 percent of the total number of positions held by Hispanics in 1994—a percentage higher than that for women officeholders nationally (24 percent).[39]

The combined effect of reapportionment and redistricting bolstered Hispanic political representation in the 1990s. At the congressional level, reapportionment after the 1990 U.S. census generally added congressional seats in states with large Hispanic populations. At the same time, redistricting created more predominantly Hispanic districts. As a consequence, Hispanic representation in the U.S. House of Representatives increased from 11 to 17 members after the 1992 elections. NALEO reported that redistricting had a major effect on state legislative races as well.[40]

Though impressive, such gains have not rectified the long-standing pattern of underrepresentation for Hispanics at every level of government. Indeed, in 1994, HEOs overall constituted only slightly more than 1 percent of the total number of elected officials in the country (511,039).[41] Increasing Hispanic political representation thus remains of critical importance for the future empowerment of the population and provides a compelling goal for furthering Hispanic political participation.

Three considerations loom large for future increases in Hispanic political representation. Legal challenges to the creation of majority-minority legislative districts under the Voting Rights Act gained momentum in the 1990s. In a series of rulings, the U.S. Supreme Court showed its disapproval of redistricting plans that had sought to preserve or enhance minority candidates' chances of winning elective office. In major decisions in 1995, the Court struck down Black-majority congressional districts in North Carolina and Georgia. At the same time, legal challenges to Hispanic-majority congressional districts in Illinois (Chicago) and New York (New York City) were upheld by the Court. Legal questions regarding redistricting for purposes of enhancing minority representation are far from resolved and will no doubt continue into the next millennium. Should the courts find majority-minority districts invalid or unconstitutional, an important avenue for increased Hispanic representation would be eliminated.

Two additional considerations should be noted. To date, Hispanic elected officials tend to represent majority Hispanic districts. In 1994, NALEO found that, overall, HEOs were more likely to be elected from constituencies that were at least 50 percent Hispanic.[42] Although the creation of Hispanic-majority districts has proved essential to furthering Hispanic representation, it remains a limited strategy.[43] To increase their numbers in office over the long run, Hispanic candidates will have to win in more heterogeneous districts where Hispanics do not constitute a majority of the population. To be sure, should the creation of Hispanic-majority districts be curtailed by the courts, the ability of Hispanic candidates to win in non-Hispanic districts will be all the more imperative.

Finally, the future status of the Voting Rights Act is questionable. Congress will reconsider the VRA in 2007, when it is up for renewal. In all likelihood its critics will seek to curtail its provisions or eliminate it altogether. Without a doubt, the VRA has been indispensable to Hispanic political empowerment. In addition to eliminating many obstacles to Hispanic voting, the VRA has authorized bilingual ballots and, as mentioned, the creation of majority-minority districts. Further, it has allowed legal challenges to at-large election systems and gerrymandering schemes that have diluted the Hispanic vote. The results of the political battle over the VRA will necessarily have tremendous effects on Hispanic empowerment strategies.[44]

Political Mobilization: Parties and Interest Groups

Political Parties

Political parties serve as important mechanisms to both stimulate and channel Hispanic political participation in U.S. politics. The extent to which the Democratic and Republican Parties include Hispanics among their constituent groups and respond to their political agendas carries implications for Hispanic empowerment in the long run. As previously noted, Hispanic groups are highly partisan. Mexican-Americans and Puerto Ricans form core constituencies of the Democratic Party; Cuban-Americans are a key element of the Republican Party. In both parties (but more so in the Democratic Party), Hispanic leaders and activists can be found at all levels of their respective party structures. To be sure, Hispanic activism within the mainstream political parties is both long-standing and enduring. However, the ability of the parties to incorporate increasing numbers of Hispanics and mobilize new constituencies on their behalf remains open to question.

Lessons from the 1996 presidential election are instructive. In their study of the 1996 presidential race, de la Garza and DeSipio described how the Democratic presidential campaign of Bill Clinton and Al Gore reached out to Hispanics in unprecedented ways. The outreach effort, *Adelante con Clinton-Gore!,* reflected new levels of sophistication, funding, and integration with the overall campaign. In the end, the Democratic Party ticket enjoyed decisive levels of support from Hispanics, but the Democrats failed to turn out the Hispanic vote to a greater degree than in the past. As a percentage of eligible voters, Hispanic voting in 1996 was lower than in 1992. De la Garza and DeSipio faulted the "high-tech" outreach strategy employed by the Democrats for its limited success in mobilizing Hispanic voters. In addition, Bill Clinton's support for congressional legislation on immigration and welfare reform—two stands criticized by Hispanic groups—perhaps tempered Hispanic enthusiasm for the ticket.[45]

In contrast, the Republican presidential campaign of Bob Dole and Jack Kemp proved highly problematic with Hispanic voters, including Republicans. Notably, some breaks within Republican ranks on issues involving immigration, public benefits for legal immigrants, affirmative action, and "English-only" laws surfaced. Nevertheless, the Republican Party and its presidential ticket ultimately embraced what many perceived to be an anti-immigrant and anti-Hispanic agenda. Furthermore, Republican efforts to engage in Hispanic outreach were limited in scope and funding.

In the end, Hispanics voted overwhelmingly (72 percent) for Clinton's reelection in 1996. Most surprisingly, Clinton won in Arizona and Florida, two states that had long voted Republican in presidential contests. In both cases, the Hispanic vote appeared key to Clinton's margin of victory. In Florida, the Hispanic vote went for Dole over Clinton, 46 percent to 42 percent, but the margin of victory was much less than what Hispanic Floridians had helped Republican candidates gain in past elections. Political observers posited that a somewhat diminished Cuban vote for the Republican candidate, along with Democratic voting among non-Cuban Hispanics, provided the Democratic Party with an important margin of success.[46]

To what extent the major parties will seek to include Hispanics under their respective "tents" will constitute a significant issue for years to come. For the Democratic Party, the main challenge appears to be mobilizing a core constituency toward higher levels of participation. For the Republican Party, the question of inclusion appears more complex and problematic.

In the aftermath of the 1996 election, internal battles raged within the GOP over an appropriate and effective Hispanic outreach strategy. Republican opposition to immigrant rights, affirmative action, language rights, and bilingual education became contentious issues among the party faithful. Hispanic Republicans, among others, protested their party's stands and noted their deleterious effects on Republican outreach efforts.[47] Importantly, differences within the Republican Party emerged at the state level, with California Republicans most clearly endorsing issue positions at odds with Hispanic policy preferences. In other states, the Republican Party supported Hispanic positions or sought to avoid such "wedge issues" altogether.

Overall, scholars of American politics contend that the ability of American political parties to engage the citizenry in politics has declined over time. Moreover, these parties hardly resemble the political parties of the past, which sought to incorporate new immigrants and new voters into the electoral process through local-level organization. Their effectiveness as agents of mobilization for Hispanic empowerment, though clearly important, may be limited in the long run unless they reinvigorate themselves as mediating institutions between the people and their government.

Interest Groups

Interest groups, like political parties, provide a means for people to articulate their interests in American politics and bring their influence to bear on government and the political process. Defined broadly here to include a wide range of organizational endeavors, interest-group politics have provided an important avenue for Hispanic political mobilization and the exercise of power. Hispanic organizations have been key in placing Hispanic demands on the political agenda and in marshaling resources and mobilizing constituencies to pressure public officials and others influential in both the public and private sectors to respond to their demands.

Contemporary Hispanic organizational endeavors involve a multiplicity of goals, memberships, strategies, and tactics. They include national civil rights organizations (several to be cited later), professional and business associations (e.g., National Association of Hispanic Journalists, National Hispanic Bar Association, Hispanic Chambers of Commerce), labor unions (e.g., United Farm Workers of America), and a plethora of single-issue groups (such as immigrant rights groups) and community-based organizations. Their tactics range from the more conventional activities of litigation, lobbying, candidate endorsement, and voter mobilization to protest activities that include labor strikes, sit-ins, marches, demonstrations, and boycotts. Among their many functions are advocacy and representation for their members and/or the Hispanic population at large, the provision of services to their members (e.g., information, technical support), public education, and access to public policy-making arenas.

Working for the economic, political, and educational advancement of the Hispanic population, a number of Hispanic organizations have risen in national prominence. They include the League of United Latin American Citizens (LULAC), touted as the nation's oldest and largest Hispanic organization. Founded in 1929 by Mexican-Americans in South Texas, LULAC in 1998 claimed a membership of more than 160,000, with over 600 local councils that extend to every state in the Union and Puerto Rico. Similarly, the National Council of La Raza (NCLR), founded in 1968 as an advocacy group for Mexican-Americans in the Southwest, now includes a pan-Hispanic focus in its advocacy efforts. One of the most visible Hispanic organizations lobbying in Washington, D.C., the NCLR draws upon a multimillion-dollar budget to represent the Hispanic population at large and its affiliate network of more than 220 community-based organizations across the United States.

The Mexican American Legal Defense and Educational Fund (MALDEF) and the Puerto Rican Legal Defense and Education Fund (PRLDEF) have become prominent public-interest law firms representing the interests of Hispanics, primarily through litigation on a number of issues involving, for example, affirmative action in education and employment, immigration, minority vote dilution, and redistricting. The National Association of Latino Elected and Appointed Officials (NALEO) pursues a variety of strategies to increase the number and efficacy of Hispanics in public office. NALEO has enjoyed increasing visibility as the number of Hispanic men and women in public office has increased. Although regionally focused, both the Southwest and Midwest Voter Registration and Education Projects, respectively, have produced important results for Hispanics at the national as well as state and local levels, through their voter registration drives and their advocacy for Hispanic interests in the redistricting process.

Indicative of organizational success has been the increasing number of influential persons from the public and private sectors who have attended the national conferences or fund-raising banquets of the organizations described here. High government officials, including the president, vice-president, and members of the Cabinet, prominent politicians, and corporate and foundation executives have increasingly appeared at Hispanic organizational events. At the 1998 LULAC convention held in Dallas, Texas, prominent speakers included Speaker of the House Newt Gingrich (R-GA), House Minority Leader Richard Gephardt (D-MO), Texas Governor George W. Bush (R-TX), and the Reverend Jesse Jackson. Vice-President Al Gore sent a videotaped address to the convention. In short, as group representatives of Hispanics' increasing political power, prominent Hispanic organizations now draw the attention of political and economic elites in unprecedented ways. In like manner, these organizations draw most of their funds from federal, foundation, and corporate grants.

Overall, research on Hispanic interest groups suggests several important developments over the past two decades. First, an advocacy explosion has fostered the emergence of hundreds of new groups, on the local, state, and national levels. Second, Hispanic groups are more diverse and geographically dispersed, representing the interests of an increasing number of Spanish-origin groups. Third, through more formalized and sophisticated politics, Hispanic groups have become political players in a number of new policy arenas, including immigration, free trade, and foreign policy.[48]

Nevertheless, questions regarding the future evolution of Hispanic interest-group politics arise. The sustainability of Hispanic organizations over the long term involves questions of funding, membership support, and organizational effectiveness, for groups from the national to the local, grassroots level. Furthermore, as Hispanic politics enter the next millennium, the development of coalitions among Hispanic groups, as well as with non-Hispanic groups, and the problems of bureaucratization and co-optation will most likely command increasing attention.

With regard to political participation, perhaps one of the most important functions of interest groups is their ability to engage various sectors of the Hispanic population in the political process. Accordingly, the role of women as leaders and activists in community struggles has claimed particular attention from scholars, who note their importance as agents of political mobilization at the grassroots level.[49] The work of the Industrial Areas Foundation (IAF), under the leadership of organizer Ernesto Cortés, has been recognized for its success in spurring political activism in low-income Hispanic barrios and other local communities across the country. Utilizing the organizing principles of its founder, Saul Alinsky, the IAF follows a well-developed methodology for teaching individuals the art of politics—that is, how to build relationships and engage in political discussion, debate, compromise, and negotiation with community leaders and public officials. Over time, IAF efforts have resulted in the political mobilization of thousands of barrio residents on behalf of their families and neighborhoods in local-level politics. Notably, working-class Hispanic women figure prominently as leaders in IAF organizations.[50]

In the long run, Hispanic interest groups will continue to function as important mechanisms to channel Hispanic participation in the political process. To the extent that they connect people to politics and generate broad participation in the process—the goal of IAF organizations—they will further the democratization of American politics. At the same time, Hispanic interest groups may increasingly reflect the class bias that is prevalent in interest-group politics at large. That is, rather than generate broad participation among the Hispanic population, they may mobilize only the relatively narrow middle-class and professional sectors of the Hispanic population.

Researchers have noted how interest-group competition in American politics tends to favor groups with the most resources, such as money, status, and members. Moreover, individuals with higher socioeconomic standing are more likely to participate in interest-group activities than those at the lower end of the socioeconomic scale. In general, then, interest-group advocacy in American politics tends to reflect a class bias—the interests and preferences of the more affluent. Such a scenario raises a significant challenge for Hispanic groups who seek to represent and mobilize vast sectors of the Hispanic population, which are working class or working poor. Ultimately, the extent to which Hispanics organize their communities with both breadth (broad representation of various sectors of the population) and depth (high quality of participation) will provide evidence of their ability to wield influence within the political system and move American politics toward greater inclusiveness and participation.

A Public Policy Agenda for the Twenty-First Century

The Politics of Demographics

Hispanic demographics underlie the construction of a public policy agenda for the next millennium. The availability of accurate and reliable data on the Hispanic population and its political attributes is imperative for understanding the politics and public policy needs of this population. Although major advances in data collection and dissemination on Hispanics have been made over time, the need continues for additional information, improved methodologies, and timely reports. To be sure, the issue of data collection became highly politicized in the 1990s over the design and implementation of the 2000 census.

Noting the significant undercount of the Hispanic population in the 1990 census, Hispanics joined a number of groups calling for improved statistical methods and outreach efforts to ensure a more accurate count of the U.S. population in the year 2000. At the same time, partisan battles were waged within Congress over the enumeration process and its implications for reapportionment, redistricting, and federal funding formulas. Republicans opposed statistical sampling procedures as unconstitutional and untested and sought to block funds for the 2000 census. Democrats charged that Republicans did not want to see more people counted in poor, urban, and minority—and hence largely Democratic—areas.[51]

Beyond the political jousting over census counts was debate over the U.S. Census Bureau's use of racial and ethnic classifications. Public debate focused on the creation of a "multiracial" category for use in the 2000 census, as well as changes in selected ethnic designations. The Office of Management and Budget ultimately ruled against the addition of a multiracial category, but the 2000 census will allow individuals to designate more than one racial category for themselves. The 2000 census will also incorporate changes in ethnic categories and terms.[52] It is unclear what these changes imply for the Hispanic population, but their use and impact will be closely monitored for years to come. In the end, data collection must be guided by the scientific imperative for accurate and complete demographic information on the U.S. (and Hispanic) population, regardless of partisan and political interests.

Demographics should also figure in the political strategies and mobilization efforts Hispanics undertake to further their participation in the political process. Research has revealed how the disadvantaged socioeconomic status of Hispanics constrains and limits their political involvement. Mobilization efforts and public policies that seek to improve the material circumstances of Hispanic families—and challenge structural inequities in the nation's political economy—would address fundamental obstacles to Hispanic political participation. Likewise, attention should focus on Hispanic youth, who constitute a significant proportion of the Hispanic population and yet are one of its most disconnected and disengaged sectors. Some political scientists have identified public education as the number one priority on the Hispanic policy agenda. Advancing the educational attainment of Hispanic youth alone will provide multiple opportunities for group advancement. Given the close connection between education and political participation, such an agenda in the long term promises to convert large numbers of Hispanic youth to perhaps the Hispanic community's "greatest political asset."[53]

The conversion of immigrants to citizens, and subsequently to active participants in the political process, stands as another policy imperative for the twenty-first century. Voting and election studies have identified noncitizenship as a major impediment to Hispanic political empowerment. As a consequence, naturalization drives must become important components to Hispanic voter registration and get-out-the-vote efforts. Meanwhile, the governmental system must remove bureaucratic impediments to the naturalization process, whose complexity and administration discourage many Hispanic immigrants from initiating or completing the process.[54]

Demographic considerations also pertain to Hispanic relationships with other minority populations, especially Blacks. Hispanics' growing numbers and visibility have led in some cases to strained relations and competition between Hispanics and Blacks over such issues as jobs, immigration, public school policies, public sector employment, and political representation. As Hispanics surpass Blacks as the nation's largest racial/ethnic minority group, political tensions and competition between both groups may well increase. The Hispanic agenda must address the political consequences of changing demographics in such a way as to foster cooperation and coalition among disadvantaged groups.[55]

Research Questions and Issues

A research agenda for the twenty-first century must include further investigation of Hispanic political orientations and behavior. Questions regarding Hispanic ethnic identity and policy preferences carry important implications for understanding the parameters—the possibilities and limits—of building a common agenda across diverse Hispanic groups. Moreover, assessments of political outreach and mobilization strategies employed by political parties and interest groups can point to the more successful ways to engage Hispanics in the political process. Research into the social backgrounds and political trajectories of Hispanic elected officials can reveal factors that both obstruct and facilitate the election of Hispanic women and men to public office.

Finally, research can pinpoint structural and procedural changes that must be made in American politics to enhance the political participation of Hispanics and other underrepresented groups. Electoral arrangements must continue to be examined and evaluated for their accessibility and impact on minority political participation and representation. Types of election systems (e.g., at-large, single-member districts, cumulative voting), political party nominations and the slating of candidates, the drawing of district lines, and voting procedures (e.g., bilingual ballots) promise to figure prominently as salient issues in the next millennium. Furthermore, Hispanic political activists and scholars have raised the issue of voting rights for legal resident aliens to further the inclusion and integration of Hispanics in the political process.[56] Although a few locales already allow noncitizens to vote in local and school board elections, this recommendation has not met with much favorable response. However, it may well constitute an important item on the Hispanic agenda in the next millennium.

Ultimately, the political system's response to Hispanic demands for political inclusion will determine how Hispanics will figure in the political processes and structures of this country. Research in the 1990s points to a Hispanic population, composed of native-born and immigrants alike, who hold participatory attitudes toward American politics—yet their levels of participation remain low. Hence, enhanced material and political resources and structural opportunities for participation are needed to convert potential participants to actual participants in American politics. Mobilizing agents remain important to motivate people toward participation and to transform their political interests into political action. As a "politics of inclusion" provides a compelling theme for a Hispanic agenda in the next century, it also poses a necessary challenge to the U.S. political system to respond affirmatively to Hispanic interests to further the incorporation of this population into the body politic.

Notes

1. See Harry P. Pachon and Louis DeSipio, *New Americans by Choice: Political Perspectives of Latino Immigrants* (Boulder, Colo.: Westview Press, 1994) for analysis of the National Latino Immigrant Survey. A description of the Latino National Political Survey and presentation of the overall findings appear in Rodolfo O. de la Garza, Louis DeSipio, F. Chris Garcia, John Garcia, and Angelo Falcon, *Latino Voices: Mexican, Puerto Rican, and Cuban Perspectives on American Politics* (Boulder, Colo.: Westview Press, 1992). Louis DeSipio, *Counting on the Latino Vote: Latinos as a New Electorate* (Charlottesville, Va.: University of Virginia Press, 1996) analyzes data from both national surveys. The *Hispanic Journal of Behavioral Sciences*, volume 18 (May 1996), devoted a complete issue to additional analyses of the Latino National Political Survey.
2. For a review and critique of the literature relevant to Hispanic women in politics, see Christine Marie Sierra and Adaljiza Sosa-Riddell, "Chicanas as Political Actors: Rare Literature, Complex Practice," *National Political Science Review* 4 (1994): 297–317.
3. Aníbal Yáñez-Chávez, "Introduction: The Beat Goes On," in *Latino Politics in California,* ed. Aníbal Yáñez-Chávez (San Diego, Cal.: Center for U.S.-Mexican Studies, University of California, San Diego, 1996), 1.
4. United States Bureau of the Census, "The Hispanic Population in the United States," Current Population Survey—March 1996, Summary Tables, Table 1, Internet posting, February 3, 1998.
5. F. Chris Garcia, "Introduction," in *Pursuing Power: Latinos and the Political System,* ed. F. Chris Garcia (Notre Dame, Ind.: University of Notre Dame Press, 1997), 2.
6. Rodolfo O. de la Garza, *"El Cuento de los Números* and Other Latino Political Myths," in *Latino Politics in California,* ed. Aníbal Yáñez-Chávez (San Diego, Cal.: Center for U.S.-Mexican Studies, University of California, San Diego, 1996), 12.
7. Garcia, *Pursuing Power,* 8.
8. Rodolfo O. de la Garza and Louis DeSipio, "Latinos and the 1992 Elections: A National Perspective," in *Ethnic Ironies: Latino Politics in the 1992 Elections,* ed. Rodolfo O. de la Garza and Louis DeSipio (Boulder, Colo.: Westview Press, 1996), 6.
9. United States Bureau of the Census, "Hispanic Population of the United States," Table 1.
10. Paraphrased from an observation made by John A. Garcia, book prospectus, February 26, 1998.
11. See Robert R. Brischetto and Rodolfo O. de la Garza, eds., *The Mexican American Electorate Series* (San Antonio, Tex.: Southwest Voter Registration Educa-

tion Project and the Hispanic Population Studies Program of the Center for Mexican American Studies, University of Texas at Austin, 1982–1984).

12.   Rodolfo O. de la Garza, ed., *Ignored Voices: Public Opinion Polls and the Latino Community* (Austin, Tex.: Center for Mexican American Studies, University of Texas at Austin, 1987).

13.   For a provocative critique of the Latino National Political Survey, see Luis Fraga, Herman Gallegos, Gerald P. López, Mary Louise Pratt, Renato Rosaldo, José Saldívar, Ramón Saldívar, and Guadalupe Valdés, *Still Looking for America: Beyond the Latino National Political Survey* (Stanford, Cal.: Stanford Center for Chicano Research, Stanford University, 1994).

14.   De la Garza et al., *Latino Voices*, 39–40, Table 2.27.

15.   Analyses of the politics involved in the construction of ethnic identities, as well as their instrumental uses and contextual underpinnings, are also important to consider. See, for example, Martha E. Giménez, "The Political Construction of the Hispanic," in *Estudios Chicanos and the Politics of Community: Selected Proceedings of the National Association for Chicano Studies*, ed. Mary Romero and Cordelia Candelaria (Ann Arbor, Mich.: National Association for Chicano Studies, 1989), 66–85; several essays in *Latin American Perspectives*, volume 19 (1992), that address the issue's theme, "The Politics of Ethnic Construction: Hispanic, Chicano, Latino … ?"; Felix M. Padilla, *Latino Consciousness: The Case of Mexican Americans and Puerto Ricans in Chicago* (Notre Dame, Ind.: University of Notre Dame Press, 1985).

16.   Michael Jones-Correa and David L. Leal, "Becoming 'Hispanic': Secondary Panethnic Identification Among Latin American-Origin Populations in the United States," *Hispanic Journal of Behavioral Sciences* 18 (May 1996): 220.

17.   Ibid., 214, 239.

18.   Rodney E. Hero, *Latinos and the U.S. Political System: Two-Tiered Pluralism* (Philadelphia, Pa.: Temple University Press, 1992), 60–61.

19.   John A. Garcia, "Political Participation: Resources and Involvement Among Latinos in the American Political System," in Garcia, *Pursuing Power*, 49; John A. Garcia and Carlos Arce, "Political Orientations and Behaviors of Chicanos: Trying to Make Sense Out of Attitudes and Participation," in *Latinos and the Political System*, edited by F. Chris Garcia, 125–51 (Notre Dame, Ind.: University of Notre Dame Press, 1988).

20.   De la Garza et al., *Latino Voices*, 79–81, 162; Rodolfo O. de la Garza, Angelo Falcon, and F. Chris Garcia, "Will the Real Americans Please Stand Up: Anglo and Mexican-American Support of Core American Political Values," *American Journal of Political Science* 40 (May 1996): 335–51; DeSipio, *Counting on the Latino Vote*, 55.

21.   Hero, *Latinos and the U.S. Political System*, 60–61; Carol Hardy-Fanta, *Latina Politics, Latino Politics: Gender, Culture, and Political Participation in Boston* (Philadelphia, Pa.: Temple University Press, 1993); Garcia, *Pursuing Power*, 35; John A. Garcia, "Political Participation."

22.   De la Garza et al., *Latino Voices*, 84, Table 6.7.

23.   Paula D. McClain and Joseph Stewart, Jr., *"Can We All Get Along?" Racial and Ethnic Minorities in American Politics* (Boulder, Colo.: Westview Press, 1995), 63; de la Garza et al., *Latino Voices*, 90; DeSipio, *Counting on the Latino Vote*, 50.

24.   De la Garza et al., *Latino Voices*, 88–89, Tables 7.1 and 7.2.

25.   Ibid., 97 and 99, Tables 7.15 and 7.19 respectively.

26.   See Kevin A. Hill and Dario Moreno, "Second-Generation Cubans," *Hispanic Journal of Behavioral Sciences* 18 (May 1996): 175–93; Lisa J. Montoya,

"Latino Gender Differences in Public Opinion: Results from the Latino National Political Survey," *Hispanic Journal of Behavioral Sciences* 18 (May 1996): 255–76.

27. De la Garza et al., *Latino Voices*, 127, Table 8.24.

28. Maria Torres, "Will Cuba Be Next? What About Miami?," in Garcia, *Pursuing Power*, 464.

29. McClain and Stewart, *"Can We All Get Along?,"* 77; United States Bureau of the Census, "Voting and Registration: November 1996," Table 23, Internet posting, October 17, 1997.

30. Institute for Puerto Rican Policy, "Latino Gains in Voting and Registration Higher than Whites and Blacks in 1996," Internet posting, October 25, 1997.

31. De la Garza et al., *Latino Voices*, 123, Table 8.14.

32. McClain and Stewart, *"Can We All Get Along?,"* 77; United States Bureau of the Census, "Voting and Registration," Table 23; Institute for Puerto Rican Policy, "Latino Gains."

33. The following sources were consulted for data on Hispanic voting: United States Bureau of the Census, "Voting and Registration," Table 23; Institute for Puerto Rican Policy, "Latino Gains"; DeSipio, *Counting on the Latino Vote*, 59; De la Garza and DeSipio, "Latinos and the 1992 Elections," 29. Also see Rodolfo O. de la Garza and Louis DeSipio, "The Best of Times, The Worst of Times: Latinos and the 1996 Elections," *Harvard Journal of Hispanic Policy* 10 (1996–1997): 4–5. Written prior to the release of census data on voting in the 1996 election, De la Garza and DeSipio's prediction of the number of Latinos voting in 1996 is lower than the actual turnout.

34. Ruy Teixeira, "The Real Electorate," *American Prospect*, no. 37 (March–April 1998): 82–85, Internet posting.

35. DeSipio, *Counting on the Latino Vote*, 59; Institute for Puerto Rican Policy, "Latino Gains."

36. Carole J. Uhlaner, "Latinos and Ethnic Politics in California: Participation and Preference," in Yáñez-Chávez, *Latino Politics in California,* 45.

37. DeSipio, *Counting on the Latino Vote*.

38. De la Garza and DeSipio, "The Best of Times, The Worst of Times," 24, their emphasis.

39. NALEO Educational Fund, *1994 National Roster of Hispanic Elected Officials* (Washington, D.C.: National Association of Latino Elected and Appointed Officials, 1994), vi–xi.

40. Ibid., xi.

41. Ibid., viii.

42. Ibid., xi–xii.

43. See Rodolfo O. de la Garza and Louis DeSipio, "Save the Baby, Change the Bathwater, and Scrub the Tub: Latino Electoral Participation After Seventeen Years of Voting Rights Act Coverage," *Texas Law Review* 71 (June 1993): 1514–17, 1520, for a critique of Hispanic-majority districts as a strategy for Hispanic mobilization.

44. Ibid., 1479–1539.

45. De la Garza and DeSipio, "The Best of Times, The Worst of Times," 3–26.

46. Ibid., 14; and personal conversation with Wayne Smith, Carleton College, Northfield, Minnesota, February 14, 1997.

47. Carroll J. Doherty, "GOP Initiatives Hamper Efforts to Reach Out to Minority Groups," *Congressional Quarterly* (March 1998), Internet posting; "Chastised GOP Softens Stance on Immigration," *Los Angeles Times*, Sunday, November 23, 1997, Internet posting; Paul A. Gigot, "GOP Confronts Future Without His-

panics: Adios!," *Wall Street Journal*, Friday, August 22, 1997, at A14; Marc Sandalow, "State GOP in Quandary over Minority Vote; Convention Ends with Few Solutions," *San Francisco Chronicle*, Monday, September 29, 1997, at A1, Internet posting.

48. Christine Marie Sierra, "Latino Organizational Strategies on Immigration Reform: Success and Limits in Public Policymaking," in *Latinos and Political Coalitions: Political Empowerment for the 1990s*, ed. Roberto E. Villarreal and Norma G. Hernandez (Westport, Conn.: Greenwood Press, 1991), 61–80; Magalí Murià, "La comunidad latina estadunidense y la aprobación del TLC," *Revista Mexicana de Política Exterior* 52 (October 1997): 111–30; Maria Torres, "Latinos and U.S. Policies Toward Latin America: A Case Study of the 1988 Presidential Campaign," *Latino Studies Journal* 1 (1990): 3–23.

49. Mary Pardo, "Mexican American Women Grassroots Community Activists: Mothers of East Los Angeles," *Frontiers* 11 (1990): 1–7; Hardy-Fanta, *Latina Politics, Latino Politics*.

50. Benjamin Marquez, "The Industrial Areas Foundation and the Mexican-American Community in Texas: The Politics of Issue Mobilization," in *Minority Group Influence: Agenda Setting, Formulation, and Public Policy*, ed. Paula D. McClain (Westport, Conn.: Greenwood Press, 1993), 127–46; Laurie Goodstein, "Harnessing the Force of Faith: Movement Spreads the Gospel of Community Power," *Washington Post*, February 6, 1994, at B1, B4.

51. Lawrence L. Knutson, "Gore Slams GOP's Immigration Stance," Cable News Network, Inc., Internet posting, September 15, 1997.

52. Randolph E. Schmid, "Multiracial Census Category Nixed," Associated Press, Internet posting, October 29, 1997.

53. Ronald J. Schmidt, "Latino Politics in the 1990s: A View from California," in Garcia, *Pursuing Power*, 457–61.

54. DeSipio, *Counting on the Latino Vote*, 143–52.

55. James Jennings, "Blacks and Latinos in the American City in the 1990s: Toward Political Alliances or Social Conflict," in Garcia, *Pursuing Power*, 472–78; Rodolfo O. de la Garza, "Latino Politics: A Futuristic View," in Garcia, *Pursuing Power*, 453.

56. De la Garza and DeSipio, "Save the Baby, Change the Bathwater, and Scrub the Tub," 1522–23.

Bibliography

Brischetto, Robert R., and Rodolfo O. de la Garza, eds. *The Mexican American Electorate Series*. San Antonio, Tex.: Southwest Voter Registration Education Project and the Hispanic Population Studies Program of the Center for Mexican American Studies, University of Texas at Austin, 1982–1984.

"Chastised GOP Softens Stance on Immigration." *Los Angeles Times*, Sunday, November 23, 1997. Internet posting: http://www.latimes.com

de la Garza, Rodolfo O. *"El Cuento de los Números* and Other Latino Political Myths." In *Latino Politics in California*, edited by Aníbal Yáñez-Chávez, 11–32. San Diego, Cal.: Center for U.S.-Mexican Studies, University of California, San Diego, 1996.

———. "Latino Politics: A Futuristic View." In *Pursuing Power: Latinos and the Political System*, edited by F. Chris Garcia, 448–56. Notre Dame, Ind.: University of Notre Dame Press, 1997.

———, ed. *Ignored Voices: Public Opinion Polls and the Latino Community.* Austin, Tex.: Center for Mexican American Studies, University of Texas at Austin, 1987.

de la Garza, Rodolfo O., and Louis DeSipio. "The Best of Times, The Worst of Times: Latinos and the 1996 Elections." *Harvard Journal of Hispanic Policy* 10 (1996–97): 3–26.

———. "Latinos and the 1992 Elections: A National Perspective." In *Ethnic Ironies: Latino Politics in the 1992 Elections*, edited by Rodolfo O. de la Garza and Louis DeSipio, 3–49. Boulder, Colo.: Westview Press, 1996.

———. "Save the Baby, Change the Bathwater, and Scrub the Tub: Latino Electoral Participation After Seventeen Years of Voting Rights Act Coverage." *Texas Law Review* 71 (June 1993): 1479–1539.

de la Garza, Rodolfo O., Louis DeSipio, F. Chris Garcia, John Garcia, and Angelo Falcon. *Latino Voices: Mexican, Puerto Rican, and Cuban Perspectives on American Politics.* Boulder, Colo.: Westview Press, 1992.

de la Garza, Rodolfo O., Angelo Falcon, and F. Chris Garcia. "Will the Real Americans Please Stand Up: Anglo and Mexican-American Support of Core American Political Values." *American Journal of Political Science* 40 (May 1996): 335–51.

DeSipio, Louis. *Counting on the Latino Vote: Latinos as a New Electorate.* Charlottesville, Va.: University of Virginia Press, 1996.

Doherty, Carroll J. "GOP Initiatives Hamper Efforts to Reach Out to Minority Groups." *Congressional Quarterly* (March 1998). Internet posting: http://www.cq.com

Fraga, Luis, Herman Gallegos, Gerald P. López, Mary Louise Pratt, Renato Rosaldo, José Saldívar, Ramón Saldívar, and Guadalupe Valdés. *Still Looking for America: Beyond the Latino National Political Survey.* Stanford, Cal.: Stanford Center for Chicano Research, Stanford University, 1994.

Garcia, F. Chris, ed. *Latinos and the Political System.* Notre Dame, Ind.: University of Notre Dame Press, 1988.

———. *Pursuing Power: Latinos and the Political System.* Notre Dame, Ind.: University of Notre Dame Press, 1997.

Garcia, John A. "Political Participation: Resources and Involvement Among Latinos in the American Political System." In *Pursuing Power: Latinos and the Political System*, edited by F. Chris Garcia, 44–71. Notre Dame, Ind.: University of Notre Dame Press, 1997.

Garcia, John A., and Carlos Arce. "Political Orientations and Behaviors of Chicanos: Trying to Make Sense Out of Attitudes and Participation." In *Latinos and the Political System*, edited by F. Chris Garcia, 125–51. Notre Dame, Ind.: University of Notre Dame Press, 1988.

Gigot, Paul A. "GOP Confronts Future Without Hispanics: Adios!" *Wall Street Journal*, Friday, August 22, 1997, at A14.

Giménez, Martha E. "The Political Construction of the Hispanic." In *Estudios Chicanos and the Politics of Community: Selected Proceedings of the National Association for Chicano Studies*, edited by Mary Romero and Cordelia Candelaria, 66–85. Ann Arbor, Mich.: National Association for Chicano Studies, 1989.

Goodstein, Laurie. "Harnessing the Force of Faith: Movement Spreads the Gospel of Community Power." *Washington Post*, February 6, 1994, at B1, B4.

Hardy-Fanta, Carol. *Latina Politics, Latino Politics: Gender, Culture, and Political Participation in Boston*. Philadelphia, Pa.: Temple University Press, 1993.

Hero, Rodney E. *Latinos and the U.S. Political System: Two-Tiered Pluralism.* Philadelphia, Pa.: Temple University Press, 1992.

Hill, Kevin A., and Dario Moreno. "Second-Generation Cubans." *Hispanic Journal of Behavioral Sciences* 18 (May 1996): 175–93.

Hispanic Journal of Behavioral Sciences, vol. 18 (May 1996).

Institute for Puerto Rican Policy. "Latino Gains in Voting and Registration Higher than Whites and Blacks in 1996." October 25, 1997. Internet posting: http://www.ipmet.org/IPR/vote96.html

Jennings, James. "Blacks and Latinos in the American City in the 1990s: Toward Political Alliances or Social Conflict." In *Pursuing Power: Latinos and the Political System*, edited by F. Chris Garcia, 472–78. Notre Dame, Ind.: University of Notre Dame Press, 1997.

Jones-Correa, Michael, and David L. Leal. "Becoming 'Hispanic': Secondary Panethnic Identification Among Latin American-Origin Populations in the United States." *Hispanic Journal of Behavioral Sciences* 18 (May 1996): 214–54.

Knutson, Lawrence L. "Gore Slams GOP's Immigration Stance." Cable News Network, Inc., September 15, 1997. Internet posting: http://www.cnn.com

Latin American Perspectives, vol. 19 (1992).

Marquez, Benjamin. "The Industrial Areas Foundation and the Mexican-American Community in Texas: The Politics of Issue Mobilization." In *Minority Group Influence: Agenda Setting, Formulation, and Public Policy*, edited by Paula D. McClain, 127–46. Westport, Conn.: Greenwood Press, 1993.

McClain, Paula D., and Joseph Stewart, Jr. *"Can We All Get Along?" Racial and Ethnic Minorities in American Politics.* Boulder, Colo.: Westview Press, 1995.

Montoya, Lisa J. "Latino Gender Differences in Public Opinion: Results from the Latino National Political Survey." *Hispanic Journal of Behavioral Sciences* 18 (May 1996): 255–76.

Murià, Magalí. "La comunidad latina estadunidense y la aprobación del TLC." *Revista Mexicana de Política Exterior* 52 (October 1997): 111–30.

NALEO Educational Fund. *1994 National Roster of Hispanic Elected Officials.* Washington, D.C.: National Association of Latino Elected and Appointed Officials, 1994.

Pachon, Harry P., and Louis DeSipio. *New Americans by Choice: Political Perspectives of Latino Immigrants.* Boulder, Colo.: Westview Press, 1994.

Padilla, Felix M. *Latino Consciousness: The Case of Mexican Americans and Puerto Ricans in Chicago.* Notre Dame, Ind.: University of Notre Dame Press, 1985.

Pardo, Mary. "Mexican American Women Grassroots Community Activists: Mothers of East Los Angeles." *Frontiers* 11 (1990): 1–7.

Sandalow, Marc. "State GOP in Quandary over Minority Vote; Convention Ends with Few Solutions." *San Francisco Chronicle*, Monday, September 29, 1997, at A1. Internet posting: http://www.sfgate.com/news/

Schmid, Randolph E. "Multiracial Census Category Nixed." Associated Press, October 29, 1997. Internet posting: http://www.ap.org

Schmidt, Ronald J. "Latino Politics in the 1990s: A View from California." In *Pursuing Power: Latinos and the Political System*, edited by F. Chris Garcia, 457–62. Notre Dame, Ind.: University of Notre Dame Press, 1997.

Sierra, Christine Marie. "Latino Organizational Strategies on Immigration Reform: Success and Limits in Public Policymaking." In *Latinos and Political Coalitions: Political Empowerment for the 1990s*, edited by Roberto E. Villarreal and Norma G. Hernandez, 61–80. Westport, Conn.: Greenwood Press, 1991.

Sierra, Christine Marie, and Adaljiza Sosa-Riddell. "Chicanas as Political Actors: Rare Literature, Complex Practice." *National Political Science Review* 4 (1994): 297–317.

Teixeira, Ruy. "The Real Electorate." *American Prospect*, no. 37 (March–April 1998): 82–85. Internet posting: http://epn.org/prospect/37/37teixfs.html

Torres, Maria. "Latinos and U.S. Policies Toward Latin America: A Case Study of the 1988 Presidential Campaign." *Latino Studies Journal* 1 (1990): 3–23.

———. "Will Cuba Be Next? What About Miami?" In *Pursuing Power: Latinos and the Political System*, edited by F. Chris Garcia, 463–65. Notre Dame, Ind.: University of Notre Dame Press, 1997.

Uhlaner, Carole J. "Latinos and Ethnic Politics in California: Participation and Preference." In *Latino Politics in California,* edited by Aníbal Yáñez-Chávez, 33–72. San Diego, Cal.: Center for U.S.-Mexican Studies, University of California, San Diego, 1996.

United States Bureau of the Census. "The Hispanic Population in the United States." Current Population Survey—March 1996. Summary Tables, Table 1. February 3, 1998. Internet posting: http://www.census.gov/population/socdemo/hispanic/cps96/sumtab-1.txt

United States Bureau of the Census. "Voting and Registration: November 1996."

October 17, 1997. Internet posting: http://www.census.gov/population/socdemo/voting/history/wot23.txt

Yáñez-Chávez, Aníbal. "Introduction: The Beat Goes On." In *Latino Politics in California,* edited by Aníbal Yáñez-Chávez, 1–9. San Diego, Cal.: Center for U.S.-Mexican Studies, University of California, San Diego, 1996.

About the Contributors

Pastora San Juan Cafferty is Professor at the School of Social Service Administration, The University of Chicago. She has degrees in American literary and cultural history and teaches in social welfare policy and analysis, with special interest in the fields of race and ethnicity in American society. Her publications include *Hispanics in the United States: A New Social Agenda, The Dilemma of Immigration in the United States: Beyond the Golden Door, Backs Against the Wall: Urban-Oriented Colleges and Universities and the Urban Poor and Disadvantaged, The Politics of Language,* and *The Diverse Society,* as well as many monographs, articles, and contributed book chapters. Dr. Cafferty currently serves on the boards of directors of several corporations and public/nonprofit groups.

David W. Engstrom is Associate Professor of Social Work at New Mexico Highlands University. His career of study and teaching in social work and research has been accompanied by personal involvement and service in community and public service groups such as La Familia Medical Center and the Albuquerque Border City Project. Dr. Engstrom is a frequent guest lecturer whose publications include *Presidential Decision Making Adrift: The Carter Administration and the Mariel Boatlift* and *Asian Immigrant Entrepreneurs in Chicago,* as well as numerous contributed book chapters and articles.

Barry R. Chiswick is Research Professor and Head of the Department of Economics, University of Illinois at Chicago, whose many publications and awards reflect his international reputation for his research in economics, human resources, immigration, and minorities. He is a former chair of the American Statistical Association Census Advisory Committee, a frequent consultant to government and international agencies, and a member of the editorial boards of several academic journals.

Michael Hurst has been a labor economist for the past fourteen years in Alaska and Illinois, and is currently a senior business analyst for Household Finance Corporation and a lecturer at the University of Illinois at Chicago. Dr. Hurst's areas of research and publication have included unemployment and labor force dynamics, the economic adjustment of immigrants in the United States, wage differentials of minority groups, and credit risk policy.

Alvin Korte is Professor of Social Work at the School of Social Work, New Mexico Highlands University. His long career of teaching and publishing has encompassed subjects from social research methodology and statistics to the family life of Hispanic rural elderly and the inculcation of moral behavior.

David Maldonado, Jr. is Professor of Church and Society at the Perkins School of Theology, Southern Methodist University. Since receiving his doctorate in social work from the University of California at Berkeley, his research emphasis has been on the Hispanic elderly, as reflected in his many publications and his service with national and community groups.

Katie McDonough, Associate Professor of Social Work at New Mexico Highlands University, applies her interdisciplinary background in psychology, social work, and political science to teaching, grant writing, and administration in the areas of mental health, gerontology, and children/family. A frequent lecturer and conference presenter, Dr. McDonough presently serves on National Council on the Aging and with Catholic Charities, USA, among others.

Cruz Reynoso, a Professor of Law at UCLA School of Law, has been an Associate Justice of the California Third District Court of Appeal and the California Supreme Court, as well as a practicing attorney in private, government, and public service positions. He is currently Vice-Chair of the United States Commission on Civil Rights and sits on the boards of directors of the Latino Issues Forum and the Natural Resources Defense Council.

Melissa Roderick is Associate Professor at the School of Social Service Administration, The University of Chicago, and a director of the Consortium on Chicago School Research. Dr. Roderick's numerous publications, papers, and presentations document and augment her research projects and statistical analyses of student and school performance, adolescent development, and school dropout.

Christine Marie Sierra is currently Associate Professor of Political Science at the University of New Mexico, following a visiting scholarship with the Mexican American Studies and Research Center at the University of Arizona. Dr. Sierra teaches, researches, and publishes in the areas of American race and ethnic politics, Hispanic politics, and women in American politics.

Zulema E. Suárez is Associate Professor at Fordham University's Graduate School of Social Service. In addition to her teaching and many presentations and publications on minority and health care issues, Dr. Suárez is a clinical consultant at Freedom House in Detroit, a former board member of the Midwest Migrant Health Information Office, and a consulting editor of *Social Work*.

Teresa A. Sullivan is Vice President and Graduate Dean of the University of Texas at Austin, where she is Professor of Sociology, Professor of Law, and the Cox & Smith, Inc., Faculty Fellow in Law. She is an elected Fellow of the American Association for the Advancement of Science and the Sociological Research Association. Dr. Sullivan has been the Chair of the U.S. Census Advisory Committee on Population Statistics and a member of National Research Council panels on statistics and census policy.

Index

Department of Health and Human Services (HHS), 248
Deportation, 208, 209
DeSipio, Louis, 324, 325, 330, 333
Dhooper, Surjit Singh, 265
Diabetes, 22
Diagnostic and Statistical Manual (DSM), 249
Diaz-Briquets, Sergio, 34
Diaz-Stevens, Ana Maria, 101
Discrimination, 238; basis of, 9; in education, 149; effect on political participation, 324; in employment, 46, 59; ethnic identity and, 71; hate crimes, 292–93, 303; in health care, 205, 219; in incarceration, 284; in jury service, 290; language-based, 73; by police, 280, 281, 285; within religious denominations, 103, 105; in sentencing, 295. *See also* Prejudice
Displacement, 19–20
Dominicans, 5, 8; emigration factors, 52; immigrants, 49, 52; political culture, 323; refugees, 39–40
Donato, Katharine M., 37
Dropout rates, 17, 79, 83–84, 131, 156, 240–41; factors in, 148, 300; perception of, 301
Drug abuse and crimes, 296–98
Due process. *See* Civil rights
Duran, Jorge, 37

Earnings, 20, 189–92; education and, 126–27; ethnic gap in, 127; gap, 181, 189, 191–92. *See also* Income level
Economic development, 33
Economic immigrants, 7, 8
Economy, 245, 246; inequity in, 261
Ecuador, 7
Education, 14–17; accountability in, 155; anti-discrimination, 293; aspirations re, 129, 139; bilingual, 16, 257, 319; bilingualism in, 78–84; community information re, 146; cultural issues re, 150–51, 152; early childhood, 131–34; early twentieth-century, 125; effect on political participation, 328, 339; equal, 78, 80; health care and, 197, 217; high school, 142–43, 148–49, 156; higher

(*see* Higher education); immigrants' knowledge of system, 142; immigrants' view of, 152; improving, 158; issues re, 25; juvenile delinquency and, 300–301; labor force success and, 197, 217; motivation for, 152, 153; non-school opportunities, 16; payoffs for, 126–27; about politics, 337; program orientation, 138; reforms, 134–35, 157–58; religious, 108–9; sufficiency of, 79; value placed on, 14, 15, 142, 150, 151–52, 300
Educational achievement, 125, 126, 133, 136–38; compensatory study for, 152; constraints on, 139–53; ethnic gap, 155; family support for, 139–40, 141–42, 145, 150–52; improving, 144–45; lack of, 240, 241, 242; performance expectations and standards, 134–38, 142, 155–56; school support for, 145–49, 153
Educational attainment, 14–15, 17, 123–24, 189; adults, 139–41; college, 126–27, 129–31; comparative rates, 177–79; criminals, 294; effect on employment, 242; elderly, 241; high school completion, 127–29; immigration and, 131, 157; increasing, 148, 154–59; labor market success and, 176–77, 191; LEP students, 153; of parents, 139, 143, 144, 151
Educational disadvantage, 123, 152–53
Educational opportunity, 14, 15–16, 152, 153; equalizing, 155
Eisenstadt, S. N., 87
El Salvador, 7, 43, 52
Elderly, 12, 241–42; poor, 238; welfare/SSI use, 54–55
Elmore, Richard F., 135
Emigration, 74
Employers, sanctions on, 37, 44–45, 45–46, 58
English as a Second Language (ESL), 81, 83, 217
English-language skills, xvi, 70, 78, 189; assimilation and, 73–74, 78; educational opportunity and, 80–81; elderly, 242; health care needs and, 205; labor market success and, 179–